SOPHIA
GODDESS OF WISDOM

The Divine Feminine from
Black Goddess to World-Soul

CAITLÍN MATTHEWS

Mandala
An Imprint of HarperCollins*Publishers*

Mandala
An Imprint of Grafton Books
A Division of HarperCollins*Publishers*
77-85 Fulham Palace Road,
Hammersmith, London W6 8JB

Published by Mandala 1991

1 3 5 7 9 10 8 6 4 2

© Caitlín Matthews 1991

Caitlín Matthews asserts the moral right to be
identified as the author of this work.

British Library Cataloguing in Publication Data

Matthews, Caitlín, 1952-
Sophia, goddess of wisdom: the divine feminine from
black goddess to world-soul.
1. Goddesses
I. Title
291.2'11

ISBN 0-04-440590-1

Printed in Great Britain by Bath Press, Bath, Avon

CONTENTS

LIST OF ILLUSTRATIONS

ACKNOWLEDGEMENTS

Without Wisdom, nothing! To all lovers of Wisdom: the many, unnamed peerers through the lattice and the public proclaimers in the street alike. They have been my guides and companions. Thanks are also due:

To my sage husband, John, for untold encouragement and support over this book's long gestation, and Emrys, for his sophianic forebearance of a mother hitched to her computer for what must have seemed untold Gnostic aeons.

To Maureen Ballard, the unwitting but wise originator of this text. It was she who called the first Goddess Conference in the British Isles in 1979 at which I spoke along these very lines. To my canny agent, Barbara Levy, for giving me the courage to get moving. Truly, Necessity may be the Mother of Invention but she is also the Midwife of Deadlines! To my wise-weaving editor, Marion Russell for her belief in my abilities to construct a platform for Sophia.

To Catherine of Alexandria, Lady of Wisdom's Wheel, and my patron saint, for keeping me moving. To Kathleen Raine, a spiritual grandmother and defender of the ancient springs of the sacred and imaginal arts, for her understanding and encouragement. To the harmonious memory of Dr. Deirdre Green, late of Lampeter University: she was a true soul-friend whose light still shines in dark places.

To Stratford and Léonie Caldecott for Sophianic support over the years and for the loan of books. To Ean Begg who shares my dark but dazzling obsession with Black Virgins, for sharing the fruits of his research with me. To Dick Temple of the Temple Gallery for his kind assistance in tracking down obscure icons, and to Donald M. Fiene for his expert and friendly conversation on the Russian and iconic appearances of Sophia. To Tau Rosamonde Miller for her cooperation.

To Rev. Gereint ap Iorwerth and all within the *Order of Sancta Sophia* for sharing their inner lives with another follower of the Lady. To Aurora Terrenus for letters of Sophianic comfort and support. To Peter Taylor for alchemical advice. To all priestesses and priests within the Fellowship of Isis and to all friends and readers for unfailing companionship, rituals and for sharing Wisdom's picnic lunch with me. May we enjoy uninterrupted symposiums in the joy of the Pleroma!

The following individuals, museums, institutions and libraries are thanked for their permission to reproduce the illustrations:

The British Library, BM ADD 30337; Nikos Stavroulakis; Mary Beth Edelson, *See for Yourself*; Philosophia, from Neumann, Erich, *The Great Mother: an analysis of the Archetype*, trans. Ralph Manheim, Bollingen Series 47. Copyright 1955 © 1980 renewed by Princeton University Press; Tau Rosamonde Miller of the *Ecclesia Gnostica Mysteriorum*; Robert Lentz, 1989, New Mexico, USA; National Trust, Arlington Court, Devon; Jennifer Begg; Oxford University Press; Elisabeth Collins; Judy Collins, Tate Gallery; Bibliotèque Sainte-Geneviève; Biblioteca Nacional, Madrid; Nicholas Roerich Museum, New York.

Lilith by Chesca Potter, *Isis of Corinth* and *Goddess of Sovereignty* by Stuart Littlejohn, *Sophia on the Shore* by Bryce Muir: these artists are contactable via BCM HALLOWQUEST, London WC1N 3XX.

Veneror itaque inventa sapientiae inventoresque. . . mihi laborata sunt. – I therefore venerate all the works of Wisdom and all her artificers . . . for me have they laboured.
Seneca

AUTHOR'S NOTE

In this book I have attempted to give an overview of the Goddess in her many manifestations as mediator of wisdom. Concentrating on the Western tradition, it explores the development of the Goddess of Wisdom, Sophia, from earliest times up to the present day. It deals primarily with Sophia *on her own terms* and, where possible, in her own words. It is the metahistory of an idea and its metaphors.

In this study, I have chosen to draw upon a far wider framework of reference than is normally usual. The Biblical and philosophical guises of Wisdom are, I believe, not the only ones. Most books on the Goddess deal with her pre-Christian appearances or with her twentieth century reappearances. I have purposely chosen to go into what many consider blind alleys or areas irrelevant to Goddess studies, chiefly because they remain unexplored and because Sophia has left her calling card en route. Sophia is a guerilla combat Goddess, attired in camouflage veils so complete that many orthodox spiritualities never realized that the Goddess was still accompanying them.

I do not believe, as is often fashionably assumed, that the orthodox spiritualities totally took over the Divine Feminine and nullified all her subsequent appearances. The influence of salvific stories and myths of the Goddess is more subtle and pervasive, more likely to be stubbornly retained in unlikely places.

I have attempted to give a shape to the vast hinterland of mythic and philosophic ideas which led to the formation of Sophia as we know her; giving equal weight to the mythological and hermetic testimony as to the scriptural and philosophic. The ways of Wisdom have a serendipity all of their own. I have striven to give shape and coherence to the complex tangle of Wisdom-Sophia as she appears in Biblical, Apocryphal and Gnostic traditions. The Biblical books of Wisdom have their own commentators, but other areas are less documented and here I have tried to bring out relevant comparisons and themes which have too long lain hidden.

I have worked from the premise that all ways to Wisdom are valid paths. In speaking of spiritual experience, we have to use the language of the heart, not the mind. If this 'spoils' an academic study of Sophia, then so be it, it is the language I prefer. I have

1

treated Christianity with respect for its mystical traditions – a view which few non-Christians, and fewer feminists, share. In doing so, I have been sensitive to the fact that mystical Christianity has always kept open the gates for Sophia to go in and out: where Sophia has been, there have I followed. Those who view Christianity with contempt will, I hope, read deeper and find the 'treasures of darkness'.

I am also painfully aware that the restatement of the Divine Feminine as Goddess has often entailed the rejection of many aspects of worship which still sustain many people and keep them connected to the Divine Wisdom. This need not be so, for I believe that wherever Sophia has walked, the spirit of the Goddess has penetrated, even to the hearts of what many might consider as 'the ultimate patriarchal religions'. Gnosis speaks of Sophia as the woman with three measures of leaven: I believe that she knows just when her dough is risen, and when that time comes, every form of spirituality will know about her in ways now undreamed of. Let us trust her to judge the ripeness of that time.

I have regretfully traced the Goddess of Wisdom only through-out the Western European world; to have drawn upon the far more cohesive Goddess traditions of the East and the native earth traditions of the West would have doubled this book's length. If the emphasis is loaded for the West it is because Sophia is most needed and least appreciated here. My purpose is to give Wisdom a voice, for she calls aloud in the city looking for her beloved and few listen.

Wisdom – whether as Black Goddess or Sophia – is a wise mediator who can be approached, without fear, *by both sexes*. This is particularly true as we emerge from the twentieth century into the New Age of a Sophianic millennium.

A few words about semantics are appropriate here. The histori-cal placing of the word Sophia (Greek for wisdom) is squarely within the period between the early centuries BC and the 4th–5th centuries AD. There are many forward references in the early chapters to the Gnostic Sophia, who appears in this period as a fully fledged Goddess. In this book, I have sometimes chosen to speak of Sophia and at other times of Wisdom. Where she appears in capitalized form, *Wisdom* signifies Sophia. Throughout I have capitalized Woman and Man, to signify womankind or mankind as distinct genders. Rather than using the grammati-cally ubiquitous and now devalued 'man' for both genders, I have prefered humankind. There is a glossary of specialist words on page 345 for which there are no adequate English equivalents.

The search for Sophia's origins is widespread, many scholars claiming the precedent of their own theory and usually treating her as a textual abstraction: rather, I believe, she is the result of the fragmentation of the original Goddess mirror whose shards have fallen through time and space to be reassembled in our own time.

As well as being the most evasive goddess, Sophia is also one of the most pervasive ones. I have not hesitated to draw upon folk-tradition, legends and mythology, which pertain to Sophia, being concerned to tell stories which move the soul towards its destined path – that wise way which all lovers of wisdom (the real *philosophias*) need to find. Sophia plays, hides, adapts, disguises, brings justice. But though I have treated her many appearances as a mythic unity, collecting stories and placing them with lapidary care into their fit shape, it is only to find that they reorganise themselves when I next look. This may go to show that Wisdom is not stupid: she knows that my attempt to impose form upon her movements is a doomed undertaking, and so she turns the kaleidescope when I'm not looking.

In accordance with her wishes, I have attempted to write with this criteria in mind. If corners have been cut, and abysses of understanding leaped, then it was only because she held my hand and assured me it would work. Believe me, I would never have jumped unless she made me!

What follows is a journey in the steps of Sophia, giving the background and itinerary of her journey. Because of its length, I have reserved practical explorations of her territory to a further book, called *Sophiance*, where Sophia can be experienced at first hand.

For those who like to know at the outset where the author is coming from, I shall say that I am a traveller in the mystical realms of the Western spiritual tradition. I enter wherever I am welcome and make myself at home, but I am as likely to rush out into the street again because I think I have heard Sophia's voice calling. Wherever her song is sung, there am I.

Caitlín Matthews
13th February 1989 – 1st May 1990

PROLOGUE

The Lost Goddess

The West is exiled of the Goddess – her features are unknown to us, guessed at, hoped for, rejected as aberration, feared as monstrous or deformed. We in the West are haunted by the loss of our Mother. Our mother country is a place many have never visited, though it is endlessly projected as a golden matriarchy, or a paradise, but though the house of the Goddess is in disrepair after so many centuries of neglect, some have begun the work of restoration while others have already moved back in and are renovating from within.

But if the Goddess has been displaced from her territorial home all this long while, where has she been residing in the interim? This book is an attempt to answer that question. The Goddess did not simply die out or go into cold storage two thousand years ago to be revived today in the same forms she manifested then. If the Goddess wanted to survive and accompany her people, surely she would have done so in a skilful and subtle manner?

Sophia is the great lost Goddess who has remained intransigently within orthodox spiritualities. She is veiled, blackened, denigrated and ignored most of the time: or else she is exalted, hymned and pedestalled as an allegorical abstraction of female divinity. She is allowed to be a messenger, a mediator, a helper, a handmaid: she is rarely allowed the privilege of being seen to be in charge, fully self-possessed and creatively operative.

Sophia is the Goddess for our time. By discovering her, we will discover ourselves and our real response to the idea of a Divine Feminine principle. When that idea is triggered in common consciousness, we will begin to see an upsurge of creative spirituality which will sweep aside the outworn dogmas and unliveable spiritual scenarios which many currently inhabit. When Sophia

5

walks among us again, the temple of each heart will be inspirited, for she will be able to make her home among us properly; up to now, she has been sleeping rough in just about every spirituality you can name.

To rediscover Sophia, we have to infiltrate a conspiracy of professional, orthodox interest in order to flush her out of hiding and liberate her from the clutches of those who say they have a vested interest in the possession of Wisdom.

Wisdom is neither good or bad, male or female, Christian or Pagan: she is no-one's personal possession. The Goddess of Wisdom reaches down to the depths of our need. Her simple being is so vastly present that we have not noticed it. Indeed, we have not known the depths of our need nor that any assuaging wisdom was near at hand.

Yet the Goddess of Wisdom is not a newcomer to our phenomenal world, so how is it we have failed to notice her? The Western world has been so busy about its affairs that only a few unusual people have had time to comment on her existence. When they have talked or written about her, it has been in such overblown esoteric language that few have taken notice. Wisdom trades under impossible titles: Mother of the Philosophers, the Eternal Feminine, Queen of Good Counsel and other such nominations do not inspire confidence. These beings are impossibly remote: they sit about all day in courts of law or in palaces, on intensive committees and government boards. They are scarcely approachable in these forms.

And yet, we have the dichotomy that this rarified being is most appreciated by the very simple and unlearned, who turn to her as naturally as to their own mothers, for she really helps us in ways that philosophy and other arcane studies do not. We feel at home with her because she has seen and heard it all before; she has the same kind of battered face as her petitioners, for she offers real wisdom, not the kind offered by lady bountifuls who are all mouth and no sense.

This is aptly borne out in C. S. Lewis's *Till We Have Faces*, his masterly retelling of the Psyche story. Here, Psyche's hard sister, Queen Orual, has gone to the temple of the goddess Ungit where she has been responsible for installing a brand new statue of the goddess. She witnesses a peasant woman cast herself down in front of the ancient stone formerly representing the goddess.

'Has Ungit comforted you, child?' I asked.

'Oh yes, Queen,' said the woman, her face almost brightening, 'oh yes. Ungit has given me great comfort. There's no goddess like Ungit.'

'Do you always pray to *that* Ungit,' said I (nodding toward the shapeless stone), 'and not to *that*?' Here I nodded towards our new image, standing tall and straight in her robes . . . the loveliest thing our land has ever seen.

'Oh, always this, Queen,' said she. 'That other, the Greek Ungit, she wouldn't understand my speech. She's only for nobles and learned men. There's no comfort in her.'[1]

It is for this very reason that this book goes down to the roots of the Goddess of Wisdom and shows her many guises, whether it be her transcendent, starry face or her workaday, primeval one. I want to show that the blackened old stones once venerated as goddesses and the crystalline virgins of esoteric spirituality are not so dissimilar, that they both represent Sophia in all her forms. Neither image is better or more achieved than the other.

Where is Wisdom to be found? asks the *Book of Wisdom*. This question is the preoccupation of philosophers and theologians who make it their profession to find out. But it is also the question of ordinary folk too: 'How can I best do this? What does this mean?' are typical questions to find the wisest course. Between the one and other there is a world of difference; it is what divides the theoreticist and the practitioner. Once we allow Sophia to become an abstraction, we lose touch with her. Our culture tells us that there is a great deal of difference between Divine and Earthly Wisdom: that one is to be sought, while the other is to be despised. My thesis is that, Divine and Earthly Wisdom, though having different appearances, nevertheless partake of the same essence. Our society has mainly lost sight of Sophia and attempted to split her into various manageable parcels. Frequently reduced to God's secretary who nevertheless still supplies all the efficiency of the divine office, she is from all time, the treasury of creation, the mistress of compassion.

Return of the Goddess

When we speak of God, no-one asks, 'which *God* do you mean?' as they do when we speak of the Goddess. The West no longer speaks the language of the Goddess, because the concept has been almost totally erased from consciousness, although many are trying to remember it. Our ancestors were very young when they were taken from the cradle and it is now difficult for us, their descendants, to speak or think of a feminine deity without the unease of someone in a foreign country. We have been raised to think of Deity as masculine and therefore a goddess is a shocking idea. But we do not speak here of *a* goddess, rather of *the* Goddess, and we speak it boldly and with growing confidence, because we find we like the taste of the idea.

When did we make up this idea? some ask. We didn't invent the Goddess. She was always there, from the beginning, we tell them. Somehow, humanity left home and forgot its mother. Perhaps our ancestors took her for granted so much that they lost touch? Well, our generation wants to come back home now and be part of the family in a more loving way, because the West has still got a lot of growing up to do and the Goddess has a lot to teach us.

What or who is the Goddess then? Deity is like colourless light which can be endlessly refracted through different prisms to create different colours. As the poet William Blake said: 'All deities reside in the human breast.'[2] The images and metaphors which we use to describe deity often reflect the kind of society and culture within which we have grown up. After two thousand years of masculine images, the time of Goddess reclamation has arrived. The Goddess is just as much Deity as Jesus, or Allah, or Jehovah. She does not usually choose to appear under one monolithic shape, however. Each person has a physical mother; similarly, the freedom of the Divine Feminine to manifest in ways appropriate to each individual has meant that she has many appearances.

The re-emergence of the Divine Feminine – the Goddess – in the twentieth century has begun to break down the conceptual barriers erected by orthodox religion and social conservatism. For the first time in two millennia, the idea of a Goddess as the central pivot of creation is finding a welcome response. The reasons are not difficult to seek: our technological world with its pollution and imbalanced ecology have brought our planet face to face with its own mortality; our insistence on the transcendence of Deity and the desacralization of the body and the evidence of the senses threatens to exile us from our planet.

The Goddess appears as a corrective to this world problem on many levels. In past ages she has been venerated as the World–Soul or spirit of the planet as well as Mother of the Earth. Her wisdom offers a better quality of life, based on balanced nurturing of both body and spirit, as well as satisfaction of the psyche. But we live in a world in which the Goddess does not exist, for a vast majority of people. They have no concept of a Deity as feminine. As Bede Griffiths has recently written: 'The feminine aspect of God as immanent in creation, pervading and penetrating all things, though found in the book Wisdom, has almost been forgotten . . . The Asian religions with their clear recognition of the feminine aspect of God and of the power of God, the divine shakti permeating the universe, may help us to get a more balanced view of the created process. Today we are beginning to discover that the earth is a living being, a Mother who nourishes us and of whose body we are members.'[3]

While Asian metaphors of the Divine Feminine may be helpful to some, there are many similar metaphors lying neglected within our Western society. The Western world is full of people who are orphaned of the Goddess. In a court of law, loss of the mother is considered as mitigating evidence for diminished responsibility. Perhaps this may go some way to explain why the Western world has perpetrated so many evils, perhaps not.

Somehow we have lost the wisdom of the Goddess and our world is a poorer place because of it. However, there are many signposts to her presence among us, and many developments leading to her reintegration of our society.

Perhaps the greatest factor in the re-emergence of the Goddess is the Women's Movement. Historically, women have been the bearers of children and the makers of the home: natural roles which have been unfailingly reinforced by the political and spiritual regimes of the past two millennia. With the advent of better technology and contraception, women have at last become free to demand equal status with men, to exercise their creativity and spirituality.

Many women have turned to the concept of the Divine Feminine in their struggle, finding a more appropriate response to their spiritual needs in a Goddess rather than in a Trinity of masculine representation. It is with a special poignancy that women turn towards the Goddess in the depths of their need. As Sophia weaves her work of restoration, many women are realizing that their spiritual needs have been particularly neglected; they are also discovering the confidence to assume spiritual existences and take their power. Many supposedly mature commentators have decried this female reaction as 'a phase women are going through'. Believe me, never was a movement so timely as this resumption of female integrity. While this book is not addressed solely to women, it nevertheless spotlights the neglect which womankind has suffered.

This resurgence of interest in the Goddess has rushed rapidly to fill an aching vacuum, often creating strident and unbalanced results as it does so. Instead of a fierce patriarchal God, many feminists have set in his place an insistently matriarchal Goddess, no less fundamental than Jehovah. This has had the effect of making all men of the human species appear culpable for women's long repression, thus creating a whole new crop of imbalances for our children to reap.

Some feminist writers have delighted in perpetuating the myth of the golden age of matriarchy – when women ruled the earth and peace prevailed. Others have done the great disservice of rewriting history in the light of fundamental, and frequently simplistic, feminist principles, without any deference to accurate research whatever. In this way many 'facts' about the nature of the Goddess have been perpetuated in this generation. This arbitrary rewriting or bending of source material does a great disservice to future generations who, whatever their approaches and opinions, will still have a necessary dependence upon primary sources.

Although the figure of the Goddess has been in eclipse, she has not been inactive. She has been working away like yeast within the chewy dough of daily bread. The foundation mysteries of the Goddess underlie later spiritual developments which are generally associated with the esoteric streams of orthodox religions. It was especially within the figure of the Goddess of Wisdom that these mysteries were transmitted into our own time, taking many strange and unexpected routes. Significantly, the major mystics of all faiths have perceived Sophia as the bridge between everyday life and the world of the eternal, often entering into deep accord with her purpose. But though such mystics as the medieval Abbess Hildegard of Bingen or the Sufi, Ibn Arabi, are hardly considered to be 'Goddess-worshippers' in the feminist sense, they nevertheless show that the channels of the Divine Feminine have been kept open and mediated by many so-called patriarchal faiths.

I have worked from the basis that Sophia or Wisdom is the practical and transcendant form of the Divine Feminine – the Goddess herself. This view is at variance with all other studies of Wisdom which see her as an allegorical or subsidiary figure to that of the Divine Masculine – God. Wisdom is not *part* of any deistic schema, she is *central* to our understanding of spirituality.

And while she may be invoked by many for purposes as various as the creation of a female priesthood within Christianity or as the inspiration of feminists in search of a broader view of the Goddess, Sophia is at the last her own self: the leaven which permeates creation, life's creative impetus and completion.

I have accordingly looked for the Goddess of Wisdom under many names and titles, including Nature, the World-Soul, the Blessed Virgin and the Shekinah, as well as under her more usual designations. Each of them has retained some part of the Goddess's image which, like a shattered mirror, waits to be reassembled.

Goddess of Wisdom

Sophia appears in nearly every culture and society. She is clearly distinguished by unique qualities and symbolic representations: she is concerned with the survival and maturation of all creation. She is the leavening influence of life. Without Wisdom, life is dull. Without Wisdom's serendipity, things remain in pieces. Wisdom connects, enlivens. She plays her game seriously, and her work playfully, while we mortals work seriously and play playfully. She is a shy Goddess and a queenly one, she is a protecting Goddess and a hidden one.

Sophia is both silent and veiled, unlike her partner, the Logos, who goes forth speaking openly. But the silence of Wisdom precedes the speech of the Logos. It is for this reason that the deacon at the Eastern orthodox liturgy cries out: 'Wisdom, let us attend!', that we might listen to the wisdom of the heart.

She is distinguishable from many popular forms of the Divine Feminine by the fact that she is a Black Goddess. She is black because she is primal. Hers is not a blackness of skin (although she is frequently represented in this way) rather, like Isis, she keeps her glory veiled. She often takes the appearance of a hag, an aged widow or a dispossessed woman. Like Kali, she can shock and terrify. But she is primarily the keeper of earthly and heavenly wisdom and the guardian of its laws. At the other end of the archetype, Sophia is gloriously beautiful, ageless, eternal, mediating, transcendent spirituality.

These polarised appearances – as Hag or Queen of Heaven – are the two sides of one coin, one archetypal power. Just as coal and diamond are both carbon – that basic substance of matter – so does the Goddess of Wisdom manifest her power through seemingly opposing appearances. By concentration upon the influence of Sophia in our daily lives, we can liquify carbon into light, coal into diamond.

The greatest strength of Lady Wisdom is that she transcends the dualism that has bedevilled our Western society since the fading of the prehistoric and Classical eras when the Goddess was last manifest as a powerful entity of wholeness.

The Goddess of Wisdom has appeared as an abstraction, a pedestalled feminization of a univeral quality, as a serene Goddess, as a philosophical nicety. When we enter theological and philosophical ground, we discover continual hair-splitting as to Sophia's real identity: she becomes a substance, an energy, an abstraction, or she is an identifiable part of the Trinity. Theologians and philosophers have gone out of their way to explain her away, to grudgingly incorporate her into the Divine economy, or else to subvert the orthodox thought processes of their tradition in order to give her a place. The way that Sophia has been treated is well paralleled in the manner with which women have been accorded respect or not. Even today, in most masculine walks of life, women are considered to be a necessary evil, a tangle of contradictions which will not accord with the masculine norm, or else, they are a wondrous species to be pedestalled in some exalted sphere, though robbed of any real power.

The solution which both Sophia and womankind have discovered refutes philosophers and gynophobes everywhere: it is their very intrusiveness. Sophia pervades everything: women, likewise, make their presence felt wherever they are.

Sophia comes to mediate between all these needs and opinions, able to go at will among them because she is a veiled Goddess; she can be everyone's mother, sister or daughter. She is at hand as a living avatara of the Divine Feminine, the Goddess whom we have forgotten and for whom we yearn so urgently.

Part One

THE BLACK GODDESS

=== 1 ===

THE BLACK MISTRESS

Nature's mother who bringest all to life and revives all from day
to day. The food of life Thou grantest in eternal fidelity. And
when the soul hath retired we take refuge in Thee. All that Thou
grantest falls back somewhere into Thy womb.

prayer to Terra Matris, third century AD

The Black Goddess

We live in an age of rediscovery and remembrance, where the
Divine Feminine as Goddess is being recalled to consciousness.
One of her key visionaries has been the poet Robert Graves,
whose book, *The White Goddess*, has awakened a sleeping world.
Though many have attempted to revamp his material, few have
been as successful at provoking response at that creative level.
Graves wrote lyrically and with poetic awe about the inspiring
White Goddess and her priestess-muse representative, Woman.
He wrote as a male poet, totally in love with and in the service
of an exacting Mistress. He also wrote, in less detail, about the
challenging Black Goddess, she who 'is so far hardly more than
a word of hope whispered among the few who have served their
apprenticeship to the White Goddess.'[1]

The Divine Feminine may indeed be discerned as a White Goddess of love and inspiration by men who, reasonably enough, are
drawn to her attractive and fascinating qualities. But the Goddess
of Wisdom, the Black Goddess who is at the heart of the creative
process, cannot be so easily viewed, as Graves himself remarked:
she 'may even appear disembodied rather than incarnate.'[2] Why
should this be so?

The Black Goddess is the veiled Sophia who, in many forms,
is the primal manifestation of the Divine Feminine. She may be
more readily discerned by women, because her hidden processes
and powers accord to their own unspoken but instinctive qualities.
Men rarely approach her, except in fear, for she is manifest not
as a sensuous and desirable muse (although she may sometimes

choose that shape) but as a Dark Mother, immanent and brooding with unknown and unguessable power, or as a Virago, a potent virgin. Fear of the feminine stems from this avoidance and so it is that there are few texts speaking of her qualities, for few men have stayed long enough in her vicinity to record their findings and even fewer women have written about their organic experience of her. It is so that I write this text as an introduction to the idea of the Black Goddess who is the powerful foundation for our understanding of the Divine Feminine, for it is only by homage to her that we may find the Goddess of Wisdom.

Sophia has been on the stage since the beginning, for she is a Creating Goddess. She lies waiting to be discovered within the Black Goddess who is her mirror image, knowing that, until we make that important recognition, she is going to have to come again and again in many shapes. She is waiting in the wings patiently to emerge, knowing that she will have to play many parts – including breeches parts – in the forthcoming scenario.

An appreciation of the Black Goddess is coming slowly into perspective within the West. Throughout the last two thousand years when the Goddess has been marginalized, most appearances of the Divine Feminine have been understood in a dualistic and problematic light. We have not had the safety valve of feminine metaphor in our spiritual understanding, consequently, the Feminine, both Divine and human, has appeared monstrously contorted, threatening and uncontrollable.

The fact that our metaphors of deity can change or have different faces is foreign to Western understanding. The Goddess can be viewed in many ways, a fact which has caused many philosophers and theologians to call the Goddess fickle and mutable, changeable as a whore with her many clients.

It has always struck the Western mind as aberrant that Hinduism can accept so repellent a form as Kali. If the Black Goddess is denied, as she has been in our culture, she will make her appearance in ways that will remind us to respect her in the future – if there is a future. In the Hindu succession of ages, we are in the time of the Kali Yuga, the age of destruction.

We have so often only stressed the beneficial and the beautiful that we have created a false archetype out of the Divine Feminine. The Goddess, to be acceptable to our culture, has had to appear as sweetness and light, a cross between Marilyn Monroe and Venus de Milo, sexy and largely unintelligent. Such dangerous polarisations have hit hard in the West. Not only has this image set the norm for how womankind are viewed, it has unbalanced our relationship with the whole of creation. Western culture, like its orthodox spiritual forms, is dominating, dictating and patriarchal. It does not allow the basic human freedoms to develop in a balanced way, warping even the qualities of wisdom, love, knowledge and compassion.

It is traditionally believed in Hindu culture that when someone establishes a spiritual relationship with Kali, a sacrifice will be demanded. Commitment to the Black Goddess is not to be taken lightly, certainly, for she leads us in many ways which we will find hard. However, if there is mutual respect between us and her, she will also lead us to the heart of truth and justice. Perhaps it is here that we find the beginning of wisdom within ourselves?

If we start with the Black Goddess, rather than with one of her more 'socially acceptable' faces, we will never be led astray. If we embrace her as she is, we will find her wise love will transform us. And as we change, so she also will change into a transcendently beautiful and wise metaphor which we have chosen to call Sophia. This subtle alchemy is our spiritual task.

The way of Sophia is the way of personal experience. It takes us into areas which we may call 'magical reality' – those creative realms to which ordinary mortals are called by right of their vocational and creative skills. However, the poetic, the magical, the creative inscapes of vision are often denied us by our culture. Anyone who has been into the world of vision, defined by many as 'unreal', knows that its power can enhance our lives. It is Sophia who acts as a way-shower and companion on this inner quest, especially helpful for women. Because Sophia's creativity has been denied, we see her in the cloak of the Black Goddess, moving silently and mysteriously about her work.

The Black Goddess lies at the basis of spiritual knowledge, which is why her image continually appears within many traditions as the Veiled Goddess, the Black Virgin, the Outcast Daughter, the Wailing Widow, the Dark Woman of Knowledge. Our own search for the Goddess is one which is begun in darkness and unknowing. Ours is the knowing ignorance of the child in its mother's womb: we have to be born and we are frightened of the extra-womb dimension. Once out of that womb, we begin to be terrified of our origins. But one of the prophecies of Sophia is, 'I will give thee the treasures of darkness, and hidden riches of secret places.'[3] Those treasures of the Divine Feminine lie deep within us, waiting to be discovered.

We have only to consider the mystical experience of the Dark Night, as exemplified by John of the Cross and other mystics. Within the darkness of night or the cloud of unknowing, we discover the heart of our spirituality. This is the seed experience of spiritual growth, to be held fast in the dark earth, to suffer the coldness of winter that germination may take place. It is return to the spiritual womb, in which we find the dazzling darkness spoken of by the mystical poet, Henry Vaughan:

> There is in God, some say,
> a deep but dazzling darkness . . .[4]

Re-entering this womb is both a rebirth of the spirit and a death of the ego:

> Dear beauteous death! the jewel of the just,
> Shining nowhere but in the dark;
> What mysteries do lie beyond thy dust;
> Could man outlook that mark![5]

This school of Dark Night spirituality is found in most traditions that venerate the Black Goddess, not because she is sinister or evil, but because she is the power-house from whence our spirituality is fuelled. It is a way of unknowing, of darkness and uncertainty. Yet the experience which is obtained by this path is one of illumination, when the sun shines at midnight. This is the kindling of Sophia, who is the transcendent pole of the Black Goddess, though finding the connection between the two sometimes takes a long time because of our dualistic conditioning.

We fear the Black Goddess because we project our terrors upon whatever we do not know and what remains hidden from us. Her image has been pushed away so long and now we are reencountering her wherever we look, for she takes the face of Nature to remind us of our responsibility for creation. Once our vision of Nature and of the Goddess was integral to ourselves: 'We participate in her substance, her nature, her processes, her play and her work.'[6]

Our divorce from this total participation is one of the effects of civilization. One of the chief problems is our disdain of matter, our own bodies and their functions, for they remind us of the humbling fact that we are matter. Communion with the Black Goddess is usually non-verbal, non-intellectual – it derives through the body itself for she is our basic prima materia. 'Do you know . . . what matter is? Have you tried taking the word back to its roots? It goes right back to Sanskrit . . . Push through the fissive nature of matter and where do you find yourself? Not, I assure you, in the kingdom of the Leptons and the Quarks, but in the black hole of Magna Mater. Yes, the Great Mother herself, and it is a terrible thing to fall into the lap of the living Goddess.'[7]

Our fear of being exploded, diffused, or made chaotic may be our reaction to the idea of the Black Goddess who, like dark matter, 'controls the structure and eventual fate of the Universe.'[8]

The Black Goddess is the mistress of the Web of creation which is spun in her divine matrix. She is not separate from it, for she *is* it. One of the great spiritual mysteries is the way in which a mystic identifies with the deity: this is considered to be the highest state of mystical awareness. The Goddess, similarly, identifies with her creation. Many Goddess mystics already acknowledge that identification with the Goddess is also identification with the whole of creation. As science strives to uncover the mystery of dark matter, the Creating Mother as Black Goddess is already activated in the imaginations of spiritual seekers.

The Wisdom of the Serpent

The Goddessly creation myths usually take one of two elemental forms – creation from water, the amniotic waters of the womb when the primal soup is mixed, or creation by and from the earth.

Chaos is frightening, and the Goddess first manifests in chaotic images in many cultures, just as she also manifests in ordered images also. The Wisdom of the Bible who makes everything with her partner, delighting in the fashioning of creation, is acceptable within our society – it is a metaphor we have chosen to adopt, based on ancient, pan-cultural symbolisms which we will examine shortly. Set against this image is the real birthing mother like Tiamat who produces the creation from her body when Marduk rips her into clouds, water and earth. We have chosen to retain this metaphor for Nature, red in tooth and claw, chaotic, elemental, unpredictable. It is an aspect which we can identify as the Black Goddess, our primal Wisdom.

Nature is always metaphored by female images; she is present both as Dame Kind, the beneficent and providing mother, and also as the Great Dragon, her terrible aspect which roams through all things. With these dual expressions of the Goddess goes a fear of chaos and a love of order – which is why we see the polarization of the Black Goddess and Sophia.

Which is the oldest myth of creation: the heterosexual or the parthenogenic? Science tells us that single cells divide to reproduce themselves. Whether we look to older or later myths, the chaotic feminine is in there at the beginning, either as the Goddess riven in two or the Orphic darkness of Night laying her solitary egg.

The Babylonian Creation myth tells of the God Apsu and the Goddess Tiamat, who are the spiritual essence of the sweet waters and the bitter waters. These may be seen respectively as fresh-water and sea-water. By the mingling of these pure waters, the gods were created. Eventually Anu, the Sky-God, begot Ea, the God of Wisdom. There arose a tumult between the first-begotten Gods; Apsu was for destroying them, Tiamat for biding their time until their children were mature. Like the Gnostic Sophia, 'she was stung, she writhed in lonely desolation, her heart worked in secret passion.'[9] Like Zeus with Kronos, Ea arose and drowned Apsu, thus taking on the role of first father of the Gods. He lay with Damkina, his wife, and she conceived Marduk. Anu sent storms to torment Tiamat and her rebellious children who begged their mother for help. She accordingly made eleven monsters to fight on their side, taking one of them, Kingu, to be her captain and husband. She hung the tablets of fate about his neck to empower him.

Ea 'took the short road, went the direct way to Tiamat', but he could not face her.[10] No-one could be found to face her save Marduk. Anshar, God of the Horizon, sent his messenger Kaka 'to primordial sediments, (to) call together the generations of the gods.'[11] Kissing the primordial silt, Kaka called upon the male and female deities of silt and told them what had befallen, inviting them to come and decide the nature of the world. They met with the younger gods and appointed Marduk as king and leader of the gods, bidding him: 'Slit life from Tiamat, and may the winds carry her blood to world's secret ends.' Armed with magical weapons, Marduk flew to meet Tiamat, calling in the midst of the fray: 'Mother of all, why did you have to mother war?'[12] Tiamat was netted and the wind-god blew into her body so that it became inflated. Marduk pierced her belly with an arrow which cut out her womb. He then smashed her body into pieces, scattering her organs to the directions. Splitting the carcass in two, he set up the upper half to create the arch of the sky, setting the celestial lights to cross over it. The lower half was heaped up with mountains and pierced for water-courses. Tiamat's spittle became the rain. 'High overhead he arched her tail, locked in to the wheel of heaven; the pit was under his feet, between was the crotch, the sky's fulcrum. Now the earth had foundations and the sky its mantle.'[13] The titanic monsters were imprisoned and their likenesses set up as guardians to the Abyss. In the assembly of the gods, Marduk proclaimed: 'In the former time you inhabited the void above the abyss, but I have made Earth as the mirror of Heaven',[14] and he made Babylon his chief abode where the Annunaki, the fallen gods, made his temple. Kingu was sacrificed in order to provide the matter for the first human beings.

We see here that Tiamat is a primordial sea-goddess whose body creates the earth, which does not exist prior to the god's rebellion. Hebrew qabalistic tradition calls her Marah, the bitter sea: a name which is etymologically linked with both Miriam and Mary. Tiamat is the Elder Mother of all, she who is the essential moisture from which life proceeds. Her husband, Apsu, gives his name to our word 'abyss' frequently used as a term for the Underworld. The Akkadian *Tiamat* and the Hebrew *tehom* are closely associated, meaning 'the deep'. It is upon the waters of the *tehom* that God's spirit moves in *Genesis* 1:2. The overlaps between this creation myth and the Hebrew and Gnostic ones are considerable. Kingu is very much a demiurge and Tiamat, like Sophia, creates her offspring by herself.

Myths of how the Goddess was split into many fragments are told throughout the world.[15] Feminist exegesis frequently reads such myths as patriarchal take-over bids or heroic one-up-manship of god over goddess. The ubiquity of these myths cannot lie, but they may bear other interpretations. Do they arise from cultures who strive to leave their mother and discover metaphors of male-ness and fatherhood in the process of maturation? The cutting of the umbilicus is essential for physical survival, but whether this metaphor may be also applied to spirituality is unclear. Sometimes the myth supports the Mother Goddess at the expense of her consort.

War between the older gods and their offspring is a common mythic theme. In Greek myth, Ouranos as father sky and Gaia as mother earth lie together nightly, but Ouranos hides away all children born of their union. Gaia hides her son Kronos who then castrates Ouranos. Gaia receives the blood into her womb and the Erinyes are conceived. But no longer do sky and earth meet in union.[16] The same pattern of devouring or hiding children is enacted by Kronos, and Rhea's son, Zeus castrates his father.

Further echoes of the myth are discernible throughout Mediterranean tradition, notably the manner in which Oceanus and Tethys create the gods. Plato sees them as 'the offspring of flux and motion'. Their story precedes all other Greek creation myths. It is not difficult to see the parallels between Oceanus and Apsu and Tethys and Tiamat. The trail of Tiamat survived within Christian scripture as Leviathan, the sea-monster of chaos, where she is likened to Rahab, the harlot,[17] and also in Egyptian tradition as the crocodile of Set. It is ironic to identify this same beast as the serpent of knowledge in the Garden of Eden who tempts Eve and as the devouring serpent of *Revelations* 12 that combats the Virgin.

The dragon energy of the Black Goddess recurs in the myth of St George and the Dragon. This story is often taken as implying the overthrow of both the earth and of women, but its subtext is more subtle than that. The dragon of the Black Goddess is transformed into the maiden Sophia who, with her symbol of the dove, is released from her primal form by love, a theme recurring in the Grail cycle.[18]

The overcoming of the dragon or serpent occurs also at Delphi. The Earth Mother has always spoken through her oracle, often housed in a cave or cavern to be nearer the source of power, and where better than at Delphi, a word deriving from the Greek *delphys*, or womb. The Delphic oracle, called the Pythoness, now associated with the Sun God, Apollo, was once the servant of Gaia, as well as of Hera or Juno. It is told how Hera, shamed by Zeus bringing Athene to birth without her maternal assistance, called upon the ancestral gods to aid her to bear a child as strong as Zeus. Remaining apart from him for a year, she bears Typhon, who has a man's shape but two serpents' tails for legs.[19] She takes Typhon to Delphi to be fostered by the *drakaina* or Pythoness.

The *drakaina* was an earth-speaker whose veiled words represented the views of the earth, the Black Goddess herself. Similarly, vows were always witnessed by the earth, who would hear and remember. Our ancestors made such oaths to the earth which we have forgotten to uphold and the *drakainas* of our time now speak urgently of the wronged earth in ways we cannot fail to hear. Many people now fear for the end of human existence: not that life itself will cease.

Diodorus Siculus reported that 'the Chaldeans say that the substance of the world is eternal, and that it neither had a first beginning nor . . . will at a later time suffer destruction.'[20] The image of uroboros, the serpent with its tail in its mouth is emblematic of this eternal chain of life. Tiamat, the chaotic creating mother and the dragon of the Apocalypse are one and the same.

The earliest forms of the Goddess of Wisdom lie far back in the metamemory of ancestral heritage, a tradition to which there are two possible approaches: through the agency of archaeological research or through inspired analeptic memory. Many matriarchal feminists have used the latter method to intuit the roots of the Goddess. It is not an academically acceptable practice, but when archaeology runs out of ideas, such analepsis must take over.

This seed of memory is that very motherwit with which all living things are imprinted. It is genetically encoded within us and, whatever our conditioning, it frequently emerges, giving us access to survival skills and unbidden instincts which help us in necessity. This kernel of motherwit allows us access to skilful wisdom – not the high-flown and academically acceptable kind of Wisdom, but the homely and immediate kind. It is arising spontaneously in the peoples of the earth who are becoming earth-speakers of the Black Goddess.

Like the prophet Jonah, or like the coiled infant awaiting birth, we are also in the belly of Tiamat-Leviathan, contemplating our destined vocation. Maybe somewhere locked in the intertwining strands of DNA which are sealed with the unquestionable signature of the Goddess , we will find the indwelling motherwit of the womb-oracle and act upon it.

Earth Mother: Mountain Mother

The creation of the world is often expressed in primal cosmogony by means of a birthing Goddess who is shown in the position of birth, her vulva spread, her legs akimbo. Through the sacred gateway of her vulva all life proceeds and is incarnate. This image is the Sheila na Gig, the *fons ex origo*, whose image was placed over church doorways, a continual reminder that we are all born of the earth and that her womb will also become our tomb.

In primal society, birth is a sacred activity and is accordingly granted special privileges and rituals. It is not until the classical Hellenic age that we find a disdain for the reproductive organs as

1 *Earth Mother* Here the Goddess of the Earth arises from the ground. As the Mistress of Generation, verdancy springs up from her very body and a winged serpent, representing the life-force itself, comes to drink from one breast, while a bull drinks from the other. She is Nature herself. From an eleventh century Exultet Roll of Monte Cassino Abbey. B.M. Add. Ms. 30337.

unclean, for birth as an abomination. Indeed, since those times, we may trace the degradation of the body and all things pertaining to it.

Within our own time, the attempt to re-evaluate the birth experience has gone hand in hand with feminism. It is no longer necessary for most women in the West to endure the most painful of birth positions which has been the Western 'norm' in hospitals: that of lying on the back. Creative application of 'primitive' birth positions – walking, squatting and kneeling – have been adapted by Western women with great results. Birth is, after all, something a woman does herself, not something that is done to her.

We have tended to treat cosmology in the same way – it has been laid on its back and the forceps applied to produce a strange metaphorical product. The birthing Goddess has been replaced by the Father, Son and Spirit. Physical creation, the Goddess and Woman have been polarized to the preferred metaphors of mental creativity, the Divine Masculine and Man.

The earth wisdom of the surviving native traditions of our planet speaks of a simplicity which our world lacks. It is a wisdom which addresses the heart, recognizing our kinship with each other and the rest of creation. It is sacramental and incarnational rather than transcendent in its approach to spirituality. It has a humility which frequently underscores our 'civilized' Western paranoia. For the native traditions, the Earth Mother is a reality: the earth which feeds us and gives us plentifully all that we need.

The 'primitive' experience of the Goddess is not one of fear and torment, it is one of perfect familiarity and respect. When the Nez Perce Indians of North America were presented with the prospect of agriculture as a means of survival, their spokesman, Smohalla, very rightly replied: 'My young men shall never work. Men who work cannot dream and wisdom comes in dreams. You ask me to plough the ground. Shall I take a knife and tear my mother's breast? Then when I die She will not take me to her bosom to rest. You ask me to dig for stone. Shall I dig under her skin for bones? Then when I die I cannot enter her body and be born again. You ask me to cut grass and make hay and sell it and be rich like the white man. But how can I cut off my mother's hair? it is bad law and my people cannot obey it. I want my people to stay with me here. All the dead humans will come to life again. We must wait here in the house of our ancestors and be ready to meet in the body of our mother.'[21]

The tombs of Tarxien in Malta, whose floor-plans reflect the bodily shape of the Goddess, remind us that, for our ancestors also, the earth was both the womb and the tomb of humanity.[22] Many land features such as the Paps of Anu in Kerry, Ireland, and Silbury Hill, near the prehistoric complex of Avebury in South-West England, recall the physical shape of the Creating Goddess.

The native peoples of the world have always lived, and in some places still live, with the earth. It is an integral part of their lives. Its diverse lifeforms are both food, medicine and companion. They do not despise their bodies or their habitat in the way in which we often do today. Western society must find its way back to this harmony, if necessary by finding a balance within the Black Goddess, for the spirit of the earth speaks aloud in our own time, in simple syllables for those simpletons whose greed wrecks the earth and her resources, raping her store of mineral, grain, forests, and animals for short-term and short-sighted ends, which will leave our ecology forever depleted. The Black Goddess moves in the shape of the elemental weather which afflicts us as earthquake, sand-storm, hurricane, drought; as Oya, the Cailleach, as Rhea, Cybele and Kali, she exhibits an outraged face.

The cult of the earth mother celebrates the fact that we are surrounded and enclosed by the creation of the Mother. If we threaten creation, then it fights back, as James Lovelock, using the ancient Greek earth mother's name as metaphor for the planet, has expressed: 'Gaia . . . is no doting mother tolerant of misdemeanours . . . she is stern and tough, always keeping the world warm and comfortable for those who obey the rules, but ruthless in her destruction of those who transgress.'[23] Ge or Gaia combines both the nurturing and destructive aspects which polarize the Goddess being the nurse of the young, the providing mother, and also the sender of ghosts and demons, the Goddess of death whose realm lay within her own body.[24] One of her titles is Melantho (the Black One).[25]

The West has exiled itself from the primal experience of native spirituality. There is no space to detail the destruction wrought by colonization where natural spiritualities, habitats and cultures have been ruthlessly overlaid by Western patterns, 'because they were good for progress.' This is not a feminist argument only, but one which is arising in many hearts. The manipulative and destructive patterns of the West have now been successfully inculcated throughout the Third World – a heritage which we still have to reap.

Despite the New Science which allows spirituality and technology to inhabit one domain once again, science is tending to look beyond the earth for answers, seeing our earth as expendable and the Western pattern of 'progress' and expansion as being planned for another solar system.

The titanic powers of our earth, the children of Tiamat whom Marduk sought to chain, are being reassembled in the shape of uranium. The dissecting tendency of Science may be seen as no better than the slicing up of Tiamat by Marduk, regarded by some as the primordial rapist. However, the interaction of male and female deities in cosmogony is a necessary one.

The nature of the Goddess is more subtle and various than many allow. She has transformative qualities which few have guessed at. In our rediscovery of the Goddess, it might be easy to remain with a single terrestial metaphor, to define her solely in terms of a monolithic figure on whom the legend of 'Supreme Goddess' can be pinned. In the reclamation of the Divine Feminine, many have made of the Goddess a single entity, in imitation of monotheism. There have been many cults of the Goddess, just as there have been many cults of the God, the Divine Masculine. Yet deity is deity, a colourless light which may be refracted in different ways through the different prismatic lenses of metaphor.

Into recorded history we can trace the development of one Goddess who survived from early times to be called Magna Mater, among other titles. She who is called Cybele, Rhea and many other names. She is a mountain mother, one who forms the world from rocks thrown from her apron. She inhabits the inaccessible regions of the earth, on mountains and in caves, surrounded by her beasts. She is the Mistress of the Steppe (*belit seri*) and Mistress of the Beasts, aspects of whom are reflected in Artemis, Inanna, Anath, Atargatis.

We see her first in some of the earliest remains of the ancient world, of Çatal Hüyük in Anatolia. A statue from this site, dated 6000 BC shows the Great Mother seated on her throne or birth-stool which is supported by leopards or lionesses; her child's head is in the process of crowning.[26] This image is echoed by later statuary, which shows the Great Mother standing upon a hill, between two lions or supported by dancing lionesses.[27]

Cybele is primarily associated with the earth, specifically a rock. Her cult constellated around the black meteorite which was enshrined at Pergamum. She was chiefly venerated in her cities of Troy, Pergamum and Pessinus by the people of Phrygia[28] where her name was originally Kubaba, 'Lady of the Cube', later Hellenized to Cybele.[29] However, the Greeks avoided calling her by name, preferring to call her *Meter Theon*, Mother of the Gods, being happy to associate her with their native goddess Gaia and Rhea.

The poet Lucretius (*c.* 99–55 BC) explained the natural power of Cybele in her lion-chariot as being like the earth, which hangs in airy space, 'for earth cannot rest on earth'. The mural crown on her head is hers 'because earth in select spots is fortified and bears the weight of cities. Decked with this emblem even now the image of the holy mother is borne about the world in solemn state.'[30]

How Cybele came to Rome is interesting. The Delphic oracle had been consulted concerning the Roman war against the Carthaginians. It foretold that if the Phrygian Mother were brought from Pergamum she would aid the Roman cause. Accordingly, a deputation was sent out and the great black stone which was worshipped as the statue of Cybele was loaded onto a ship. The ship could not, however, be moved up the Tiber but became stuck through no apparent cause. People began to mutter that the priestess Claudia was not pure. In vindication, Claudia removed her girdle and, fastening it about the ship's prow, prayed the Goddess to clear her name. The ship accordingly moved and the black stone of Cybele was reverently installed in the temple of Victoria on the Palatine in 204 BC. There was great rejoicing in Rome, since Cybele was the Goddess of the Trojans, ancestors of the Romans according to tradition.[31]

Sabina, a Roman priestess of Cybele, wrote of the Goddess's mysteries:

> Deo's orgies
> and the terrifying
> Hekate nights
> I experienced.[32]

The ecstatic worship of Cybele, with its throbbing drums, wild flutes and animal howling, represents the chaotic and untameable aspects of the Great Mother. Like Nyx, in the Orphic mystery, the dark drum of the Black Goddess beat the rhythms and cyclicities of life. At Epidaurus, a third century BC song is inscribed on stone: 'When the sovereign Zeus caught sight of the Mother of the gods he hurled the thunderbolt and took up the *tympanum* (drum), he shattered the rocks and took up the *tympanum*', bidding her go hence, but Cybele replied: 'I shall not go hence to the gods, unless I am given my territories, half of the heavens, half of the earth, a third part of the sea. Only then shall I go hence.'[33] This fragment suggests a rivalry between the ancient Earth Goddess and the Sky Father, to whom she stands in the relationship of a grandmother, although she is sometimes described as the *paredros*, or throne-companion, of Zeus.

The myth of Cybele in the later Classical world told how the Great Mother was sleeping on Mount Ida in the form of a rock, or, some say, as the earth itself. Her son, Zeus, tried to lie with her but only succeeded in spilling his semen onto the earth, whereupon Cybele conceived and bore an androgyne called Agdistus. This monstrous being was so dangerous that the other gods determined to chain it. Making Agdistus drunk, they tied his genitals to a tree so that when he woke he would castrate himself. The place where the testicles lie sprouted up as a pomegranate tree. Gathering fruit from it one day, the nymph Nana became pregnant from contact with the tree and bore Attis. He grew up, fell in love with a maiden, and Agdistus drove Attis mad, so that he castrated himself.[34] This complex myth sets the scene for many future scenarios, notably the Gnostic one in which Sophia plays so great a part.

The experience of Cybele is an intensely matriarchal one. Gudea, the Sumerian ruler of Lagash, addressed Gatumdug, the city's Goddess, thus:

> I am one who has no mother, you are my mother.
> I am one who has no father, you are my father.
> You have taken my seed into the womb, have given birth to me in the shrine.[35]

Such words might indeed have come from the lips of any of Cybele's *galloi*, whose seed was shed and permanently enshrined within the Earth Mother herself.

The experience of the *galloi* is one fearful to most men. These priests were inspired at the annual rites of Cybele and Attis to castrate themselves and serve the Goddess, to give their power in the form of their male virility to the Goddess's keeping. Cybele is, in many ways, the Goddess who was predominant in the expression of feminism during the sixties and early seventies. The results of this are still to reap, for many men were symbolically castrated at that time. Such imbalances will adjust themselves when we focus our attention upon the mediating presence of Sophia.

At that time, the voice of the Goddess was upraised in the West in one gigantic shout, her tympanum throbbed with uncontrolled urgency. While feminism has sought more acceptable faces since, the shadow of that first feminist impact is still cast across the Western world: a many-headed, many-armed female with instruments of war in her hands, her mouth wide open to expel a long-suppressed scream of birthing anguish. This is the popular image which lurks beyond the threshold of many minds.

There are other, equally potent, voices upraised on behalf of the earth itself, which is being raped of its resources, its natural habitats (including humanity's own), polluted, its fair face made as ugly as technology and population explosion can make it. The ecological movement projects as monstrous an image of the Black Goddess as any that lies dormant in popular spiritual metaphor.

The rites of the Great Mother show the fearsome aspect of the Goddess which operates on the fuel of raw energy and sacrificed virility. She is our Western Kali: the one who gives us birth and who receives us at the end. The prayer addressed to the

Great Mother which heads this chapter observes that 'all that Thou grantest falls somewhere back into Thy womb.'[36] The Black Goddess wastes nothing, but reprocesses all.

The Black Goddess is terrifying because she does not just nurture her offspring, she makes them change by challenging them. This is also the action of Sophia: although she is responsible for the Fall, in Gnosticism, she is also the companion to every soul, leading it to wisdom. She is both creator and receiver of creation.

This Black Goddess aspect of Sophia is not evil. Like the wrathful images of Buddhist deities, the dark face of Sophia is there to warn and admonish, to exhibit her reflected aspect with more effect. The petrifying face of Medusa did not harm Perseus, as long as he looked at her reflection in his polished shield, given him by Athene, the Goddess of Wisdom. So it is with the dual aspects of Sophia. Some can only look at the Black Goddess by viewing her reflected face of Sophia.

Refracting the Image

The Goddess is as old as time and as young as eternity: a pair of complementary forms which runs throughout the mythos of Sophia as the dark Mother of Earth and the bright Virgin of Heaven. We can call her Sophia Nigrans, Black Sophia, and Sophia Stellarum, Sophia of the Stars.

How are Sophia and the Black Goddess associated? We may use an image of sparks of fire running through the blackness of charcoal, to illumine this mystery. The Black Goddess is the metaphorical appearance of the Goddess in matter. Sophia is the metaphorical appearance of the living spirit within matter. Sophianic images usually resort to fire at some point, as we shall see. The Black Goddess, meanwhile, is expressed by means of stones, rocks and earth, as well as in the very flesh we all inhabit. Sophia has seeded her sparkle of fire in us all. When we are spiritually kindled, then her pathway of fire spreads throughout the charcoal of our physical being.

When we deal with Sophia, we will find ourselves alternately dazzled and blindfolded – the effect is the same, whether we stand in darkness or light. We must trust to her voice within us to guide us forward.

Goddess spirituality shows us the matched pair of Black Goddess and Sophia, inverse poles of the same archetype. The Keres Indians of New Mexico still revere two such images, knowing them to be one and the same: Tse che nako, or Thought Woman, who, like Sophia, conceives of, thinks and creates everything. She is also believed to be the creative power of thought within everyone. She 'was the first to work with creative visualization. She is ever spinning her web, developing the possibilities of life. She is far away, but ever near,' a frequent characteristic of Sophia.[37] Her mirror image is Spider Woman, who is a more familiar and earthy figure who helps those in need. Among the Hopi she is called Kokyang Wuhti, most often portrayed as an elderly woman of great wisdom who is the guardian of the earth.[38]

These figures are but two among thousands of examples. The manner in which we envisage the Goddess is important for tomorrow. In stressing the aspects of Black Goddess and Sophia in this book, I am attempting to throw light on the issues of creativity, knowledge and wisdom – qualities associated more generally with benign Goddess metaphors and upon destruction, ignorance and foolishness – qualities frequently associated with the wrathful aspects of the Goddess. This over-simplified paradigm is doomed to failure, because there is no duality of purpose within the Goddess, only a rhythmic filling and emptying of our consciousness of which the Black Goddess and Sophia are the regulators. Between these poles we learn true wisdom.

The Black Goddess helps us in the process of *kenosis*, or emptying: in this phase we are stripped bare, reduced to basics, forced to lie fallow that knowledge may be seeded in the bare, cleansed fields of Wisdom. Sophia helps us in the process of *plerosis*, or filling: in this phase we experience the growth and replenishment of our resources, when we are reinvigorated and our knowledge strengthened. This is a rhythmic process where one phase succeeds the other. We cannot choose to experience only Sophia and to ignore the Black Goddess.

The poles of the Goddess may be visualized as colour: everything from black to white is possible. She may manifest so, or she may choose to work via one of her many guises – the liberal arts as notes of music, as gifts of the Holy Spirit – thus showing herself as the full spectrum of the rainbow between the poles of black and white. Here black and white do not equate with evil and good; they have no moral qualitative weight.

The Goddess has liked to operate under more than one set of colours. At this latter day, we mainly observe her major three: white, red and black, Maiden, Mother and Elder. These are the sacred colours of life itself, out of which creation is woven:

> I wove it once with colours white,
> With black I wound it through
> Then I did dye it with a red
> That binds the life in you.[39]

The three moon phases and the triple sisterhood of the Parchae or Fates, spinning, weaving and cutting, lurk in the recesses of our rusty symbolic treasuries. Many people have attempted to pigeon-hole Sophia into one of these, but the problem is that the Goddess is more complex than that. We formulate endless metaphors, but end up using a miserable vocabulary of 'nice, pleasant and not so pleasant.'

Sophia is capable of appearing in all or any of these circum-scribed symbolic categories. For the purposes of this book, it is more helpful to see Sophia as multi-form, appearing throughout three ages, which are typified by the three sacred colours. These are derived from earliest symbolism and appear elsewhere as the *gunas,* or three fundamental tendencies, in Hindu ideology, the three alchemical stages of the Great Work, the three cups which are offered by the Grail Goddess, among others. The three aages of Sophia are also applicable to our individual condition annd spiritual experience:

The first age/experience is Black – the essential darkness of knowledge, wherein we are within the womb oof the Goddess. This age is typified by initiatory rites withiiin caves, temples and underground cells – the experience of the 'sun shining at midnight' is sought. This state of darkness is not evil, rather it is the darkness of innate knowing, the 'divine darkness' of apophatic spirituality. In this age everyone experiences spiritual vision directly through the body, soul and spirit: we know the Black Mistress.

The second age/experience is White – wherein the forgetting of the Goddess occurs when we emerge from her womb into the light. A blindness descends upon our physical faculties and there is a greater emphasis on the intellectual processes. This age is typified by rituals of light's celebration, in structures which tower higher and which keep the people and priesthood separate. Nevertheless, the Goddess proceeds with her creation in the form of a pillar of cloud. There is a renunciation or distrust of the body as untrustworthy and a sense of matter as unclean: we are aware of the White Virgin.

The third age/experience is Red – the remembrance and reanimation of the Goddess' mysteries. This age is happening now. It is typified by enthusiasm and fervour, often working through extant spiritualities and deities who express pure spirit as fire. It has diverse rituals whose purpose is to kindle the spirit by practical means. There is a rediscovery of wholistic experience, the union of separated metaphors. The Goddess leads her people in the form of a pillar of fire, which shines in the night. People gather in circles, in open places, usually about a fire or centralized altar which symbolizes the spirit's kindling. Sophia appears in the form acceptable to each heart as the Red Queen, winged and radiant as the sun.

The pre-patriarchal appearances of Sophia are to be found aspected in many goddesses worldwide. While women have sought the early images of these primal goddesses in order to help enhance and rediscover their spirituality, these are metaphorically remote from our modern conditions and problems. Sophia is not Woman, but she very much represents the state of womanhood. In her post-patriarchal manifestation, Sophia often appears as the Goddess 'tidied up' and regularized. Her wild, playful side has been denied so long that now she remains abstract, veiled, blackened, subject to sudden disappearances, chastisements and victimizations. As more women and men meditate upon Sophia, they discover their own lost wisdom. It is a long process of stripping off the veils one by one. It is a journey of descent, of valorous fall in order to remember.

═══ 2 ═══
THE SACRED MARRIAGE

I believe that most of what was said of God was in reality
said of that Spirit whose body is Earth
AE (George Russell), *Candle of Vision*

Marriage to the Land

The metaphor of Earth-Mother permeates our consciousness of
the Goddess at many levels. She is one who is riven apart to create
matter itself. She is understood in every country as the Goddess
of the Land, a sub-personality of the Goddess of the Planet,
who has distinct geological features, meteorological conditions,
and a cultural colouring all of her own. Sometimes queens and
priestesses assume her personality and attributes as, for example,
where Egyptian queens manifest the Goddess Isis in her life-giving
function as patroness of the Nile.[1] The abiding presence of the
Goddess is also understood to reside in certain sacred places,
temples, land-features and, by later association, she is perceived
to be the Mistress of the whole globe. This concept eventually led
to the birth of the *Anima Mundi* or World-Soul. The mythos of the
Goddess who makes the earth, associates closely with it and then
leaves it to become a guardian entity, is that of Sophia.

In the early prefigurings of Sophia, two qualities epitomise the
Goddess of the Land: she rules by love and justice. Somewhere
between these joint principles, the image of Sophia arises to bear
the major burden of the Divine Feminine in successive centuries.
The myth of Sophia, known to us in fragmentary form through the
texts and scriptures of early Jewish, Christian and Gnostic sources,
is a salutary tale of loss and finding; underlying the myth is the
reality of union, hoped-for, actual or remembered. Exile in flesh
is everyone's birthright, runs the chorus of the myth; the flesh is
not seemly, matter is misfortune, runs the refrain of those who
suffer this exile.

However, we can go beyond this planctus and strike a chord
which is both wholesome and familiar: the exile of men and
women from wholeness is briefly evaded by the joys of sexual

union. The conjoining of flesh and its embraces are our birthright and mode of continuance. Before the speculations of philosophers come to darken the scene, the early Western world knew this homely wisdom well.

We currently inhabit a society which rapes the earth, scorns women and denies Deity a female face. If we are to understand just how and why the Goddess of Wisdom, almost alone of representatives of the Divine Feminine, has survived within Western orthodox spiritualities we must come to a basic understanding about the body and the spirit.

It was William Blake who outlined the three truths which are overthrown by all sacred codes as heresy:

1 Man has no Body distinct from his Soul; for that call'd Body is a portion of Soul discern'd by the five Senses, the chief inlets of Soul in this age.
2 Energy is the only life, and is from the Body; and Reason is the bound or outward circumference of Energy.
3 Energy is eternal delight.[2]

This is a gnostic understanding that exoteric religion usually finds a way of denying. It is also a way of contemplating the Goddess of Wisdom as a whole being, not a pair of polarized sisters, or as a petrified statue of antique worship. The experience of the body is critical in our spiritual journey. If we only take the evidence of the spirit as true, Sophia does not inhabit us. Before Sophia came to be symbolized as a transcendent virgin, she was the Black Mistress of life.

In pre-patriarchal times, the wisdom of the Goddess was understood primarily through the body. The rituals which bound humankind to the Divine Feminine were enactments of sacred sexuality: a state wherein wholeness is experienced. The Goddess of the Land was contracted as the divine bride of the earth's people. This ritual enactment was performed by the priestess of that Goddess's cult and by the appointed king or ruler.

In the early egalitarian societies where men and women lived in partnership rather than in successively polarized social roles, the marriage of the land played an important part in the rituals of the Goddess. 'The goddess and her hero were the two cosmic powers, and, as priestess and king, also the two social powers.'[3]

In earlier times, the Goddess of the Land was herself represented by a queen and the ruler was *her* husband. The kingly sacrifice which

35

figures in many Middle Eastern cultures from Dummuzi/Tammuz through to Osiris and Christ is a remembrance of this theme. The Goddess of the Land requires a new husband every seven years in order to remain young. This ancient wisdom lay in the fact that any ruler could become a restrictive despot if allowed to remain unchallenged. Sometimes the challenger killed the old king, becoming the new king. Sometimes the old king killed the challenger and remained worthily in office another seven years. This theme endlessly repeated in seasonal mythology shows how the Goddess replaces her consort with a new, virile lover who, full of love for her, will renew and uphold the land, even as she herself is pleasured.

This was the rationale behind the sacred marriage of the ruler to the land. Those who are horrified by the kingly sacrifice might well consider how today we sacrifice political leaders to the expediancy of the moment, for the marriage of the Goddess to the land continues to this day, with democracies electing and casting down their appointed representatives with the same casual unconcern as Inanna with her many consorts.

The union of the land and the king was enacted quite literally from Sumer to Ireland. The remembrance of this ritual is recalled in the Biblical *Song of Songs*, in the Gnostic passion of Sophia and her union with the Logos; it remained an integral part of Jewish marital Sabbath customs as well as in the mystical speculations of the qabala.

The erotic nature of Sophia has been carefully tidied away as not consistent with her virginal stereotype. However, the primal essential quality of sex is part of her function. 'Erotic energy is the eternal source of creativity', wrote Nicholas Berdyaev. 'The erotic shock is the way of revealing beauty in the world.'[4] When we long for the fulfilment of sexual desire or the appeasement of hunger, there can be no denial of our orientation. Real spiritual response is as raw as these.

It is so that Enkidu, the Sumerian wild man of the *Gilgamesh* epic, was 'civilized'. Gilgamesh sent a *hierodule* to sleep with Enkidu. After six or seven nights of sexual activity, 'Enkidu had wisdom, broader understanding.'[5] However, the wild beasts no longer came to him, in this story. He gained wisdom at the expense of instinct. Sexual knowledge and sacred knowledge have already been separated in the *Gilgamesh* epic, a dichotomy which was to exercise the Gnostics in later centuries.

Sophia has been called by many 'the Virgin Wisdom', after Pallas Athene, but the fact of the matter is, Sophia yearns after the marriage bed. As transcendent mother, she is exiled from her co-creator; as manifest daughter, she is exiled from her lover, the Logos. The ancient mysteries saw the intrinsic epiphany of wisdom in the image of the bridal chamber. This feature was taken into Gnosticism, where the Valentinian baptistry was called the *nemphon* or bridal room.

Initiates of the mysteries could look forward to having 'angels as their spouses . . . they will enter the bridal room of the *ogdoad* in the presence of the spirit; they will become sympathetic aeons; they will participate in spiritual and eternal weddings.'[6] This language may seem far removed from the primal experience of the sacred marriage.

During the highest initiations of the Eleusinian Mysteries, the candidate experienced the *epopteia*, where the gods of Eleusis were portrayed by the priests and priestesses in a ritual which dramatized the sacred wedding of the gods Zeus and Demeter. The saying by which the highest initiates recognized each other was preserved by Clement of Alexandria:

> I have eaten from the *tympanon* (drum),
> I have drunk from the *kymbalon* (skin),
> I have carried the *kernos* (fan),
> I have crawled under the *pastos* (bridal-bed).[7]

The Orphic mysteries bear out that last statement, for the initiate is there said to have 'entered the bosom of Despoina', the subterranean persona of the Kore or Persephone. The experience of the bridal chamber, the 'little death' of orgasm where union is experienced as a temporary death of the ego, was a profound mystery of non-duality and therefore of spiritual illumination. The initiate's journey was as mysterious as the passage of the virgin beyond the gates of hymen.

But while humankind sought the divine experience of life, divinity sought the human experience of death. The developing mythos of the Goddess began to speak of her descent into materiality in a way which expressed concern about the separation of body and spirit. This is manifested in the story of Inanna who, although lauded as Mistress of Heaven and Earth, is nevertheless unacquainted with the very human experience of death.

Inanna

Inanna is the Sumerian name for the Goddess whom the Babylonians called Ishtar. Both names are associated with Astarte of the Phoenicians and the Hebrew Esther. She was mystically considered to be the bride of each king. 'Ishtar is indeed thy beloved, may she lengthen thy life, may the good genius of kingship faithfully stand by thy side.'[8]

Ishtar is called 'creatress of wisdom' and 'counsellor of the gods', the 'guardian spirit of life'.[9] Inanna combines aspects to show herself as a warrior and as a beloved mistress. She is described as being as high as the heavens and as wide as the earth.[10] As Ishtar she is likewise 'she who gives sceptre, throne and royal power to every king.'[11] The sacred wedding was performed by Inanna's priestessly representative and the king, of course. The rites of Inanna/Ishtar were similar to those of Aphrodite or Venus who passes into European tradition as the Mistress of Love.

Inanna has many Sophianic resonances. Here, she is a wanderer beseeching Enlil:

> I, the woman who circles the land – tell me where is my house,
>   Tell me where is the city in which I may live . . .
>   I, who am your daughter . . . the hierodule, who are your bridesmaid – tell me where is my house . . .
>   The bird has its nesting place, but I – my young are dispersed.
>   The fish lies in calm waters, but I – my resting place exists not.
>   The dog kneels at the threshold, but I – I have no threshold.[12]

This Sophianic complaint is reiterated by Maat, Astraea, the Shekinah, and Sophia as Christ. The eviction of the Goddess from her proper place and the dispersal of her qualities permeates our story.

Ishtar's symbol is the eight-pointed star. As we will see in subsequent chapters, Sophia is the Mistress of the *Ogdoad*, dwelling in the eighth region superior to those of the seven planetary levels or experiences. She proved herself to be likewise mistress of the eight bright ways to wisdom by her descent to the Great Below through seven levels. She underwent the stripping of the seven levels. The mystical number seven is crucial in unfolding the mysteries of Sophia. The seven levels, pillars, sorrows or sleepings are integrally part of her universal mythos. They are states which we undergo, pass through and understand.

The motivation of Inanna's descent to the Underworld is not given in the text; it has been assumed that she wished to overcome death, in the manner of Saviour Goddess, but let us follow her down. She determined to travel from the Great Above, her own realm, to that of the Great Below, which was ruled over by Ereshkigal, whom she called her 'elder sister'. Inanna polarizes as a White Goddess, while Ereshkigal takes the Black Goddess role. Inanna took her leave of her seven chief temples and we can imagine her coming from the Great Above down these seven levels as Sophia descended. She fastened about her the seven *mes* (pronounced *mays*), which are the divine rules symbolized by her regalia.

When Ereshkigal heard of Inanna's impending visit, she bade her gatekeeper lock the seven gates of the Underworld against her. At each of these Inanna was stripped of one of the seven *mes*, the crown, the two necklets, the breastplate, the ring, the measuring rod and line and lastly her royal robe. It was so that she came naked into Ereshkigal's realm. The Annunaki, the Underworld's assessors, found her guilty, as though she had been any mortal soul brought to judgement. Ereshkigal 'fastened on Inanna the eye of death'[13] and condemned her to be hung on a spike like rotting meat. Ninshubar, Inanna's faithful vizir, entreated Enki, the god of Wisdom, to help restore Inanna. He accordingly took dirt from his fingernails and fashioned two beings called *galatur*, to whom he entrusted the food and water of life.

They arrived to find Ereshkigal as it were in labour. The *galatur* moaned in sympathy until Ereshkigal was moved to offer them a reward. They refused everything she offered, asking only for Inanna, on whom they sprinkled the food and water of life. As Inanna sprung up towards her own realm, demons followed her whose task was to replace Inanna with another human creature. Inanna forbade them to take her vizir or her children. They came upon Dumuzi, Inanna's husband, lounging in magnificent splendour on his throne. Just like Ereshkigal, Inanna, 'fastened the eye of death upon Dumuzi' and the demons tortured him preparatory to dragging him away to the Great Below. Dumuzi's spirit fled away to Geshtinanna, his sister, who hid him. Here the seven demons found him and dragged him away.

Inanna lamented over the body of Dumuzi with Geshtinanna

but a fly showed them where his spirit still lingered. Inanna finally took his hand and commanded that he would spend only six months in the Great Below and then return again.[14]

This myth is the pattern for many underworld descents, including those of Adonis and Osiris. We note that Inanna and Ereshkigal may stand as aspects of Sophia and the Black Goddess, respectively. The myth is wound up with the issues of life, death and rebirth. Inanna had to relinquish all her royal prerogatives and powers, descending through the seven levels of the Underworld in order to arrive at the experience of death. Immortal gods are ignorant of death. Death, for them, is ultimate knowledge. To have personally suffered death is to be supremely powerful. It is so that Inanna was empowered.

The converse experience is so with Ereshkigal. As Inanna span slowly like a side of beef rotting on her hook, Ereshkigal was seized by the pangs of birth. The Black Goddess, so famed for her destruction and the processing of dead things, was filled with life which was supremely painful to her. She groaned in travail like a common woman. As Inanna rose from the Underworld, Ereshkigal was symbolically delivered of her child – Inanna was born anew to the world from the maw of Ereshkigal.

Dumuzi had neither mourned nor cried in Inanna's absence. He was spelled in the illusion of his shepherd's reed pipe which he was found playing idly when his wife returned with her avenging demons. He was the rightful prey of the Black Goddess, a role which Inanna assumed at this point. She dethroned him and committed him to death in a seemingly cruel way. However, wisdom was not arrived at without pain. Dumuzi eluded the demons, fragmenting his spirit in the manner of Osiris, so that they were initially confounded of their prey. Although his physical body lay dead, Dumuzi's spirit eluded them until Inanna herself could be moved to offer him escape. Like Persephone, he was to remain half the year in the Underworld. The poem ends:

> Inanna placed Dumuzi in the hands of the eternal.
> Hail Ereshkigal! Great is your renown!
> Hail Ereshkigal! I sing your praises![15]

Ereshkigal means 'Lady of the Great Earth' or 'Queen of Hell'; she has overtones of both Cybele and of Persephone. A fragmentary poem speaks of her house as one 'which separates the wicked and the just.' The threshold 'is a monster with jaws that gape.' Yet 'here also lie / the rainbow gardens of the Lady.'[16] The house of Ereshkigal can be both fearful and delightful, but Inanna experienced only its terrors. When she returned from the house of her sister and opposite, Inanna became as hard and judging as Ereshkigal. She assumed the just and stern face of an assessor because the justice of her loving covenant with Dumuzi had not been renewed. Her solution was to allow him a similar sojourn with Ereshkigal, the better to balance his loving trust by the human initiation of death.

The sacred marriage was celebrated in Sumer on Spring Equinox, which is still New Year's Day in Persian custom. We may imagine it as a time of great rejoicing when the king ascended to the chamber in the ziggurat where he was seven levels higher than the earth. The eighth level, that of the bridal chamber itself, was where he lay with the priestess who embodied the Goddess:

> The king goes with lifted head to the holy lap,
> He goes with lifted head to the holy lap of Inanna,
> The king coming with lifted head,
> Coming to my queen with lifted head . . .
> Embraces the Hierodule of An.[17]

The ziggurat was an artificial holy hill, the sacred platform which betokened the contract between humanity and the gods. The locus of the Sacred Marriage was witness to the symbolic meeting of creation with its Goddess of the Earth and Heaven.

The sacred marriage opened the gates to the Goddess and her ecstatic healing energies through the communion of the body. Men received this energy in deep communion: women mediated this energy, partaking of the nature of the Goddess as priestess-hierodules. The rites of sacred marriage took place all over the Mediterranean and beyond until sacred sexuality was viewed as an unsuitable mode of spirituality. However, although the Israelites attempted to discard the old fertility ceremonies, no better example of the marriage of the King to the land can be found than in the story of Solomon and Sheba whose sacred coupling is the perfect conjunction of bodily and spiritual wisdom.

Queen of the South

It is indeed here that we might look for some kind of ultimate prototype of Wisdom, within the cluster of desert Goddesses whose reign was so long and now so totally subsumed. Is it not the Queen of the South who comes to stir up Solomon, the manifestation of the Holy Spirit incarnate, to blow his wisdom to greater conflagration?

The Queen of the South is invoked in *Song of Songs* 4:16 to stir up the urge to love: 'Come, O south wind!' In Hebrew tradition, the northern region was that of the Adversary, while the South was the direction associated with the Holy Spirit of God, the Shekinah. It is the wind of awakening desire. It is also the direction from which Sheba visited Solomon, for Sheba is believed to be either Saba in the southern Yemen or else in Tigre. The Queen of the South is she who will come to condemn unbelievers on the last day, according to Jesus.[18]

Just as Isis subsumed all lesser Egyptian goddesses within her, so too did Solomon subsume all manner of benign and just kings in his exercise of wisdom. His historical reign was marked by the building and furnishing of the Temple which would act as a house for the Shekinah, God's Holy Spirit. The finance required for this enterprise, the dwelling place of God and his resident Shekinah, was considerable. Solomon's skill in finding exotic materials to furnish the temple brought him into close links with many countries who, to placate the king, sent ambassadorial gifts, including female slaves. Solomon's harem of wives and concubines, by which his political links were maintained, exceeded 5,000 women. Yet, legend attributes to him one prime wife who has become the manifestation of Sophia, Sheba.

I Kings 10:1–13 tells how Sheba heard of Solomon and, laden with many gifts, 'came to test him with hard questions,' all of which he was able to answer. She praised him for his wisdom and 'King Solomon gave to the queen of Sheba all that she desired.' This statement has been taken to imply that Solomon 'knew' Sheba. Certainly, in Ethiopian tradition, Sheba was tricked into sleeping with Solomon, who desired her. She conceived Menelik, from whom descend all the Ethiopian kings.[19] In the Bible, Sheba is satisfied with Solomon's knowledge, but not outdone by him, as she is within the *Koran*.

The Ethiopian queen, Sheba, also known as Bilqis in Islamic tradition, was the mistress of wisdom. She came to see Solomon as an equal, to confer and dispute with him.

In Islamic tradition, the queen set various impossible tasks for Solomon, one of which was a casket whose contents he had to guess. Inside were a white pearl with no hole and an onyx stone with a crooked hole. After guessing these correctly, he had to further advise how to pierce the pearl and thread the onyx. Using the services of a woodworm, which bores a hole in the pearl, and a maggot with a thread in its mouth, Solomon solved the puzzle.[20]

This test contains two images of the Goddess of Wisdom: the virgin pearl is Sophia and the onyx with a crooked hole is the Black Goddess, her reflection. As we shall see in Chapter 9, the Black Stone of the Ka'aba was originally a white pearl.

But in the *Koran* we find a less flattering portrait of the Queen of Sheba. The hoopoe was one of Solomon's bird-messengers; he told Solomon of Sheba's queen and how she worshiped the sun. Solomon sent messages to her, bidding her appear before him. He then bade one of his djinn to bring Sheba's throne to him and to disguise it. Entering the glass-paved hall where it stood, Sheba thought that the hall was filled with water and lifted her skirts to wade across to it, thus shamefully revealing her body.[21] Islamic tradition elaborates this incident to show Sheba had hairy legs. Here Solomon's superior wisdom defeated Sheba by means of mirrors: she could not tell what was glass and what was water.

The test of crossing water is a recurrent feature of Sheba's story. The *Golden Legend* celebrates Sheba's recognition of the cross. Solomon made a bridge, anachronistically, out of the wood of the True Cross to see if Sheba would cross over it. But Sheba recognized it as the tree of paradise, for she had been the serpent, and so she waded across the stream. Her pious avoidance of the Cross was rewarded and her goose-footedness, the European substitute for hairy legs, was cured.[22]

Sheba remained a popular medieval figure and appears throughout time, even in the Grail legends where she became the motivation behind the making of the time-travelling Ship of Solomon which would bear the Grail-winner, Galahad, to his final Grail nirvana at Sarras.[23] Divining that Solomon had had a vision of Galahad and wished to aid his descendants in future times, she caused a ship to be made, and a canopy to go upon it made out of the wood of the Tree of the Knowledge of Good and Evil, slips of which were brought out of Eden by Eve. The ship sailed down time, bearing with it wood from the First Garden for this critical task of Grail restoration.

Sheba showed herself to be a priestess of wisdom. She tested Solomon and found him equal to her in knowledge and so she celebrated the Sacred Marriage with him in a meeting of both carnal and sacred knowledge. Her concern to preserve wisdom, displayed in the *Quest del San Graal*, is perhaps echoed in the Ethiopian *Kebra Nagast* where Menelik, their son, abducted the Ark of the Covenant and took it to Aksum; thus fortuitously saving it from destruction.[24]

For Solomon, Sheba *is* Wisdom. She exhibits the two faces of Sophia; her great wisdom is contrasted with her devilish femaleness, which manifests in her animal-like hairy legs. Both Islamic and Jewish tradition elaborate Sheba's hairiness, so that she becomes a creature of European folklore: La Reine Pédauque, Mother Goose, with her woman's body and her bird's feet. Medieval tradition calls her 'lady of Sheba and also of Ethiopia, and a Sibyl, with goose-like feet and eyes shining like a star.'[25] The goose-foot or pentagram is the five-pointed star, the magical sigil of Solomon. It betokens the mystical knowledge which the first man received from the first woman, and remains a symbol of hermetic wisdom to this day. Needless to say, with the usual duality attributed to Wisdom, the pentagram is also seen as the foot-print of the great female demon, Lilith, the woman of knowledge and the first wife of Adam.

The descent of Sheba from Queen of Wisdom to female demon may seem abrupt, but it stems from Judaic demonology which polarized the Divine Feminine into fearful roles. Solomon is the supreme arbiter of wisdom in Judaic lore. The arrival of the Queen of Sheba to ask him riddles was therefore seen in the most plausible light – she was not a wise queen but a demon, since what woman could be called wise? Solomon revealed her demonic nature by making her show her give-away bestial feet.

Sheba, as queen of wisdom, lodges happily within the Bible, not so the mistress of dynamic sexuality, Lilith.

Lilith was the first woman to be created, becoming 'the bride of Satan, now the consort of God, ever flaming at the gates of paradise.'[26] According to Talmudic legend, Lilith was created at the same time as Adam. When they came to make love Lilith refused to lie down under Adam because she was of equal status to himself. She thereupon uttered the name of God and flew away to the desert where her sexual fantasies were realized with demons.[27] In this, Lilith is like Sophia, for she flew away to her own place, there to resolve her inequity. For the Gnostic Sophia, this means the engendering of the Demiurge; for Lilith, it means becoming the mother of countless demons. According to another tradition, she desired to be one with the cherubim,

but God forcibly detached her, making her seek the earth. Then
she saw that Adam was already partnered by Eve and sought
to rise back to the cherubim, whereupon she was cast out into
the desert to lament the diminishment of the moon and women's
power.[28]

She is often equated with the serpent of the temptation in the
Garden of Eden. She is about knowledge. As in shamanic tradition
where 'the climbing of the magical tree is the heavenly journey of
the shaman, during which he encounters his heavenly spouse,'[29]
she is the Goddess of Kundalini, the hidden fire of sexuality which
lies coiled as a serpent at the base of the spine, waiting to be
aroused.

In Lilith we find the Black Goddess depicted as the fearful
possessor of both wisdom and sexuality – a dynamic and, for
most learned Jews, a horrific combination in a female. 'In Lilith
the symmetry of "as above, so below" is completed, for she has
the female lips of the mouth which can pronounce the magic
name of God and the female lips of the vulva below which can
receive the semen of Adam . . . The revolt of Lilith therefore
expresses the rising up from below of all that would be denied
by the rational male consciousness. Like the uroboric serpent
which bites its own tail, the spinal column brings the mysteries
of languages and sexuality, mouth and genitals together.'[30]

In Lilith we see the physical and spiritual wisdoms in one figure.
She is the Goddess complete within herself, an abomination to
those who also fear and despise lesbian and solitary women as
dangerous. The power to conceive is hers. The orthodox texts
only stress Lilith's negative side: it has been for modern women
to rediscover her power within themselves, to go apart for a while
and to discover the ability to engender children of thought, just
as Lilith and Sophia do.

The libidinous aspect of Lilith as a nymphomaniac succuba
shows the extreme polarization of the Yahwist position, for in
Jehovah there is no apparant eros. However, the bride of the
Sacred Marriage does put in one orthodox appearance as the
Shulamite.

The authorship of the *Song of Songs* is often accorded to Solomon. Composed about the second half of the 5th century BC,
it draws upon traditions of the Sacred Marriage and has many
echoes reminiscent of Sumerian sequences. It was traditionally
read at Passover, significantly marking the renewal of God's
contract with Israel.[31] Rabbi Aquiba revered the text as 'the Holy

THE SONG OF SONGS

2 *I am Black but Beautiful* The Shulamite is the sensuous maiden from the Biblical *Song of Songs*, who is 'Black but Beautiful'. From the sacred marriage rite of the Middle East to the erotic encounter of Solomon and Sheba, the Shulamite is an image of the Goddess, whose embrace confers wisdom. She depicts the erotic face of Sophia. Picture entitled *The Shulamite* by Nikos Stavroulakis.

of Holies of scripture.'[32] The Church has traditionally taken the erotic symbolism to apply solely to the marriage between God and Ecclesia. The rarified translations appearing in most Bibles overlay the literal eroticism of the original text. Here we meet Wisdom as the bride of the sacred marriage, not yet separated from her sexuality.

The *Song of Songs* is a dialogue between the Shulamite who is 'black but beautiful',[33] and her lover. This blackness is the classical antithesis of beauty throughout the West. Blackness is not usually desired, whether appearing in brunette women, skin-pigment or other aesthetic considerations. This blackness is the sign of the Black Goddess herself who, like an Ethiopian Aphrodite, speaks plainly of her erotic desire throughout this text.

> Upon my bed by night
> I sought him whom my soul loves;
> I sought him, but found him not;
> I called him, but he gave no answer.[34]

Like Lady Wisdom in *Proverbs*, she rushes through the streets, calling for her beloved in urgent frustration. But:

> The watchmen found me,
> as they went about in the city;
> they beat me, they wounded me,
> they took away my mantle.[35]

This mantle is nothing other than the veil of the *qedesha*, the hierodule, which covered the head and shoulders and fell to the ankles.[36] The implication is that the watchmen raped her. The removal or rending of the veil is one of the primal myths of the violated innocence of Sophia which is continually repeated throughout the history of the West.

The Shulamite longs to bring her lover:

> into the house of my mother,
> and into the chamber of her that conceived me,[37]

just as Inanna longed to take Dumuzi home to her mother.[38]

This longing is like that of the Shekinah to be seated upon the throne of the Matronit in qabalistic tradition, or like the fallen Sophia, Achamoth, to be raised up to the bridal chamber (see Chapters 6 and 8).

47

The scholar Hartmut Schmökel has persuasively rearranged the sequence of the text to read as a liturgy for the Sacred Marriage, scored for priest, priestess and male and female choruses.[39]

The blackness of the Shulamite will be met again in both Isis and the Black Madonna. Hers is a particular kind of blackness which sparks remembrance of light:

> Thou still abidest so entirely one,
> That we may know thy blackness is a spark
> Of light inaccessible.[40]

The Shulamite and her song have furnished generations of mystics with acceptable images portraying the sacred marriage of the soul to God. She is one of the last authentic links with the bride of the Sacred Marriage who upholds the contract between the Goddess of the Land and its people. In subsequent theology, however, both the Shulamite and Sophia herself represent the earth *and* its creation, becoming the bride of God who is imaged as the Divine Masculine, Master of Heaven. It is at this point, perhaps, that the Goddess of Justice leaves the earth and starts her wanderings.

The Eye of Justice

The right ordering of creation is one of the tasks most appropriate to the early forms of Sophia in pre-Christian understanding. The ruler must be married to Wisdom. She is his *paredros* – the throne-companion or assessor. She tells her heart on every matter and is the arbiter of justice. This role, once directly experienced by the marriage contract between the ruler and the Goddess of the Land, was taken primarily by a royal woman of the tribe or a priestess of the Goddess. It later devolved upon an adviser or counsellor.

Justice is one of the guises of the Goddess of Wisdom; sometimes it is the searing, chaotic justice of the Black Goddess who, as Anath, Sekhmet or Ishtar, sends destruction upon the earth; sometimes it is the gentle and withdrawing Sophia who, as Maat, Astraea and the Enochian Shekinah, departs sorrowfully, so that the absence of justice will provoke response.

Ancient oaths were frequently sworn 'by the earth' who could be expected to hear and witness all. The Erinyes are the chthonic avengers of the Greeks. The Goddess of Love and War is a title which the Goddess of Land takes when love and justice are in the balance. When she manifests as the Black Goddess, it is like Inanna, Ishtar or the Ugaritic Goddess Anath. She delights in the blood of the slain:

> She washed her hands, did Virgin Anat,
> Her fingers the Progenitress of Peoples;
> Washed her hands of soldiers' blood,
> Her fingers of soldiers' gore.[41]

In an episode which parallels the action of Sekhmet, who feasted on corpses until she was beguiled by floods of beer dyed red, Anath strikes fear into the heart, just as do Kali or the Irish Morrighan. The face of the Goddess of the Land is metaphored as either a desirable virgin or else a virago – a strong virgin-warrior.

In a clear prefiguring of the nature and relationships of Sophia, the Egyptian Goddess, Maat, represents right order. She is the daughter of the sun-God Re, protecting him and destroying his enemies, embracing him night and day. The image of Maat was worn upon the breast of the highest judges who called themselves 'the priests of Maat'.[42]

Maat's role is a complex one within Egyptian cosmology. She is said to stand in front of Re on the day of the New Year festival, where she represents the right ordering of the cosmos and the patterns of destiny on that day. The hieroglyph for Maat's name has been shown to represent 'the platform on which the rites of the sed-festival (New Year) are performed.'[43] It has been suggested that this sign is connected to the hieroglyph of the stairway, a symbol of the primeval mound upon which the New Year festival was celebrated. (We are reminded of the ziggurat of Sumerian tradition on which the sacred marriage takes place.) Maat ensures the regular rising and setting of the sun, and acts as the navigator of Re's solar barque in both the heavens and the underworld.

Maat, like Sophia, represents Re's vital essence, without which he can find no rest or energy to perform:

> I (the king) come to thee, I bring to thee Maat.
> Thou livest by her. Thou rejoyest in her,
> thou art perfect by her, thou unitest by her,
> thou givest by her, thou restest upon her . . .
> thou art powerful by her, thou art stable by her
> thou art adorned with her, thou risest by her.[44]

49

It is in 'the hall of the double Maat' that the dead person's soul is judged. The double Maat, depicted with the distinctive feather of Maat's judgement against which the dead person's heart is weighed in the balances, is clearly similar to the Mazdaean concept of the Daena who is likewise of dual appearance (see Chapter 9).

One of the chief components of the Sophia myth is that of her flight from evil. This leitmotif can be traced from early Hellenic and Egyptian sources, which further stress the relationship between Wisdom and justice.

In the time of the primeval gods, Maat descended from heaven:

> Abundant food was in the bellies of men.
> There was nothing wrong in the country,
> no crocodile did snatch away,
> there was no sting of a serpent
> in the time of the Primordial gods.[45]

This recalls the myth of the Greek Golden Age when gods and humans lived in mutual harmony. But, as in Greek myth, worse was to follow. In order to improve conditions, 'Maat came down from heaven and joined those who lived on earth. At that time there was no injustice, no pain, no hunger.'[46] This myth of Maat is fragmentary but the implication is that she later returned to the Otherworld.

The myth of the Golden Age is the Classical paradigm of the Judaeo-Christian Fall. Once everything was harmonious, but some act or a succession of worsening affairs intervenes between the communion of the divine and the human. Hesiod gives one such act of mischief as the opening by Pandora of the jar of all ills. Her curiosity let these loose upon humanity.[47] But the legacy of Pandora's jar is hope: 'Hope is the one good God yet left among mankind; the rest have forsaken us and gone to Olympus. Gone ere this was the great Goddess Honesty (Pistis), gone from the world was Self-Control (Sophrosyne).'[48]

Hesiod speaks of the two Goddesses *Aidos* (Respect) and *Nemesis* (Just Retribution), who 'with their sweet forms wrapped in white robes, will go from the wide-pathed earth and forsake mankind to join the company of the deathless gods.'[49] We may compare this with the flight of Diké (Justice) in Aratus' *Phaenomena* 96–136. Diké or Astraea was the daughter of Zeus and Themis, being one of the Horae. She is the witness of wrong-doing: 'And there is virgin Justice, the daughter of Zeus, who is honoured and reverenced among the gods who dwell on Olympus, and whenever anyone hurts her with lying slander, she sits beside her father, Zeus, the son of Kronos, and tells him of men's wicked heart, until the people pay for the mad folly of their princes.'[50]

During the Golden Age, she lived with humankind, withdrawing during the Silver Age to the mountains where she exhorted them to reform their evil-doing or else she would never answer their prayers again. During the Bronze Age she abandoned the world to become the constellation of Virgo.[51] Diké is the mistress of the normal order. When she is absent from any enterprise, we say that chaos has set in. Indeed a remark of Heraclitus confirms this: 'Sun will not overstep his measures . . . if he does, the Erinyes, the minions of Justice, will find him out.'[52] The Erinyes are none other than the Furies, who punish blood-guilt. They are the conscience of the earth itself and may be seen here in their context as servants of the Black Goddess herself.

Similar is the flight of Wisdom in the *Book of Enoch* I:42:

> Wisdom went forth to make her dwelling
> Among the children of men,
> And found no dwelling place;
> Wisdom returned to her place
> And took her seat among the angels.[53]

The *Bereshith Rabbah* says: 'The main dwelling of *Shekhinah* was originally below, but after the Fall of Adam, she took off to the first heaven.'[54]

The loss of Astraea from the world was known by Virgil whose Fourth Eclogue celebrates Diké's return:

> Now has the last great age begun,
> by Cumae's seer foretold;
> new born the mighty cycles run
> their course, and quit the old.
> Now too, the virgin re-appears,
> and Saturn re-controls the spheres.[55]

This prophetic utterance, from the lips of Virgil himself – deemed in medieval times to be a seer-magician – has been taken to allude to the coming of Christ. This understanding has perhaps filtered through on many levels for the just Virgin Sophia is believed to be none other than Christ himself.

The loss of Wisdom in her Justice aspect is even found within the Gospels. The German scholar R. Bultmann suggests that two of Christ's sayings in *Matthew* 23:34–39 and *Luke* 11:49–51 are extracted from a lost Sophia narrative which speaks of the withdrawal of wisdom. The true saying of Sophia is recorded in Matthew: 'O Jerusalem . . . how often would I have gathered your children together as a hen gathers her brood under her wings, and you would not! Behold your house is forsaken and desolate. For I tell you, you will not see me again, until you say, Blessed is he who comes in the name of the Lord.'[56] But even in the *Haggadah*, the legends and commentaries upon the Pentateuch, justice does not leave altogether:

'When God dismissed (Adam and Eve) from Paradise, He did not allow the divine quality of justice to prevail entirely. He associated mercy with it.'[57] It is because of this that Jews say, 'Behind each law mercy is concealed.'

The Virgin Justice, either as an autonomous figure or as the *paredros* of a God, is an early manifestation of Sophia. She stands for the primal harmony between creation and creator, an intermediary character between heaven and earth. She is strangely no longer an autonomous Goddess, nor even one who bears equal status, she no longer manifests as the Goddess of the Earth, but she does still represent its people. Something in her innate justice forbids her own union unless her creation may also partake of it. Sometimes it is wise to pack your bags and leave, the better to return in strength and compassion. The symbol of this compassionate relationship is anciently the dove, an image which is central to Sophia.

The dove was sacred to Aphrodite, Ishtar and Atargatis, the awakeners of love. It is the bird of erotic propensities which is nevertheless faithful to its chosen consort. Its image adorned the temples of this Goddess's aspect in Babylon, Beth-shan and Paphos.[58] Our society retains this symbol of Sophia as one of peace but nothing can make the dove nestle under the eaves of peace, any more than love may be commanded. The peace-war dichotomy of the dove-Goddess similarly follows Sophia's mythos.

Derceto, the Syrian Goddess, with the head of a woman and the body of a fish, was supposedly the mother of a child whom she exposed in her shame. The baby was nourished and protected by doves and later found and fostered by a herdsman and his wife. They called her Semiramis, which means 'doves'. After a brilliant career in which she conquered India and Ethiopia (shades of Sheba!), Semiramis, so legend says, 'turned into a dove and flew off in the company of many birds which alighted on her dwelling, and this, they say, is the reason why the Assyrians worship the dove as a god, thus deifying Semiramis. Be that as it may, this woman, after having been queen over all Asia with the exception of India, passed away . . . having lived sixty-two years and having reigned forty-two.'[59]

These same doves return to give notice of Sophia's presence, both in the Grail legends (see Chapter 11) and in the dove which symbolizes the Holy Spirit – god's messenger. The dove was the common bird of sacrifice at the Judaic Temple, the agreed price for the purification of a woman after childbirth: she must offer either a lamb and a pigeon or a turtle dove for a sin offering, or else two pigeons or two turtledoves – one for a sin offering, the other for a burnt offering.[60] This curious custom of burning the dove contrasts strangely with our contemporary custom of releasing doves in a token of freedom or peace. *Psalms* 74:19 speaks of the innocent: 'Deliver not to the beasts the life of your turtledove.'

Doves were sacrificed to Tiamat in a particular way, showing how close was their association with the Goddess of Creating Chaos: a dove was dedicated to Tiamat and, at the annual recitation of the Babylonian creation myth, it was ritually sliced in half, in imitation of Marduk's action.[61]

The Biblical dove is the bird which returns to Noah's ark with the olive branch in its beak after the Deluge. Just as the rainbow signifies God's covenant with humanity never to let loose further inundations, so the olive-branch signifies the green and living earth which has been purified. Both dove and olive tree are symbols of Wisdom.

The dove descends to become a symbol of Mary in the Coptic *Life of the Virgin*. As Mary, like Sophia the workwoman, sits weaving the veil of the temple, angels minister to her in the shape of doves.[62]

The fact that the Holy Spirit takes the form of a dove, and is seen descending upon Christ at his baptism at the hands of St John the Baptist, is an interesting comment on the action of Sophia. Here the dove of renewal hovers over the restored image of humanity.

Sophia is not all head and no heart: she works through the agency of love to bring intellect to its senses. The image of the dove remains a potent reminder of Sophia who returns to earth out of faithfulness and love. She abides in the cleft of the rock which is the heart of us all. The ancient peace of the Goddess of Wisdom is typified by the dove. If we are at peace with the earth, then we are at peace with each other.

Resacralizing the Body

The loss of the Divine Feminine from consciousness is a wound which we all carry. Without her dimension of love and justice, we exile ourselves from the earth, from physicality and from each other.

The resacralization of the body and of womanhood is essential in the West. The incidence of rape increases as the spiral of violent disaffection from the earth grows to a vortex of destruction. The sacred integrity of Sophia which dwells in the shrine of the heart, is being dragged out and degraded in the rape of every woman, child and man. 'Both "abuse" and "the sacred" seem to beckon' to us in our society.'[63] And is there any wonder for 'we have, at present, no festivals of sacred sexuality'.

Sexual love lies like an unexploded bomb in our society. It is potentially the most creative of acts but, robbed of its sacred dimension, it may also be the focus of the most destructive acts. The evils of pornography, which excise all love for the profit of lust, daily endanger women, children and men the world over. Couples are encouraged to buy and read sex manuals which depict the manifold positions of the sexual act but which totally fail to inculcate any sense of responsible love. And because sex is not taught as a sacred skill, it becomes secretive and guilty. The old nurturing societies where a woman learned to experience the space of the Goddess within herself, where men and woman discovered the 'alchemical fusion in the perfect marriage' are no more.[64] The engendering of life is no longer seen as a holy act; the calling down of a divinely-fired soul into the vessel of the womb is not a skill now taught by orthodox spiritualities. Our lust to possess the earth has spread our kind across the world in greater and greater numbers until its population is now more than it can sustain.

We have come a long way from the ancient regard for both physical virginity and sacred marriage, whereby the hymen was analogous to the veil of the temple of the Goddess, and where those who entered into the experience of the holy of holies were considered initiates. The desacralization of the body is nowhere more apparent than in the barbaric practice of infibulation – one of many practices common to parts of the Middle East and Africa – whereby the labia minora and clitoris are excised from women. It is sometimes called 'pharaonic circumcision' and does not exactly replicate male circumcision in that it denies the woman sexual fulfilment. It requires the excision of the exterior genitalia of women and the sewing up of the vagina, which is then cut open upon marriage and childbirth, whereupon it is then resewn. The principle behind this barbarism is that women are sexually indiscriminate, both in their bestowal of favours and also in their enjoyment of the sexual act.

This notion was shared by the Greeks as we find in the myth of Teiresias where Zeus and Hera were arguing about who received greater enjoyment from love. Teiresias was the arbiter, proclaiming:

> Of ten, the man enjoyeth but one part,
> Nine parts the woman fills, with joyful heart.[65]

This was clearly the correct answer, but Hera, furious with him for having given away one of woman's closest guarded secrets, struck him blind. Another myth tells how Teiresias came across serpents coupling and, striking them with his staff, was turned into a woman. The serpent is the emblem of the Black Goddess of the Earth, and indicates her creative, sexual powers.

Fear of the feminine is often fear of the chaotic and ecstatic nature of sexuality itself, in which men and women temporarily 'lose control' of their rational, ordered being. The burden of sexual responsibility has been laid upon women who are urged, in many traditional religions, to veil themselves lest they stir up uninvited passion which threatens the self-control. The view of woman as unconscious temptress is unconsciously endorsed under the law of many lands which sees the female victim of rape as partially if not wholly culpable.

Sacred engendering, sexuality, etc, depend on our acceptance of life. If we do not accept life as wholesome, then we become agents of our own desacralization.

One of the chief areas which is seen as unclean in many spiritualities is menstruation. The blood of life is much feared. It is said by shamans that 'spirits fly off the woman's belly', meaning that the source of power is within the womb.[66] The menstruating woman is locked away or ignored in many societies and, in Eastern Orthodoxy, refused communion. She is dangerous, like Lilith. 'Lilith's sexuality is the kind women know a few days before menstruation when the female hormones have stopped flowing and the male hormones are at their raging peak. It is a pulsating, throbbing, primal, wordless state of being.'[67]

The voluntary sequestration of many women from patriarchal affairs is in many ways like the moon lodge experience of native American spirituality, whereby menstruating women go apart to commune with their source of power, to listen to dreams and receive visions. At such times, women listen to the wisdom of their bodies. They have pressed their bellies against the world, so that they can experience the drum-beat of its motion.[68] It is through this sacred centre that women feel the earth and know the will of the Black Goddess.

The need for the Goddess to be mediated through the art of the priestess-hierodule has not diminished, although our society denies it. The basic freedom to choose the sexual freedom of the monastery, where sacred relationship is practised, or the sexual responsibility of a personal, rather than a communal, family is not an open option in our time. The spiritual vocation of women is extremely straightened in our age, for the freedom to mediate the Goddess physically as hierodule has been degraded into the sexual economy of prostitution.

The mystic, AE (George Russell) wrote: 'Some renewal of ancient conceptions of the fundamental purpose of womanhood and its relations to Divine Nature, and that from the temples where women may be instructed she will come forth, with strength in her to resist all pleading until the lover worships in her a divine womanhood, and that through their love the divided portions of the immortal nature may come together and be one as before the beginning of the world.'[69]

As women resume their power – guardianship of the secret fire which the Shulamite, Sheba, Inanna and Lilith manifest – a more dynamic and just society will result in which the Black Goddess will be joined with Sophia freely and effectively. Though the tantric teachings of Shakti are still taught in the East, the West has denied the Black Goddess her role as awakener and arouser, has applauded Sophia in her role as the virgin of divine love. It has polarized the Goddess as either profane or sacred, as eros or agape. The secret of the hidden fires of the Goddess has been virtually forgotten in the West. The subsequent dualistic view of sex is at odds with the message of Sophia, who urges us to love and break down the barriers between each other.

By splitting off the functions of the body from the workings of the soul, the West has created a fragmented, sometimes schizophrenic, society. It has created a Fall as devastating as the myth of Adam and Eve. The primordial condition of innocence and mutual honour between species is reflected in sexual customs. This was apparant in the ancient world in the practice of sacred marriage. When such a relationship no longer existed between the land and its people, the further breakdown between the sexes and the species followed. Sometimes seen as a Golden Age, this early period is usually assigned to full honouring of the Divine Feminine in many forms, who presides over this sacred marriage. At the end of the Golden Age, the Goddess took more just and severe forms and left the earth, as has clearly fallen out. She nevertheless left tokens of her return – one of which is the rainbow or dove, or a pattern of sacred behaviour as exemplified still in some of the mystical enclaves of Western religion.

The sacred marriage was a ritualized re-enactment of the marriage of the divine and created, the very aim of Sophia herself to which she calls us again and again. In all subsequent histories and traditions the symbolism of marriage, mystical union and the entry into the bridal chamber of initiation, into the Mysteries, are emblems of Sophia's work among us.

It was once the custom for brides to remain unseen by their husbands until after they were married – a practice which still occurs in Moslem and Hindu custom today. What lay behind the veil might be beautiful or terrifying. Sophia is still a veiled Goddess, for she is the unknown bride of the soul. Until we acknowledge her among us once more as the primal Goddess of the Earth, in equal love and justice, she will remain veiled.

=== 3 ===

THE SAVIOUR GODDESS

Isis: Come thou to me quickly,
Since I desire to see thy face after not having seen thy face . . .
My heart is hot at thy wrongful separation;
I yearn for thy love toward me.
Come! Be not alone! Be not far off!
Nephthys: Draw nigh, so please you, to us;
We miss life through lack of thee.

The Lamentations of Isis and Nephthys

The Mysteries

The return of the Goddess in our time acts as a corrective to our long absence from her presence. In the last thirty years there have been innumerable feminist histories of the Goddess that attempt to acquaint our society with what it has lost, to reconnect us to the Goddess by ties of learned familiarity. We all need a continuum, something which connects us with our mother country and which will accompany us into the uncertainty of the future because, for most of us, the Goddess remains a lost country.

The tradition of a Saviour Goddess – one who is attuned to our condition, who reaches out to us and bears us up – is absent from our society. The Saviour as a male Messiah, Prophet and Spiritual Teacher has intervened. But our ancestors certainly recognized and were initiated into the mysteries of the Saviour Goddess. The body of wisdom associated with each deity was guarded and administered by local shrines, temples and confederations dedicated to the Goddess of the locality. The Mystery Religions gave direct initiation into the myth of their presiding deities, so that each individual knew what it was like to mourn for Osiris, search for Kore, descend to the Underworld and be reborn. Sometimes these cults attracted a good deal of attention from further afield, such as the Eleusinian and Isiac mysteries, and though the former remained localized to Greece, the cult of Isis spread throughout the Roman Empire after the fashion of a religion, providing one

58

model for the state religion that was to follow. The mystery initiations of these cults were prefigurings of the sacraments which replaced them.

Many scholars have mooted that each or any of the Goddesses in this chapter may have furnished models for Sophia. As we trace the myth of the Goddess through her salvific guises, we are aware of a cohesive set of metaphors which suggest a family likeness, as though a great mirror has shattered, prismatically retaining the original image. Indeed, the way in which Wisdom appears in the Bible is by means of 'reflective mythology' – not the representation of an actual myth but by a theological appropriation of mythic language and patterns which have been repackaged from the pagan models.

With the Goddesses Demeter and Isis, the myth of the Goddess takes on a greater urgency which resonates to our contemporary spiritual response to the Divine Feminine: we find a common theme of loss and finding, of seeking for pieces of the shattered mirror of the beloved. Only when the divine daughter or husband is found and reconstituted can earth function again. Kore and Osiris are lost and found again: but they cannot be reconstituted entirely as they were. So it is with our own search for the Goddess. In the period of loss, exile or death, something transformative has happened. As we see below, Kore and Osiris, like Ishtar, descend to the underworld and become way-showers for all who go beyond death to spiritual rebirth. In the story of Psyche, this search is personally exemplified by a woman who becomes a Goddess, but only after total loss and dereliction. In Psyche, the portrait of Sophia becomes clearer. In each of these saving stories, it is the urgency of love, the enduring patience of the seeker, which restores the lost beloved. These are the prime qualities of Sophia which remind us always, though we do not see her face clearly because she is veiled or disguised, that the Goddess accompanies us wherever we go.

Demeter amd Kore

Demeter and her daughter Kore represent a primal tradition of the Saviour Goddess which survived the demise of the Eleusinian Mysteries, established in their honour. Elements of the story were incorporated by the Hellenic dynasties of Egypt into the myth of Isis and Osiris, as well as permeating the Neo-Platonic and

Hermetic traditions who revered Kore as the ultimate initiator or Virgin of Light.

The names Demeter and Kore are not personal names at all, but titles. They mean Mother and Daughter or Girl, respectively. The names of deities are usually veiled and given only in the heart of the initiation into the mystery, which in the case of the Eleusinian Mysteries was a personal enactment of the phases of the following story.

Demeter's daughter Kore was gathering flowers when she was abducted by Pluto to Hades. Only Hecate heard the girl at first but soon Kore's lamentations filled the mountains and seas, and Demeter understood that Kore was lost. Searching everywhere for her daughter, Demeter at last sat exhausted by the Maiden's Well at Eleusis looking like a crone. The daughters of Metaneira took her home to be nurse to their baby brother Demophoön. Unsmiling and refusing sweet wine to slake her thirst, Demeter was roused from her sorrow by Iambe (or Baubo).[1]

In his commentary upon this episode, Arnobius relates: 'Baubo . . . received Ceres, wearied with complicated evils, as her guest, and endeavoured to soothe her sorrows . . . she entreated her to pay attention to the refreshment of her body, and placed before her (the *kykeon*) to assuage the vehemence of her thirst . . .'[2] Being unable to divert Demeter, Baubo then uncovered her vagina: 'upon which the goddess fixed her eyes, and was delighted with the novel method of mitigating the anguish of sorrow; and afterwards, becoming cheerful through laughter, she assuaged the ardour of her thirst with the (*kykeon*) which she had before despised.'[3]

This episode is crucial to an understanding of the Eleusinian mysteries, for Demeter cannot be heartened by any act of kindness. Baubo, in the earthing role of the Black Goddess, reminds Demeter of the origin of life by revealing her vulva in the manner of a Sheila na Gig. She reminds Demeter of the Black Goddess's role as life-bringer and of the delights of sexuality: the reversal of death and decay. Demeter is able to accept the refreshing drink and the Eleusinian mysteries are established.

Demeter nursed the child Demophoön and, in an attempt to give the child immortality, she held him in the fire each evening, burning away his mortality. However, Metaneira interrupted this ritual, believing her child to be endangered. Demeter thereupon resumed her Goddessly stature and rebuked her hostess. So the Eleusinian Mysteries were thereafter established to appease Demeter, who initiated her hosts into the mysteries of the earth and agriculture.

In the meantime, the earth's seasons had ceased and in mourning for Kore, Demeter 'caused a most dreadful and cruel year for mankind', so that no seed grew. All the gods implored Demeter to relent and Zeus instructed Pluto to let Kore go. Demeter and Kore were restored to one another but, because Kore had eaten pomegranate seeds in Hades, she was obliged to remain a third part of the year in that place. Thereafterwards, Hecate became Kore's companion.

Another tradition survives of Demeter's wanderings in Arkadia, and this gives us Demeter Erinyes, Black or Angry Demeter. The story tells how Demeter was raped, while hiding in the form of a mare, by Poseidon, in the form of a stallion. Grieved both at this event and by the loss of Persephone to Hades, she put on black and retired to a cave in Phygalia. The earth was stricken with famine. Eventually the Gods sent the Fates to ask her to relent, which she finally did. She gave birth subsequently to a son, Arion, and to an unnamed daughter called, merely, Despoina (the Mistress). The Phygalians honoured the cave of Black Demeter with a mare-headed statue, which held a dolphin in one hand and a dove in the other.[4]

Despoina was worshipped as the Mistress of the Underworld among the Orphites, understanding her to be the subterranean Persephone, while Kore was seen as the trancendent maiden of the mysteries. This two-fold Persephone gives us a Black Goddess and her Sophianic counterpart.

The three Goddesses of the Eleusinian mysteries, Kore, Demeter and Hecate, comprehend the realms of heaven, earth and the underworld between them. They may also be associated with the three phases of the moon, as Proclus remarks of Diana in his commentary on the *Timaeus*: 'She presides over the whole of generation into natural existence, leads forth into light all natural reasons, and extends a prolific power from on high even to the subterranean realms.'[5] This is the nature of the Goddess of All, whose wisdom encompasses every realm; those Goddesses whose realm of operation is restricted to one region of existence seldom accord with the Goddess of Wisdom, who incorporates all within her.

The later Orphic traditions which incorporated the traditions associated with Demeter and Kore, utilized the Eleusinian mysteries to great effect. Proclus tells of the inner mysteries: 'Persephone abides on high in those dwellings of the Mother which she prepared for her in inaccessible places, exempt from the sensible

61

world. But she likewise dwells beneath with Pluto, administering terrestial concerns, governing the recesses of the earth, and supplying life to the extremities of the Kosmos.'[6]

This precisely corresponds with the unfolding pattern of Sophia who is both transcendent and manifest, withdrawn and always among us. It also leads us to consider the manner in which the Orphic mysteries developed the ancient idea of the Goddess weaving the web of life. Using the deities' Roman names, it tells of a tradition whereby Ceres, fearful that harm might come to Proserpine, secretes her daughter in a house in Sicily, while she herself withdraws to the temple of Cybele. In order to draw Proserpine forth, Jupiter sends Venus to beguile her, along with Diana and Minerva, the Virgin Goddesses, to set her suspicions to rest.

'The three goddesses arriving find Proserpine at work on a scarf for her mother, in which she had embroidered the primitive chaos, and the formation of the world.'[7] Thomas Taylor defines the three Goddesses thus: Venus represents Desire, Minerva Reason, and Diana is Nature. They led her out where she could be abducted and the story falls out as above. This image of betrayal may seem a contradictory one, but here the three Goddesses are responsible for the experiential descent of Persephone.

Demeter's loss of Kore is akin to the earth losing the World-Soul. Hence, Demeter's journey and Kore's finding remain two powerful paradigms for spiritual experience. We note that when Kore returns to the realms of earth once more 'Hekate becomes thereafter the constant attendant of Persephone . . . Until the Soul falls into matter, she has no Fate, or Karma.'[8] It is thus that the Black Goddess is received into Saviour Goddess within this mythos, and seen to be part of the salvific process. For the Orphics, Persephone remained the inimitable Goddess of Nature, weaving the web of the world. She is distracted from her Mother's task and enters the realm of experience. In this she is like both Pandora and Eve. The mystery narrative of Psyche and Cupid (Eros) similarly tells of the way in which Psyche, another clear paradigm of the soul, fell into experience. As we will see in Chapters 8 and 12, the Fall – so often seen as a terrible fate – has its meaning reversed. Is this the way Sophia intends us to understand our lives – not as the terrible exile we have been led to believe, but as a wonderful adventure?

The mystery of the Virgin Mother lies in her *fiat*, her acceptance of life's experiences. She assents, not personally or preferentially, but unreservedly, for all creation. It is so that she is remade and renewed, becoming inviolate because she has so willingly given herself. It is this experience that links Inanna, Kore, Mary and Sophia who each descend into life and become of one nature with it. The descent of the World-Soul, of the Goddess, was a familiar theme throughout the ancient world. We note that the emphasis is no longer upon the marriage of the Goddess to the creation. The physical union of lover and beloved is not forgotten, but the metaphor is now one of the body seeking its soul. The foundation myth of the soul's search for her beloved is told about Psyche, whose name means, simply, 'soul'.

Psyche and Cupid

The story of Psyche and Cupid appears in Lucius Apuleius's *The Golden Ass*. Psyche was the youngest daughter of a king and was so beautiful that people likened her to the Goddess Venus. At this piece of hubris, Venus herself intervened, and sent Cupid to make Psyche fall in love with an outcast. Since Psyche's great beauty was so awesome, no suitor appeared to court her and her father sent to Apollo's oracle to learn her fate. The oracle darkly bade Psyche to prepare for her marriage: she should be left on a barren rock where a monstrous bridegroom, not of mortal kind, would claim her. Left alone, Psyche found nearby a house prepared for her, where she was invisibly tended. Her invisible husband visited her bed and bade her not to listen for the mourning voices of her family who assumed her death. He warned her particularly against her sisters who would, he said, demand to know what Psyche's husband looked like.

But Psyche was visited by her sisters who were exceedingly jealous of her good fortune. The pregnant Psyche listened to her sisters' surmise that her husband was a monster and that she must find out what he looked like and then slay him. Psyche prepared a knife and hid a lamp in her bedroom. She kindled the lamp that evening: 'At once the secret was revealed. There lay the gentlest and sweetest of all wild creatures, Cupid himself, the beautiful love-god, and at sight of him the flame of the lamp spurted joyfully up and the knife turned its edge for shame.'[9] She accidentally pricked her finger on one of his arrows and so fell in love with Love. Cupid awoke and told how he had disobeyed his own mother because he had been wounded with one of his own

63

arrows. Because she had refused to heed his advice about her sisters, he left her alone. Psyche cast herself on the mercy of her two sisters who, hearing that Cupid was now unattached, went to the forlorn rock and independently fell to their deaths.

Neither Ceres nor Juno, to whom Psyche prayed for help, were inclined to aid her since Venus had sent a proclamation asking for the return of Psyche as her runaway slave-girl. Venus captured Psyche and set her four tasks. She was to separate a sack of mixed seeds into piles, and was helped by a company of ants. She was told to go and fetch a hank of golden fleece from a herd of wild sheep. In despair, she intended to drown herself but was prevented by a reed which told her to wait until the afternoon. Venus then demanded a cup of icy water from the waters of the Styx. It was guarded by dragons, but an eagle helped her. Venus then ordered her to Hades to request from Persephone a little of her beauty for Venus' own use. Psyche was about to spring from a high tower when the tower itself counselled her.

Psyche was told not to open Persephone's box, which of course she did. She immediately fell into a Stygian sleep, but Cupid himself roused her and, begging Jupiter for help, secured immortality for Psyche and her child.[10]

The outcast whom Psyche married was, of course, Love. Love is the unknown and unimaginable quality until it is personally experienced. For virgins it is another country. Psyche was too immature to insist on the evidence of her own senses and could be swayed by her sisters into believing that her love was nothing more than a monster. The experience of Sophia is like this, for the face of the Divine Mistress is veiled, sometimes imagined to be a terrible Medusa who will devour or petrify.

Psyche and Cupid together depict the dual role of Sophia. Cupid or Eros is pure love which cannot be seen but only apprehended. Psyche is subject to the tests of love, which she seeks by dogged patience. Like the manifest Sophia, she must go in suffering and sorrow about the world, seeking to bring about the perfect conditions by which she will know her love once more.

It is a story in which the soul seeks for union with Deity. But Eros is like the God of the New Testament, dwelling in inaccessible light, 'whom no man has seen and whom no man is able to see.'[11] Love can only be experienced personally, never vicariously.

Psyche, like Pandora and Eve, shows us the pagan myth of the falling feminine. The Fall, so often considered to be a terrible thing, is a fall into experience; like the falling of the epileptic to earth, it may also have its other face, for then we fall into the embrace of our dreams and fears and know them for what they are face to face. The Senoi Indians, experts in dream-leading, tell us not to be afraid of dreams of falling because: 'the falling spirits love you. They are attracting you to their land, and you have but to relax and remain asleep in order to come to grips with them. When you meet them, you may be frightened of their terrific power, but go on. When you think you are dying in a dream, you are only receiving the powers of the other world, *your own spiritual power which has been turned against you*, and which now wishes to become one with you if you will accept it.'[12]

The Lord of the Underworld, Ereshkigal and Venus are all teachers in these salvific pagan stories; they show that the fearful face of the Black Goddess is really the veiled Sophia. The rebirth of the mystery initiation brings us into contact with our own power, which we have failed to take in our own time. Part of the reason for this is that we live in the shadow of the Judaeo-Christian Fall, for which Woman bears the blame. The experience of Psyche and Kore shows the vulnerable face of Sophia, who is not afraid to fall, to learn by seeming mistakes. They show that the descent into death is the only possible pathway to ascent or spiritual rebirth. This is why Hecate as Black Goddess stands with her torch to guide Persephone as Sophia and all other souls who pass that underworld way thereafter.

The Lady who passed the torch of this mystery knowledge into mystical Christianity was Isis.

Isis

The connections between Isis and Sophia are very significant and show us Sophia's strongest links to the ancient Goddess tradition. Isis is a Saviour Goddess par excellence, one who combines the elements of the Black Goddess and the Hellenic philosophies which went to create the definitive Sophia.

Isis was a potent Goddess as early as the 3rd millennium BC. She was the sister-wife of Osiris, with whom she mated in the womb of their mother, Nuit, the sky goddess. Theirs was an eternal balanced partnership and may stand as a model for the ideal Sophianic relationship to the Divine Masculine. Isis was primarily the Lady of the House of Life, the possessor of the *ankh*, which was the symbol of both divine authority and also the key to the house of life itself. Her name in Egyptian was really Auset (Isis is a Hellenicized version), which means throne. The hieroglyph which represents Isis is the throne, and this image shows her as literally the power of the earth, of which the royal seat is but a representation. Pharoahs were established on the throne of Isis. The dead went into the Otherworld, their sarcophagi guarded by Isis with her wings outstretched. Was it a memory of this image that caused the writer of the Pentateuch to write: 'The eternal God is thy refuge and underneath are the everlasting arms'?[13]

The cult of Isis was wide-ranging and deeply-rooted in the Classical world. She epitomized the Great Mother, as well as taking on the attributes of lesser goddess-forms and subsuming them into her cult. In her aretalogy or self-praise, Isis utters as comprehensive a list of her abilities as any which appear in the mouth of Wisdom within the Bible:

> I gave and ordained laws for men, which no one is able to change . . .
> I am she that is called goddess by women . . .
> I divided the earth from the heaven.
> I showed the paths of the stars.
> I ordered the course of the sun and the moon.
> I devised business in the sea.
> I made strong the right.
> I brought together women and men.
> I appointed to women to bring their infants to birth in the tenth month.
> I ordained that parents should be loved by children.
> I laid punishment upon those disposed without natural affection toward their parents.
> I made with my brother Osiris an end to the eating of men.
> I revealed mysteries unto men.
> I taught men to honour images of the gods . . .
> I made the right to be stronger than gold and silver.
> I ordained that the true should be thought good . . .
> I am the Queen of rivers and winds and sea.
> No one is held in honour without my knowing it.
> I am the Queen of war.
> I am the Queen of the thunderbolt.
> I stir up the sea and I calm it.
> I am in the rays of the sun . . .
> I set free those in bonds . . .
> I overcome Fate.[14]

This comprehensive list enumerates the pagan virtues as understood in the ancient world. Isis shows herself in the likeness of
Maat, or Demeter Thesmophorus, as well as an upholder of justice,
a law-giver and creator, as well as one who reforms the nature of
spirituality and even fate, *heimarmene*, which was most feared by
the ancients for its capricious convolutions. Significantly, another
aretalogy says of her: 'thou didst make the power of women equal
to that of men.'[15]

The turning point in Isis' career happened when Alexander
the Great conquered Egypt. The Ptolemaic dynasty, founded by
Ptolemy I, a Macedonian, brought a Greek influence to bear upon
Egypt. The Ptolemaic dynasty immediately assimilated itself to
Egyptian modes of kingship, but the assimilation of Egyptian
and Greek religious traditions was more difficult. The Greeks
were keen to understand the universal language of symbolic
correspondence between their own deities and those of the
Egyptians. Ptolemy I appointed two priests to modify the disparate
polytheisms into a coherent order: Manetho, an Egyptian, and
Timotheus, a Greek. The long history of Egyptian tradition
had, over the centuries, accommodated itself to some strange
inconsistencies which these two ironed out, incorporating Greek
concepts and deistic analogies which made the Egyptian worship
more ecumenical.[16]

Plutarch took up the Egyptian Isis and Hellenicized her in his
study *Isis and Osiris*. The Greek-Egyptian experience is truly a
catalyst in this study of Wisdom, for the strong character of Isis
the Goddess became the Sophianic touchstone of both Hermeticism and Gnosticism, as well as a major influence within Neo-
Pythagorean philosophy.

The myth of Isis is typified chiefly by her long search for the
body of her husband/brother, Osiris, who is riven in pieces by
Set, his opponent. Isis' long task is the reassembling of Osiris'
body and the magical conception of her child, Horus, through
whom the teachings of the gods will be vindicated. Plutarch
speaks of this esoteric wisdom: 'The Egyptians place sphinxes
before their shrines to indicate that their religious teaching has in
it an enigmatical sort of wisdom.' In Saïs, the statue of Athena,
whom they believe to be Isis, bore the inscription: 'I am all that
has been, and is, and shall be, and my veil no mortal has yet
uncovered.' The statue of Neith at Saïs betokens the nature of
Isis, whose mantle she is – the mysteries of the Goddess are
eternal and ever-renewing. It is not given to any mortal to view

these mysteries in their totality, save only in part and by the light of their own understanding.

The Goddess Neith, once venerated as the Creating Mother who wove the loom of the sky with her shuttle, was associated with another creating God, Khnum, who made the gods on his potter's wheel.[17] This association of a veiled goddess with an artificer god prefigures the Gnostic Sophia and her son the Demiurge.

In the *Hermetica* Horus asked his mother: 'How did Earth attain to the happy lot of receiving the efflux of God?' And Isis answered: 'Mighty Horus, do not ask me to describe to you the origin of the stock whence you are sprung; for it is not permitted to inquire into the birth of gods. This only I may tell you, that God who rules alone, the fabricator of the universe, bestowed on the earth for a little time your great father Osiris and the great goddess Isis, that they might give the world the help it so much needed.'[18] Here, we see the hermetic concept of Godhead of artificer; exactly the same term is used to describe Lady Wisdom in *Proverbs* 8:

> As for the robes, those of Isis are variegated in their colours; for her power is concerned with matter which becomes everything and receives everything, light and darkness, day and night, fire and water, life and death, beginning and end.[19]

Isis was the great saving Goddess under whose many-coloured cloak were subsumed the attributes and abilities of myriad lesser deities. Plutarch comments: 'There are those who declare that Isis is none other than the Moon; for this reason it is said that the statues of Isis that bear horns are imitations of the crescent moon, and in her dark garments are shown the concealments and the obscuration in which she in her yearning pursues the Sun (Osiris).'[20]

The black Isis is none other than the Black Goddess, Isis in her role as estoeric instructor as well as in her sorrowful mantle of mourning. Generally, the Black Goddess aspect of Isis is polarized upon Nephthys, her sister, who was originally Mistress of Heaven and the Underworld, but these roles became later split in Isis as Queen of Heaven.[21]

Isis was the skilful avoider of the net in which Set attempted to trap her. The net was seen as the symbol of the Adversary of Wisdom, for it was believed to exist in the Underworld where the dead had to learn its every part: the poles, ropes, weights and hooks whose names they had to learn in order to become 'true fishers'. In other words, the initiate was supposed to learn about the net of life not solely in order to avoid being caught in its toils, but also to learn how to fish for real nourishment.

With the onset of Christianity as the Roman state religion in the 4th century AD, the cult of Isis declined only in name, for the potency of her ritual worship flowed into the cult of the Blessed Virgin Mary to whom the same qualities, divine works of mercy and love, are attributed. Like the fertile waters of the Nile which brought life to Egyptian people then as now, the Goddess Herself returns to enliven Her people. Now that we are experiencing a reappraisal and reverence for the Goddess, it is only right that we should approach Her once again, in whatever form She appears to us.

The statues of Isis suckling Horus formed the early iconic model for all subsequent Madonna and Child states of Christian tradition. The Roman emperors, prior to Christianizing Constantine, venerated Isis, as is shown in a mural at Philae where Augustus is shown offering Isis myrrh, while Tiberius offers milk and incense, as well as animals sacred to Isis. Without any reservation one can transpose this nativity to that stable frequented by three kings![22]

As Isis is the sister-spouse of Osiris, so the *Gospel of Philip* observes: 'Mary is the name of his (Jesus') sister, and his mother, and it is the name of his partner.'[23] Mary inherits the role of *Nympha Dei* (bride of God) from Isis, along with numerous other titles, the most important correlation being: 'Throne of the King' as Mary is called in the Eastern Orthodox *Akathist Hymn*.[24]

Isis is opposed to Set and all his works, in much the same way that Mary is opposed to the serpent of Satan. 'The adversary who spies on us lies in wait for us like a fisherman.'[25] Statues of Isis show her crowned with the moon and with a crocodile under her feet – the infamous Set thrown down – this image is translated in its entirety in the *Book of Revelations* where Mary is similarly depicted, only as the Maiden crowned with the Sun and with the Moon under her feet, trampling on the serpent representing Lucifer. Mary's veil of sunlight is the true *doxa* or glory of Sophia.

The Beatus Apocalypse of Ferdinand I of Spain (see page 70) shows the Woman Clothed with the Sun, the Christianized Isis. Mary appears as Lower Sophia, totally black and with her eagle's wings ready to lift her to safety; one of the heads of the seven-headed dragon about to devour her has a net-like flood to entrap her.

3 *The Woman Clothed With the Sun* appears in *Revelations* 12. Upper left, we see her in her glory, assailed by a seven-headed dragon. Lower left, she appears again as the Black Goddess with wings, while one of the heads spews forth a flood with which to drown her. However, 'the earth helped the woman' and swallowed the waters so that she was able to fly to safety. The retreat of Sophia to a safe place is a continual theme in her mythos. This episode is paralleled in the stories of both Isis and Leto. These two images of Sophia show her in her glorious and veiled guises. From the eleventh century ms. *Beatus Apocalypse* of Ferdinand I. Biblioteca Nacional, Madrid.

The identification between Set and Typhon was readily made in Hellenic Egypt.[26] It is surprising that Nephthys, the sister of Isis and her mirror-image, should not have partaken of Set's nature, for she is Set's wife. She remains on Isis' side, as Black Goddess to her Sophia throughout her battle with Set, just as Ge Melantho does with Hera in her battle against Zeus.

The House of the Net was the title of the god Thoth's temple. The term 'net' was used in a symbolic sense to denote that which shuts humankind 'into the limitations of the conventional life of the world' and which keeps us from memory of our true selves.[27] Here the veil of Sophia keeps the unprepared from experiencing initiations which will overturn their world. This veil is usually seen as an entrapping net, as when Tiamat was trapped in a net by Marduk.[28] So Zeus sought his mother Rhea in marriage until she assumed serpent form, but he bound her in 'the Noose of Hercules' and united with her. In contradistinction to the entrapping net is the protective veil of Isis, the veil of Neith.

> In the Panathenaea the famous Peplum, Veil, Web, or Robe of Athena, the Goddess of Wisdom, was borne aloft like the sail of a galley; but this was the symbol only of the Mysteries. Mystically it signified the Veil of the Universe, studded with stars, the many-coloured Veil of Nature, the famous Veil or Robe of Isis, that no "mortal" or "dead man" has raised, for that veil was the spiritual nature of man himself, and to raise it he had to transcend the limits of individuality, break the bonds of death, and so become consciously immortal.[29]

That same veil was inherited by Isis from her mother, Nuit, the Sky Goddess, whose body arches over the heavens with a veil of stars. The veil of sunlight which Mary wears in *Revelations* is truly the *doxa* of Sophia, the glory which was once that of Isis.

The Peplos was one of the names of heaven, according to the hymns of Orpheus.[30] It was said to have been woven by Persephone, when her mother left her in a cave to learn the arts of embroidery and weaving. Persephone was seen as presiding over creation, and her web is the weave of heaven itself. This continual reference to the garment or veil of Wisdom reminds us that Sophia is found everywhere, under the forms of nature or else hidden in the symbols and images which speak to the heart. This is the veil which cannot be rent assunder by rape, only by personal understanding.

4 *Isis of Corinth* Isis is traditionally understood to be the Goddess of the Heavens, the Underworld and of the Earth itself. She appeared to the initiate of her mysteries, Lucius Apuleius, in this guise. Along the track of the full moon reflected upon the waters, Isis returns to comfort her creation. Clothed in a multi-coloured garment, and cloaked with the mantle of stars, the Goddess is crowned with the fruits of the earth. She holds in her hand the vessel of the soul's rebirth. Picture by Stuart Littlejohn.

72

Isis was a way-shower through the mysteries of spirituality. As Isis Pelagia, Queen of the Sea, the famous Pharos of Alexandria, the lighthouse which is one of the Seven Wonders of the World, was dedicated to her. It is indeed like a *pharos* that she appeared across the sea to Lucius Apuleius.

Lucius Apuleius (*c*. AD 120–180) was an initiate of the mysteries of Isis about which he wrote in his allegorical story *The Golden Ass*. In this, Lucius tells how he was accidentally transformed into an ass by his girl-friend, the servant of a Thessalian witch. The antidote to this unfortunate condition was the eating of roses. However, the assinine Lucius was taken away before he was able to be transformed and spent a year in ass-shape. After thrilling and frightening adventures, he was condemned to become the object of an obscene spectacle: with a condemned female criminal he was fated to mate with her publically in the arena. He made his escape and found himself by the sea. A full moon rose over the waves and he purified himself seven times in the sea and addressed Isis, imploring her to help him.

She appeared crowned with the headdress of the moon and two vipers, with corn-stalks woven in her hair. Her multi-coloured robe was woven with flowers and fruit, and her black mantle embroidered with stars and the moon. She carried a sistrum in her hand and addressed Lucius: 'I am Nature, the universal Mother, mistress of all the elements, primordial child of time, sovereign of all things spiritual, queen of the dead, queen also of the immortals, the single manifestation of all gods and goddesses that are.'[31]

The next day turned out to be the *Navigium Isidis*, the annual dedication and launching of a ship to Isis. During the ceremonial procession, Lucius was instructed to go forward and eat of the rose-garland which the high priest bore. Isis said: 'Only remember, and keep these words of mine locked tight in your heart, that from now onwards until the very last day of your life you are dedicated to my service. It is only right that you should devote your whole life to the Goddess who makes you a man again.'[32]

Lucius was duly transformed and received the three rites of initiation, which brought him fully into the worship of Isis and Osiris. He upheld the reticence of the initiate in his reported initiations, and spoke in veiled language of his revelation of Isis: 'I approached the very gates of earth and set one foot on Persephone's threshold, yet was permitted to return, rapt through all the elements. At midnight I saw the sun shining as if it were noon: I entered the presence of the gods of the underworld and the gods of the upper-world, stood near and worshipped them.'[33]

This allegory of Lucius' transformation is a mystery story. Its inclusion of the labours of Psyche reinforces the nature of initiation. Lucius intended to be transformed briefly into an owl, the bird of wisdom, but instead, due to his irregular life, became transformed into an ass, the beast of foolishness. Like Bottom in *A Midsummer Night's Dream*, he underwent mockery and degradation; he was brought into close relations with the fairest women who, in his human condition, he would have longed to embrace. He was cast in the part of Typhon, the Ass, to experience to the full his disordered lusts. Isis taught him wisdom and continence, and finally showed herself his Saviour Goddess.

What then is the task of Isis? Plutarch tells us '(Typhon or Set) tears to pieces and scatters to the winds the sacred writings, which the Goddess collects and puts together and gives into the keeping of those that are initiated into the holy rites.'[34] Isis is, then, the re-assembler of lost knowledge. To us also is entrusted the sacred task of re-assembling the scattered wisdom of the Goddess into a body of knowledge. This image is a compelling one for contemporary women who have no Goddess heritage to draw upon. Let them look to Isis and know her as queen of their search, who will take off her crown, wrap her hair in a scarf and go out looking with them.

If we leave Isis here, it is not farewell. We will meet her again, in other guises and in other centuries, coming over the seas of time in visionary splendour as brilliant as ever Lucius saw. Sophia now stands at the point of embarkation, leaving behind her self-evident salvific status to go into strange countries. She goes as a traveller, as a pilgrim Goddess, wearing a cloak which will not draw attention to herself, in the mode of all women travelling alone. During this exile, Sophia will emerge from each culture and country until a cumulative image of Divine Wisdom arrives back on the shores of consciousness as Isis returning with much baggage besides.

Part Two

THE WHITE VIRGIN

=== 4 ===

WISDOM AMONG
THE PHILOSOPHERS

> Great goddess, hear! and on my dark'ned mind
> Pour thy pure light in measure unconfin'd;
> That sacred light, O all-protecting queen,
> Which beams eternal from thy face serene.
> My soul, while wand'ring on the earth, inspire
> With thy own blessed and impulsive fire:
> And from thy fables, mystic and divine,
> Give all her powers with holy light to shine . . .
> Hear me, and save (for power is all thine own)
> A soul desirous to be thine alone.
>> *Hymn to Minerva*, trans. Thomas Taylor

> Learn at first concentration without effort; transform work
> into play; make every yoke that you have accepted easy and every
> burden that you carry light.
>> *Meditations on the Tarot*, Anon

Stolen Fire

We stand at the turning point where the Goddess no longer manifested in her full glory. The millennium between 500 BC and 500 AD saw the steady assimilation of the attributes and images of the Goddess into philosophical modes of thought which were later to influence the development of Christian theology. As she retreated from public consciousness slowly but inexorably, images of the empowering Saviour Goddess were drawn directly into the mythos of Mary, while Western philosophy reprocessed other Goddess images into abstract ideological forms. It was not until the Middle Ages that these abstractions re-emerged clothed in new personifications; Natura, Fortune, Dame Kind, Fate, the Seven Liberal Arts (see Chapter 12). Effectively, only Sophia retained the full empowerment of the Goddess, while her regalia was borrowed to adorn Mary whose power, at least on paper, was minimal.

Sophia became the Goddess of philosophers. Hers is a philosophy of fire for she kindles the inner fire within the soul; without her enthusiasm (literally 'god-inspiration') there is no warmth in our actions. Formerly, many cults of the Goddess, such as Hestia, for example, involved the ritual guardianship of sacred fires. The fire of the Goddess had burned in every hearth for thousands of years. It was a Greek law that no new city or colony could be founded unless fire was brought from the foundation city temple of Hestia. From this new fire, all domestic hearths were lighted. Just as Prometheus had stolen fire from heaven, now the sacred hearth was to be robbed of Wisdom's light. Philosophy kindled its embers on that sacred hearth, then stole the Goddess's fire to make conflagrations of its own. After a while, the sacred hearths were nothing but dead ash, for the fire was kindled elsewhere and guarded by professional lovers of wisdom.

Although many ancient philosophers retained their allegiances to the mystery cults of the Gods, even as some philosophers are still adherents of religions today, many more took the Gods back to their primal atomic principles into greater and greater abstraction. The result is that, for many people, philosophy no longer bears its original meaning - literally 'love of wisdom' – but is split off from the realities of existence. The inability of philosophers to live up to the quotation which heads this chapter is lamentable. Wisdom is the mistress of the game, indeed, but her game is a productive one, leading to life. Philosophy has a tendency to remain an empty and cerebral game unless animated by dialogue with Sophia. What is wisdom but a whole understanding which our specialist society has fragmented, just as the Goddess has been scattered? Scientists refute the allusive language of mystics, philosophers refute the eliptical language of esotericists. Isms and ologies have divided the world into their proper study and damned be she who attempts to reconcile all wisdom into one book.

Yet the study of wisdom means friendship with Sophia, and kinship with Wisdom brings immortality.[1] Traditional wisdom or philosophy is a holy and noble occupation, whereby the connections between divine and created natures are understood. It has always been in the hands of specialist priests and priestesses, as in the old mystery cults. The Gnostic text *The Teachings of Silvanus* exhorted the faithful thus: 'Clothe yourself with wisdom (*sophia*) as a garment, and pure understanding (*episteme*) upon yourself as a crown; sit upon a throne of perception (*aisthesis*). For these things are yours;[and] you will receive them again above.'[2] Thus the regalia of the ruler and of the initiate are identical, for the one enlightened by Sophia will regain her former nobility. Philosophically, the relationship between the monarch and the divine is found in Plato's *Timaeus 90a* where the king is seen in receipt of divine inspiration, becoming the bridge between the worlds for his people. The duty of the king, according to tribal and philosophical tradition alike, was to imitate the Divine in his life in every particular, by his truthfulness, justice and graciousness. Of course, the possession of wisdom was the prime requisite in the fulfilment of this onerous duty. Sages and councillors drawn from the priestly class who acted as advisors formed a quorum of elders from whom a formalized body of thought arises: from these the literature of Wisdom arises.

The desiccation of the Goddess of Wisdom is a pervasive feature of philosophy. No longer seen as the empowering and saving Goddess, the Black Goddess takes her toll: 'to those who fear her and scornfully shun her embraces, she becomes accidie, the demoness of sloth and meaninglessness . . . Without her blessing the waters of life dry up and wisdom desiccates into mere dusty, factual knowledge or airy theorizing.'[3]

I have chosen here to steer clear of philosophical abstraction where possible and concentrate upon the remythification of cosmogony and deity. Although philosophers are disinclined to use the language of story, they nevertheless are hampered in their methodological approach; to communicate their ideas to another party, they are forced to use popular concepts to carry their ideas. That some of their language is also misogynistic is to be expected, as is the assumption of Goddessly qualities to male divinities: one of the most irritating and confusing factors as we track Sophia.

There is still a tendency among philosophers such as Plato to utilize the mythic language and speak of the archetypal qualities of the Divine in terms of Greek deities, but there is a far more overwhelming tendency to avoid these mythic analogues and move further into the realm of abstraction. Early philosophy becomes an attempt to demythologize creation, to take it down to its atomic principles, to quantify and explain the work of the gods by intellectual means. It is so that the Saviour Goddess moves from autonomous entity to a mere quality. The Goddess is distilled by philosophy into pure thought, just as alchemy distills prima materia into pure gold.

The strands which went to weave together the Sophia of Gnostic and Medieval Christian thought are complex and tangled. The following attempt to uravel the muddle into which they have fallen must be considered a simplistic ordering, but the best which can be managed under the circumstances. If we are to arrive at any understanding of how the Goddess continued through the difficult years ahead and finally emerged, her power still apparantly manifest, we must start gently tugging at the ravelled loom. Where better to start than with the Goddess who bridges the two regimes, in whose mythos Sophia is firmly based?

Athene

All Classical philosophies are united in deriving Sophia, whether as World-Soul or some other abstract, from the mind of a male Creator. This feature is also the myth of a Goddess who, in her own person, shows how the Divine Feminine journeyed from divine autonomy to an abstraction of herself. She is the Greek Goddess of Wisdom, the model for some major strands in the Sophianic tapestry: Athene, the Goddess of Wisdom.

The earliest representations of Athene are found in Minoan-Mycenean culture where she frequently takes the form of a snake, being associated with the guardianship of houses and palaces.[4] When we look more closely at her mythos, it becomes clear that, like Cybele, she is a mountain-mother, for she drops the rock which forms Mount Lykabettos.[5] These two early symbolisms connect Athene to the Black Goddess energy. However, they are soon overlaid and complicated by successive developments. Early representations of Athene show her as a winged Goddess, which significantly connects her also with the future image of Sophia in Orthodox tradition, where she appears as a fiery angel (see Chapter 15).

Athene's birth is surrounded by many stories. Her mother Metis ('Wise Counsel') was the most far-seeing of the gods, the daughter of the originating deities, Oceanus and Tethys. Metis helped Zeus overcome his father Kronos who was devouring all his children. She provided the sleeping potion so that Zeus could castrate him. Because of a prophecy which said that Metis should bear a son who would overpower him, Zeus put the pregnant Metis in his own belly, and took her power as his own. Hephaistos smote Zeus' head with his axe and so enabled Athene to be born of her father's skull.

'But Athena sprang quickly from the immortal head and stood before Zeus . . . great Olympus began to reel horribly at the might

80

of the bright-eyed Goddess . . . until the maiden Pallas Athene had stripped the heavenly armour from her immortal shoulders. And wise Zeus was glad.'[6] As Hephaistos was the son born to Hera, without the aid of a father, so Athene was the daughter born to Zeus, without the aid of a mother.[7] These two parthenogenic cousins are further related, as we shall see.

Athene is the virago – the strong virgin – the untouched because untouchable one. Only three Greek Goddesses are avowed virgins: Athene, Hestia and Artemis. Paradoxically, Athene is also called mother as well as virgin. When Hephaistos helped Athene's delivery from the head of Zeus, he asked that she be made his bride. He led her to the bridal chamber but when he went to lie with her, she vanished and his seed fell on the earth. Gaia received it and so the child Erichthonios was born. Although actually born of Gaia and Hephaistos, the child was entrusted to Pallas Athene who behaved as its mother.[8] The seeds of this story took root in the Gnostic scriptures, for Erichthonios is sometimes said to have taken the form of a snake, rather as Ialdabaoth does in the Gnostic cosmogony. He grew up to become the one who institutes worship of the gods and state government. As we shall see, there are significant parallels between this story and that of subsequent Gnostic schemas.

One important ritual activity associated with Athene's 'wedding' to Hephaistos, which was celebrated with bridal ritual, was the festival of Chalkeia. Nine months later, the Panathenaia was celebrated, whereat an enactment of the mysteries of Erichthonios's birth were played out. The covered basket played a central part in the mysteries. In the intervening nine months after Chalkeia and before Panathenaia, priestesses of Athene rewove the *peplos* or tunic of the Goddess.[9]

It may seem strange that the Athenian in Plato's *The Laws* should call Athene 'our Kore and our Despoina', titles which apply to Persephone.[10] Kerenyi has proved that Athene had another aspect which has been rarely discussed: the dark Athene who, as the maiden Aglauros, had the keeping of the sacred basket of the mysteries and whose representative priestess might well have once been the maiden sacrifice in earlier days. He bases his theory upon the fate of the Lokrian maidens who, 'in archaic times were sent from Lokri to Troy as atonement for the crime which Aias had committed against the Palladium.'[11] The Trojan men had ambushed and slain the maidens. 'If the Lokrian maidens remained unrecognized and reached the temple of Athene, they became priestesses of the Goddess.' This episode was re-enacted in mystery form at the festival of Plynteria when the temple of Athene was cleansed. On the night preceding the *apophras emera* or ominous day, the Kallynteria was performed, whereby the priestess representing Aglauros was decked with ornaments prior to her ordeal in darkness. The priestess of Athene-Aglauros was originally called 'Agraulos', or 'one spending the night in the field,'[12] testifying to her descent into darkness. The exact rites are not known, but they seem to presage the sufferings and descent of the Gnostic Sophia, the daughter who descends into darkness. Thus Athene does indeed partake both of the nature of the transcendent Sophia and of the Black Goddess in her Persephone-like descent to suffering – an act moreover associated with the shame of having borne (mystically or otherwise) a child which is neither of heaven nor of earth – the Erichthonios or Ialdabaoth of the piece.

In imitation of Zeus's conception of Athene, Gnostic Sophia produced a self-conceived offspring. As we read on, it may be thought that the Goddess has perpetrated a great joke. In the Valentinian Gnosis the Demiurge – the alleged creator of the world – thought that he had created everything out of himself. However, Achamoth (Sophia) wished to be seeded everywhere, without his knowledge. Accordingly, she conceived an embryo and secretly inserted it into the Demiurge, 'that it might be sown into the soul created by him and into the material body . . . and might become ready for the reception of the perfect Logos.'[13] Accordingly, humanity does not derive its soul from the false Demiurge, but from the Mother Above. This Gnostic joke may perhaps be translated into Athenian terms, for Metis was pregnant with Athene when Zeus swallowed her and Zeus remains forever afterwards in her mighty shadow. Metis is derived of an earlier breed of gods, like Gnostic Sophia, and her influence is absorbed by Zeus. Zeus acts like a divine creator, though it is his foremothers who are the real shapers.

Athene as patron of wisdom, arts and crafts was called *Ergane*, the Work-Woman, a phrase reminiscent of 'artificer' which Wisdom holds in *Proverbs* 8:22 (see Chapter 5). If we look briefly at the associations between Athene, the Goddess of Crafts, and Hephaistos, the God of Smithcraft, we will discover some interesting patterns which will be further explored in Gnosticism. Socrates calls Hephaistos 'the princely lord of light' (*phaeos istora*) – perhaps the earliest Greek reference to Lucifer.

Hephaistos was, moreover, a premature baby, like the Gnostic Demiurge. He was conceived at a time when Hera and Zeus' relationship was kept secret. It was said he was incubated in her thigh, but that Zeus discovered him – a baby whose feet were on backwards – and hurled him to earth. Thetis, the sea-goddess, received him. In his later career, Hephaistos was famed for his craftsmanship, making him a true Demiurge or artificer. He fashioned golden virgins who moved and acted as though they were alive. He was the maker of the first woman, Pandora – she who carries the burden of Eve in Classical tradition.

It is Prometheus who stole divine fire from Zeus and the crafts from Pallas Athene. The stealing of divine crafts and skills by humankind is at the epicentre of all stories about the Fall, in whatever culture. here we may see how the Titans acted in a restrictive manner similar to that of the Gnostic Aeons.

Athene was always invoked in Greek prayer with two other gods in this order: Zeus, Athene and Apollo. These three deities may be seen as the triple godhead of Gnosticism: the father, virgin mother and glorious child who, under many different names and titles, invade Gnostic cosmogony. Athene also acquired the name *pronoia*, or providence, which is also one of the given names of the transcendent mother of Wisdom. The snakes of Athene's aegis are also reminiscent of the Gnostic Zoë, who takes the form of a snake in order to protect the integrity of Adam and Eve.

Athene became the bearer of the aegis – the protective goatskin which awakens fear in all who see it. She came by this in a variety of ways, according to legend, but the prime legend tells how Medusa, one of the Gorgons, was raped by Poseidon in Athene's temple. Athene made Medusa ugly and gave her the ability to turn to stone all who looked at her.[14] When Perseus had successfully beheaded Medusa, with Athene's help, the Goddess took the flayed skin and set the Gorgoneion, Medusa's head, upon her breast to complete the protective and horrifying aspect of the aegis. On statues, the aegis is shown as a flexible goathide, with the Gorgoneion over Athene's breast, while about the edge many serpents curl. The aegis is another example of Sophia's veil, by which we are shielded from too much knowing.

The fact that the Olympian Goddess of Wisdom should have the head of the Black Goddess upon her breast is most intriguing. To misquote *Sirach* 1:14, 'The fear of the Lady is the beginning of wisdom.' Like the Cailleach of Celtic tradition, Athene is a battle-Goddess and prime protectress. She is described as 'male and female, begetter of war, counsellor, she-dragon of many shapes.'[15] This last epithet is inherited from Metis who is a shape-shifter.

A medieval miniature shows Athene as the Goddess of Wisdom, bearing her palladium shield and giving it to a suppliant. The title of the picture is 'Wisdom renders us invulnerable to attack'. It reminds us of Sophia's function as companion and helper of the soul. Many heroes called upon Athene as 'the ever-near'; for example, Perseus received her shield to guard him against the petrifying gaze of Medusa. It is interesting that Athene, who started her existence as a form of the Black Goddess, should end it by guarding heroes from the threat of the Black Goddess.

5 *Against Wisdom Evil Does Not Prevail* This quotation from *Wisdom* 7:30 is illustrated by this medieval picture in which Athene is shown arming her suppliant with an invincible shield, rather as the Goddess armed Perseus against the Medusa. This is the warrior aspect of Sophia. Illumination from fourteenth century French text *Le Livre des Propriétés des Choses* by Barthélemy Anglais. Bibliotèque Sainte Geneviève, ms. 1029, fol 8v.

In many eyes, Athene is a traitor Goddess who sells her sisters down river. It is Aeschylus who puts the words of betrayal into Athene's mouth, when she is called to testify against Orestes' murder of his mother Clytemnestra:

> There is no mother bore me for her child,
> I praise the Man in all things (save for marriage),
> Wholehearted am I, strongly for the Father.[16]

She upholds Orestes, the mother-killer, against the Erinyes, the avengers of blood-guilt, the just daughters of the Black Goddess. It is for this reason that Athene is not generally held to be a popular archetype for modern women to follow. Though Athene was originally a Goddess of wise and practical craft, she has been transmuted over the centuries into a Goddess of transcendent and philosophical wisdom. When considering Athene, we must remember the hidden mother, Metis, Goddess of Wise Counsel. Her voice must be balanced against Athene's more intellectual wisdom.[17]

Athene is a prime example of the way in which the powers of the Goddess are subverted and then assumed by male deities. The Goddess of Wisdom is about to become the sacrificed daughter, the suffering soul who requires the saving act of another to rescue her from error. For not only does Gnostic Sophia derive from a Father, she is also rescued by a Son. Philosophy is about to show us another cosmogony in which the prime maker is not female but male, where Hephaistos is the Demiurge and Athene is the misguided mother.

World-Soul

Ancient philosophy was almost entirely dedicated to the under-standing of what animates the universe and how it works. Religions call this enquiry 'theology', scientists call it 'physics'. Philosophy unpicks myths in the pursuit of the pure and archetypal idea of what the Goddess and indeed, Deity, really is. The ancient notion that the whole earth partook of the Goddess's substance was subtly altered, producing the philosophy of the World-Soul, or *anima mundi*. The goddessly metaphors are stripped of their mythological garments and reduced to skeletal and sometimes deformed frameworks.

85

Socrates in *Philebus* asks about the soul: from where could the body have acquired a soul unless the body of the universe itself were not possessed of a soul also?[18] This question is answered in the *Timaeus*.

It is in Plato's greatest work of cosmogony, that we discover the World-Soul – a model which was to be followed and improved upon by succeeding philosophers. *Timaeus* may be described as 'notes for a cosmology'. It is an unfinished work, largely theoretical in content, which attempts to describe the formation of creation without recourse to the language of Greek myth. It was also the model for much of medieval philosophy. Plato tells us the world was 'like the fairest and most perfect of intelligible beings, framed (like) one visible animal comprehending within itself all others animals of a kindred nature.'[19] This accords closely with James Lovelock's view of the earth as Gaia.

Plato describes first the making of the world out of the four elements by God: 'He made it smooth and even, having a surface in every direction equidistant from the centre, a body entire and perfect and formed out of perfect bodies. And in the centre he put the soul, which he diffused thoughout the body, making it also to be the exterior environment of it, and he made the universe a circle within a circle . . . *He made the soul in origin and excellence prior to and older than the body, to be the ruler and mistress, of whom the body was to be the subject* . . . The soul, interfused everywhere from the center to the circumference of heaven, of which also she is the external envelopment, herself turning in herself, began a divine beginning of never-ceasing and rational life enduring throughout all time. The body of heaven is visible, but the soul is invisible and partakes of reason and harmony, and being made by the best of intellectual and everlasting natures, is the best of things created.'[20]

The idea of the World-Soul as circular or spherical, of having a cyclic movement, is implicit within mystic visionaries as diverse as Julian of Norwich with her hazelnut-vision of the world and William Blake, who saw eternity in a grain of sand.[21] The circle is an image of completion and wholeness, of integral harmony. Many mystics have echoed the Gnostic Poimandres' statement: 'God is a spiritual sphere, whose centre is everywhere and whose periphery is nowhere.'[22]

For Plato, the World-Soul is the supreme mediating entity, of which the human soul is a microcosm. Created by the Platonic Demiurge (not to be confused with the Gnostic Demiurge – a being who perpetuates the evils of life), the World-Soul is here conceived to be the most perfect created thing. There is also suggestion that she is pre-existent. As we shall see, many parallels to the Platonic World-Soul exist, not least in the Books of Wisdom. It has been suggested that Plato drew his inspiration for the creation from the Persian Zoroastrian creation myth, whence derives the greater part of Western dualism.

It is clear also that Plato's doctrine of the *anima mundi* is a rational and coldly logical one. It has been given to successive cultures to animate and personify the World-Soul so that she is truly present among us, sharing and empathizing with our pain and frustrations, a personification which the romanticizing academics of the medieval Chartres school promoted (see Chapter 12). But however powerful the World-Soul may be as an image, she is not a supreme entity. Sophia's major problems stem from the Platonic doctrine of the Monad and Dyad. The Monad, or first originating principle is always male, while the Dyad derives from the Monad and is usually female: it is a role which Sophia as World-Soul normally occupies. God replaces Goddess centre stage.

The Monad is understood to be the active principle which imposes limit on the formlessness of the opposite principle. The Dyad is a duality, infinitely extendable or divisible. The Dyad is manifest throughout the natural world and is subject to the limiting principle of the Monad. Around these two principles, certain metaphors have accumulated, a body of imagery which philosophical thought has used as a convenient packaging for these abstractions. Into this framework of two principles, the World-Soul appears as an intermediate and mediating entity. 'This is basically the entity whose creation is described in the *Timaeus*, but traces appear, in such men as Philo and Plutarch, or a rather more august figure, which almost seems to reflect a Speusippean Dyad, a figure not evil but simply responsible for multiplicity, and thus for all creation.'[23]

This 'more august figure' is none other than the Goddess, who becomes subsumed in the complex webs of the philosophers. It is so that Philo's Sophia is almost interchangeable with the Dyad, while in Plutarch's vision Isis is presented as the World-Soul. We owe Plutarch the notion of a 'maleficent World-Soul'. 'For if nothing comes into being without a cause, and if good could not provide the cause of evil then nature must contain in itself the creation and origin of evil as well as of good.'[24] This piece of dualism is probably largely responsible to the Gnostic dualism surrounding Sophia. This maleficent, or lower World-Soul appears as Set-Typhon in the Hermetic derivations from this tradition.

Plato's implicit dualism supported a cosmological view which has had far-reaching consequences. For Plato, reality was to be found in the world of ideas, not in their manifestation in the world of forms. This gives us our current notion of the natural world as inferior to the uncreated world. In fact, Plato avoids defining Nature at all: Natura was to emerge as but one female personification of a grander cosmographic mythology during the Middle Ages. Natura is daughter to the Dyad, or World-Soul, endlessly multiplying forms without integrity.

This implicit philosophical dualism was reflected in the subsequent Western understanding of both the earth, the natural world and Woman. Today, we are still suffering from this misunderstanding and its concomitant problems. It is a legacy which Sophia can help us reduce to a more balanced understanding.

Speusippus, (407–339 BC), the nephew of Plato and the head of his uncle's academy, supported the view of a female principle in the universe which manifested itself at different levels of being, right the way from the Dyad through the Soul into Matter.[25] We find traces of this diffusionist theory of the Divine Feminine in both neo-Pythagoreanism and in Gnosticism, where the remythification of these philosophical terms took place.

'Xenocrates . . . held as Gods the Monad and the Dyad. The former, as the male principle, has the role of Father, ruling in the heavens. This he terms Zeus . . . and it is for him the supreme God. The second is as it were the female principle . . . in the role of the Mother of the Gods ruling over the realm beyond the heavens. This he makes the soul of the universe.'[26] So writes the doxographer Aetius. But Xenocrates' Dyadic World-Soul is not a supreme Goddess sitting next to Zeus, for she receives informing intelligence from him and is thus what philosophers term 'an irrational World-Soul', serving in the role of God's secretary. If we turn to Plutarch's *Isis and Osiris*, a work clearly influenced by Xenocrates, we find that there the World-Soul is represented by both Isis as World-Soul, and Seth-Typhon as the evil principle of disorder. These roles will be played out upon the Christian stage by Mary and Satan, and by Sophia and her son the Demiurge in Valentinian theology.

Plutarch tackles the nature of Isis from a Platonic point of view, rationalizing the Egyptian Goddess into an irrational World-Soul. 'Thus Isis is the female principle in nature and that which receives all procreation, and so she is called by Plato, the Nurse and the All-receiving . . . Imbued in her she has a love of the first and most sovereign principle of all, which is the same as the Good, and this she longs for and pursues. The lot which lies with evil she shuns and rejects; she is, indeed, a sphere of activity and subject matter for both of them, but she inclines always of herself to what is better, offering herself to it for reproduction, and for the sowing of herself of effluxes and likenesses. In these she rejoices and she is glad when she is pregnant with them and teems with procreations. For procreation in Matter is an image of Being and imitation of That which is.'[27]

Plutarch here translates Isis into a womb of procreation, a metaphor of Nature herself, who continually receives the impressions of the Monad in successive reflections which can mutate into evil influences, though Isis herself does not partake in any evil, but offers herself continually in the hope of a perfect reflection. This makes Isis like Eve whose female descendants went on bearing children endlessly until Mary brought Christ to birth to set right the ancient ancestral sin of humankind. Isis' many-coloured garment becomes, like Persephone's web or Athene's peplum, a reflection of the multiplicity of nature. As we have seen, Isis set herself up in opposition to Set-Typhon who was the manifestation of evil in Plutarch's dualistic cosmology, as Mary was to do later in *Revelations*.

In the Graeco-Roman world, as well as in the Judaeo-Hellenic world, the concept of Wisdom was seized upon and applied to its resident archetypes. Philo, the Alexandrian Hellenist and Jewish philosopher, identified the Mother of the divine Logos with Isis. In this amalgamation, Isis-Sophia was the mother of Harpocrates as the Logos.[28] Philo 'transforms the cosmological mythology derived from the Isis-Osiris cult into psychological realities. The Logos as priest and king of the cosmos becomes the priest of the soul.'[29]

Confusion similarly dogs the steps of Sophia, for she is frequently presented as at once transcendent, a kind of Dyadic Goddess, but also manifest – an epiphany of the World-Soul, lost and wandering in sorrow. Among the philosophers there is consistent fudging of the female principle which is elided into daemonic, planetary and auxiliary entities, while the male principle is forthrightly defined and upheld.

In Albinus' philosophy, the World-Soul is virtually a yawning slut, a passive mirror of the Monad whose function is to merely reflect ideas and who has, moreover, to be awakened by the

Demiurge. 'The Soul of the World, which exists eternally, God does not create, but merely brings into order; he ccould be said to create it only in this sense, that he rouses and turns towards himself its Mind and itself from, as it were, a sort of trancelike sleep, that it may look upon the objects of his intellection and so receive to itself the Forms and shapes, in its striving towards his thoughts.'[30]

The dynamic action of the Goddess is here made passive, capable only of reflection, a feature which recurs within the *Bible*. If the World-Soul can be imaged in this way, are the images of the human soul itself any more uplifted?

The Soul and the Spirit

The nature of the soul was at the basis of philosophical speculation. In many cultures, especially those where the Divine Masculine occupies the forefront of religious consciousness, the soul is conceived of as feminine – a natural polarization of genders which is reflected in mystical works throughout all levels of Islam, Christianity and Judaism.

The pre-Socratics grappled with the nature of soul and spirit. Anaximenes understood the soul to be composed of air (*pneuma*) which 'holds us together, so do breath and air surround the whole universe.'[31] This aerial theme was later applied to the Virgin in Gerard Manley Hopkins' poem *The Blessed Virgin Compared to the Air we Breathe*:

> I say that we are wound
> With mercy round and round
> As if with air: the same
> Is Mary, more by name.
> She, wild web, wondrous robe,
> Mantles the guilty globe . . .
> And men are meant to share
> Her life as life does air.[32]

Here is a truly philosophical and theological poem where Mary is the World-Soul and the soul's life.

Heraclitus preferred to conceive of *pneuma* as fire. It is he who first spoke of the spirit as *logos* or 'word'. His description of its action should be compared to Plato's description of the World-Soul: '*logos* is spirit, which is thought and yet deeper than mere thought;

it travels the same circle in the consciousness, even at the edge of consciousness as fire in the cosmos. The *logos* runs in a circle from opposite to opposite, thus shattering the proposition that opposites exclude one another.'[33] By the pervasive *logos*, we are made intelligent, according to Heraclitus.

It was Pythagorus who further set the trend for the polarity of matter and spirit. For him, *pneuma* was pure spirit, in contradistinct polarity to matter. For Pythagoreans, the spirit was a numerical abstraction, for all things arise from the One, the Monad, and the mathematical progression of number gives the world its harmonious proportion. This obsession with numbers remained a Hellenic preoccupation where deity is geometricized. Plato's *Timaeus* is firmly based within it, the early church doubtless derived its complex Trinitarian arguments from this stream, and the Gnostics brought the numbers game to the brink of absurdity.

The Classical world regarded the descent of the soul into the body as a supreme misfortune. In Stoical vein, Plotinus summarizes human existence: 'This is the life of gods and of the godlike and blessed among men, liberation from the alien that besets us here, a life taking no pleasure in the things of earth, the passing of solitary to solitary.'[34] This joyless statement concludes the *Enneads*.

We may compare a late Jewish *midrash* which describes the soul being summoned before God. 'She bows forthwith before the King of Kings, whereupon the Holy One, blessed be He, commands the soul to enter into the drop of semen contained in so and so; but the soul replies: "Lord of the universe, sufficient for me is the world in which I have dwelt from the moment you created me, why do you wish to install me in this fetid drop, since I am holy and pure and hewn from your glory?"' God then directs the soul to obey him. '"The world into which I am about to place you will be more lovely for you than the world in which you have dwelt hitherto, and when I created you, it was only for this seminal drop that I created you." The Holy One, blessed be He, then immediately installs her *against her will*.'[35]

This *midrash* shows not only a reliance on the mistaken physiology of Aristotle which understood generations of life to derive solely from male sperm, rather than its admixture with the female ovum, but also upon the widespread notion that the descent into matter is abhorrent to the spiritual nature. Orphism, Manicheanism and branches of Gnosticism concurred with this notion, as the text, *The Hymn of the Pearl* testifies.

91

'Wise men of old gave the soul a feminine name. Indeed she is female in her nature as well', says Gnostic *Exegesis of the Soul*.[36] All who possess a soul are female, is the Gnostic argument. Gnosticism likens the soul to Sophia who, like Psyche, undergoes torments until her beloved rescues her.

The soul nearly always takes a feminine metaphor in relation to Deity, regardless of whether that soul is enshrined within a male or female body. Plotinus exemplifies this concept in a nutshell in the following myth. 'The soul in its nature loves God and longs to be at one with Him in the noble love of a daughter for a noble father; but coming to human birth and lured by the courtships of this sphere, she takes up with another love, a mortal, leaves her father and falls. But one day, coming to hate her same, she puts away the evil of earth, once more seeks the father, and finds her peace.'[37] This metaphor can only be sustained if the source of Creation is seen in male images and, indeed, the Gnostic text, *The Exegesis of the Soul* accords with Plotinus' scenario. It will be interesting to see, as Goddess spirituality gradually spreads into the 21st century, whether the new thealogy will retain the notion of a female soul or not.

Somehow, in seeking for the soul, the world lost the Goddess whose wings had sheltered it for so long. To all intents and purposes, the Goddess *became* the human soul, as well as the World-Soul, or could be seen as the soul's companion angel, undergoing the sufferings of life.

Returning to the Cave

The ancient philosophers give a stilted and somewhat gloomy picture of existence. The World-Soul which animates our globe is seen as sluggish or bestial, and the soul itself is an unwilling female entity, then what of the body itself?

Porphyry (205-269 AD), the commentator of Plotinus, wrote Concerning the Cave of the Nymphs, a mystical commentary upon an episode in the thirteenth book of the *Odyssey*. Porphyry, standing in the line of Neo-Platonic philosophy and speaking the old language of the mystery schools, returns the Goddess to us, in simple and unambiguous metaphors. In this text, Odysseus' ship comes into the Cave of the Nymphs where he meets and recognizes Athene, his patron. In order to effect his secret homecoming, Athene transforms Odysseus into an old beggar. The fact that she transforms him in the Cave of the Nymphs is significant, for it is here, according to Porphyry's reading, that souls come in order to have the garments of mortal bodies woven for them.

Porphyry speaks about the image of the cave, reminding us that Plato also used this image to describe the world. 'For as they consecrated temples, groves and altars to the celestial gods; but to the terrestial gods and to heroes altars alone, and to the subterranean divinities vaults and cells; so to the world they dedicated caves and dens. The ancients not only considered a cave as the symbol of this generated and sensible world, but as the representative of every invisible power . . . Thus Ceres (Demeter) educated Persephone with her nymphs in a cave.'[38]

At the entrance to the cave stands an olive tree, a not insignificant symbol . . . 'for as the world was not produced by the blind concurrence of chance, but is the work of divine wisdom

6 *Cave of the Nymphs* This painting by William Blake portrays Porphyry's *De Antro Nympherum*. Here Odysseus kneels, casting back the girdle which Leucothea, the sea-goddess, gave him. Behind him, Pallas Athene, the Goddess of Wisdom and patron of the hero, indicates the northern portal of the mysterious cave where mortals are ensouled. The Parcae (Fates) are at the water's edge, weaving garments for the soul. National Trust, Arlington Court, Devon.

and an intellectual nature, hence an olive, the symbol of divine wisdom, flourishes near the present cavern, which is an emblem of the material world. For the olive is the plant of Minerva, and Minerva is wisdom.'[39]

There are two gateways within the cave: the Northern one corresponds to the egress and exit of humanity, the Southern one corresponds to the passage of the gods. This concept, familiar from Macrobius, is explained by the gateways of the solstices: the Southern gate of Cancer at midsummer, when the Gods are manifest, and the Northern gate of Capricorn at midwinter, when humanity is restored at Saturnalia.

The work of the nymphs within the cave (illustrated by William Blake as the Parcae), 'weaving on stony beams purple garments wonderful to behold', is explained as the flesh being woven about the bone. Porphyry directs us to remember: 'Persephone, who presides over every thing generated from seed, is represented weaving a web; and the ancients called heaven by the name of *peplos*, which is as it were the veil . . . of the celestial gods.'[40]

It is within this busy cave that Wisdom herself appears, to reclothe her wanderer in fresh mortal garments. We will recall that one of Athene's emblems is the *peplum*, the veil or tunic of the Goddess by which humanity is clothed. It was an object of veneration in her temple. Here, Athene shows herself the mistress of this task which is nothing more than the formation and incarnation of the soul.

Plato's *Symposeum* tells us that as Pallas Athene established her loom through longing and desire, so also did Hephaistos take to smithcraft.[41] It is thus that the Gnostic Sophia becomes the foremother of created life-forms.

This important text places the Greek Sophia in her context. She is the creator of the physical fabric of life, the Athene *Ergane* and also its guardian upon earth, where she may appear in numerous forms as Persephone, the World-Soul, as Love or Beauty.

Philo

The most influential figure upon the appearance of Sophia is the 1st century philosopher Philo (20 BC–50 AD). A Hellenized Jew living in Alexandria, he single-handedly reforged metaphors of Wisdom, drawing on a variety of images which were to hand. Working from a close knowledge of Plato, 'he developed the doctrine of a distant God whose "powers" or "powerful agents" (*dumameis*) mediate between him and the world.'[42]

Philo was one of the first to weave together the strands of philosophy, Judaic and Goddess lore, and in so doing promoted a theological exegesis which was to be a bridge by which early Christianity crossed over from Middle Eastern obscurity into European prominence.

To Philo, pre-existent Wisdom is a divine power with the form of a woman, whose gift is fecundity of spirit rather than of body. She is an intermediary being, or *dunameis*, between God and matter. She is equated with images as diverse as the Law, the Tabernacle, Eden and the Promised Land.

He resorts to many allegorical instances of Wisdom from Biblical examples. Wisdom is the daughter of God; sometimes, his wife. The perfect man, Isaac, is the son of Sarah, a type of divine Wisdom. His wife, Rebekah, represents manifest Wisdom. She is coveted by Abimelech, the incomplete man who, like the Fool, cannot possess Wisdom. Philo embodies Wisdom in the persons of Sarah, Rebekah, Zipporah and Hannah who are all representatives of the fecundity of Wisdom.

Philo, a man of his time, believed in the inferiority of the feminine and accordingly exalted his Wisdom as Bethuel, 'Daughter of God', who is nonetheless called 'Rebekah's father'. He explains: 'But how can Wisdom, the daughter of God, be rightly said to be a father? Is it because, though Wisdom's name is feminine, her nature is masculine? Indeed all the virtues have women's designations, but powers and activities of truly perfect men.'[43] Like the masculine virgin, Athene, Bethuel is necessarily androgynous in metaphor, as Philo carelessly tells us: 'Let us then pay no attention to the discrepancy in the terms, and say that the daughter of God, Wisdom, is both masculine and the father, inseminating and engendering in souls a desire to learn discipline, knowledge, practical insight, noble and laudable actions'.

This view permeated Gnosticism to the extent that the writer of the Gnostic *Tripartite Tractate* recast the story of Sophia into a story of the Logos – a significant change which is echoed in the way in which Christ as Logos takes over the role of Sophia also.

To follow Philo's track into the tangled theologies of Gnosticism is a task beyond this book, but he did observe that the Pythagoreans likened the number 'seven to the motherless and ever-virgin Maiden (Athene), because neither was she born of the womb nor shall she ever bear.'[44] We may note here the codification of the sevenfold imagery which attaches to Sophia in all her aspects. Philo observes that some philosophers liken seven to Nike (Victory) who, like Athene, came from the head of Zeus. He employs this Classical argument to exemplify the dignity of the Sabbath, the seventh day of rest, as the bride of Moses who found the Sabbath to be a virgin begotten of a father alone: 'he recognized in her the birthday of the world, a feast celebrated by heaven, celebrated by earth and things on earth as they rejoice and exult in the full harmony of the sacred number'.

The inconsistencies of motherhood and virginity are echoed in Rebekah who is called 'the motherless wisdom'. Bethuel's house becomes a bridal chamber of Athene's Panathenaia in order that Isaac might be joined in union with Rebekah, the virgin Constancy.

Philo was frequently confused by his own rhetoric, and unclear in his thinking about Sophia, who veers wildly from being a kind of earth-mother to a transcendent entity. For instance, he describes Sophia Platonically as 'the Mother of all things in the Universe, affording to her offspring, as soon as they are born, the nourishment which they require from her own breasts.'[45] Yet, on the other hand, Sophia is the partner of God sitting beside him as *paredros* (assessor), like Diké beside Zeus, or Wisdom beside Jehovah.

Before the Greek properties are made over and wheeled onto the Gnostic stage, we must take a journey into the Judaeo-Christian desert, to discover what elements Philo drew upon and how they became part of the Sophianic package which the Gnostics unwrapped at Alexandria. It is here that the Biblical Lady Wisdom met the philosopher's Sophia, and the Goddess found a circuitous method of survival.

═ 5 ═

WISDOM BUILDS HER HOUSE

I will again make instruction shine forth like the dawn, and
I will make it shine afar;
I will again pour out teaching like prophecy, and leave it to
all future generations.

Sirach 24:32–3

The Untarnished Mirror

No matter how many tributaries of Sophia's myth we follow, the
principle river undoubtedly flows through the sapiential books of
the Bible. These consist of *Job, Proverbs, Song of Songs, Wisdom,
Sirach* or *Ecclesiasticus*. Of these, only *Wisdom* and *Sirach* appear
in the Septaguint, the Greek translation of the Hebrew scriptures.
As a result, these two books, along with some others, are excluded
from the canonical Bible and are relegated to the *Apocrypha*. Their
influence has been considerable, since within *Proverbs, Wisdom*
and *Sirach* are all the major references to Sophia as Lady Wisdom.
Most Marian liturgies and devotions draw upon these books. The
metaphors presented in the sapiential books become the *lingua
franca* of Sophia in succeeding centuries, providing an array of
poetical veils with which to shroud Wisdom.

Since each of the sapiential books has a vast critical corpus, I
have chosen, in assessing its theological implications and parallel
texts, to uncover only those themes which provide a full portrait of
Sophia. The influence of the metaphors established in these books
is potent, flowing into the liturgies of the Christian church, into
esoteric Jewish thought and Hellenic philosophy, as well as into
the well of Gnosis.

Within the sapiential books, Sophia appears in various forms,
consistent to the Hebrew tradition. Sometimes she is a fully fledged
personality, as in *Proverbs* where she is the companion of God,
or as the Skilful Woman opposed to the Foolish Woman. At
other times, in *Sirach*, she appears merely as a hypostasis, an
abstraction, a quality to be desired and sought after, no more.
Each in their own way has influenced the direction of Sophia's

97

acceptance within orthodox and mystical spirituality, which is why we consider their evidence briefly here.

We have seen how the Goddess of the Land was married to the king to be his *paredros*, or assessor. The laws which marked this marriage contract became the traditions of wise counsel or sage advice which were further codified into summaries or proverbs. These were taught and upheld by priests, prophets and sages, all educated men with a professional interest in effective methods of life. Such wisdom was the lore preserved by the ancestors and taught by the elders of the tribe. The codification of tribal wisdom is the direct ancestor of philosophy under the patronage of the just Goddess of the Land. It is so that the most ancient texts are frequently framed in the manner of laws rather than creation mythology, which arises usually from later speculation. These laws are the integral part of tribal society, keeping it alive and healthy, regulating and sometimes terminating the lives of criminals who would harm the common good. Holy law therefore precedes scripture.

The ancient laws of the Goddess are restated within Biblical scripture, reframed in Judaic terminology. The authors of the sapiential books give us tantalizing glimpses of a vanished world where the Goddess was still actively part of creation; what remains to us are the metaphorical fragments, still potent today, that reshaped the way our ancestors viewed the Divine Feminine.

Proverbs

Proverbs presents us with a sublime portrait of Sophia as the creative ground of existence, as messenger and instructor of Wisdom. It was collated in about 700 BC and is the earliest of the sapiential books.[1] Most of the text is an exhortation to act wisely, in a similar manner to Polonius' advice to Horatio in *Hamlet*. Three chapters deal specifically with Wisdom who begins forthrightly in the street:

> Wisdom cries aloud in the street;
> in the markets she raises her voice;
> on the top of the walls she cries out;
> at the entrance of the city gates she speaks.[2]

She calls everyone to listen to her and reproves them for being so slow in attending:

Because I have called and you refused to listen,
have stretched out my hand and no one has heeded . . .[3]

But she is no mild and ineffective presence. In words which will
be echoed in *St Matthew* by Jesus, and which have already been
spoken by Astraea, she promises:

> I also will laugh at your calamity;
> I will mock when panic strikes you like a storm . . .
> When distress and anguish come upon you.
> Then they will call upon me, but I will not answer;
> they will seek me diligently but will not find me.[4]

This is Wisdom speaking with the harsh voice of the Black Goddess
in her judgmental aspect. But she shows herself more merciful in a
later passage:

> I love those who love me,
> and those who seek me diligently find me.[5]

For this reason, she stands in the way, obviously and approachably
at the thresholds of life:

> On the heights beside the way,
> in the paths she takes her stand;
> beside the gates in front of the town,
> at the entrance of the portals she cries aloud.[6]

The rest of Chapter 8 of *Proverbs* is nothing other than an
autobiography of Wisdom, in which she is shown to be a separate
entity, the companion of God:

> The Lord created me at the beginning of his work,
> the first of his acts of old.
> Ages ago I was set up, at the first,
> before the beginning of the earth.
> When there were no depths I was brought forth,
> when there were no springs abounding with water.
> Before the mountains had been shaped,
> before the hills, I was brought forth;
> before he had made the earth with its fields,
> or the first of the dust of the world.
> when he established the heavens,

> I was there,
> when he drew a circle on the face of the deep,
> when he made firm the skies above,
> when he established the fountains of the deep,
> when he assigned to the sea its limit,
> so that the waters might not transgress his command,
> when he marked out the foundations of the earth,
> then I was beside him, like a master workman;
> and I was daily his delight,
> rejoicing before him always,
> rejoicing in his inhabited world
> and delighting in the sons of men.[7]

Wisdom was clearly not existent prior to God, but she was the first of his actions. There is no sense of her being a co-equal Goddess or co-creator, as such, though the 'play of Wisdom' before God suggests that her creative faculty stimulated creation.

This passage inspired the Slavonian *Book of Enoch*: 'On the sixth day, I (God) commanded my Wisdom to create man.'[8] This and the *Clementian Homilies* 16:11f give Wisdom a greater power than the original text: 'One is He who said to His Wisdom: "Let us make man." But Wisdom, with whom He is always, rejoiced as with His own spirit, is united with God like a soul, and is stretched out from Him like a hand, creating everything.'[9]

The word 'master-workman' is sometimes substituted by 'child' in some translations. Both readings make sense. One of Athene's titles is *Ergane* or work-woman, indicating the way in which divine wisdom underlies all patterns of creation. In qabala, Binah, the Great Mother, is the producer and shaper of matter. But Wisdom may equally play before God like a child. This is one of her unsung abilities – her creative facility which is appreciable in all children who have a natural access to wisdom in their play that we adults lack. Wisdom as child acts as a counterpoise to God's creation.

Rather like the servants who are sent out to invite everyone to the wedding feast in *St Matthew* 22, Wisdom invites her own guests:

> Wisdom has built her house,
> she has set up her seven pillars.
> She has slaughtered her beasts,
> she has mixed her wine,
> she has also set her table.
> She has sent out her maids to call
> from the highest places in the town,

7 *Wisdom Has Built Her House* This sixteenth century icon is a pictorial representation of *Proverbs* 9:1–6. Above, is shown Wisdom's temple of seven pillars, while below, she has slaughtered her beasts, poured her wine and set her table. She calls everyone to leave foolishness behind and sit at the table of wisdom. Sophia appears as the full manifestation of the Divine, the cup of redemption in her hand, while Mary as Theotokos (God-Bearer) and her Son appear outside the temple.

"Whoever is simple, let him turn in here!"
To him who is without sense she says:
"Come, eat of my bread
and drink of the wine I have mixed.
Leave simpleness, and live,
and walk in the way of insight."[10]

Whence come these Seven Pillars of Wisdom? Rabbinical commentaries state that the Israelites were continually accompanied on their journey by seven clouds of glory: one in front, one behind and one on either side of them, one above to keep off rain, hail and sun and one under them. The seventh preceded them, making the pathway clear and ridding it of snakes, thorns etc.[11] This is the action of the Shekinah, yet another persona for Wisdom, she who is God's dwelling. Wisdom's house is analogous to the Jewish Temple, or to the Christian Ecclesia, the Church. This much is clear from a later passage:

By wisdom a house is built and by understanding it is established;
by knowledge the rooms are filled with all precious and pleasant riches.[12]

The number seven appears frequently in our study of Sophia. It is applied to Wisdom also by the Jewish philosopher, Aristabulus of Paneas, who regards 'the Preexistent Wisdom or Logos, to be symbolised by seven, representing the true Sabbath rest which may be enjoyed by followers of Wisdom.'[13]

But in the light of Gnostic textual evidence, Wisdom's temple of seven pillars may be seen as none other than the wedding chamber wherein the mysteries of creation are folded away (see Chapter 8). The juxtaposition of the creation with its ending in *Proverbs* may seem shocking; but Wisdom is concerned with both beginnings, and endings, as well as effective middles. *Proverbs* ends with an alphabetical poem which has been commonly taken as praise of the perfect wife. In the context of this text, it must apply to Wisdom herself who is shown to be a perfect provider and businesswoman, who is charitable to the poor and who clothes all her household with her own weaving. This much we may apply to any Middle Eastern woman, but in addition: 'She opens her mouth with wisdom and the teaching of kindness is on her tongue.'[14] She is a wise instructor clothed in strength and dignity, who 'laughs at the time to come.'[15]

We find in *Proverbs* the polarization of Lady Wisdom with Folly, the harlot – a polarization which follows Wisdom and her sisters throughout her long succession. Philo's Two Ways – the way of life and happiness, the way of disobedience and death – probably derive from *Proverbs* where the way of Wisdom is called 'the path of uprightness'[16] and Folly's way is 'the path to Sheol.'[17]

Wisdom is the true wife to be sought after, while Folly is like a roaming prostitute who is to be avoided.[18] The ordered banquet of Wisdom is contrasted with Folly's orgies.[19] The first is an invitation to the wedding feast, of the kind celebrated in Gnostic belief; the second is an invitation to hell. 'Wisdom builds her house, but Folly with her own hands tears it down.'[20]

The manner in which Wisdom calls aloud in the street is reminiscent of the way in which the Shulamite goes about the streets looking for her Beloved in *Song of Songs*. The line between the street-walking whore looking for trade and the diligent wife seeking her husband is a fine one. The Shulamite is in fact beaten up like any streetwalker, her great love mistaken for arbitrary lust. This allegory of the soul's journey is reworked many times in the mythos of Sophia.

Wisdom's role as street-walker is astounding, considering the social context of the time. In the Near East, women did not walk about uncovered, let alone proclaim themselves as prophets. The only kind of woman walking the streets would be veiled female servants, street performers and prostitutes. Wisdom cries aloud like any Middle Eastern *hakim* chanting line-by-line instruction in a courtyard classroom. The nobility of Lady Wisdom is evident from the text – she is used to being obeyed, to running a large household. The fact that she should take to the streets is both shocking and liberating. Both Wisdom and Folly show themselves to be women outside the social rules. While Folly is seen as particularly dangerous, Wisdom is rarely socially acceptable in female guise, and may be seen as equally dangerous. This is all part of Wisdom's subversive character however.

Her bottom line as 'street-wise' Wisdom is not about basic survival tactics; her gift of free instruction for all who want to go beyond this level of living. The dichotomy for women has hitherto been the choice between being a housewife in purdah or else a dangerous woman whose sexuality and integrity are her own. The Wisdom of *Proverbs* shows a third way which many women are now seeking: to enter the marketplace and cry aloud, whether in print, workshop or media, the message of

Wisdom which has been so long ignored. The reader can judge the contemporary aptness of the last verse of *Proverbs* which is beginning to apply to all women:

> Give her of the fruit of her hands, and let her works praise her in the gates.[21]

The Wisdom of Solomon

The Wisdom of Solomon occupies a uniquely free place in the Biblical canon. Quoted widely by Church Fathers as various as Origen, St Augustine and St Jerome, it was written probably about 30 BC. Its author, despite the title, was a Hellenized Jew of Alexandria who derived his themes from the hotbed of speculative philosophy which flourished in that city. He was probably a contemporary of Philo of Alexandria, many of whose ideas he echoes. He takes the persona of King Solomon, the wisest of kings, so that his words take on a dramatic import: Wisdom is a royal attribute, so that association with her ennobles its possessor.[22] What is most exciting about the text is its enthusiastic portrayal of Wisdom and its extraordinarily daring assumptions about her relationship to both God and the individual soul.

The author begins his portrait of Wisdom:

> I will tell you what wisdom is and how she came to be, and I will hide no secrets from you, but I will trace her course from the beginning of creation.[23]

Speaking as King Solomon, he tells how he sets Wisdom above everything else, even health and beauty. He has learned that 'all good things came to me along with her, and in her hands uncounted wealth. I rejoiced in them all because wisdom leads them; but I did not know that she was their mother.'[24] This important understanding is critical, for the pursuit of Wisdom does not imply disdain of this world or of its benefits: these are implicitly bestowed.

The virgin nature of Wisdom is upheld: 'She is a breath of the power of God, and a pure emanation of the glory of the Almighty; therefore nothing defiled gains entrance into her.'[25] Wisdom appears as the Egyptian Maat, the Mazdaen Daena, and the World-Soul combined, for she hears what is said, throughout the whole world; she will judge, convict and bring life or death on the strength of a person's deeds.[26]

The vocabulary employed by the author of *Wisdom* is redolent of the cult of Isis. He speaks of her[27] as being a radiance (*aparantos*) of everlasting light: a word utilized in the magical papyri and borrowed from Egyptian practice. Isis speaks of herself: 'I am in the rays of the sun.'[28] But Wisdom 'is more beautiful than the sun, and excels every constellation of the stars. Compared with the light she is found to be superior, for it is succeeded by the darkness, but against wisdom evil does not prevail.'[29] This light is only yet beginning to dawn in our own age.

Wisdom is praised in a litany of twenty-one epithets, many of which are similarly applied to the worship of Isis *myrionymos* (many named): intelligent; holy; unique; manifold; subtle; agile; lucid; unsullied; clear; inviolable; loving goodness; keen; unhindered; beneficent; humane; steadfast; unfailing; untouched by care; all-powerful; all-surveying; pervading all spirits.[30] Wisdom is described as 'a pure emanation of the glory of the Almighty.[31] This compares interestingly with *Songs of Isis and Nephthys* 9:26 where it is said that 'the Nile is the efflux of Osiris' body.'[32] The life-giving waters of the Nile were, of course, associated with the loving wisdom of Isis herself.

However, this leaves in question Wisdom's actual existence, for she is described as a reflection, a mirror of God's work, as a personification of God's goodness.[33] Her extensive abilities make her God's active agent, not a Goddess. Her activity reflects and transforms the idea of God: she is therefore the thrustblock of creation, but not the Creator. This mirror symbolism reminds us of the action of the Spirit of God moving upon the face of the waters in *Genesis*.[34] The Divine Masculine is passive and uncreative until the movement of the Divine Feminine Wisdom gets to work. *Wisdom* says: 'Wisdom is more mobile than any motion; because of her pureness she pervades and penetrates all things.'[35] The mystic, Nicolas of Cusa (1400-64), writes: 'There is only one mirror without flaw: the divine, in whom what is revealed is received as it is. For this mirror is not essentially different from any existing thing. Rather in every existing thing it is that which is: it is the universal form of being.'[36] The World-Soul's reflective quality is like Wisdom who, like a Dyad, reflects the creative ideas of the Monad.

Drawing upon the portrayal of Wisdom extant in *Proverbs* 8:22ff. and *Job* 28:12ff., the author gives her new status as a hypostasis of

God: one who has assumed the attributes proper to God and whose knowledge of God is so extensive that, to all intents and purposes, she is of one substance with God. 'She magnifies her noble birth by enjoying intimacy with God, and the Master of All loved her'[37] but, as Philo points out, God had union with her, not like human men, but still begat created life.[38] He re-echoes *Proverbs* 8 and reminds God that Wisdom knows all his works and was present when he created the world. Philo describes Wisdom as mother and nurse of the All.[39] By means of Sophia God created the world.

Wisdom is foremost 'an initiate of the knowledge of God and an associate in his works.'[40] She passes down into devout souls through succeeding generations in the manner of the Pythagorean transmigration of souls: 'Though she is but one, she can do all things, and while remaining in herself, she renews all things; in every generation she passes into holy souls and makes them friends of God and prophets.'[41] This 'passing down' will become clearer when we turn to Chapter 8 and consider the Gnostic Sophia. For the rest, Wisdom inspirits all souls, making them lovers of Wisdom – literally, philo-sophias. The inheritance of Wisdom can be left to all who come afterwards, for 'in kinship with Wisdom there is immortality.'[42]

This kinship is established in the manner of a husband looking for a bride. In a long prayer to obtain Wisdom, the author is audacious enough to ask God for his companion: 'Send her forth from the holy throne of thy glory, send her, that she may be with me and toil, and that I may learn what is pleasing to thee.'[43] Wisdom is the Bride of God whom Solomon seeks to court. Our author is, however, more ambitious! He asks God: 'Give me Wisdom, your throne-companion.'[44] This expression echoes the position of Themis, the Goddess of Order, as the *paredros* of Zeus:[45]

> There Saviour Right is honoured
> at the side of Zeus . . .

The latter half of *Wisdom* is concerned with the assimilation of Israel's history. The remainder of the text praises Wisdom as a saviour Goddess, as the rescuer of Adam, Noah, Abraham, Lot, Jacob, Joseph, and the Israelites from Egypt. The myth of Sophia is reiterated in clear terms. How she accompanied Adam into captivity:

> She descended into the dungeon with him,
> and when he was in chains she did not leave him.[46]

Sophia comprehends the last atom of matter and accompanies it as surely as she became the guide of the Israelites – the Pillar of Cloud by day and Pillar of Fire by night. 'You provided your people with a blazing pillar as a guide for their uncharted journey, a benign sun to accompany them on their glorious pilgrimage.'[47]

The occasion of the exodus from Egypt brings another of God's attributes into the drama: the Logos (the Word) leapt forth from heaven[48] to protect Israel and deliver it from the Egyptians. And here we have the first mention of Sophia's counterpart in the Bible. The *Logos* came like a warrior, described in terms of Athene. 'On his full-length robe there was a representation of the entire cosmos, and the glories of the fathers upon his four rows of carved stones, and your splendour on the diadem upon his head.'

Such a dynamic picture will not be seen again in the Bible until the scourging of the moneychangers in the temple and in the final drama of the Apocalypse, when the Logos will enter into the bridal chamber of the New Jerusalem and be joined once more to his Sophia.

A close reading of *Wisdom* uncovers a coherent spiritual life-direction for all seekers. Wisdom is the destined bride of the soul, the holy immortal part that accompanies all flesh. This attempt to make the soul a partner or co-operator with the divine permeates mystical Western thought from the hermetic arts through to the Assumption of Mary to heaven. 'Late magical texts show that pagans tried to obtain union with their throne-partner by magic.'[49] This magical art, sometimes called 'the knowledge and conversation of the holy guardian angel', attempts to bring about a conscious relationship with the interior guiding spirit, whether this is conceived of as the conscience, the angel or the daemon. This is one of the most important functions of Sophia in that she is the angelic presence whom all may seek. Because she is established in these texts as the partner both of God and of the soul, she is likewise the symbol of divine union – the sacred marriage of heaven to earth.

Sirach

Ecclesiasticus or the *Wisdom of Jesus the son of Sirach* (called here *Sirach* for short) was probably written about 190 BC. Although it is not canonical to either Hebrew or Christian scripture, it is widely quoted in rabbinical writing and is probably the most quoted book in the whole of Christian liturgy. When the feast of Mary's Assumption was first introduced into Rome in the mid-seventh century, the texts were drawn extensively from Chapter 24 of *Sirach*. These texts were later incorporated into the *Little Office of Our Lady* as readings, thus strengthening the sapiential character of Mary.

The text begins with a statement that all wisdom comes from God, but that Wisdom was created before everything else. 'The Lord himself created wisdom, he saw her and apportioned her, he poured her out upon all his works. She dwells with all flesh, according to his gift.'[50] She is our mother-right and inheritance: 'The fear of the Lord is the beginning of wisdom; she is created with the faithful in the womb.'[51] This statement, the first half so often quoted, has a deeper interpretation, for Wisdom has, as we have seen, two appearances. We do not come to wisdom unless it is by experience, which is given by the Black Goddess. If we respect her, we will come to Sophia. *Sirach* is virtually alone in stressing the admonitory and instructive side of Sophia, so that the hard centre of the Black Goddess shows through.

She is the companion of all flesh, but her ways are not easy. 'For at first she will walk with him on tortuous paths, she will bring fear and cowardice upon him, and will torment him by her discipline until she trusts him, and she will test him with her ordinances.'[52] Like Sheba, she will set hard questions: 'She seems very harsh to the uninstructed . . . for wisdom is like her name and is not manifest to many.'[53]

Wisdom is a garment to be assumed. She may appear to be a slave-mistress at first, but 'her fetters will become for you a strong protection, and her collar a glorious robe. Her yoke is a golden ornament, and her bonds are a cord of blue. You will wear her like a glorious robe, and put her on like a crown of gladness.'[54] She is to be pursued as though one was a hunter, or an obsessed lover: 'he who peers through her windows will also listen at her doors.'[55] She will be like a mother or a wife, feeding the bread of understanding and the water of wisdom.

The whole of Chapter 24 is the boast of Wisdom. It reads very like the aretalogies of Isis in its boldness and scope. The mellifluous and exalted language of the Goddess of Wisdom speaks forth unashamed:

> I came forth from the mouth of the Most High, and covered the earth like a mist.

I dwelt in high places, and my throne was in a pillar of cloud.
Alone I have made the circuit of the vault of heaven and have
walked in the depths of the abyss.
In the waves of the sea, in the whole earth, and in every people
and nation I have gotten a possession.
Among all these I sought a resting place; I sought in whose territory
I might lodge.[56]

She is appointed a place in the people of Israel, and in words
which are later put into the mouth of Mary, she says:

From eternity, in the beginning, he created me, and for eternity I
shall not cease to exist . . .
In the beloved city likewise he gave me a resting place, and in
Jerusalem was my dominion.
So I took root in an honoured people . . .[57]

She compares herself to incense and fruit-bearing trees and bids
all people, as in *Proverbs* 9, to come eat and drink of her.

But, for all these assertions, she remains a virgin of unknown
potential: 'Just as the first man did not know her perfectly, the last
one has not fathomed her.'[58] Adam's knowledge is incomplete,
and the Logos will not be joined with her until the *apocatastasis*.
Sophia must remain accessible to all people and for this reason
she boasts: 'Observe that I have not laboured for myself alone,
but for all who seek instruction.'[59] She is like the craftspeople
who are listed in Chapter 38 of *Sirach*, diligently applying herself
to her mystery. Wisdom the workwoman, like Athene *Ergane*,
walks unseen because her craft is in all places: it is nothing less
than the fabric of the world itself. Craftspeople are therefore under
her protection. They may not join in the disputes of sages and
philosophers, 'but they keep stable the fabric of the world, and
their prayer is in the practice of their trade.'[60]

Throughout the sapiential literature, Sophia remains illusive,
like a shy, veiled creature. We hear her laughter in *Proverbs*,
while she plays before God like a joyful child; we hear her glorious words as the radiant Divinity of *Wisdom*; we are awed by
her voice in *Sirach*, yet we do not *see* her as we can visualize
the Shulamite or Sheba. Truly her path is as tortuous as *Sirach*
implies: hard to discover. But she promises to anyone who walks
in her footsteps the glad revelation of her secrets. Her legacy is
for all future generations, descending even to our own age of
unwisdom.

The sapiential books are unconscious of their pagan metaphorical debts, although theologians and rabbis have since pointed them out and disputed the right of Wisdom to exist autonomously within scripture. The result is a tapestry of Wisdom which successive spiritualities will copy and re-embroider, ever rejoicing that God may appear in feminine as well as masculine guises. Within the severely patriarchal regime of Judaism, Wisdom was reinforced by her sister, the Shekinah, whose long journey we now trace.

═══ 6 ═══

THE CLOUD ON THE SANCTUARY

The divine Sophia is Israel's God in the language and form of
the goddess.

Elisabeth Schüssler Fiorenza

Merciful Law

Sophia is no stranger to the tents of the Israelites. Indeed, one
might say that she slept rough in them for many generations
before finding a home in the Temple of Solomon.

Exoteric Judaism does not, at first glance, seem a fruitful place
to find the Goddess. However, its esoteric traditions preserve the
footsteps of Sophia more than adequately. It is often the way that
the most patriarchal of faiths, which exclude women from active
roles within worship, turn to feminine images of the Divine, such
as the Shekinah and Wisdom, or are typified by cyclic and rhythmic
prayer forms, such as *davenin* – the rapid chanting of scriptural and
midrashic texts while rocking or swaying over the book.

The patriarchal spiritualities respond to their anti-feminine structures by investing them with curious femininity on many levels.
Judaism has its own celebrations which recall the Divine Feminine
in many ways. The scrolls of the law become the bride of the faithful, the faithful are submissively female in relation to Yahweh the
Father, even the temple or shrine becomes an enclosing mother.
The feast of Succoth, or Tabernacles, when Jewish families make
a booth in accordance with the remembrance of their escape from
captivity in Egypt, is a time of great rejoicing. Alexander Susskind
of Grodno (*d.* 1793) observed: 'When a man sits in this dwelling
(i.e. the *sukkah* booth) the shadow of faith, the *Shekinah* spreads
out Her wings over him from above.'[1]

By adhering closely to a study of its mystical and legal teachings,
Judaism has preserved its traditions. The exoteric teachings are
represented by the Torah, the scrolls of the Pentateuch, and by
the *mishnah* and *talmud* which support scripture. It is the minutiae
of these laws and observances which have typified the Jew to the
outsider. However, there is another side of the story. The esoteric

111

teachings, preserved by qabalists, who are the mystics of Judaic tradition, are found in the study of the Tree of Life. The Torah – the scrolls of the law – occupies a unique place in spiritual tradition. Most spiritualities revere their scriptures as divine, or imbued with their prophet's or scribe's holiness. The Jews are unique in according a divine *persona* to the Torah. It is none other than the Bride of God. Following the inherited pattern of Wisdom, the Torah has two such personas or voices: 'one recondite and on high, and the other more accessible.'[2] According to the *Zohar*, to the transcendent or Supernal Wisdom is accorded the silent Voice; the manifest Wisdom speaks through the Torah of the oral law. *Baruch* 3:9ff. speaks of God's hidden Wisdom, concealed from the rulers of nations, but vaunts the Torah (law) as her representative.

Early Jewish creation stories represent the Torah as the wife of God : 'In the beginning . . . the Torah (was) written with black fire on white fire, and (was) lying in the lap of God.'[3] God decided to create the world and asked Torah's counsel. She said that no king is without armies and attendants to do him homage. But her advice was 'given with some reservations. She was sceptical about the value of an earthly world, on account of the sinfulness of men, who would be sure to disregard her precepts.'[4]

The feast of Simcat Torah celebrates the Torah, the scrolls of the law, which are clasped in the arms of adult male Jews and danced with about the synagogue. This ancient custom stems from the dance of Wisdom with her faithful hearers.

Knowledge of the law is true wisdom within Judaism and the nuptial celebrations of Simcat Torah vindicate the legalistic bond which is between Jews and their Torah. It is an ecstatic justice at this festival, not the narrow *lex talionis* of 'an eye for an eye'. The Torah represents the *logos* or 'letter of the law' within Judaic tradition, just as the qabalistic teachings of the Tree of Life represent its *sophia*.

These mystical cyphers for the Divine Feminine are all very well but is there any coherent body of lore acknowledging the Goddess which precedes the formalized Judaism we know today?

Throughout the Bible, we come across ubiquitous Baals and Asherahs; these titles were generic for any pagan god or goddess in the vocabulary of the Yahwist school. We know these archetypes already for they are none other than the local forms of the Lord and Lady of the sacred marriage. The Dumuzi and Ishtar of Babylon became localized in the Middle East as El or Baal and Astarte or Ashtoreth. The devotion to the Divine Couple of the Sacred marriage was widespread throughout the Middle East. Religious leaders among the Israelites found it near impossible to prevent their people celebrating the old fertility and vegetation rites at different times, when recourse to hierodules or seasonal orgiastic coupling was considered normal.

In a chapter which treats on the nature of celebrating festivals, *Deuteronomy* forbids the planting of 'any tree as an Asherah beside the altar of the Lord.'[5] The Asherah was the sign of fertility in the desert: sometimes a tree or a dolmen pillar would be set up in honour of the Divine Couple. Solomon and Sheba are the models for this partnership, in straight inheritance from early pagan Semitic tradition as the Baal and Ishtar of their day.

Under the reforms of King Josiah, the high priest of Jerusalem was commanded to bring out of the temple the vessels dedicated to the use of Baal and Asherah and burn them. The Asherah which adorned the temple was also removed and burnt. The houses of the *qedeshim*, the male hierodules serving Baal and Asherah, were broken down: this was where women wove hangings to adorn the Asherah.[6]

When Jeremiah sought to warn the Israelites living in Egypt that they should adhere to Mosaic law and leave off their worship of foreign deities, they refused to obey, saying: 'We will do everything that we have vowed, burn incense to the queen of heaven and pour out libations to her . . . for then we had plenty of food, and prospered and saw no evil.'[7] They complained that since they had stopped performing these accustomed rituals they lacked food and had been subject to war and famine.

Obviously such practices were extracurricular to orthodox Judaism, but were considered by the people to be beneficial and natural. There was no way of serving the Divine Feminine within orthodox Judaism, and so the people turned to the neighbouring deities of their location, whether it be the gods of Egypt or the deities of Canaan. But the absence of the Goddess within Judaism was compensated for by the incorporation of the Shekinah within its esoteric understanding. This late development came about in the post-exilic period when not only had the Solomonic temple fallen to the Babylonians but the Herodian temple had been razed by the Romans. The Spirit of God no longer had a house. Without the tangible symbol of the temple to define 'deity' to the Israelites, qabalistic Jews, assimilating philosophic and Hellenic ideas, reverted to their ancestral resources and personified the exiled Spirit of God and the community of Israel as the Shekinah – a female persona for God who was, like Wisdom, not quite a Goddess.

Shekinah

The acceptance of the Shekinah within Judaism was by no means universal. In *Middrash Haggadol,* Rabbi Eliezer said: 'He who translates a verse (from the Bible) literally is a liar. He who adds to it, commits a blasphemy . . . If he translated, "And they saw the glory of the Shekinah of the God of Israel," he commits

8 *The Shekinah* Here the guiding figure of the Shekinah, who led the Israelites through the desert as a pillar of cloud by day and a pillar of fire by night, is shown leading her people by the light of the stars. The journey into wisdom is often one of darkness and exile from the familiar daily round. The inner companionship of Sophia accompanies all souls, just as the Shekinah accompanies the Jews of the Diaspora. Picture entitled *Wisdom Leading Her People* by Cecil Collins.

blasphemy, for he makes three, *viz*: Glory, Shekinah and God.'[8] This is the very accusation which was later levelled at the Russian Orthodox priest, Sergius Bulgakov, this century, whose theological speculations about the nature of Sophia and the Trinity suggested a somewhat closer relationship than Orthodox theologians could tolerate (see Chapter 15).

The history of the Shekinah (my preferred spelling, though quotations may vary) throughout Jewish tradition is complex. The Shekinah has become the female hypostasis of God: his Holy Spirit and *paredros*, but not a Goddess in her own right. This narrow avoidance of heresy within Judaism has kept its mysticism washed with the waters of Sophia.

The word *shekinah* first appears in the so-called *Targum Onkelos* of the first to fourth centuries AD. It renders the more usual reading of *Exodus* 25:8, 'let them make me a sanctuary, that I may dwell in their midst', as 'let them make before me a sanctuary that I may let my Shekinah dwell among them.'[9]

The word *shekinah* derives from 'dwelling-place'. The notion of a deity as a house or sanctuary is widespread among Middle Eastern Goddesses: the Babylonian Tashmit, whose name means 'the merciful hearing' is called 'Lady of the Dwelling Places' – possibly a metaphor for the heavens. Islamic tradition also recognizes the *sakina* or spirit of Allah as resident both within the human soul and the tent of the Ka'aba (c.f. Chapter 9). The metaphor of shelter in connection with deity is deep-seated. In his death-bed blessing of the twelve tribes, Moses speaks of God as an eagle or chariot-borne being riding through the heavens: 'the eternal God is your dwelling place, and underneath are the everlasting arms.'[10] The meaning of this image is central to understanding of the Shekinah – she is the true home of the soul. But while the soul is exiled from the dwelling-place, she accompanies the soul, lodging where she can, and stretching out her arms, like Isis, to protect and guard.

As we shall see by comparison with Gnostic texts, the Ark of the Covenant was regarded as the mid-place wherein the spirit of God's Wisdom rested. She was literally between the worlds. The emblems of the cherubim on the chest of the Ark were derived from the Babylonian *karibu*, half-human, half-animal beings which guarded the doorways of temples.[11] Yet they also resemble images of the Egyptian Goddess Hathor with her outstretched and protecting wings. The Ark was placed inside the sanctuary of the holy of holies, which only the high priest might enter.

115

We have seen how the *Song of Songs* exemplifies the primordial experience of the Sacred Marriage. This was echoed by the annual visit of the high priest into the holy of holies in the temple of Jerusalem, when he alone entered into the sanctuary as the representative of all Israel to acknowledge the contract of people and God.

The tent housing the Ark of the Covenant in the desert was analogous to the tents wherein the Sacred Marriage took place. The Jewish historian, Josephus, was very reluctant to speak about the interior of the holy of holies, asserting that it was empty, or rather, contained something. His reluctance may be viewed as an initiate's caution, since many sanctuaries are empty of image but full of meaning. It has been suggested that, within the holy of holies, the cherubim upon the Ark of the Covenant, itself the *ketubah* or marriage contract between Israel and God, were shown in erotic embrace. A Talmudic tradition of the third or fourth century related that: 'When Israel used to make the pilgrimage, they (the priests) would roll up for them the *paroketh* (the curtain between the Holy and the Holy of Holies in the Second Temple) and show them the Cherubim which were entwined with one another, and say to them: "Behold! your love before God is like the love of male and female."'[12]

The symbol of human sexual union for divine and human relations holds good throughout Judaic mysticism. Here the image of the veil, the *paroketh*, is shown as the sacred veil of Sophia which shrouds the Mysteries. Traditional Jewish mysticism acknowledges the rightful partnership of male and female: 'the Holy One, blessed be He, will not set up His tabernacle in a place in which male and female are not united.'[13] Philo attempted to exemplify this partnership between God and his Shekinah by polarizing their aspects on the two cherubim in the following way:[14]

The Left Hand Cherub	The Right Hand Cherub
Mother	Father
Bearer	Begetter
Nurturer	Creator
Wisdom (*Sophia*)	Reason (*Logos*)
Sovereignty	Goodness
Legislative	Peaceable
Gentle	Chastising
Correcting	Beneficent

When the Solomonic temple was destroyed, the Shekinah fled the sanctuary, passing in ten stages from the ark cover to the desert.[15] 'When the Shekhina left the Sanctuary, she returned to caress and kiss its walls and columns, and cried and said, "Be in peace, O my sanctuary, be in peace, O my royal palace, be in peace, O my precious house, be in peace from now on, be in peace".'[16]

The Shekinah repeats the words of *Jeremiah* 3: 23 three times from the Mount of Olives: 'Return you backsliding children, I will heal your backsliding'. Then, before retreating to heaven like Astraea, she flies about saying: 'I will return to My place until they admit their guilt and seek my face.'[17]

The prophets of the post-exilic period are almost unanimous in presenting the community of Israel as an erring wife, running after foreign lovers (*Hosea*), or as a lamenting widow (*Jeremiah*). The exception to this is a passage in *Isaiah* which scholars agree is an interpolation dating from after the Babylonian captivity. It prophesies the loving return of God the husband of the bride; the bride symbolizes the cast-off widow, Jerusalem, but here we may also read the welcoming of the Shekinah:

> Enlarge the place of your tent, and let the curtains of your habitations be stretched out;
> hold not back, lengthen your cords and strengthen your stakes.
> For you will be spread abroad to the right and to the left, and your descendants will possess the nations . . .
> Fear not, for . . . the reproach of your widowhood you will remember no more.
> For your Maker is your husband . . .
> For the Lord has called you like a wife forsaken and grieved in spirit, like a wife or youth when she is cast off, says your God.
> For a brief moment I forsook you, but with great compassion I will gather you.[18]

It is impossible to slip a knife between the metaphors of the exilic Israelites and the wandering Shekinah. She is God's bride, cast off, yet she is so completely the soul of the community of Israel that it is impossible to tell who or what is meant here. Well indeed might the Israelites 'enlarge their tent' to accommodate the children which will be born to this union, yet so might the Shekinah spread her sanctuary wings wider to encompass her spiritual children. Such will be the rejoicing of this union, says *Isaiah*, that 'the mountains and the hills before you shall break forth into singing, and all the trees of the field shall clap their hands . . . instead of the brier shall come up the myrtle; and it shall be to the Lord for a memorial.'[19] The myrtle is the plant which is borne in the hands of Yemeni brides going to their husbands, and the prophet acclaims it as an anamnesis of God and his Shekinah, just as the olive is a sign of God's covenant with humanity at the time of the Flood.

The spiritual privation of Israel hits hard and somehow penetrates to the very depths of human need, ultimately symbolized by the separation of man and woman. The sapiential books reiterate the protective love of Wisdom for humanity:

> When a righteous man was sold, wisdom did not desert him, but delivered him from sin.
> She descended with him into the dungeon, and when he was in prison she did not leave him, until she brought him the sceptre of a kingdom.[20]

Wisdom accompanies her children wherever they be. A later Tannaitic passage speaks of the ten descents of the Shekinah, one of which has been lost:

1　At the Fall, when she entered the Garden to punish Adam, Eve and the serpent.
2　When she confounded the builders of Babel.
3　At the destruction of Sodom and Gommorah.
4　When she liberated the Israelites from their Egyptian captivity.
5　When she drowned the Egyptians.
6　On Sinai, when she appeared to Moses.
7　As a pillar of cloud and fire, when she led Israel through the desert.
8　When she entered the Holy of Holies.
9　In future times she will appear at the battle of Gog and Magog.[21]

These ten descents correspond to the qualities upon the qabalistic Tree of Life: 'By ten things the world was created: by wisdom and by understanding and by knowledge and by power and by rebuke and by might, by righteousness and by right, by grace and by mercy' says the *Hagiga*.[22]

We see that the Shekinah exercises the wrathful and punishing aspects of the Divine, as well as the nurturing ones. The esoteric convention in the West is to stress the beneficent and mothering qualities of the Divine Feminine. However, within qabala, the different aspects of God's bride are detailed in an orderly way, so that we are able to see the more active face of the Shekinah.

Tree of Life

The image of the tree has ever haunted the Middle Eastern imagination. Everywhere the sacred trees of the Goddess grew: the *asherahs* so often fulminated against by prophets. Israel cut down the sacred trees of neighbouring tribes, but perhaps it was only to erect one of their own – the Tree of Life, which still stands triumphant within Judaism's esoteric discipline of the qabala.

From the Sumerian Goddess Siduri-Sabatu and her vine of life in the *Gilgamesh* Epic through to Wisdom's hymn of self-praise in *Sirach* where she likens herself to many trees, commanding all to come and eat of her fruits,[23] the image of the Tree of Life is one which is many times given over to Wisdom herself. *Genesis* begins with the Tree of the Knowledge of Good and Evil, by which the Fall is brought about. But this tree is contrasted with that of *Proverbs* 3:18, which says of Wisdom: 'She is a tree of life to those who lay hold of her.'

The Tree of Life, the blue-print of qabala, is a comprehensive cosmological system of far-reaching effect. In it is encoded creation, the manifestations of the Godhead and the history of Israel, among other things. It may be regarded as the living body of Adam Kadmon, the microcosmic man, who represents creation. Studying the qabala brings knowledge of the self, the realization of Adam Kadmon, and hastens the return of the Shekinah.

Qabala literally means 'from mouth to ear', indicating its authentic oral esoteric tradition. It manifested as an esoteric discipline in medieval Spain, though its antecedents are credited to the second century AD. Qabala is a method for coping with the strictures of monotheism: while it apportions the qualities and powers of God into definitions, it does not seek to quantify them or to create anything other than hypostases of God. Similar esoteric methods may be discerned within Islam, which has its own lore concerning the names and qualities of Allah.

Qabala has become the province of gentiles who have utilized its esoteric structures, though rarely its mystical insights, for magic, self-improvement, meditation and so on. Serious qabalistic schools of both orthodox Judaic and gentile persuasion still open the ways to wisdom in our own day.

Each sephiroth (sphere) of the Tree of Life has a designated title and set of symbolism, but none is conceived of as a separate deity, rather they are all hypostases of God. In this regard, Wisdom or Chokmah is merely one of nine others. Philo speaks of the ten curtains of the Tabernacle of the Holy of Holies as giving egress to the whole of wisdom.[24] The arrangement of the sephiroth is explained thus:

> All the powers of God are arranged one atop the other (in layers), thus resembling a tree; just as it is through water that the tree produces its fruits, so, too, it is through water that God increases the power of tree. And what is God's water? That is [female] khokmah [wisdom], and that [namely the fruit of the tree] is the soul of the righteous, which [all] flow from the wellspring to the great channel, and it rises up and hangs on the tree. And what is it through which the tree blooms? Through Israel: if they are good and righteous, then the shekina dwells among them, and through their works they abide in God's womb.[25]

The Jewish titles of the sephiroth of the Tree of Life and their transliterated meanings are:

Kether	Crown	**Tiphareth**	Harmony
Chokmah	Wisdom	**Netzach**	Victory
Binah	Understanding	**Hod**	Splendour
Chesed	Mercy	**Yesod**	Reverberation/ Foundation
Geburah	Severity	**Malkuth**	Sovereignty

In the *Zohar*, God creates a Wisdom-gushing fountain (Chokmah). But, because Wisdom cannot be comprehended in abstraction, the waters spill into the vessel of Understanding (Binah). Then, 'he directs it into seven precious vessels, which he calls Greatness (Chesed), Strength (Geburah), Glory (Hod), Victory (Netzach), Majesty (Tiphareth), Foundation (Yesod), Sovereignty (Malkuth).'[26] It is so that the images of the Goddess are dispersed, becoming ever more diluted and less efficacious, although even the lowest spheres upon the Tree of Life are considered equally holy with the highest. We have here a parallel with the Greek philosophical and Gnostic models, where the three supernal spheres of the Tree of Life, together with the seven lower sephiroth, reproduce the cosmology of the Monad, Dyad and Logos, with seven aeonic powers or archons of the planetary spheres.

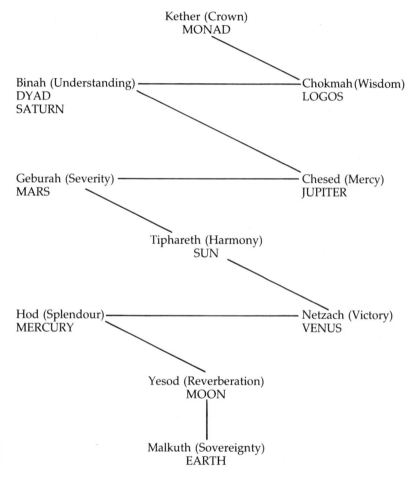

Kether (Crown)
MONAD

Binah (Understanding)
DYAD
SATURN

Chokmah (Wisdom)
LOGOS

Geburah (Severity)
MARS

Chesed (Mercy)
JUPITER

Tiphareth (Harmony)
SUN

Hod (Splendour)
MERCURY

Netzach (Victory)
VENUS

Yesod (Reverberation)
MOON

Malkuth (Sovereignty)
EARTH

The interconnections between the spheres of the Tree of Life are subtle. Qabalists spend most of their lives working within the pathways which these interconnections open to them.

The pronouncement of the holy name of God, *Yod He Vau He*, (Yahweh) pronounced on the Day of Atonement by the High Priest, is, qabalistically, a weaving together of the four worlds of the Tree.[27] The utterance of the holy name, in which the syllable

He appears twice, was thus a summation of the Tree of Life. When the High Priest emerged from the Holy of Holies, the light of the Shekinah was supposed to shine from his countenance, much as Moses' did when he descended Mount Thabor.[28]

The tetrad of the Divine Name was further characterized by four personas:

Divine Name	Sephiroth	Symbolic Persona	Titles
Yod	Chokmah	Father	Zaddik (Spiritual Master)
He	Binah	Mother	Supernal Mother
Vau	Tiphareth	Son	the King
He	Malkuth	Daughter	Matronit/Shekinah

Binah is called the Supernal Mother and is mystically considered to be the mother of the Shekinah whose sphere is that of Malkuth, which is called the Lower Mother or Matronit.[29] Binah, like Demeter, equates to the creative Sophia, while Malkuth, like Kore, equates to the hidden erotic aspect of Sophia. Within the mystical personas of the Tetragrammaton lies a cosmogonic myth, almost the recreation of Israel's own mythic past. The hidden mythos accorded to the Tetragrammaton tells the story of the marriage of heaven and earth, of God and Shekinah. The Father and Mother conjoin and create two children, the King and Matronit, the Lesser Mother. The transcendent couple play little further part in the scenario and must be considered as harmonically resonant with the Son and Daughter who are destined to be each other's spouse, in a complete and mythic disregard of incestuous barriers.

Because the Matronit associates herself with the community of Israel, who fall into sin, she herself is separated from the King. The King used to unite once a week with his bride in the holy of holies in the temple. However, after its destruction, this act no longer took place. The qabalistic practice of marital love on the Sabbath was undertaken in conscious imitation of this Divine Union.

The prime image for qabalistic philosophy is the vision of Ezekiel[30] where the prophet sees the four winged creatures within many wheels which have the ability to go in any direction. These are the mystical manifestations of God's power. Significantly these come accompanied by a great cloud with fire flashing out of it and the brightness of a rainbow about it. These symbols indicate the presence of the Shekinah.

Similarly, in *Sepher Hekalot*, we read about a warlike Shekinah who is responsible for God's campaigns. Her four flaming wheeled chariots stand in the heavenly halls, awaiting their orders.[31] Like a Jewish Kali, or reminiscent of the Ishtar of love and war, the Shekinah appears in the *Zohar* as a fearsome aspect of the Godhead, a titaness to whom mountains are but a bite and who can swallow rivers at one gulp. From her hair issue troops who are sent to be a scourge to sinners. From her vulva issues Metatron, the greatest Angel of the Presence, and the two female demons, Lilith and Naamah.[32] This aspect of the Shekinah incorporates the quality of Geburah, or Severity, upon the Tree of Life. She acts like Maat, Anath, Sekhmet or Ereshkigal.

The *Zohar*, or 'Book of Splendour', typifies the aspects of Sophia as both Transcendent Maiden and Black Goddess. 'In the flame . . . are two lights: one light is a bright white and one light is united with a dark or blue . . . this dark light, or bluish colour, which is below, is the precious throne to the white . . . it unites to the above, to that white upper light, and unites itself below to the thing which is under it, which is the burning matter . . . And on this white light rests above a Hidden Light which is stronger. Here is the above mystery of that flame which comes out from it, and in it is the Wisdom of the Above.'[33] This quotation is summed up by the qabalistic aphorism: the Lesser Mother sits upon the throne of the Supernal Mother, for this is the destiny of the Shekinah who will rise from her earthly position at Malkuth to become once more the bride of God at Binah, and where divisions between Black Goddess and Sophia will cease. Similarly, when Kore returns from Hades to the embrace of Demeter, never more to be parted, the Eleusinian Dyad will be dynamically one with creation.

The darkness of the Black Goddess is sometimes seen as resulting from a fallen or deprived situation. 'The lowest *sefirah*, the *Shekhinah* has no light of its own, but is nothing more than a mirror that reflects the light shed upon it from above. In this respect, the *Shekhinah* is also seen as the moon, entirely and utterly dark except when it conveys the light that it receives from the sun, who is the central *sefirah*, *Tifaret*, also called "the Holy One, blessed be He", around whom all the others revolve.' Thus the full meaning of the *Song of Songs* becomes clear: '"I am black but comely" is the appeal made by the *Shekhinah*, who is female, to the male *Tifaret*, expressing her forlorn state when she is deprived of light.'[34]

But Rabbi Levi ben Haytha knew that the blackness of the Shekinah was transformative: 'I am black on the days of the week and comely on the Sabbath; black all the days of the year and comely on the Day of Atonement, black in this world and comely in the world to come.'[35] Just as in Islamic tradition, where the Black Stone was originally a white pearl, so too the Shekinah reflects a different image of herself. Indeed, 'pearl' was one of the Shekinah's many titles.[36]

This esoteric comprehension of the poles of Sophia as Shekinah did not extend to the rest of exoteric Judaism for whom the Divine Feminine was marginalized as demonic and fearful. The chief protagonist in the supernatural world was Lilith, apocryphally the first wife of Adam. The word *lillu* is Sumerian for 'underworld spirit'. The fear of Lilith was widespread; it was particularly exacerbated among the Ashkenazi Jews living in Central Europe, wherein the ancestral woodland spirits were understood to be alive and active. Amulets, charms and spells against Lilith and her kin were commonplace, for Lilith was believed to be a succuba, living off the nocturnal emissions of men in order to create countless more demons; she was a child-snatcher, a bringer of disease.[37] And yet we have seen that, according to one text, she was born of the Shekinah!

The metaphorical polarization of divine male and demonic female must always be extreme where the Divine Feminine is marginalized. However, Sophia cannot help but drift into the forefront of esoteric veneration, whether as woman, female abstraction or hypostatic Goddess. It is in her most transcendently beautiful of guises that she enters the soul of the qabalist.

Sabbath Bride and the Lost Princess

The Sabbath has long been personified as God's bride. The Ethiopian Jews, the Falashas, said of the Sabbath: 'The mediatrix of the Christians is Mary; ours is the Sabbath.'[38] The Sabbath is the holiest day of the week, celebrated by Jews the world over in token of God's rest after the labour of creation. From the eve of Friday night when one colour cannot be distinguished from another, the Sabbath is in force until the next evening; no inessential work is done and there are many proscriptions about certain forms of activity which may be undertaken. Each of the 'religions of the book' celebrates its Sabbath: the Muslims on

Friday, the Jews on Saturday, the Christians on Sunday. Friday is associated with Venus, of course, but the derivations of the sabbath-day might shock many fundamental Christians.

The word 'sabbath' derives from *sa-bat* or heart's rest.[39] In Babylon, one day of *sabbatu* marked each quarter phase of the moon and was regarded as the day on which Ishtar menstruated; on these days people abstained from certain activities, as though they were menstruating women.[40] The enforced rest of the sabbath is, therefore, an imitation of the restrictions and privileged rest-period once associated with menstruation in the Middle East – restrictions which apply to many women of Semitic and Moslem background today. It may have been Philo who set the trend for the personification of the Sabbath, but it soon became a widespread concept. The custom of 'gladdening the Shekinah,' or of enjoying marital union on the Sabbath, was anciently attested.

Abraham ibn Ezra(1092–1167) relates how, while in England, he had a dream in which he was handed a letter from the Sabbath. On opening it, he found a poem in which the Sabbath spoke of herself as 'the crown of the religion of the precious ones'.[41]

The chief exponent of the Sabbath Bride concept was Isaac Luria (1534–72), a contemporary of St John of the Cross (1542–91). Their two forms of spirituality overlap remarkably. Luria presided over a qabalistic community at Safed in Palestine where his famous hymn to the Sabbath Bride was sung with great fervour, as it still is at Sabbath services today:

> Come let us go to meet Sabbath,
> for she is the source of blessing,
> Pouring forth from ancient days.
> The act was the end, in thought the beginning . . .
> Come, my friend, to meet the Bride,
> Let us receive the face of Sabbath.[42]

The rite of *zivvuga kadisha* or sacred marriage is the union of the spheres Tiphareth and Malkuth. It was performed by qabalists at the beginning of the sixteenth century. The night of the mystical marriage, celebrated in the Feast of Weeks, the fiftieth day after Passover was spent in prayer and song. The next morning, the marriage contract between the bridegroom (God) and the Virgin (Shekinah or Israel) was read out.[43]

But it is the welcoming in of the Sabbath each Friday which celebrates the Shekinah, when she is invited as the Bride to come and join the company. Elaborate processions were performed at

Safed and the Sabbath psalms were sung with closed eyes because 'the Shekinah . . . as "the beautiful virgin who has no eyes" . . . has lost her eyes from weeping in exile.'[44]

The Shekinah has become totally identified with the Community of Israel. Since the expulsion from the Garden of Paradise, she has accompanied her people into Egypt, into Babylon and, subsequently, into many other kinds of exile and diaspora. Within the qabala, the Shekinah is the most approachable aspect of God. 'The chain of processes that links the unknowable God to the Shekhinah and thence to the terrestial world, has a continuous dynamism.'[45]

Many great qabalists have had close relationship with the Shekinah. Rabbi Joseph Karo (1488–1575) was one of the Safed School of mystics. His *maggid* or spiritual mentor, was the Shekinah herself. Fasting from sleep and praying, he heard her voice: 'Happy are you in this world . . . that you resolved to adorn Me on this night. For these many years had my head been fallen with none to comfort Me . . . but now you have restored the crown to its former place.'[46] She bade him, 'Cease not from studying, for a thread of mercy is stretched out over you'. With his companions Karo cried out: 'Blessed be the name of His glorious Kingdom for ever and ever.'[47] They fell weeping because they had heard the voice of the Shekinah. Many subsequent messages were received, including the injunction: 'Sanctify yourself and all your limbs to My service by day and night. Let your limbs form a camp within which the Shekinah can rest.'[48]

Rabbi Abraham Berukhim was advised by Isaac Luria to pray at the Wailing Wall. For three days and nights fasting, he wept and prayed. 'Suddenly he raised his eyes and saw on the Wailing Wall the image of a woman, from behind, in clothes which it is better not to describe, that we have mercy on the divine glory.' When he had seen her, he immediately fell on his face and cried and wept and said, ' "Zion, Zion, woe to me that I have seen you in such a plight." '[49] He fainted and then fell asleep. 'Then he saw in a dream the image of a woman who came and put her hands on his face and wiped the tears of his eyes . . . and when Isaac Luria saw him he said: "I see that you have deserved to see the face of the Shekhinah." '[50]

Nahman of Bratislav (1772–1810) was one of the Hassidim, a sect of pious Jews which began in medieval Germany. The Hassids were and are very like the Shakers in their exuberant manifestations of devout joy into song and dance. It is not surprising, therefore, that the Hassidim should have also employed didactic tales to spread their teachings. These tales, like the parables of Jesus, were compelling to their hearers. Nahman was in the line of the Ba'al Shem Tov, the great miracle-worker and founder of the modern Hassidim, of whom so many tales are told. Nahman was a contemporary of William Blake (1757–1827), with whom he shared an emblematic imagination. His many folk stories always have a qabalistic content, and some of them are directly about the Shekinah and her exile.

The most famous is that of *The Loss of the Princess*.[51] There once was a king with six sons and a daughter, whom he deeply loved. However, one day she annoyed him and he exasperatedly said: 'May the Not-Good take you away!' The next day she was not to be found. The king sent his viceroy to find her. He came at last to a castle where the ruler's wife was none other than the princess. The castle was the place of the Not-Good (Nahman's euphemism for the Adversary). She could not be freed unless the viceroy stayed put for a year, yearning for her and fasting, until on the last day he should fast and not sleep from sunset to sunset.

All went well until the last night when the viceroy craved an apple, immediately falling asleep. He awoke and was told he had to repeat the year of yearning. On the last day, he saw a spring which looked strange. Tasting it, he discovered it was filled with wine and he fell asleep for seven years. The princess passed by, but was unable to wake him, so she left her kerchief. He awoke and read the kerchief which told him to seek for a golden mountain and pearly castle. He searched for years and eventually met a giant to whom he told his errand. The giant was master of all animals and they had never heard of the castle. However, he sent the viceroy to his brother, the giant master of birds, but with similar success. He sent the viceroy on to the giant who was master of winds. One of the winds was late arriving when summoned, because he had been transporting a princess to a golden mountain. The viceroy was bourne by the wind to that place and rescued her.

Nahman makes the Shekinah the princess in exile and the viceroy is the pious person in pursuit of her. The viceroy fails at first to rescue her because he succumbs to the sins of Adam (the apple) and Noah (drunkenness). The kerchief may indicate the study of the Torah. The pearly castle is the abode of the Shekinah herself. The final act of redemption, the *tikkun*, is not fully explained by Nahman since this cosmological story's end is that of humanity's also.

The Shekinah has also been a prophetic voice. It is reported by Kalonymus Kalman Epstein (*d.* 1823): 'when the great *zaddikim* (outstanding leaders of mystic quality) attach themselves to the worlds on high and have the garments of the body stripped off from themselves, the *Shekinah* rests upon them and speaks from out of their throat so that their mouth utters prophecies and tells of future events.'[52]

In all of these narratives there is a sense of mystical exaltation, rarely of true practical expressions of love for women, although, in essence, communion with the Shekinah should bring a heightened compassion for every created being. This is the problem of mysticism: how to actualize vision. In Martin Buber's novel, *For the Sake of Heaven*,[53] the hero is Yehudi. He loves his first wife, Foegele, but leaves her in order to emulate the exiled Shekinah. He is obedient to Foegele's legitimate deathbed request that he marry her sister, Schoendel, although she is enraged by his treatment of her sister and his distance from everyday problems. Eventually, one night, Yehudi has a vision very similar to Lucius Apuleius' of Isis. The blackness of the night is transformed by the blast of a heavenly shofar (horn) into the appearance of the Milky Way. From within this pool of white radiance emerges a woman, veiled in black, with bleeding feet. She says that it is the holy men who are causing her torment and excluding her: 'each of you exiles his comrades, and so together you exile me.' With a directness which cannot be gainsayed she tells him: 'one cannot love me and abandon the created being.' As she lifts her veil, Yehudi beholds Foegele in the shape of the Shekinah. Reconciliation with the earth and human responsibility is the call of Sophia, and it is to that long-overdue appointment that the Shekinah calls Jewish women and men. For, 'she so pervades this lower world that if you search in deed, speech, thought and speculation, you will find *Shekhinah*, for there is no beginning nor end to her.'[54]

Tikkun – the Great Restoration

Like the Gnostics and Christians, qabalistic Jews look towards the *tikkun*, the 'putting-right', or restoration, of all things. All good works hasten the tikkun: all evil works lengthen the exile.

There is a Hassidic story which sums up this realization. It is told how Rabbi Isaac of Kalig was a master of music. He studied night and day to rediscover the perfect music that had been in Paradise since, at the time of Adam's sin, that music had been dispersed about the universe. One day he overheard the song of a shepherd: the tune turned his soul over with delight, for it was the very cadence he had been looking for. However, the words puzzled him:

> Oh wood so high, how vast you are,
> Rose so sweet, how far.
> If the wood were shorter,
> My rose would be near.
> If I could leave the forest
> And smell the rose,
> I would live in love forever more.

He went home and put sleep from his eyes until he had unravelled this riddle. In the manner of Abraham Abulafia, the great Sephardic qabalist, he made permutations of the words until they became meaningless. Towards midnight, he turned once more to the actual words themselves and his mystical sight was stunned by the simplicity of the riddle. The wood was nothing more than the exile of the Israel. The rose was the Shekinah. In his great rejoicing he was able to sing the correct words to the tune of the shepherd:

> O exile great, how vast you are!
> Spirit of God how far.
> If the exile were shorter
> Shekinah would be here.
> If we could leave the exile
> And find the Shekinah,
> We would live in love forever more![55]

The work of qabala is nothing less than the realization of the microcosmic body of humanity, symbolized as Adam Kadmon, upon the tree of life. Likewise, its work is to recreate the ladder of ascents by which the Shekinah may return to union with the Creator. When the Shekinah returns, it automatically follows that the creation is likewise restored.

Every Sabbath is a microcosmic *tikkun*, for it encompasses the quietness and refreshment of the seventh day of creation, completing and beginning each week. One of the few duties of worship enjoined upon women is the lighting of the Sabbath candles, whereat the Shekinah is invited into the home. This act is central to the spirituality of many Jewish women

> Happy are those of steadfast faith
> who still can bless the light of candles
> Shining in the darkness . . .
> Rejoice, O Earth, in those who keep the way,
> For there is still song for them within you.[56]

Women have been almost totally excluded from spiritual ministry in Judaism apart from the faithful performance of their *mitzvot*, or domestic obligations. The condition of femaleness has been shunned by men and walled about with proscriptions which stress Woman's guilt. She must go veiled because she is ashamed of wrongdoing, she precedes corpses because she brought death into the world, she menstruates in memory of her guilt in shedding Adam's blood. She must set aside the *challah*, or priestly tithe of dough, when she bakes because she seduced Adam who is 'the world's *challah*'. For the same reason she extinguishes the Sabbath candles.[57]

More and more women within Judaism are awakening to the power of the Divine Feminine. They may not call her Goddess, but the effect is still the same. Deena Metzger, a contemporary novelist of Jewish birth who has had to rediscover her tradition, awoke to the realization that: 'there had been a tradition which was before the forefathers, a tradition of the foremothers and forefathers together, that could be (and was) vital, and is emerging again.'[58]

Remarking upon the absence of female qabalists, Gershom Scholem, one of the most influential of modern qabalistic commentators, writes that, as a result of this, Judaism has remained remarkably free from the 'hysterical extravagance which follow(s) in the wake of this influence.'[59] This paranoia about the female is instanced throughout Judaism which has exalted the Divine Feminine as secondary to God, and which sustains a tradition of the demonic as deriving from the female.

Ya'qub ibn Yusuf, a Sufi graduate of Jewish studies, recently remarked on what he feels to be a distressing practice among feminist Jewish circles of addressing the Shekinah in prayer, thus: 'Blessed are you, Shekinah,' instead of the more usual 'Blessed are you, O Lord.'[60] However, unless the faithful are free to address their petitions through the correct burning glass, the essential fire of Sophia will not be kindled.

The numerous male testimonies given above to the influence of the Shekinah are beginning to be balanced by the number of women who are now celebrating their spirituality with greater confidence. What they already knew and practiced is being given a voice at last.

Rabbi Leah Novick writes of giving workshops on the Shekinah and finding that people – Jews and non-Jews alike – 'carry concepts, feeling and images of the Shechinah within them . . . when we share these experiences, we find that individuals "know" or uncover most of the traditional characteristics of Shechinah themselves.'[61]

The wings of the Shekinah have not ceased beating, nor will they while there are women like Rabbi Lynn Gottlieb, who has written a prophetic cycle called *Navia, Voice of the Prophet Woman*. In the tradition of all great Jewish storytellers, she finds a tale which is relevant to the needs of today.

It tells of Serach, the woman who shares the enslavement of Israel in Egypt. She is a prophetic storyteller, and takes the symbol of her slavery, the grinding stone, and smashes it to pieces. The fragments become birds, bearing shards of a great mirror. As each woman looks into this mirror, it melts into their foreheads. 'And each one saw Her, in a moment held forever. Yehoyah, the midwife woman, would enable freedom in their own time.'[62]

In this powerful fable, Gottlieb has taken the four letters which make up the the name Jehovah (YHVH) and created the name Yehoyah, the midwife creator of all things. And so it is that the prophecy runs that:

> Every one thousand years
> there is born a woman
> who does not die
> but lives forever
> she comes from the root soul
> of the Ancient Mother of Days.
> When seven such women are born
> and seven Houses rise
> this circle of knowledge
> will be
> complete.[63]

As Judaism is reappraising itself in our own age, so too is Christianity uncovering the roots of its inheritance. We leave the Shekinah and go to seek her Christian counterpart, who comes in the shape of the long-prophesied Messiah.

THE DIVINE ANDROGYNE

Cease, cease, O you who tread upon matter!
For behold, I am coming down into the world of mortals
For the sake of that part of me which has been there since
the day that they overcame the innocent wisdom (Sophia) who
descended;
(I am coming) so that I might thwart their goal that was
ordained by the one that was shown forth because of her.

Gnostic Logos from *Triple Protennoia*

God of Love

In a book dealing with Sophia as a Goddess, it may seem extraordinary to give space to Sophia as a masculine deity. But this chapter cannot be omitted from the story, because Sophia's escape routes pass through it.

The female images of Wisdom from the Bible and the steadily diffusing influence of the Goddess in the ancient world entered Christianity and the figure of Christ in a way which is both extraordinary and baffling. The transposition of female metaphor to male image frequently happens wherever the female images are expunged from a tradition: the many-aspected names of Allah and Yahweh are, for example, nearly all derived from qualities which are popularly credited to the Divine Feminine. It has been part of orthodox mystical theology to assign the female relationship with God to humankind as a whole; it is seen to yearn towards God in a spousal relationship which avoids any necessity for us to reframe the Trinity in anything but masculine symbology.

To write of Christ at all is problematic, since a welter of separatist metaphors are woven about him, each claiming to be the only true image. Twentieth century culture has produced some of the most flattened and undynamic images of all, which have little spiritual currency in the New Age. Christ is reinvented in every generation, but we cannot help but be influenced by the images which have been traditionally employed.

Most brands of Christianity claim that Christ alone holds the power to redeem the Fall and show the way to heaven: an exclusivism which has been the cause of much war and suffering, as well as dubious political self-justifications. If we are able to edit out the Church's political investment in Christianity and look at the textual and traditional evidences, the influence of the Goddess of Wisdom can be observed, like a yeasted dough which has seldom been left long enough to rise. The discovery of the Goddess within Christianity has been long announced but is only now being proclaimed. It is not an avenue of discovery welcomed by either orthodox Christians nor certain feminists, because the metaphors are loaded with explosive issues that are dangerous to handle. It is perhaps possible to sidle up to Christianity through the image of the divine androgyne, the mediating deity who connects divine and human realms in a bond of love.

The Greek Eros, god of love, who is called *Protogonos* 'the firstborn', and *Phanes*, 'revealer of the light', brought heaven and earth together to create Oceanus and Tethys, the originating deities of the Greeks.[1] Eros has been somewhat absent in Christianity. He has been replaced by Caritas, the inclusive and encompassing love of Christ who has preserved Eros' ability to bring heaven and earth into harmony by means of love. Christ does not marry or raise children, according to orthodox tradition: his task is to kindle the dormant spirit in each person he encounters, not to provoke erotic attachment. In this respect, while manifesting as a human man, Christ is available to both women and men – a feature that he exemplifies in the Gospels. The refusal to entertain even metaphorical sexuality is echoed by St Paul's 'in Christ there is no male or female.'[2] Christianity is theoretically inclusive of both sexes by transcending sexuality, though the practice is widely variant from this reading.

The foundation ritual of Christianity is not the sacred marriage – though that may take place within the thalamus of the soul and is the apocalyptic prophecy of *Revelations* – it is the ritual whereby the faithful partake of the slain god under the form of the Eucharist, albeit in an unbloody manner. Like the descents of Dumuzi, Adonis, Attis and Dionysius into the realm of death, to be reborn in another manner, Christ's descent to hell overcomes death itself. This act shows a love for creation and the institution of rites of *anamnesis*, for recalling and reinstituting the act of Sophianic love in daily life. The sacrifice of the divine for the creation manifests in many ways: the Creating Mother is rent apart, Ishtar and Dumuzi descend into death, Christ dies on the cross, Osiris is dismembered. Likewise, the ritual dismembering of Dionysius by the titans,[3] symbolized by the Egyptians as the crushing of grapes for wine, has parallels with Christ's aretalogy of himself as the True Vine.[4]

Christ's aretalogy is not so dissimilar from that of the ancient Goddesses, for he is 'the bread of life' and 'the living water'.[5] As Good Shepherd, he follows in the footsteps of the Sumerian shepherd, Dumuzi, with his 'mother flute'.

Each revelation of the God of Love is accompanied by a certain blurring of gender barriers. Christ is no exception to this rule. The Irish philosopher, John Scotus Erigena (c. 810–877 AD), held that the resurrected Christ was androgynous in his *Periphyseon*: 'the Lord Jesus united in himself the division of our nature, that is, male and female . . . For in Him there is neither male nor female, although it was in that masculine sex in which He was born of a Virgin.'[6] He speaks of the way in which Christ, 'in Himself united us with ourselves in Himself by taking away the difference between male and female and instead of men and women, in whom the mode of division is most apparent, exhibited men as such properly and truly . . . bearing immaculate their image which marks of corruption do not touch at all.'[7] *Periphyseon* is a dialogue conducted between an instructor and a student. The student confesses himself puzzled about how and whether human sexual differentiation will translate to the paradisal condition. His instructor replies: 'For if Christ Who understands all things, (Who) indeed is the understanding of all things, really unified all that he assumed, who doubts but that what first took place in the Head and principle Exemplar of the whole of human nature will eventually happen in the whole?'[8] Statements such as these did not make John Scotus very popular and his writings were held to be heterodoxical. This view of Christ's androgyny was upheld in Gnosticism and in the works of Boehme (See Chapters 8 and 14).

How did this androgyny of Wisdom come about? We have seen how persistent is the tradition of the sacred marriage between the Goddess of the Land or her representative, and the God or his kingly stand-in. In the person of Christ, we see the fusion of Word and Wisdom, Logos and Sophia, in a distinct way. This has two manifestations: Christ and his hidden, suffering Ecclesia interact during his ministry; after his resurrection, he is understood to conjoin with his restored Church, the Sophianic Ecclesia. Christ is both the sum of Logos/Sophia in his own person, but is also understood to mystically join with the Blessed Virgin – his own mother – in a mystical union.

Christ is not born of a Goddess, although Mary assumes attributes of the Divine Feminine in her later cult. The prime image which permeates Christ's story is Sophia who makes her appearances in many guises. As she is not bound by shape, nor is she restricted to gender. Sophia, like the Holy Spirit, is the presence of Deity among us: a travelling presence which penetrates both the earthly and otherworldly realms.

It is the maternal Spirit which hovers over the waters of the deep in *Genesis* 1:2 and over Christ at his baptism;[9] it is the paternal Spirit which descends upon Mary at her Annunciation, a feast which St John Chrysostom called 'the Feast of the Seed'.[10]

The sacred marriage of Christianity lies in the mystical partnership between Christ and the soul, or Christ and his Mother, who is seen as the representative of all humanity. The coronation of the Virgin is seen as the crowning of humanity. As Cabasilas has remarked: 'It is the Master who has leaned down towards the earth and has rediscovered his own image.'[11] This is in direct relationship with 2 *Corinthians* 3:18: 'And we, with our unveiled faces reflecting like mirrors the brightness of the Lord, all grow brighter and brighter as we are turned into the image that we reflect; this is the work of the Lord who is Spirit.' Scripture calls us to become reflective mirrors, like Sophia.

It is to this Holy Spirit that we now turn, to discover if the Divine Feminine has lodged therein like a dove in the cleft of the rock.

The Sex of the Holy Spirit

The Holy Spirit of Wisdom has frequently changed its gender. It has been suggested that, because of the changes in language and culture within the early Church, 'this feminine aspect (*ruach*) to the inauguration of Jesus is neutered to *pneuma* in Hellenistic Christian communities and eventually masculinized to *spiritus* in the Latin church.'[12] This led to a shift from feminine to masculine metaphors. As Jung has remarked: 'the Holy Ghost is not subject to any control,'[13] but blows where it will, like the wind. This disobedient and wayward movement is the true creative spirit of Sophia. Imagination and creativity cannot be commanded. The gifts of the Spirit are markedly identifiable with those of Wisdom. In *Isaiah* 11:2 we read the prophecy of Christ's coming: 'And the Spirit of the Lord shall rest upon him, the spirit of wisdom and understanding, the spirit of counsel and might, the spirit of knowledge and the fear of the Lord'. This list is supplemented in *Book of Enoch* 49:3 by 'the spirit of those who have fallen asleep in righteousness'. These are the seven gifts of the Spirit, analogous to Sophia's seven-pillared temple. Sophia, as Ecclesia, keeps the seven gifts of the Spirit in her lap like doves, ready to wing down to whoever is need of them, just as she keeps open the seven pathways of the sacraments which are their physical signature: the paths of baptism, confirmation, confession, communion, marriage, ordination and annointing. Like the old mystery initiations of the Classical world, the Christian initiate could go down into the waters of the Jordan and receive the confirmation of the Holy Spirit, be deeply one with Christ at the Last Supper, rejoice in the marriage of Cana, perform the ministry to the sick and travel through the sacred pathways of the sacraments.

The Holy Spirit has a confused metaphorical ancestry. We have seen how Biblical Wisdom is the mother, companion, bride or *paredros* of God.[14] The 4th century Church father, Apraates, even accorded a parental relationship between humanity and God the Father with the Spirit as wife: 'Man, as long as he has not led home the Bride, loves and worships God, his Father, and the Holy Spirit, his Mother, and he has no other love.'[15]

The accompanying Spirit of God as companion of the soul is affirmed in I *Corinthians* 3:16: 'you are God's temple and . . . God's spirit dwells in you'. But the Holy Spirit also acts as daemon between heaven and earth: 'As one that constitutes the "innermost" aspect of the Trinity, the Holy Spirit is, at the same time, the connecting link between Father and Son. Of course, the Son, too is a bond between the First and Third Divine Persons, insofar as he mediates the divinity of the Father to the Spirit. But whereas the Son is first engendered and then mediates, the Spirit is identical with his mediatory function.'[16]

The feminine metaphors of the Holy Spirit are diverse. The 3rd century liturgy of Didascalics calls the deaconess 'image of the Holy Spirit', perhaps enforcing the prevailing feminine perception of the Spirit at that time.[17] The Gnostic *Gospel of Philip* however is scornful of a feminine Spirit: ' Some say that Mary conceived by the Holy Spirit: they are mistaken . . . When did a female ever conceive by a female?'[18] Nevertheless, the maternal nature of the Holy Spirit has been an abiding presence, sometimes almost providing the lost Eros to Christianity. 'A very early tradition stated that the Holy Spirit is like the kiss of sacred love exchanged by lovers.'[19]

In the 19th *Ode of Solomon*, the cooperation of Mary with the Holy Spirit sets up a real resonance between herself and Sophia:

> The Son is the cup,
> and the Father is he who was milked;
> and the Holy Spirit is she who milked him;
>
> Because his breasts were full,
> and it was undesirable that his milk should be released without purpose.
>
> The Holy Spirit opened her bosom
> and mixed the milk of the two breasts of the Father.
>
> Then she gave the mixture to the generation without their knowing,
> and those who have received it are in the perfection of the right hand.
>
> The womb of the Virgin took (it),
> and she received conception and gave birth.[20]

Possibly due to this confusion about the Holy Spirit's gender, it is possible to speak of Sophia as both male and female within Christianity, working through Christ and Mary. The language of faith is its liturgy. Mary gains most of the sapiential references in her liturgies, while Christ is viewed as both Word and Wisdom in a theological way. But the ordinary Christian does not tend to think theologically, but responds liturgically. It may seem extraordinary, in the light of Sophia's development in the West, but we must now see how even in the person of Christ, Sophia is manifest.

Christ as Sophia

Christianity is currently a much devalued religion and the figure of Christ himself has been disempowered for many by a very human depiction of his attributes and qualities. The rather faded and nauseous figure who emerges from pious tracts and tub-thumping evangelism has little to do with the figure who emerges from the Gospels.

With the development of Christianity, Wisdom, as derived from the Saviour Goddesses of the Middle East, fades to become a hypostasis with no manifest symbolism. But as she fades from the stage, other characters take over. More specifically, Christ comes to inherit Sophia's mantle in an extraordinary way.

It is evident, from internal references within his work, that Philo was well acquainted with most of the Books of Wisdom, except perhaps *Ecclesiastes*. It is in the works of Philo that we first begin to notice the preferential treatment, not of Sophia, but of the Logos; not Wisdom, but the Word: 'To the Logos was apportioned a divine . . . pair of parents, God himself as father . . . and Sophia as mother . . . The divine Logos issues forth like a stream from the well-spring of Sophia.'[21] But while Sophia is the Logos' mother, she is also shown to be his spouse or opposite. Philo's doctrine of opposites (*syzygies*) held that everything had its polarized opposite. Yet he also concludes that each pair of opposites forms, or is derived from, a whole. Yet Philo conceived of the Logos-Sophia to be a kind of fertile masculine image: the Logos is the chief mediator between the Divine and Human realms and is the fountain of wisdom, whose perpetual streams nourish and fructify the spirit.

Philo conceived God to be so transcendent that he needed intermediaries of a cosmological or mythological stature: Sophia; Logos; Moses; Israel. Philo's habit of transposing Sophia with Logos has led, within Christianity, to some peculiar theological distinctions. Working primarily with Isis and Osiris as the mythological models for his Sophia and Logos in a creative, but wholly Jewish, manner, the fertile power of Sophia is appropriated by the Logos in true patriarchal fashion.

This trend was continued in the writings of St Paul and St John. Paul insists in I *Corinthians* 1:23,25: 'We are preaching a crucified Christ . . . a Christ who is the power and the Sophia of God.' (Most Biblical translations offer 'wisdom' but the original Greek gives 'Sophia'.) He continues: 'But still we have a Sophia to offer those who have reached maturity: not a philosophy of our age, it is true, still less of the masters of our age, which are coming to their end. The hidden Sophia of God which we teach in our mysteries is the Sophia that God predestined to be for our glory before the ages began. She is a Sophia that none of the masters of this age have ever known.'[22]

St John squarely affixes the sign of the Logos to the mast of his gospel: 'In the beginning was the Word'. Through this Logos, all things were made, just as, through Wisdom, creation takes place in *Proverbs* 8. However, in 'the Eastern Church, the icon of St John of Silence is worshipped'; he presses 'his curled finger to his lips signifying silence. He is cross-eyed, signifying the inward gaze. A winged figure is whispering something in his ear. It is Divine Wisdom, Sophia.'[23] Logos and Sophia may not be separated or, if they are, they must polarize in any given scenario. Philo's action of assigning Wisdom to the Logos meant that the *paredros* of God must find another figure to inhabit. The role eventually fell to Mary, whose nuptial relationship to Christ is discussed later.

Gnostic sources tell us that Christ has two aspects: 'his male name is called "First-Begetter Son of God"; his female name is "First-Begetress Sophia, Mother of the Universe". Some call her "Love".'[24] That this concept might find a place in Biblical scholarship might seem unlikely, but that is the case.

It was Rudolf Bultmann, the German Biblical scholar, who cited certain passages in the Gospels, notably *St Luke* 11:49-51, 13:34 and *St Matthew* 23:34–37, as interpolations of Sophia herself, put into the mouth of Christ. He suggested the influence of a no longer existent text which he called *Q*, German for 'source', as a source for some of the sayings of Jesus.[25] These sayings, or *logion* were collected by the faithful and collated long before the Gospels came to be written. These *logion* were incorporated into the canonical Synoptic Gospels, and also appeared in the Gnostic *Gospel of Thomas*, in somewhat different forms. Many such *logion* are also found in the Dead Sea Scrolls, which were the sacred scriptures of the Jewish mystical sect, the Essenes.

The presence of *Q* in the Gospels, said Bultmann, proved that 'the myth of the divine Wisdom' was intrinsically part of Jesus' ministry, that Jesus identified himself with Wisdom herself.[26] This opinion has both delighted and outraged Biblical theologians. The intricacies of this argument are beyond this book, but the theory is both Gnostically and mystically tenable.

The descent of the dove upon Jesus as he was baptised by John is perhaps significant, as the dove is Sophia's own symbol. An Orphite text, quoted by St Irenaeus, describes how Sophia, knowing that her brother Christ (conceived as a separate divine entity to the human Jesus) was coming down to her, 'prepared a baptism of repentance, and prepared in advance Jesus, so that when he came down Christ would find a clean vessel . . . As Christ descended into this world, *he first put on his sister Sophia . . .* Bound up with Sophia, Christ descended and so Jesus Christ came to be.'[27]

We have seen how, in *Wisdom*, Sophia is described as being the protector of prophets who are her mouthpiece. Both Jesus and John the Baptist stand in this tradition as, indeed, do all revealers of wisdom. The parable about the vineyard owner in *Mark* 12:1–9, who sent his servants to the vineyard tenants, tells how they were both beaten up; he therefore sent his only son whom the workers killed. This parable is about Jesus' own experience of visiting the earth. Already knowing the outcome of his mission, Jesus spoke for the whole earth, from the depths of the World-Soul itself, when he lamented over Jerusalem: 'O Jerusalem, Jerusalem, killing the prophets and stoning those who are sent to you! How often would I have gathered your children together as a hen gathers her brood under her wings, and you would not!"'[28]

In *St Matthew*, this saying is immediately followed by the last of Jesus' teachings in the Temple concerning the Last Day. It includes the parable of the five wise and five foolish virgins who must greet the bridegroom. Shortly after this, Jesus was arrested and tried.

Sophia says in *Proverbs* 1:28: 'Then they will call upon me, but I will not answer; they will seek me diligently but will not find me', which is comparable with *Luke* 11:49–50: 'Behold, your house is forsaken. And I tell you, you will not see me until you say "Blessed is he who comes in the name of the Lord!"' The *Gospel of Thomas* likewise refers to the withdrawal of Sophia: 'Jesus said, Many times have you desired to hear these words which I say to you, and you have no other from whom to hear them. There will be days when you will seek me, and you will not find me.'[29]

However, Jesus confirms his disciples as witnesses of a great happening: 'I tell you that many prophets and kings desired to see what you see, and did not see it, and to hear what you hear, and did not hear it.'[30]

This gives us a skeletal mythic framework whose trajectory is aimed through the *Gospel of St Matthew*, deriving from close attention to the sapiential literature which underpins this gospel: *Wisdom came to earth, offered herself and her prophets and was refused. She prepared the way for Jesus to come, joining herself to him as a syzygy or as the Holy Spirit in the form of a dove. She was with him throughout his life and she returns to earth, after his ascension into heaven, as the inspiring presence of the Spirit among all people. In the day when the 'house' of the earth is indeed uninhabited by her/their spirit, Sophia and Jesus will return in the persons of the apocalyptic couple and dismantle creation.*

140

This gives us a considerable edge with which to cut the Sophia myth open, here at this critical interchange between what we can call Goddess culture and God culture. If this myth is at all tenable, we see that, prior to Christ's incarnation, the prevailing Divine influence upon Western culture had been cast in the feminine image of Wisdom. From the point of Christ's incarnation, the Divine influences have appeared in masculine images. Neither are essentially antagonistic to the other: both work harmoniously to make the earth and its inhabitants wise. The disharmony has arisen through the West's insistence on one half of the syzygy, preferring God to Goddess over the last two millennia.

One reading of this myth would give us a messianic brother and sister relationship similar to that of Isis and Osiris, except in our

9 *Sophia* Here Wisdom appears as a black woman, attired in the garments of the earth. She holds up a neolithic statue of the Goddess discovered at Willendorf, to show her continuity with all expressions of the Divine Feminine. This modern icon by Robert Lentz is entitled *Christ-Sophia*. Within Christianity, Christ shares the attributes of the Biblical Wisdom. (See also cover.)

myth the rule seems to be that only one sibling may be incarnate at a time. When one withdraws, another is incarnated. We speak here of a Christian Sophia, not of the Goddess of Wisdom in her more general appearances. Here, Christ and Sophia have a joint being, or one is superimposed upon the other.

The ascription of Wisdom texts to Jesus show a sensitivity to the Messianic kingship, as administered by Sophia's earlier Middle Eastern models. It is not by force of arms that the Messianic King completes his mission, but because Wisdom *himself* has invested him with *herself*.

The Son of Sophia

Sophia frequently speaks through the humble, the weak, the oppressed: 'Blessed are the poor in spirit, the meek, those who mourn, who hunger and thirst for justice, the merciful, the pure in heart, the peacemakers, the persecuted.'[31] These are the friends of Sophia, whose lot she shares. They are the salt of the earth. The Beatitudes reveal a face of Wisdom which underlies esoteric and practical Christianity. They are the building bricks of the Kingdom of Heaven with which Sophia plays before God in *Proverbs* 8. They seem flimsy and insubstantial as building materials, but they have an unappreciated strength: 'The Kingdom is the blossoming of the paradisal seed whose growth was arrested by the pathology of the Fall, which Christ comes to heal.'[32]

The Incarnation of Christ as a human baby is still one of the most profound features of Christianity. We can tell that Sophia is present because of the prophecies surrounding his birth and the amount of opposition which greets his epiphany. Christ is hailed by philosopher-kings, the magi, whose duty is to read the message of the heavens. He is taken secretly to Egypt, the place of esoteric teaching, and there raised in security. He returns to dispute in the temple with the sages of his people.

Sophia speaks through a child, in the person of Christ in the temple. The child is the indisputable sign of Sophia – whether it be male or female. 'At various times in the past and in various different ways, God spoke to our ancestors through the prophets, but in our own time, the last days, God has spoken to us through the child, the child that God appointed to inherit everything and through whom was made everything that is.'[33]

This epiphany of the child permeates the Gospels:

> The Word was made flesh
> and pitched its tent among us.[34]

This gives the game away, for here Wisdom, who once dwelt in the tabernacle in the desert as the Shekinah, is fused with the Logos, the Word, who is now incarnate in Christ.

Here the eternal pattern of Wisdom's epiphany is clearly manifest. She says in *Sirach* 24:3:

> I came forth from the mouth of the Most High
> and I covered the earth like mist.
> I had my tent in the heights,
> and my throne in a pillar of cloud.

The moment of the Incarnation, the enfleshing of Christ within the womb of Mary, used to be symbolically acknowledged during the recitation of the Creed at the *et incarnatus est*, when the faithful would bow, acknowledging the interpenetration of the Divine among them.

Within the child in the manger is also present all the potent wisdom of the Ancient of Days. Christmas is a popular feast among non- or nominal Christians, for it is easy to accept the Nativity of the Child and the joy that all new children bring. Within the Nativity is present the promise of better days, of sweeter loving, of a return of an innocence from which we believed ourselves forever banished.

Juxtaposed to the feast of the Nativity, but less visible, is a commemoration which each of us should observe: the Feast of the Holy Innocents. These are the children which Herod succeeded in having killed, while failing to kill Christ. It is not the historical event that we should observe here, rather the continuing loss of innocence and joy among both children and adults. Here the voice of Sophia cries out in unbearable lamentation:

> A voice was heard in Ramah,
> wailing and loud lamentation,
> Rachel weeping for her children;
> she refused to be consoled,
> because they were no more.[35]

Christ as Sophia bids us all become guardians of the innocent: 'Whoever receives one such child in my name receives me; but whoever causes one of these little ones who believes in me to sin,

143

it would be better for him to have a great millstone fastened about his neck and to be drowned in the depth of the sea . . . See that you do not despise one of these little ones; for I tell you that in heaven their angels always behold the face of the Creator who is in heaven.'[36]

The symbolism of the dove plays an important part in Christ's epiphany: Mary conceives by the Holy Spirit, and Christ is confirmed in his power by the dove of the Spirit descending at his baptism. 'The power of the Most High will cover you with his shadow', says the angel to Mary in *Luke* 1:35. The same expression is used to describe the Shekinah's presence in the tabernacle. Mary becomes as a tent, a sacred tabernacle herself.

But sometimes the voice of Sophia takes on the accents of the Shekinah. According to the Gnostic *Gospel of the Hebrews*: 'It came to pass when the Lord had come up out of the water, the whole fount of the Holy Spirit descended upon him and rested on him and said to him: My Son, in all the prophets was I waiting for thee that thou shouldest come and I might rest in thee. For thou art my rest; thou art my first-begotten Son that reignest for ever.'[37]

The miracle of Cana reveals Christ in conjugal mode. The actual and subtextual references to the marriage feast are scattered throughout the Gospels and taken up in the Apocrypha. 'The Spirit and the Bride say "Come".'[38] In this miracle, we see the transmutation of water into wine, just as Christ himself is the image of humanity's own transmutation into Deity. Mary points out that the guests are thirsty, thus sophianically creating the first opportunity for Christ to give himself as the living water. This is the antiphon of the *Gospel of the Hebrews* where Zoë-Eve gives herself as the Tree of Life (See Chapter 8).

The nature of Jesus' sayings is after the fashion of the Goddess of Wisdom. He stresses the inclusive nature of life: 'As often as you do this to the least of these you do it to me.'[39] The justice of Astraea is upheld in *Matthew* 23:4: 'You have neglected the weightier matters of the Law – justice, mercy, good faith', qualities which give life their sacred dimension.

The parables of the Kingdom also stress the pervasive nature of Wisdom – it is the seed which is sown in the field, it is leaven in bread, it is the salt which gives flavour to the food. *Mark* 9:50 says: 'Have salt in yourselves and be at peace with one another'. The Gnostic *Gospel of Philip* 59:27–60:1 adds: 'The Apostles said to the disciples, "May all of our offering get salt".' They were referring to wisdom as salt. Without it no offering is acceptable. Now Wisdom is barren [without] offspring. For this reason she is called [ ] of the salt. Wherever [ ] can [ ] like them, the holy spirit [ ] and many are her offspring.[40] This fragmentary last saying of Sophia can be perhaps restored with the help of *The Thunder Perfect Intellect* 13:22: 'It is I who am the barren: and who has many children.'[41]

Salt was the pay of the Roman army, from which we still derive our word 'salary' from *cellarium*, yet the punitive act of a people whose land is being invaded is to sow their fields with salt, which renders the ground barren. If salt is not used appropriately – to add flavour to life – it causes barrenness to the earth, and its absence causes a flavourless existence. That which is ubiquitous is familiarly despised as unimportant, until it is withdrawn. Christ is described as the cornerstone that was rejected. Similarly, Sophia's influence is discounted until it is withdrawn. This saying percolates throughout the Classical Mystery schools and descends to alchemy where the prima materia is the 'despised substance' which, nonethelesss transmutes to gold (see Chapter 13).

This same transmutation is understood to occur within faithful Christians, within Eastern Orthodox tradition. Theosis or god-becoming is the recognized vocation of all Christians. The transfiguration is a doxophony, a revelation of glory. Peter and James, the only witnesses to this event, were confused, choosing to make tents to shelter from the glory, perhaps in imitation of the *succah* booth of the Feast of Tabernacles. The other participants – Elijah and Moses – had already beheld God face to face and experienced the glory of the Shekinah.[42]

At the Last Supper, when the two new commandments were given – 'love one another as I have loved you' and 'do this in remembrance of me' – we see a strange reflection of the moment of Incarnation.[43] On the eve of his crucifixion, Christ gave bread and wine to his disciples and likened them to his own flesh and blood. By taking flesh of Mary, he already shared in humankind: by the disciples' act of sharing bread and wine, they partook in Christ's divinity.

The Christian descent of Sophia is clear to see. Passing through the angelic salutation, the descent of the dove passes on down through the womb of Mary, into the baptismal waters of the Jordan, through the miracles of Christ, to the point of the Last Supper where the spirit of Sophia is at last apportioned. 'I will not leave you desolate . . . the Counsellor, the Holy Spirit, whom the Father will send in my name . . . will teach you all things and bring to your remembrance all that I have said to you.'[44] The last descent is yet to be accomplished, however.

At his crucifixion, we see the significant juxtaposition of two very Sophianic images: the rending of the Temple veil,[45] and the gambling of the soldiers for Christ's seamless garment.[46] These are symbols of the inviolable weave of Sophia, who stood at the loom of creation's web. Christ's *anastasis*, his immortality, is figured in the seamless robe: the failure of tradition to maintain spiritual life is reflected in the rending of the Temple veil. The last mystery is penetrated.

'He went down to the peoples of the past.'[47] The descent into hell to redeem the peoples of the past is a descent of profound Sophianic beauty. It is an act which reconnects the ancestral traditions with those of later times in a timelessly affirmative way.

The sacred marriage of Christ with the Black Goddess, the Mistress of the Earth and its unbreakable laws, is enacted in the earth's dark places: 'Christ, as the emblem of Compassion, offers up his own flesh for the sake of all living flesh. He is laid in the tomb, entering the dark realm of Sophia Nigrans, who is guardian of the densest kernel of creative matter at the centre of the earth. He embraces her outcast darkness, as the hero-initiate embraces the Hag; and it is in their embrace that the spark of Resurrection is enkindled.'[48]

It is not only Christ who descends to the depths of hell, for Wisdom says of herself: 'I will penetrate to all the lower parts of the earth, and will behold all that sleep, and will enlighten all that hope in the Lord.'[49] When Christ ascended, marked with the undying sign of his earthly sufferings, it was because Sophia has said to him 'keep these wounds for my sake.'[50] Wherever the Goddess of Wisdom has walked, there, too, are her teachings. Christ's descent into hell teaches us that we cannot disdain any spiritual tradition because it does not accord with ours: his action has a more cosmic function than that.

Sophia descended to the last foundations of the earth, and then began her ascent. The resurrection was proclaimed and the Holy Spirit descended as tongues of fire upon the assembled people.[51] The rest of Christian tradition has theoretically been the history of the ascent of Sophia, though there are few to bear witness to this truth. It is almost as though the witnesses to the Ascension had not heard the words of the angel: 'People of Galilee, why do you stand looking into heaven?'[52]

The Motherhood of God

It is significant in a time when Christianity, along with many other orthodox religions, has come to a point of stalemate, that the reanimation of the Christian tradition is once more abroad. Many are turning to the most traditional mystics while others are using the terminology and symbolism of pagan and non-Christian mysticism to restate Christianity's foundation mysteries. It is also ironic that this movement is also attempting to innoculate the masculine images of Christianity with the feminine ones of early belief, so that we can talk about Jesus as Sophia and God as Mother. Many orthodox Christians are alarmed by this movement, concluding that it may be all right for mystics to espouse Jesus and Mary and for scriptures to talk about a mothering God, but that it is altogether different to bring this kind of stuff into the sanctuary.

In an age where the metaphors of religion are shifting daily, many now long to see a time where 'God is also revered as woman, as mother, as wisdom.'[53] If God speaks through many people, through Christ, through priests, why not through women also?

Theologians and mystics have frequently spoken of God in female metaphor, such as Clement of Alexandria: 'Look to the mysteries of love, and then you will see the lap (or bosom) of the Father, whom the only-begotten God alone proclaimed. But God, too, is himself love, and out of love he allowed himself to be seen by us. And what was inexpressible in his nature became Father, while what was compassionate toward us became Mother. And as a consequence of his love the Father took on the nature of a woman, and the clear proof of this is the Son, whom he begot out of himself, and the fruit that was born of love is love.'[54]

In her extraordinary *Revelations of Divine Love*, Mother Julian of Norwich observed the following: 'Thus in our true Mother Jesus our life is grounded, in the foreseeing wisdom of himself from without-beginning . . . And from that time, and now, he feedeth us and furthereth us, and ever shall until doomsday: right as the high sovereign kindness of Motherhood willeth, and the kindly need of childhood demandeth . . . And I understood that there is no higher stature in this life than childhood – in the feebleness and failing of might and understanding – until the time that our gracious Mother hath brought us up to our Father's bliss. And there shall truly be made known to us his meaning, in the sweet words where he saith: "All shall be well; and thou shalt see it thyself that all manner thing shall be well." '[55]

147

Despite Julian's confident words, the practical implementation of this maternal God imagery trails a long way behind the mystical theory. The slurring of God's gender is as frightening to some as the reality of homosexual priests or female ordination. Non-sexist liturgies have been introduced in America, using inclusive language and the neutral 'Creator' or 'Parent' for God. Masculine pronouns such as 'he' and 'his' are avoided by repetition of the noun, 'Creator'. Such liturgical tools may begin to influence the modern metaphorical drift of Deity, but many see this as an undermining of Christianity's integrity.

If the Goddess of Wisdom is once recognized as the habitation of Christianity, then a revitalization of this flagging spirituality may result.

Many in the Church now turn to deep ecumenism, an acknowledgement of other spiritualities which does not rely on its own hidebound doctrines to bolster self-confidence. This is a trend to be encouraged, for with it comes a humility which is the best ground for allowing spiritual growth. The light of Sophia is recognized within deep ecumenism as a common light: 'And we all, with unveiled face, beholding the glory of the Lord, are being changed into his likeness from one degree of glory to another.'[56] And whether we look towards Christ, Kali, Allah or Sophia as our source of glorious inspiration, the same light burns in each of us, making us mirrors of that which we reflect.

The mystery of the empty tomb confesses that Christ and Sophia await the bridal chamber. They both await in the place prepared, as this enigmatical alchemical inscription vouchsafes. Of Sophia we can say that she is: 'neither woman, nor androgyne, nor maid, nor youth, nor crone, neither chaste, nor virtuous, nor whore, but all. Carried away neither by hunger, nor sword, nor by poison, but by all – Neither in heaven, nor water, nor earth, but everywhere is her resting place'. Of Christ we can say that he is: 'Neither husband, nor lover, nor kinsman, neither mourning nor rejoicing, nor weeping, neither mound, nor pyramid, nor tomb, but all. He both knows and knows not to whom he is raised. This is a tomb that has no body within, this is a body that has no tomb surrounding it. Yet body and tomb are the same.'[57]

Whether the reader credits Jesssus with an actual resurrection or chooses to side with the Gnostics, he is a son of Sophia, she who breathes inspiration into her lovers and turns them into friends of God.[58] Her message descends, via the mystical family of the Church, through the non-aligned philo-sophias and fideles d'amore of all cultures and ages down to our own time, making our own children hers.

'Wisdom is justified by all her children',[59] runs the saying of Jesus, speaking about John the Baptist. As the linking of the world's spiritual wisdoms proceeds through the slow fire of ecumenism, that saying will prove prophetically true and Wisdom will walk among us once more, unveiled by any gender.

═══ 8 ═══

THE BRIDE OF GOD

And whenever Sophia receives her consort and Jesus receives the Christ and the seeds and the angels, then the Pleroma will receive Sophia joyfully and the All will come to be in unity and reconciliation.

A Valentinian Exposition

Gnosticism

'Speak, therefore, from the heart, for it is you who are the day that is perfect, and it is within you that there dwells the star that does not set.'[1] This saying from *The Gospel of Truth* exemplifies the Gnostic approach to gnosis, which is nothing more than the uncovering of the spiritual spark within each person.

Gnosis means knowledge. It is the principle which underlies the mystical traditions of the West, for both orthodox and esoteric streams of spirituality know that their task is the unfolding of self-knowledge which is a microcosm of spiritual fulfilment. Pure gnosis is found wherever Sophia has walked; it is not dependent upon any particular school of thought.

The Gnostics, or 'knowers', were active from about the second century AD. They flourished in and around the Mediterranean and spoke mostly Greek, the educated language of the day. The Gnostics are first mentioned by St Irenaeus who was writing in Lugdunum (modern Lyon) in about 180 AD. Drawing upon many features of contemporary spirituality including Christianity, Judaic mystical speculation, Classical Mystery religions, and dependent, above all, upon Plato's *Timaeus*, the Gnostics propounded a parallel version of Christianity which survived for several centuries. Each sect was autonomous, having no centralized controlling authority as the Church came to have. The many sects stemmed from areas as disparate as Hermetic philosophy, Platonism, Judaism and Christianity. Although Gnosticism is known as a Christian heresy, there were also several non-Christian sects.

150

The majority of the Gnostic Scriptures – collected together under the title of 'the Nag Hammadi Texts' – were kept hidden, and were only discovered in 1945 in Egypt. Since then, a team of scholars has been busy translating and assessing their value. Gnosticism is notable for its complex creation myths which are often at variance to the orthodox Biblical narratives. It has a creative mythology which introduces and characterizes qualities and functions in a sometimes allegorical way. In its depiction of Sophia, the Virgin Mother of Creation, it throws a unique light upon a possible Christian view of the Divine Feminine.

Gnosticism did not exalt Mary as did orthodox Christianity; its guiding myth is focused on events long before Christ's incarnation or the creation of Adam and Eve. Gnosticism acts as a kind of prequel to the Christianity of Biblical warrant. The Divine Feminine heroine is Sophia herself and, though orthodox Christianity was to incorporate Mary into the Bridal Chamber as the *paredros* of her Son, this role is reserved for Sophia alone in Gnosticism.

The compilation of the canonical scriptures which now make up the Bible was dictated by contemporary taste, spiritual politics and cultural exigency. Of the current canon, the Apocryphal books, including the sapiential books, many scriptures are still considered uncanonical. The New Testament was canonically selected between 170–220 AD, but many texts were omitted – not just the exotic Gnostic ones, but also the harmlessly orthodox scriptures such as *The Shepherd of Hermas* (see Chapter 10).[2]

One's first glimpse of any Gnostic text irresistibly recalls one's first look into the cosmological poems of William Blake. Here are tangled narratives teeming with strangely-named characters who are at once persons, ages and qualities. It is hard to make these texts yield a comprehensible shape. Yet when we begin to polish these tarnished verbal icons, an extraordinary luminosity is revealed.

The myths which preceed Gnosis and underlie its complex cosmogony are easy to discern: the threefold creators, Male, Female and Child; parthenogenesis of Sophia's child is prefigured by the myths of Hera and Gaia; the titanic aeons are like the ancestral gods. Throughout the texts, which vary considerably in quality, the myth of the descent and restoration of Sophia is worked out. Sometimes the female heroine of Gnosis appears under other names: Barbelo, Achamoth, Zoë, Norea, Psyche, etc. These are all aliases or daughters of Sophia whose task is to penetrate to the very depths of creation.

Sophia is like the woman of the Gospel who hid leaven in three measures of dough.[3] This image is used by Jesus as an analogy for the kingdom of heaven. Similarly Sophia, under the name of Achamoth, is responsible for the 'sowing' of three crops. Achamoth secretly inserted the embryo of light into the Demiurge so that when he created life, it 'might become ready for the reception of the perfect Word. So by ineffable power and forethought the spiritual human being escaped the motive of the craftsman after he had been sown by (Sophia).'[4] These three categories of 'bread' were really the kinds of people recognized by the Gnostics: *the hylics* – pagans steeped in the gross matter of the flesh; *the psychics* – ordinary Christians not in receipt of the Gnostic mysteries; *the pneumatics* – Gnostics who were initiates of the mysteries of Christ.

The complexities of Gnosticism are all reflected in Sophia whose task is to bring the leaven of her kneading from the oven as well as the risen bread. There is no one myth of Sophia, rather there are a variety, all at odds with each other. From solely Biblical sources we can adduce the basic myth as follows: Sophia dwelt with God, in a pre-existent and companionable way, helping him with the process of creation. She sought to live on earth with humanity, but this was in vain since her message was not heeded. She therefore returned to heaven and remained hidden there. Only God knows his way to her. However, she may be sought also by the just, by prophets and friends of God.[5] However, there are a multitude of Gnostic myths to set beside this and we only have room for two of them. The first is from an early Gnostic scripture called *The Apocryphon of John* which gives a full text of the Gnostic creation myth. It it is chosen here because of its full and mature character.

The Apocryphon of John

The text begins with a dialogue between John, the brother of James (i.e. St John the Evangelist) and a Pharisee, who tells John he is deluded by the Nazarene (i.e. Jesus). Wandering confused in the mountains, John has a vision. The Saviour appears to him in different shapes but finally says: 'I am the Father, I am the Mother, I am the Son.'[6] The Saviour goes on to relate the nature of the pleroma and its inhabitants.

First there was the Monad, who is Father, the summation and abstraction of deity. From him emanated the Virgin, Mother-Father, the Womb of everything, Barbelo (another name for Sophia). She requested five co-workers to help her: Incorruptibility; Foreknowledge; Eternal Life; Intellect and Truth. Barbelo then conceived the light and brought forth Christ, the Self-Created One. Then there were four aeons or ages, under whose aegis were Ger-Adamas (the image of Adam), Seth, the Gnostic descendents of Seth and those who repented tardily. These last were under the aeon of Eleleth who was also responsible for Sophia.

Sophia wanted to create something by herself, just as the Monad had done. Her offspring was Ialdabaoth, formed with the face of a lion and the body of a serpent. He took Sophia's power and withdrew from the pleroma and went into another place, which we can understand as the Fallen World. He created twelve archons or rulers and established seven rulers over the planetary spheres and five over the abyss. Ialdabaoth rejoiced in himself and proclaimed that there were no other gods before him. At this, Sophia began to move turbulently, growing ever darker. She repented her self-created offspring and entreated the pleroma to receive her. She returned and was placed in the ninth realm until her power was restored.

Then Monad projected his image onto the waters which overlay matter in the image of a man. The archons saw this image from the underside of the waters (for they were below them) and planned to make a man in the likeness of the Monad. Each of the planetary rulers formed Adam's body, bestowing the senses, humours, and emotions upon him. But the body did not move.

Sophia still awaited the return of her vital power and the five aeons descended, taking the form of Ialdabaoth's angels, and advised Sophia's son to blow in Adam's face to inspirit him. As he blew, they stole Sophia's power from the breath which animated Adam. But the aeons took pity on Adam and sent down Epinoia, or Afterthought, sometimes also called Zoë or Life, to assist him, and she was hidden in Adam without the archons' knowledge (Zoë is the lower or manifest Sophia in this text).

They placed him in paradise but they themselves ate of the Tree of Knowledge of Good and Evil. While Adam slept, the archons formed Eve out of Adam's power – just as Ialdabaoth had been formed from Sophia. While Adam and Eve lay sleeping, a wonderful thing happened. 'And our sister, Sophia, is she who came down in innocence in order to rectify her deficiency. Therefore she was called Life which is the mother of the living. Through the foreknowledge of the sovereignty and through her they have tasted the perfect Knowledge. I appeared in the form of an eagle on the Tree of Knowledge, which is the Epinoia from the foreknowledge of the pure light, that I might teach them and awaken them out of the depths of sleep.'[7]

Thus Epinoia crept into their thoughts and Ialdabaoth saw that he was losing his creatures and he took the Life out of Eve and lay with her so that she had two children: Eloim and Yave (Cain and Abel). But Adam, recognizing Pronoia within Eve, begat Seth, 'according to the way of the race in the aeons. Likewise the mother also sent down her spirit which is in her likeness and a copy of those who are in the pleroma, for she will prepare a dwelling place for the aeons which will come down.'[8]

The descendents of Seth are those Gnostics who will return to the pleroma in the fullness of time and for this reason the Saviour descends time after time.

In a moving conclusion, the Saviour is revealed as both Logos and Sophia descending through the seed of life in all times. The Saviour identifies him/herself with Pronoia – Forethought – and tells of the mystery of the redemption of the 'immovable race': the Gnostics. This text may be set end to end with *The Reality of the Rulers*, in which we read about the Genesis story from a totally different viewpoint (see page 165).

The Apocryphon of John presents a Sophia who is innovative, inquisitive and, occasionally, helpless. Nevertheless, when she works out what has happened, she actively engages in partnership with created life to help it find the pleroma once more.

Valentinian Gnostic Myth

Valentinus was one of the greatest Gnostic teachers, one who left behind him a school which lasted until the late seventh century. He borrowed his concept of the Demiurge directly from Plato and his school of Gnosticism is very closely associated with Platonic thought. We only have the bare outline of the Valentinian Sophia myth as taught by Ptolemy, through the writings of St Irenaeus of Lyon's *Against the Heresies*. The Sophia myth of Valentinus is more abstract than that recorded in the *Apocryphon of John*, but it does provide us with the theory of a transcendent and manifest Wisdom who becomes, respectively, Sophia and Achamoth. The main characters in this drama are the Logos and Sophia: Logos acts as the Word, Sophia as the Wisdom.[9]

The first Beings were the Deep and his consort Silence. As primal mother and father they were existent within Intellect, the only-begotten and his consort, Truth, and also within Logos (Word) and Zoë (Life). Within the pleroma dwelt ten aeons, the offspring of Logos and Zoë and the twelve aeons of Anthropos and Ecclesia. These were hypostatisations of qualities: the male ones bearing such adjectival titles as 'Ageless' and 'Motionless' and the female ones being abstract nouns such as 'Hope', 'Faith', 'Unity' and, of course, 'Wisdom'.

Sophia, the last of the aeons, wished to know her origin and plunged into the abyss of Aeon, where she critically unbalanced the pleroma and was brought up short by Horus (Boundary). She was restored to her original place but the unbalance of her fall had created a formless entity. This caused intense anguish to the other aeons who caused Christos to come into being in order to deal with this entity. Christos, like Horus, ejected the entity from the pleroma where it became the lower Sophia, or Achamoth. This diminuition of the transcendent Sophia of the pleroma corresponded to the irrational World-Soul of middle Platonism. When Sophia realized her innate ignorance about the nature of the Father, she was subject to grief, bewilderment, fear and shock. These emotions became objectified and took on personas outside the pleroma. They are the ancestors of the material world, whose qualities formed the four elements while Achamoth herself produced Soul.

Out of the Soul, Achamoth produced her son, the demiurge. The Valentinian Demiurge is dissimilar to the earlier Platonic model, although he undoubtedly drew upon this. Valentinus' Demiurge is ignorant rather than evil. He created seven heavens and presided over an eighth himself.

Valentinus' Demiurge can be likened to William Blake's Old Nobodaddy – an inflated figure whose patriarchal authority is a shadow of God's. Ptolemy, in his straightforward explanation of Gnosis to a convert, Flora, spoke of the Demiurge sympathetically, telling Flora not to imagine the craftsman as evil, or as analogous to the devil.[10] The Demiurge attempted to create a reflection of the pleromic region, but it was a mere parody. His inadequacies caused him 'to follow the lie', as Irenaeus put it. The Demiurge's creation was finite and would cause him great distress. He was unable to breathe *pneuma* (soul) into the material bodies which he made and it was Achamoth who did this secretly. She desired that all created beings should find their way back to the pleroma. When every single created being was returned to source, the demiurge would cease to exist.

This complex unfolding cosmogony has style and subtlety. As with all monistic spirituality, Gnosticism had to cope with the concept of a Fall from grace, from original splendour. Valentinus' solution shows an extensive knowledge of Platonic and Judaic parallels as well as familiarity with Xenocrates and Philo. Sophia is both the heroine and the anti-heroine of this play. Indeed, she is a somewhat overactive actress within it, splitting more and more parts of herself off in order to provide continuous entertainment. This multiplicity of forms is inherited from both Plutarch's Isis and Speusippus' Dyad.

The continual proscription, 'Do not befoul your *pneuma* (spirit) nor deepen the plane!'[11] is an urging to avoid the contamination of Matter and of imitating the expulsion of Achamoth. Thus we see the nature of Sophia mirrored in successive levels by Achamoth who figured forth three appearances: Matter, derived from her Passion; Soul, derived from her 'turning back', and Spirit, derived from the light which Christos sheds upon her. Achamoth, like Eve, bore the seed of redemption within her. As Mary, Eve's descendent bore Christ to redeem humankind, so Achamoth, having caused material creation, imbued it with a soul which would help it to attain salvation and restoration in the original unity of the pleroma.

'When all this seed has grown to maturity, Achamoth their mother will . . . leave the place of the midpoint and receive her bridegroom the savior, who derives from all the aeons so that a pair is produced consisting of the savior and wisdom (Sophia) who is Achamoth: they are the bridegroom and bride, and the entire fullness (pleroma) is the bridal chamber. And the spirituals (*pneumatics*) are supposed to put off their souls; become intellectual spirits; unrestrainably and invisibly enter the fullness; and become brides of the angels that are with the savior.'[12]

Valentinus' Sophia is the unwitting mover of the Fall, like Pandora or Eve. She is helpless until helped, but this disempowerment seems only temporary, for she will welcome back all that she unwittingly let loose.

10 *Achamoth* Achamoth is one of the names given to Sophia in Gnosticism. The two aspects of Sophia, frequently seen as demonic or angelic, are shown here as a fusion in this picture of Lilith. Lilith's feet, like those of the Queen of Sheba's, are draconian, betokening her earthly and accessible side; her wings denote her transcendence. Flanked by the owls of wisdom, *Lilith* is the Mistress of creative dreams. The restoration of Lilith in feminist thealogy is important because it redeems the supposedly demonic side of Woman as well as giving access to the Black Goddess. Picture entitled *Lilith* by Chesca Potter.

157

Sophia as Goddess

These complex scriptures unfold to us a fully realized myth of Sophia in her own right. In order to comprehend the implications of what we have read here, let us consider the Gnostic Sophia in relationship to her mythic antecedents. The Judaic background for Sophia must be set against its Classical mythological and philosophical background.

The mythic pattern of Greek goddesses and heroines which may underpin Sophia's Gnostic mythos can be tabulated as follows:

1 The young woman is separated from her home.
2 There is an adolescent initiatory period of training.
3 The young woman is captured, raped and impregnated by a god.
4 She suffers the ire of her parents and is often severely punished.
5 She gives birth, usually to a boy who, when he comes to power, vindicates his mother from death or disgrace.

Most Gnostic narratives of Sophia follow this pattern, point for point. We can readily see how both Psyche and Kore are immediate successors to this archetype. But we also find that Sophia draws upon Isis. Like Isis, Sophia is a Saviour Goddess: those 'who seek truth from that female being who is truly wise will construct for themselves wings so as to fly', instructs Jesus in *The Book of Thomas*. Her boasts in *The Thunder Perfect Intellect* are equatable with those of both Isis and Biblical Wisdom. This aretalogy is of great power:

> I am knowledge and ignorance.
> I am shame and boldness.
> I am shameless; I am ashamed.
> I am strength and I am fear.
> I am war and peace.
> Give heed to me.
> I am the one who is disgraced and the great one.[13]

Here, Sophia is both the transcendent Virgin of the pleroma and the fallen Achamoth. The contradictions in this song of self-praise reflect the changing nature of the Goddess within the days following the inception of Christianity. It is popularly received that Christianity dealt the death blow to the Goddess' worship but even before Gnosticism developed, the reign of the Goddess had already been going into decline. Goddessly attributes had already been applied to God for hundreds of years in the realm of Israel. Everywhere she was given a lower place than formerly. But we can also detect another subtle infiltration technique which the Goddess used to further her influence.

Sophia has a tendency to partake of both male and female natures simultaneously – not necessarily by becoming an androgyne. This feature is found in Isis herself. A late hymn praises Isis' ability to conceive Horus from the phallus which she has made from the dismembered Osiris as 'a manly deed', and further says: 'O Osiris, first of the westerners (i.e. those who have entered the realm of the dead). I am your sister, Isis; there is no god who has done what I have done; I made myself a man, though I am a woman, in order to make your name live upon earth.'[14]

Sometimes there is even a Sophianic trace about Mary who, in *The Odes of Solomon 19* 'bore (Christ) as a strong man with desire',[15] because she wished it. This male feature of Sophia conceiving because she wanted to do something creative of her own is borrowed from both Egyptian and Greek belief where Isis, Athene and Hera produced self-generated children; it is incorporated completely within Gnosticism. Sophia is another self-conceiver, without the need of a father. We can further trace Sophia's yearning to create by herself back to Athene's birth from the head of Zeus. In Valentinian Gnosis, the first cause, the Father, was unmarried, male and alone. He produced the primal aeon, a syzygy who further produced the aeons - pairs of consorts who engage in eternal heterosexual congress. It is in imitation of the Father that Sophia attempted to bring forth. But, following the Aristotelian notion that women only produce matter, not the inspiriting soul, Sophia brought forth only a monstrous lump of flesh, a serpent with the face of a lion, Ialdabaoth, whom she hid away.

The antidote to Sophia's condition is precisely that which Classical doctors would prescribe – marital relations. The aeons jointly produced a child to be a consort for Sophia – Jesus. When Sophia received her spouse, then she would be welcome into the pleroma.

However, in Valentinian Gnosis, Achamoth 'had no father nor male consort, but she is female from a female.'[16] This statement is not borne out in the text, where Sophia is frequently depicted as disempowered, dependent upon Jesus to rescue her.

Despite the complexities of the Gnostic hierarchies, the track of Sophia, like the star-trail of Astraea which leads from heaven to earth, is easily discernable within Gnosticism. Sophia and her daughters go back in unbroken succession to the first 'looking down' of Sophia.[17]

In the *Secret Book of John* Sophia's daughter, Zoë, 'labours for the whole creation, troubling herself over it, establishing it in her own perfect temple, enlightening it about the descent of its deficiency, telling it about its ascent upward.'[18] Zoë, or Epinoia, was hidden in Adam and remained like the leaven of yeast in bread. It was she who gave light, love and life into creation, often by pretending to be vanquished by Ialdabaoth, all the time quite aware of her power.

Sophia also acquires mythic parallels within the Gospels. She is likened to 'the woman who swept the house and found the silver coin, in that wisdom lost her thinking; then later, after all things had been purified by the saviour's advent, she found it.'[19] Sophia is the seeking woman, like Isis looking for the dismembered Osiris. This feature of the myth has a modern dynamic for women looking for the Goddess.

Sophia also has her trinitarian manifestation in *Trimorphic Protennoia* where she is Father, Mother and Son (Logos). As a creator, Sophia reflects the role of Biblical Wisdom. She is described in a Valentinian fragment preserved by Clement of Alexandria as 'a painter, transferring the reality of a living being (the True God) to the image (the Demiurge).'[20]

The Sethian-Orphite sect of Gnosis was drawn to the reflective nature of Sophia's creation: 'The power which overflowed from the Woman and has the moist nature of light, fell from above . . . By its own will it has the moist nature of light, and is called Prunicos and Sophia and Male-Female. It came down directly upon the waters, when they were motionless, and set them in motion, moving boldly as far as the abysses; and it took a body for itself from them . . .'[21] Like the seed of Hephaistos which fell into Gaia, the androgynous power of Sophia expanded beyond the boundaries of the pleroma and caused creation. However, 'when it received power from the moist nature of the light which was with it, it leaped back and was borne upwards to the height. When it had ascended, it spread out and became a covering and formed the visible heaven out of its body . . .'[22] In this way, Sophia remained above, while Achamoth remained below.

The embryo, or spark of light, was secretly inserted into the Demiurge by Achamoth: he would unwittingly transmit Sophia's power to all created life.[23] It is this spark which makes a person 'gnostic'. Sophia is ultimately the Goddess who seeks to reassemble the sparks of spiritual life from created matter. St Epiphanius wrote about the Barbelo-Gnostics who, he said, practised an obscene form of worship, venerating sperm and menses as the life-bearing seed of Wisdom. Norea, as the Gnostic daughter of Barbelo (another name for Sophia), 'made clear the necessity of collecting, from out of the power within bodies, the parts plundered from the superior mother by the ruler who made the world . . . by means of the emissions of males and females.'[24] Whatever the truth of his assertions, St Epiphanius preserves for us the fragments of a very important text, *The Gospel of Eve*, the revelation of a divine being; she is probably the *Thunder Perfect Intellect* herself, since she appears to speak with a voice of thunder saying:

It is I who am you: and it is you who are me.
And wherever you are, I am there.
And I am sown in all: and you collect me from wherever you wish.
And when you collect me, it is your own self that you collect.[25]

This recalls the act of Isis, seeking for the dismembered parts of Osiris. It is the truly gnostic act, to seek for the scattered fragments of wisdom wherever they are to be found and to personally embody them. While it is possible that certain Gnostic sects took these mystical texts rather too literally, if Epiphanius' evidence may be trusted, they doubtless also comprehended the merciful command of Sophia, to become gatherers of wisdom.

The Feminine in Gnosticism

The sexual foundation of most Gnostic cosmogony is perfectly expressed in the Gnostic Sophia, who must be seen as a crucial figure in the reaffirmation of both deistic metaphor and women's spirituality.

Sophia appears chiefly in feminine guise throughout the fragmented sects of Gnosticism. The question of gender and Gnosticism is one which is likely to cause confusion among those unfamiliar with the Gnostic mind. The frequent ascription of gender to certain Gnostic emanations of Deity is also not significant or indeed helpful in determining the survival of the Goddess. Nevertheless, the use of female characters to portray the nature of Wisdom is significant in Gnosticism. Within *The Origin of the World* no less than four female characters are presented: Pronoia; Psyche; Pistis and Sophia. They each fall and are restored again.

But perhaps the best example of this use of a central female character is found in *The Exegesis of the Soul* in which we hear the story of the soul. It begins: 'Wise men of old gave the soul a feminine name. Indeed she is female in her nature as well. She even has a womb.'[26] Although the author of the text intends us to understand that the soul depicted here could be the soul of any person, the soul's journey is defiantly depicted as that of a naïve woman who was seduced, became a prostitute and who, on remembering her original nature, asked restoration of her father. He inverted her womb which, until then, had been outside her body, like male genitalia, and sent her a bridegroom from heaven. The soul waited in her bridal chamber both expectant and fearful of her impending husband. She 'dreamed of him like a woman in love with a man.'[27] They were joined in a union which was both spiritual and eternal.

The aspect of exterior genitalia in this story is a feature of Classical gynaecological speculation. Plato, Soranus and Galen – the medical authorities of their day – believed that the womb was an errant animal that roamed around inside the body. Thus women were said to be 'hysterical' – literally 'womby' – requiring the essential healing moisture of semen.[28] Galen asks us to imagine the female genitalia exteriorized: they are, he says, the inversion of male penis, scrotum and testicles. He relies on the belief of female inferiority for his argument, but is still troubled that, if his theory is true, what prevents a woman from inseminating herself?[29] As we see, this concept is explored fully in Gnosis.

In *The Paraphrase of Shem*, the womb becomes a metaphor for the world, in which we are all trapped. In concept, this is very similar to the Net of Set which Isis avoided.[30] This metaphor is at variance with the almost deification of the penis by the Naasene sect which called semen 'that first and blessed substance.'[31] The penis virtually becomes the Saviour in some Gnostic texts.

The use of female characters in Gnostic parables is at once alluring and repugnant. The presence of central female personages has frequently been praised as a liberal feature of Gnosticism, proving that women were accorded an equal role in Gnostic ministry and worship. But the more we read of the first-hand textual evidence, the more we realize that the Gnostics upheld the conventional contemporary attitude to women: that women were hysterical, uncontrolled creatures, given to passions and subject to licentious behaviour.

The Gnostic scholar, Douglas M. Parrot, considers the role of a typical Gnostic woman of this era: on joining a Gnostic group, she 'would have had a considerable hermeneutic task. She would have had somehow to discount the common belief about the nature of the female, which she would have found at every turn, and at the same time find in the statement of this belief a way of thinking about her own spiritual condition as a person.'[32] He goes on to instance the way in which religious women through the ages have had to cope with a similar burden of male language and images which exclude women. Orthodox spirituality of our own era is no different: a woman may find acceptance in the mystical sphere but the exoteric structures are polemically and symbolically opposed to her female state.

Certainly, there are sufficient instances of anti-feminism through-out Gnostic texts to suggest that some Gnostic sects required women to become as men, in much the same way that Hinayana Buddhism regards women as incapable of entering nirvana until they can reincarnate in male form! Femininity implied birth and sexuality – the means of perpetuating the endless round of existences. This feature of Gnosticism was assuredly shared with Christian sects. Within the cenobitic existence, men fled the company of women – this continues to the extreme lengths of Mount Athos today wherein no female animal, let alone woman, is allowed!

According to *Excerpts from Theodotus*, as preserved by Clement of Alexandria, Adam contained both male and female elements. He became the father of all men, and all women derive from Eve, in terms of 'male and female seed'. Similarly, 'from Sophia there stems the emanation of the Call (male) and the Called (female), also named Angels and Higher Seed. This feminine component (Called, Higher Seed), constitutes the Church of the earth, destined to union with the male Logos (Call) in the course of her return to the primordial oneness of the pleroma. This union with the male element of the syzygy actually reintroduces the female into the male principle, from which she was only temporarily separated. Accordingly, all women must be androgenized in the process of salvation. 'The female elements, changed into males, enter in conjunction with the Angels and enter the pleroma. For this reason it is said that woman becomes man and that the Church here below becomes Angels.'[33] It is so that in the *Gospel of Thomas*,

Jesus states that he will make Mary male, that she may enter the kingdom.

Women were told by Tertullian: 'You are the devil's gateway.'[34] The inviolable gate of Paradise is thus likened to the hymen – to fall out of Paradise is analogous to piercing the hymen and entering the womb of the world, wherein we are all trapped.

The Gnostic emphasis on bodily substances – blood, seed, etc. brings a consideration of women to the fore. The ancient world was fascinated by the nature of life. Aristotle's misguided ideas about the nature of reproduction (he believed that male sperm provided the form and soul of the embryo and that the female reproduction role was solely to act as giver of matter and receptacle of the embryo) coloured the whole gynaecological picture throughout the Classical world, the middle ages and beyond. Women, apart from their inherent weakness and defects – female genitalia were obviously deformed, went the argument – were merely the receptacles of children and not even deserving of the title 'mother.'[35]

This disdain of female physicality arose from a very real fear of the feminine. The feminist joke: 'If men could get pregnant, abortion would be a sacrament' gains added significance here.[36] Epiphanius, obsessively fascinated by the activities of Gnostics, accuses them of this very thing. He says the Barbelo-Gnostics did not reproduce their species and so imprison the divine spark; if a woman became pregnant, the foetus was aborted and ground into a paste which was partaken sacramentally. This lurid speculation on his part shows how unhealthy was the clerical mind of this era.

However, within the Sophia narrative we find constant references to abortions and miscarried children. The exposing of children was a social reality at this time, very often for economic reasons. Sophia suffers and shares this hardship in her wanderings, along with numerous other women.

In many ways we can view this continued metaphor of abortion as a major theme not only of Gnostic cosmology but also of the Gnostic churches themselves. James M. Robinson has spoken of the Sophianic vision as 'this aborted feminine Christology.'[37] Humanity was no longer at home in the body of the Mother, it began to view itself as an abortion, as unwanted, as unclean. The task of Sophia is indeed a soul-destroyingly hard one – to resacralize the life which we have denied in so many ways within the West. In order to go some way towards rectifying this situation, the Gnostics did strive to comprehend the two poles of human experience: knowledge and sexuality.

Knowledge and the Mother of All Living

The fall of Sophia and the Fall of the First Parents is gnostically bound together, for the fate of one is the fate of the other.

Eve desires to know what the Elohim know. She 'wishes to know what touches her most intimately: in what way, through what means, by what episodes will the house of mankind be built? Woman wishes to have a foreknowledge of the structure and the history of man . . . She wants to hold the key to these acts of God. Were it granted her, *the outcome would not be religion but magic.*'[38] So writes Father Tavard, working out of a fairly liberal reading of *Genesis*. Tavard sees the history of the Fall thus: 'Sin itself arises from this feminine aspect of mankind as something good and desirable, but premature, which should be expected as a gift rather than grasped as a possession. Following this fall, the order of history reverses the balance of mankind, making the feminine inferior to the masculine element and confuses, as well as obscures, the symbolism of the sexes.'[39]

This account of the Fall cannot help but be read as patronizing by any woman. Many more extreme fulminations against the sin of Eve abound, all based squarely on Biblical precedent. Western women, both Christian and Jewish, have lived in their shadow for many hundreds of years. Eve's punishment for her desire for knowledge is to suffer in her sexuality by bearing children. Sophia's punishment for presuming to either create by herself or to seek her origins, is to bear a child which will trap her vital power in matter. By extension, all women still suffer in their sexuality as a result of this myth's social influence.

Like the mourning and lamenting Achamoth, most women have shouldered their burden. But more recently they have been listening to the voice of Zoë, of Life itself, as well as to the voice of Wisdom crying at the gate. Although Sophia's rescue comes in the shape of the Logos within the Gnostic myth, women have realized that waiting for sexual ecumenism to come about is a waste of time unless they first institute their own search for the source of knowledge.

Knowledge, in both Christian and Gnostic Fall narratives, is preceded by sexual relations. Sexuality as knowledge is, of course, a well-known Biblical concept: and N. knew M. his wife and went into her. 'The new acquaintance' was an Elizabethan euphemism for the pox, and it is a term which is particularly apt to the Gnostics, who literally 'contracted wisdom' within sexual embrace.

Adam and Eve knew each other's nakedness and made loin-cloths. Sophia is without partner in her sexuality and, somehow, draws upon the power of God, just as God draws upon her potency to form creation in other non-Gnostic narratives.

Eve's predicament is also Sophia's, for she also desires to know. *The Reality of the Rulers* presents the first Eve or Zoë as the daughter of Sophia. She is a daughter of the pleroma and she inspirits Adam. The archons follow her down the spheres and decide to ruin Sophia's plans by raping her. Eve-Zoë, however, *becomes the Tree of Life* and leaves a sleeping semblance of herself on the ground. 'Let us take Adam's rib and say we formed his wife from it', say the archons and so the myth has ever run! The earthly Eve bears Cain and she and Adam blame the serpent for their misfortunes. However, Eve-Zoë has entered into the Serpent and told them to eat of the Tree of Knowledge of Good and Evil in order to awaken them.[40]

The act of eating of the Tree of Knowledge is thus seen as a beneficial act which is likely to awaken the descendents of Adam and Eve to find their true home for, according to this text, paradise is an invention of the archons – not humankind's place of origin, but a false paradise.

Norea and Seth are Eve's spiritual children in whom the revelation of gnosis is transmitted. Norea is specifically called 'the assistance for many generations.'[41] The following quote from the *Apochryphon of John* tells of their conception. 'And when Adam recognized the likeness of his own foreknowledge, he begat the likeness of the son of man. He called him Seth according to the way of the race in the aeons. Likewise the Mother (Sophia) sent down her spirit which is in her likeness and a copy of those who are in the pleroma, for she will prepare a dwelling place for the aeons which will come down.'[42] Seth is the mystical ancestor of all Gnostics, having many apocryphal texts atrributed to his authorship or patronage. Norea acts as the unmasker of the archons and she is given a promise by Eleleth that her descendants will find gnosis. Norea acts as a kind of priestess-sibyl for mediating the aeon Eleleth. Norea is really a grand-daughter of Sophia. Like Athene and Mary, she is a virgin who is also a mother. Indeed, it is not entirely out of the question that Norea is not herself a form of the Virgin Mary.

Norea derives from the Syriac word *nura*, or fire, and it is by fire that she destroys Noah's first two arks, since he refuses to allow her on board. It is she who understands and transmits the necessity of collecting the fragmented sparks of Wisdom's power from within each created being,[43] a significant fact when taken with her association with Noah's ark – the purpose of which is to preserve the physical life of each created species.

Zoë-Eve-Sophia is a pure virgin: 'Just as the first man did not know her perfectly, the last one has not fathomed her: for her thought is more abundant than the sea, and her counsel deeper than the great abyss.'[44] This quotation speaks of 'knowing Wisdom', yet the implication is that Wisdom retains her deep virginity, which can never be penetrated. Her fertility is the multiplicity of her inventions, and her knowledge an inexhaustible treasure. This is the true thirst of the spirit for knowledge: knowledge of another human being may slake the pangs of desire, but it does not satisfy through eternity. Such is the force underlying the Gnostics' quest.

For women, the tide is turning. Throughout the history of Western spirituality, images of the Mother of Life recur, showing that the loss of paradise is more than balanced by the quest for knowledge, the Wisdom which inhabits life.

The Wise Harlot

Sophia also appears in the surprising guise of harlot. This theme is traceable from Gilgamesh, Siduri and the hierodule who initiates Enkidu into manhood, right through to the medieval conflation of the Magdalene with the Woman Taken in Adultery. The image of harlot is perfectly reasonable in the context of gnosis for she is a woman of knowledge – again we find that pivotal word is relevant here.

'It is I who am the harlot: and the holy' says the Thunder Perfect voice of Sophia.[45] The images of the whore and the holy one are as interblent within Gnosis as they are throughout Biblical tradition. Rahab, the harlot, helped Joshua's men escape from Jericho and became an ancestor of Mary. She placed her red cord in the window as a sign.[46] Jesus himself is accorded descent from a succession of whores in Matthew's gospel: Tamar, Rahab, Ruth and Bathsheba are all mentioned. We have seen how the soul is portrayed as a prostitute in the *Exegesis of the Soul*, which calls upon the imagery of *Jeremiah* 3:1–4. The subsequent narrative is a miniature of the Sophianic passion. This same text refers to Helen of Troy's saying: 'My heart turned itself from me, it is to my house that I want to return.'[47] Here we find another part of the 'salvation of the whore' story which cross-threads Sophia's passion. Helen of Troy is woven into the Gnostic tapestry by a curious turn of fate.

The father of Gnostic heresy is purported to be Simon Magus, who is mentioned in *Acts* 8: 9–25. Little or nothing of his thought comes down to us, though he is the subject of much colourful speculation. He was a theurgist and magician. He redeemed his partner, Helena, from a brothel in Tyre. Helena was the human syzygy of Simon Magus, one who, he claimed, had been incarnated through many bodies, including Athena and the Mother of All, as well as Helen of Troy.[48] 'And on her account. . . I descended. And this is the lost sheep written of in the Gospels.'[49] The followers of Simon's cult displayed images of Zeus and Athena, representing Simon and Helena.[50] The image of poor, tempted Helen descends from this Gnostic sect down through Marlowe and Goethe, for one of Simon's many nicknames is *Faustus*, or well-beloved. Drawing on the stories of Simon, literature has created Faust the magician who conjures Helen from Elysium and who seduces innocent maidens (see Chapter 14).[51]

Simon was undoubtedly possessed of 'the secret fire' by virtue of his partnership with Helena. Esoterically, it is the female who possesses the initiating fires of creation, and who may initiate her partner into its secrets. There are many references to other Gnostic sects who utilized tantric means of identifying with their deities. However, there are few accounts of Gnostic leaders, which makes the fragmentary evidence of Simon and Helena very interesting. She was a prostitute, says tradition, but Simon translates this degraded image by visualizing her as the highest Mother of All.

A majority of Gnostic texts deals with the very elements of creation: with blood and semen. Isis herself is praised because 'she raised the slackness of the weary (the phallus of Osiris), received his seed and formed his heir.'[52]

This same relationship of Isis and Osiris has been frequently accorded to Mary Magdalene and Jesus who, according to some accounts, were the parents of a child. This obsession with physical and spiritual lineage is found frequently within post-Gnostic speculation. The theory contained in *The Holy Blood and the Holy Grail* states that the offspring of Mary and Jesus formed the root of the Merovingian kings of France, whose successors are still extant. That the Magdalene acted as the inspirer of Christ is not doubted in Gnostic tradition.[53]

Mary Magdalene is familiar to us from the Gospels as the archetypal harlot, although the evidence for this is very thin. She has been conflated with the Woman Taken in Adultery, the Annointing Woman and others. All that *Luke* 8:2 tells us is that the Magdalene was one 'from whom seven demons had gone out.' Jesus frequently exorcised the sick of such possession, but it is not without significance that Mary should possess *seven* devils - the very same number of planetary rulers that have to be overcome by the Gnostic initiate. This statement estabishes Mary as someone who has already reached perfection, according to the Gnostic ideal.

The conflation of the Magdalene with the woman who annoints Jesus is plausible, since this incident appears in *Luke* 7:36–50, and Mary Magdalene is mentioned first by name in *Luke* 8. Like Sophia, this has left Mary with two personas: as the bride of Christ in mysticism and the fallen maiden in social reality.

Mary Magdalene's role as the 'apostle of the apostles'[54] is attested in *Matthew*, *Mark* and *Luke*, when she went with other women to the tomb of Jesus and met the angels who told of his resurrection. But it is in *John* that she had a special encounter with him. After she had run and fetched Simon Peter and John to witness the empty tomb, she waited alone near the tomb weeping. The angels from within the tomb asked her why she was weeping. '"Because they have taken away my Lord, and I do not know where they have laid him." Saying this, she turned round and saw Jesus standing, but she did not know that it was Jesus. Jesus said to her, "Woman, why are you weeping? Whom do you seek?" Supposing him to be the gardener, she said to him, "Sir, if you have carried him away, tell me where you have laid him, and I will take him away." Jesus said to her, "Mary." She turned and said to him in Hebrew, "Rabboni!" (which means Teacher). Jesus said to her, "Do not hold me, for I have not yet ascended to the Father; but go to my brethren and say to them, I am ascending to my Father and your Father. . ."'[55]

The fact that Jesus did not allow her to touch him has seemed to many a betrayal of Jesus' normally expansive love in the vicinity of women, an insistence upon his Jewish male right not to be touched by them. But if he allows the woman with a haemorrhage to touch him, contrary to the most strict taboo of the Jews,[56] why does he forbid Mary? Does he not immediately after this episode appear to the disciples and invite Thomas to place his hands in the holes of the wounds, in order to strengthen his faith?[57]

The answer to this question must be sought in the Valentinian Sophia Myth, where the woman with the haemorrhage is likened to Sophia who would have been healed had she touched Christ's whole garment rather than just the fringes of it: 'she would have dissolved into her essence.'[58] The implication here is that Christ did not allow Mary to touch him at this time because the Magdalene was the lower Sophia whose restoration meant the whole restoration of creation. To have ended creation at the point of the Resurrection would have been pointless because the leaven of Sophia still had to work through the whole of life. Mary Magdalene is therefore the intended bride of Christ, but she may not enter the bridal chamber until, like Sophia, every particle of life is likewise gathered in. She remains the Sophia in exile, the mouthpiece of the Holy Spirit of God, the apostle of the Gnostics.

Mary Magdalene is not only the special companion of Jesus in Gnostic tradition, she is also the most fertile questioner among the Gnostics and the most wise. She had experience of everything. Apochryphal allusions to the Magdalene's special relationship with Christ are borne out in many texts: Christ 'loved her more than all the disciples, and he used to kiss her on her (mouth) more often than the rest of the disciples. They said to him, "Why do you love her more than all of us?" The Saviour answered: "Why do I not love you like her? If a blind person and one with sight are both in the darkness, they are not different from one another. When the light comes, then the person with sight will see the light, and the blind person will remain in the darkness.'[59]

In *Pistis Sophia*, Mary Magdalene asked 39 of the 42 questions set by the disciples. Jesus showed his preferences for her time and again: 'Mary, thou blessed one, whom I will perfect in all mysteries of those of the height, discourse in openness, thou, whose heart is raised to the kingdom of heaven more than all thy brethren.'[60] He also called her 'the inheritress of the Light.'[61] Mary told him: 'I am afraid of Peter, because he threatened me and hateth our sex.'[62] This almost prophetic passage has been proved down to our own time where the successors of Peter, 'the Rock', have been ranged against the daughters of Mary Magdalene, guardian of the Black Stone. However, Jesus ended all debate and stated categorically: 'Mary Magdalene and John, the virgin, will tower over all my disciples and over all men who shall receive the mysteries in the Ineffable. And they will be on my right and my left. And I am they, and they are I.'[63] This extraordinary statement creates Mary

Magdalene and John the Evangelist as the prime Gnostic apostles, just as Seth is the true Gnostic ancestor.

It is the Magdalene who comprehends the mystery of the wedding chamber and of the two aspects of Sophia. Interpreting a verse of Psalm 84, Mary says: ' "Truth sprouted forth out of the earth" – that is the power of Sabaoth, the Good, which sprouted forth out of Mary, thy mother, the dweller on earth. "Righteousness" which "looked down from heaven", on the other hand is the spirit in the height who hath brought all mysteries of the height and given them to the race of men." '[64]

The Magdalene exemplifies the practical voice of Sophia, she who asks the effective question. She also acts as the representative of Christ's syzygy, his intended partner in the sacred marriage chamber.

The Wedding Song of Wisdom

Gnosticism teaches that divine or pleromic beings have syzygies. This teaching is found in many systems, including those as various as Varjayana Buddhism and William Blake. It shows how a quality is never itself alone, but accompanied by its consort, who acts as helper. Many of the archangelic Gnostic beings have their consorts. Ptolemy applies the system of syzygies to the Gospel of St John, in an attempt to teach the Gnostic way. He proves, by textual breakdown, that the Word is partnered by Zoë (Life), and that humanity is truly partnered by the Church[65]. Origen flatly denies the existence of syzygies, since they are not mentioned in scripture,[66] although he does write about the hierogamy between Israel and Yahweh, the Church and the Logos. We may wonder how much the doctrine of syzygies owes to Plato's *Symposeum*, where the priestess Diotima discusses the manner in which 'lovers are people looking for their other halves.'[67]

The wedding of the divine partners becomes a central clause within Gnosticism, where it is exemplified on every level.

We have seen how the partnership of the faithful with their deity is a part of the tradition of both Goddess and revealed religion. It is John the Baptist who, on hearing of Christ's increasing ministry, said: 'He who has the bride is the bridegroom; the friend of the bridegroom, who stands and hears him, rejoices greatly at the bridegroom's voice; therefore this joy of mine is now full.'[68]

171

The call to the wedding in both the Christian and Gnostic scriptures is a recalling of creation back to its beginning and end points. This rolling up of the tapestry of creation is called the *apocatastasis*, sometimes also called 'the dissolution of the whole Mixture', in a compelling image from the *Pistis Sophia*.[69] As we have seen, the Gnostic creation of matter is like the stirring together of elements in a cup or womb, recalling Plato's idea of the *krater* (Greek bowl) wherein the elements of creation are mixed as wine and water.

The image of Sophia and Logos as the divine syzygy is repeated throughout Gnosticism. Their partnership started long before Christ's descent into the world: 'And when the annointed Christ was descending into this world, it first put on its sister wisdom (Sophia) and both rejoiced, reposing in one another: this they declare to be bridegroom and bride.'[70] Another translation gives this verse as 'and Christ . . . first put on his sister Sophia as a robe, and both rejoiced in mutual comfort.'[71]

The *Gospel of Philip* 86:4 says: 'If anyone becomes a child of the bridal chamber, he will receive the light.'[72] It likewise speaks of the bridal chamber as a metaphor for the holy of holies in the temple of Jerusalem. The events surrounding the crucifixion herald a prefiguring of the *apocatastasis* when all shall enter the bridal chamber: 'thus, its veil was torn from top to bottom, because certain people from below had to ascend.'[73]

This rending of the veil of the temple disperses the mystery of deity, continues the text: 'all deity will flee from here, but it will not flee into the holy of holies for it cannot mix with unalloyed light and the fullness that has no defect. Rather it will dwell under the wings of the cross, and under its arms'. This image is one of Sophia – no longer the veiled bride awaiting her bridegroom – but the glorious virgin of light who descends willingly from her place to partake in the drama of life's restoration to the light. Her evacuation from the holy of holies has opened 'the hidden aspects of truth. And the holy of holies was uncovered. And the bedroom invites us in.'[74]

As to the end of all things, the *apocatastasis*, Ptolemy says: 'Achamoth . . . will leave the place of the midpoint, enter the fullness, and receive as her bridegroom the savior, who derives from all (the aeons) . . . they are the bridegroom and the bride, and the entire fullness is the bridal chamber.'[75] Then all *pneumatics* will put on their true nature, become brides of thee angels. The Demiurge will acquire the position of Sophia on the eighth aeonic level, while the *psychics* will occupy the seventh level vacated by him. When that is done, 'the fire that lurks within the world will flare up, catch fire, overcome all matter, be consumed with it, and enter into definitive nonexistence.'[76]

Sophia's desire to know led her into error, according to Gnosticism. Desire for knowledge leads to sexuality, the bearing of offspring. Thus was the world began. Its *apocatastasis* will occur only when everything is folded up into the pleroma, the fullness of Sophia's own creative thought. Then, and only then, the Virgin Wisdom can enter into the wedding chamber with her Spouse. For at the end of the world, sexuality and knowledge are united and for Sophia it is the beginning of another world.

The Zone of Sophia

The question of evil or enchantment by illusion is strong in Gnosticism. Sophia stands for all that is holy and virginal: she has integrity. *Wisdom* 7:25 says, 'nothing defiled can gain entrance to her'. However, this inviolability is shattered when Sophia desires to create of herself, in imitation of her Father who also creates by himself. She becomes subject to illusion, producing a misshapen child, Ialdabaoth, the Demiurge, who is the creator of all physical life. Sophia, as it were, looses her *zone* or girdle, and the creation ensues. When she gathers it about her waist again, she will cease to be pregnant with life and will take all things unto herself again. The girdle or belt was anciently the symbol of the virgin who was physically inviolate: the ungirdling of the belt was the action of a loose woman. The anonymous author of *Meditations on the Tarot* sees the *zone* as surrounding the earth: 'as a belt of illusory mirages. It is this zone which the prophets and Apocalypse designate "Babylon". The soul and the queen of this zone is in fact Babylon, the great prostitute, who is the adversary of the Virgin.'[77] But Sophia's *zone*, like the *paroketh* of the Jewish temple, guards the entrance to the holy of holies, the pleroma. The violation of that sanctuary is rape.

We have here the dichotomy of the raped woman: is Sophia innocent or did she provoke attack? As we have seen from the history of the Shekinah, the temple was overthrown twice, proving that inviolability has its limits. We must ask, is Sophia's decision to create something of her own justifiable or does it lead to imprisonment in illusion? Is her descent really necessary? What-ever lives below the *zone* is subject to *heimarmene* or Fate; lives are circumscribed by the wheel of the zodiac and its seven planetary rulers.

The problem of evil in Gnosticism is somewhat different for Christians and Jews who may blame Eve for the Fall. Rather 'the blame for the misery of existence . . . ' may be placed 'on a structural error in the cosmos, an error which allowed the crass demiurge to produce and rule the prison-house of matter that is only a poor replica of the Pleroma.'[78] This replaces the usual guilt with a 'cosmic paranoia' for the Gnostics, causing them to behave like a 'guerrilla of knowledge fighting from within the darkness.'[79] Because the Demiurge has made the world, the Supreme God cannot thus be blamed as the author or allower of evil. However, we must remember that the Demiurge is the son of Sophia, her attempt to create something of herself. This might establish a poor reading of Sophia's performance.

The Demiurge, as we have seen, derives his mythos partially from Hephaistos. We may also trace Ptah, the Egyptian master-maker in this light. The consequent juxtaposition of the fallen Lucifer and the fallen Sophia is irresistable to archetypal mythol-ogy. The Morning and Evening Star is both Lucifer and Venus, analogous with Ialdabaoth and Sophia. The pattern of this myth stems from the avoidance of blaming the creator for evil: following the Middle Platonists, Gnosticism adopted the irrational World-Soul and clothed Sophia in her garments, while the maleficent World-Soul became Ialdabaoth.

It is hard for us to conceive of a doctrine which held birth in the flesh to be the most supreme of misfortunes. Theognis' *Elegies* 425–428 sums up this prevalent Hellenic doctrine succinctly: 'Of all things, indeed to earthly men, not to be born and not to see the rays of the burning sun, is best; but once born he should as speedily as possible pass the gates of hades and lie low, having heaped together for him much earth.'[80]

The lament of the fallen Sophia is that of the Goddess of the Classical world, a poignantly true indictment of our own time: *'They have taken my light from me, and my power is dried up. I have forgotten my mystery which heretofore I was wont to accom-plish . . . I am become as a demon apart, who dwelleth in matter and light is not in him.'*[81] The Classical notion that matter was evil and a trap of the spirit was widespread throughout pre-Christian thought.

174

Gnosticism is often promoted as a religion of sexual equality, but many sects practised a form of encratism – disdain of sexuality – combined with a cultural loathing of the feminine as much as any Christian sect.

St Augustine's doctrine on original sin – that Adam and Eve's Fall from Grace was inherited by each successive generation of the human race – brought accusations of Manicheanism against him. Indeed, on this point, there is little to distinguish the later Catholic Augustine from the earlier heretical Augustine. This doctrine has plagued orthodox Christianity ever since and has perpetuated the fearful duality from which we now suffer. The Pelagian view held that original sin was absurd and Pelagians asked the question that Augustine himself was never to answer satisfactorily: 'Why do regenerated Christians not beget regenerated children?'[82] It was thus that the doctrine of virgin birth was first developed. Mary received the 'immaculate seed' of the Holy Spirit, rather than the defective seed of a human father.[83] This reads very like a Marian parallel of the Sophia myth.

Sophia conceived a child which brought about the imprisonment of the spirit in matter: Mary conceived a child which brought about the redemption of the spirit from matter. On some levels, all that has been done within Gnosticism is to replace Eve with Sophia.

But we are still a long way from the definition of Mary as the Immaculate Conception – conceived without sin – which is what the other half of this argument requires in order to work. Indeed it was not until 1854 that the bull *Ineffabilis Deus* was ratified declaring this very definition. Augustine was attacked by Julian of Eclanum, a Pelagian bishop: 'if human nature as represented by the flesh was sinful, then Mary's flesh was sinful and Jesus should have contracted this sinfulness from her. But if only sexual intercourse, that is, male involvement, occasioned the transmission of original sin . . . then Augustine in essence made original sin a problem peculiar to males.'[84] This devastating argument works on the Classical principle that only male seed transmits the spiritual nature of humanity: the female ovum was solely the provider of the fleshly vehicle. Julian was condemned heretical and immediately made his accusation of Manicheanism against Augustine in 418. The zone or belt of Sophia the Virgin, once loosed, could only mean one thing – the proliferation of created life. This, in turn, led to the quest for spiritual restoration. This entailed overcoming the seven planetary forces which rule *heimarmene* or human fate.

In the *Acts of Thomas*, Judas baptises Thomas and confirms some young men with this invocation of Sophia:

Come, compassionate mother.
Come, communion of the male.
Come, she that revealest the hidden mysteries.
Come, mother of the seven houses, that thy rest may be in the eighth house.[85]

Here Wisdom, the house of seven pillars, is conflated with the seven days of the week and the Holy Spirit, as well as to the seven heavens; the eighth house is indeed the Pleroma, which is earnestly looked for since it is a sign of hope when Sophia passes into the Pleroma, the last home.[86] The passage through the seven levels is interesting and crucial to our understanding of Wisdom. Sophia herself falls through the seven levels or aeons. These are the planetary steps which must be passed through, purified and comprehended, if we conceive our Sophianic journey as passing back towards the plenitude of Pleroma. Within the *Corpus Hermeticum* the Demiurge's seven heavens are given seven administrators or planetary gods 'who enclose the cosmos in their circles'. Their administration is called *heimarmene*, or Fate.

St Epiphanius' full but probably inaccurate account of Phibionite Gnosis gives the following archons as rulers of these seven aeonic levels:

First	Iao
Second	Sakla
Third	Seth
Fourth	Dauide
Fifth	Eloaios
Sixth	Ialdabaoth
Seventh	Sabaoth

The eighth level is, of course, occupied by Sophia herself, for 'the luminous mother is in the highest position.'[87] This level is seen as 'a realm of repose that was given unto wisdom (Sophia) in return for her repentance.'[88] This may remind us inexorably of Astraea's exile from the earth. 'This mother they call also the eighth, wisdom (Sophia), land, Jerusalem, holy spirit, and "lord" in the masculine gender.'[89] These are some of Sophia's titles.

The zone of Sophia occupies a place midway between the Pleroma and the Hebdomad of the seven aeonic circles.

11 *Mother of the Ogdoad* Sophia is shown here holding up a seven-pointed star. In Gnostic cosmology, she overcomes the seven planetary rulers and rises to beome 'the Mother of the Ogdoad', or Eighth Realm. The descents of Sophia, like the sevenfold descent of Inanna to the Underworld, pass through all levels of experience, making Sophia a potent companion to all souls. This modern rosewood statue entitled *Sophia on the Shore* by Bryce Muir was inspired by a vision of Sophia.

177

PLEROMA   place of origination
OGDOAD   place of withdrawal and waiting of Sophia
HEBDOMAD   place of illusory planetary influence

Sophia tarries at the gateway of the worlds, neither entering into the Pleroma nor into the place of illusion: 'beside the gates in front of the town, at the entrance of the portals she cries aloud.'[90]

In the *Odes of Solomon*, composed in about the second century AD, we find Sophia as the Perfect Virgin, a dynamic Saviour Goddess once more. She opposes the Corrupter, the limiting Demiurge, and cries out like Wisdom in *Proverbs*:

> O you sons of men, return,
> and you their daughters, come.
> And abandon the ways of that Corruptor
> and approach me.
> And I will enter into you . . .
> and make you wise in the ways of truth . . .
> Through me you will be saved and become blessed.
> I am your judge:
> And they who have put me on will not be rejected,
> but they will possess incorruption in the new world.
> My elect ones have walked with me,
> and my ways I shall make known to them who seek me,
> and I shall promise them my name.[91]

Gnosticism is still a submerged factor within the history of the West. The texts have only been generally available since the 1960s and their impact is still to be fully determined. Whether they will bring a more dynamic Christianity to the fore is doubtful, for the way of Sophia is not a popular spiritual path, but one for the modern gnostic. Christianity has abandoned its mystical and Gnostic dimensions and is on the decline. We turn now to one of the fastest growing faiths which has its own mystical tradition. Sophia has walked this way as a solitary and veiled figure. As within Christianity and Judaism, she is marginalized so as to be almost invisible, but she is there nevertheless.

═══ 9 ═══

THE VIRGIN OF LIGHT

Woman is a beam of the divine Light.
She is not the being whom sensual desire takes as its object.
She is Creator, it should be said,
She is not a Creature.

Mathnawi Book 1, Jalaluddin Rumi

Light of the East

Iran and Arabia are not normally associated with the Divine Feminine, yet it is from the very heart of pre-Islamic belief that we derive important components for our study of Sophia. Nor are these wholly absent from within esoteric Islam today for, about the spare simplicity of Islamic spirituality, the ethic of ecstatic love and profound desire for spiritual union are inextricably entwined. The basis for this subtle mysticism lies in Mazdaism, the Persian belief in which Zarathustra preceded Mohammed.

In order to understand this chapter, we have to remember that militant Islam, like muscular Christianity, is only one side of the coin. The reverse is a dazzling mirror-image of Sophia who, in the persons of Fatima and Mary, upholds the Divine Feminine within Islam.

The famous Islamic *hadith* which is put into the mouth of Allah, says: 'I was a hidden treasure and desired to be known. So I created the creation in order that I might be known,'[1] presents us with an alternative way of approaching Islam. We have already posited the Orphic notion that aspects of the Goddess such as Inanna, Kore and Psyche descended into the underworld in order to have experience of creation at another level. This same notion is true of the Divine Feminine within Islam. Sophia is 'the hidden treasure', God's experience of creation, passing down through all levels of life as messenger and mediatrix of compassion. Henry Corbin called this divine movement 'theopathy', or divine empathy. This sums up the mystical approach of Islam to Sophia. She has been sought throughout the arts and sciences, and her quintessence mined from the very roots of spirituality.

Islam has its own hermaneutic studies, its alchemical arts. The great richness of the imaginal world which is the stamping ground of the Islamic mystic and artist is scarcely guessed at by the non-Moslem. There is, within Islam, a reverence for the sacred at all levels of life, especially as it is seen in the act of creation, whether it be the contemplation of artistic artifacts or the creation itself. 'The creation of concrete forms, in which one can come to contemplate the Divine, is the very reason for the existence of art. The material in the form created by the artist, and the creative process itself, are aspects of the feminine principle.'[2]

Esoteric Islam operates mainly by the practice of *ta'wil*, of understanding something on several levels simultaneously. *Ta'wil* means literally 'to take something back to its source.'[3] By this means it is possible to write a love poem which is at the same moment a cry of divine passion. When we come to look at the Ka'aba as a symbol, we will see the complexities and gradations of image which are attached to its veneration. By means of *ta'wil*, we can explore further the hidden correspondences of the Divine Feminine within Islam.

The roots of the Gnostic Sophia are to be found in the Middle East where a long tradition of prophets – Zarathustra, Mani, Mohammed – are each established as being the climactic and natural successors to those who came before them: prophets whose wisdom had both tradition and final authority. The lineage of prophets is one which is still existent in Islam: 'Not only do the Holy Imans form a chain of helpful intermediary beings, but especially Fatima, the Prophet's daughter and Mother of the Holy Imans, assumes a role which makes her a recurrence of Sophia – not only for popular piety but also for the theosophical speculations of Shi'ism, particularly Ismaeli Shi'ism.'[4]

The reverence of Moslems for both Jesus and Mary might surprise many readers, but they both appear extensively in the *Koran*. Of course, neither are accorded divine status. Just as Judaism has its *shema*: 'Hear, Israel, the Lord is our God, the Lord is One,'[5] so Islam is uncompromisingly based upon the acclamation: 'God is one. He begets not, nor is begotten.'[6]

The resistance of both Islam and Judaism to an expression of the feminine has been counterbalanced by the fact that each possesses an esoteric facet, in Sufism and Qabala, wherein the feminine is an integral part of the mystery of that faith. But Islam, while growing partially out of the Abrahamic line of Judaism, derives also from the spirituality which preceded it – Mazdeanism.

Mistress of the Bridge

'There is law in Nature. There is conflict in Nature,' is a key concept underpinning the Mazdean or Zoroastrian belief.[7]

The facts about Mazdean belief are scattered and fragmentary. Specialists are in disagreement about the original forms of Iranian religion, some seeing Zoroastrianism as an aspect of Mazdeanism, some seeing Zoroaster as the reformer of Mazdeanism.[8] It seems likely, considering the long tradition of revealed prophets in Persia, that Zoroaster (also called Zarathustra) was the latest in a long line of prophetic voices. The fusion of Mazdean and Zoroastrian belief is such that it is difficult to separate one from the other, but it is to its earlier beliefs that we now turn to discover Sophia's journey.

The supreme God in early Mazdean belief is Ohrmazd. To his right are three male deities, whose titles and responsibilities are given here:

Xshatha Variryu	Arta Vahishta	Vohu Manah
(Desirable Reign)	(Perfect Existence)	(Excellent Thought)
Metals	Fire	Animals

To his left are three female deities, given here with their titles and responsibilities:

Spenta Armaiti	Haarvatat	Amertat
(Wisdom)	(Integrity)	(Immortality)
Earth	Water	Plants

Below these divine beings are the *amahraspahds* or archangels, the *yazatas* or angels, and the *fravarti* or female spirits – literally 'those who have chosen' – who aid humanity. The Zoroastrian concept of spiritual beings or angels was further extended by the Sufi Suhrawardi. Set against these immortals are the enemy, the demonic forces of Ahriman. According to Mazdean tradition, the mixture of good and evil will be ended by the *vicharishn* or 'separation', whereat the demonic counterpowers will be thrown back into the abyss from which they came. In Zoroastrian belief, the final rehabilitation of creation is called the *frashkart*, corresponding to the Gnostic *apocatastasis*.

Elsewhere in Middle Eastern belief, including Manichaeanism, the adversaries of the immortals are led by a female demon. In Mandaean belief, Ruha deKudsa or Namrus is the mother of the world, whose sons are the seven planets. She is the mistress of midday heat, the real Queen of the South. She may be likened to the fallen Sophia, Achamoth or Barbelo. She is overthrown by Manda dHayye with the mace of light. Namrus and her sons embody the evil forces of the world. This understanding is reflected in the Gnostic Sophia who is mother of the seven archons.

The Sophia of this pantheon is Spenta Armaiti who is the immortal responsible for the earth. She is the World-Soul, in angelic form. She is 'the Mistress of the Dwelling Place', and mother of all created things upon earth. The Mazdean believer who was initiated at fifteen years of age, was taught to profess: 'My mother is Spendarmat, Archangel of the Earth, and my father is Ohrmazd, the Lord Wisdom.'[9] This creed is important, for it invests the believer with the mantle of Spenta Armaiti. The believer becomes both the child of earth and the child of earth's angel. It affirms the individual's assent to fleshly incarnation as well as confirming the soul's immortality. By affirming the immortal powers of Light on earth, the immortals will answer for the soul when it returns. It is at this moment that the Daena is awakened within the believer.

The Daena is the daughter of Spenta Armaiti, the guardian spirit of each person. It is so that Fariduddin 'Attar (d. 1221), the Persian poet, is able to state: 'Of this mother who begot me, I have in turn become the spouse. If I am called Mazdean, it is because I have made love with my mother.'[10] This paradoxical statement brings us directly into accord with the Mazdean understanding of the transcendent Sophia as Spenta Armaiti, the spiritual mother of all human beings, and the Sophia who is manifest in the soul as the Daena. Spenta Armaiti and the Daena are conceived of as one entity.

The espousal of Wisdom thus remains traditionally embedded within Persian belief and is preserved within Islam through the mediation of many Sufi poets and mystics.

Spenta Armaiti was the mother of Gayomart, the primordial man, who was tricked by Ahriman into accepting death. As Gayomart fell dying, his body, which was composed of pure metal, separated into seven metals which emerged from his body. For forty years, Spenta Armaiti, who had gathered together the gold, kept it hidden until a plant germinated from it. This plant formed the first couple who were androgynous.[11] This alchemical creation myth demonstrates Sophia's ability to gather together the essential seed or, in this case, gold of the spirit, and make it work effectively. She is the picker up and restorer of pieces, like Isis, showing that, though plans go awry, she will find an effective way to restore all things.

This story also establishes the sevenfold qualities which link the many forms of Sophia into a unity. In Mazdean belief, the sevenfold qualities are the seven immortals and their creative 'matter', the seven metals of Gayomart's body which underlie all created life. To overcome or encompass these seven qualities is the goal of most esoteric or gnostic belief.

The Daena is the daughter of Spenta Armaiti, the Mazdean Sophia, archangel of the Mazdaen pantheon and the mother of all creatures. 'And through her all the feminine figures of the Mazdean angelogy and sacred history find their meaning, including the eschatological figure of the Virgin, Mother of the Saviour to come, the Saoshyant issued from the race of Zarathustra, the one who will be named *Omnivictrix* (Vispa-Taurvairi).'[12]

The Mazdean believer looked forward to a fuller union with the Daena at death: 'I go to meet my Image and my Image comes to meet me, embraces me and holds me close when I come out of captivity.'[13] This assertion was actualized in an after-death encounter when, on the third day after death, the soul made its journey towards the Bridge of the Requiter, or the Chinvat Bridge. After numerous encounters and challenges, the soul met a beautiful maiden coming towards it, of whom the soul would ask: 'Who art thou?' Then the maiden answered: 'I am no maiden, but thine own goods deeds, whose thoughts, words, deeds and religion are all good . . . Though I was venerable, thou hast made me yet more venerable; and though I was honourable, thou hast made me yet more honourable.'[14] Then the Daena, for it is she, accompanies the soul over to paradise.

The reverse of this experience lay in store for the evil soul. Instead of the beautiful Daena, an ugly maiden awaited the soul, saying: 'I am no girl, but I am thy deeds . . . thy evil thoughts, evil words, evil deeds and evil religion . . . For though I was disreputable . . . thou hast made me yet more disreputable.'[15] She then accompanied the soul over to hell. Like Maat, the Daena is the just aspect of Sophia. She personifies the soul, accompanying every individual through life and appearing at death as she has been manifest in that individual's life. She is truly the Mistress of the Bridge. With such a companion in mind, each Mazdean believer strove to live a pure life.

The Daena is not the only eschatological maiden in Mazdean belief. According to the complex reworking of the Mazdean faith by Zarathustra, 'at the end of the twelve millennia, when our *Aeon* will come to an end, a maiden, acting as the earthly and visible typification of Ardvi Sura (Anahita), in person, will enter the waters of the mystic lake. The Light of Glory will be immanent in her body, and she will conceive "one who will master all the evils deeds of demons and men."'[16] She is none other than the Virgin Mother Eredhat Fedhri, the Vispa Taurvairi or 'all-conquering woman'. Ardvi Sura Anahita is an emanation of Spenta Armaiti, and the Vispa Taurvairi is her earthly representative. This myth is applied to the mother of Zarathustra or Zoroaster (*c.* 628–551 BC). It is myth with which we are familiar, and which may be applied to Mary within Islamic tradition.

The Black Stone

> Men seek the Kaaba's black cube
> while children game with dice.
> Now you are a man of faith
> do not turn your face
> from its black face.
> Why does it lie so still,
> so square upon the earth,
> this axis of guidance, unmoving
> as the hub of a wheel.[17]

It is ironic that the religion which has least exoteric veneration for the Divine Feminine has, at its heart, the Black Stone once venerated as the Goddess in Arabia. There were three prime Goddesses worshipped in pre-Islamic times. Al-Lat, worshipped at At Ta'if near Mecca, was in the form of a white granite stone, around which women made circumnambulations. She represented the earth in all its bounty.[18] Menat was also worshipped, though details of her cult are scant. The Goddess Al-Uzza was worshipped in the form of a black stone upon which was a mark called 'the Impression of Aphrodite' – a yoni-like indentation. The stone was taken by Mohammed and enshrined in the Ka'aba, a cubic structure which is covered by a black pall or *kiswah*. The cult of Al-Uzza was served by priestesses, but these are now replaced by the shrine's guardians called 'Beni Shaybah' or 'Sons of the Old Woman'.[19]

According to the *Koran*, the Ka'aba had been built by Abraham for the worship of the True God, but the Meccans had enshrined a number of idols, called 'the daughters of Allah,' within it.[20] The

184

Black Stone has a tutelary importance for all Arabs since it is traditionally the place where Hagar conceived Ishmael, the ancestor of the Arabic people.[21] The original direction towards which prayers were addressed was originally Jerusalem, but Mohammed changed that. He cleansed the Ka'aba of idols, re-enshrining the Black Stone, and caused prayers to be directed to the Ka'aba.[22]

It is around the Ka'aba that all Moslems on *haj* (pilgrimage) circumnambulate seven times. It is the duty of all Moslems to try and make at least one pilgrimage to the Ka'aba in their lives though few are lucky enough to actually come close enough to venerate the stone itself.

The sevenfold circumnambulation, or *tawaf* of the Ka'aba may be a remembrance of a sevenfold ascent of the ziggurat or holy mountain upon which the Black Stone may once have been prominently enshrined. This would make the original Arabic Goddess 'Queen of the Eighth' in truth.

The Ka'aba is the most powerful sacred omphalos in the world. Every mosque worldwide orients its *mihrab* or niche, wherein the prayer-leader stands to lead the faithful, towards Mecca. Thus Moslems in Russia face south-west, while those in India face northeast; Moslems in China face West and those in England face East.

The Black Stone is a sacred locus which symbolizes the meeting of earth and heaven. It is the seat of the World-Soul, the focus of spiritual aspiration for all Moslems who look towards it as alchemists towards their *prima materia*.

There is a complex symbology attached to each side of the cubic structure of the Ka'aba, which is well documented by Henry Corbin.[23] Gabriel's station is at the north-east corner where the Black Stone is enshrined. In Islamic tradition, Gabriel has one wing of light and one wing of darkness.[24] White and black are supremely important in Islamic hermaneutics, for they represent the illumination of the soul. The black light is that of the hidden treasure which will be revealed: this symbolizes divinity before creation. The white light is that which shines when the treasure is revealed.

There are apocryphal Islamic stories as to the Ka'aba's origins. One of these tells how the Stone was once the most trustworthy of God's angels who had absorbed the essence of God's pact with the angels. God accordingly placed the angel with Adam in the Garden of Eden that he might be ever mindful of his promise to God. But after the Fall Adam forgot, and God caused the angel to take the form of a white pearl which rolled towards him. The angel then appeared as before to Adam and reminded him of his promise. Whereupon Adam kissed it. God then gave it the form of a black stone, 'for such is the appearance it wears in a world given over to Darkness'. Each day Adam bore the stone until he came to Mecca. Here Adam was instructed to build the Ka'aba by the angel Gabriel and enshrine the Black Stone.[25]

Here the Black Stone becomes an angelic and alchemical touchstone, reminding humanity of its relationship with the divine. It takes on the appearance of blackness, though it can also appear as a white stone and an angel. This concept is reiterated in the Gnostic text *The Story of the Pearl*. The white pearl is sometimes also called *kuni*, the feminine for the word 'be' or 'become'. In Qarmatian doctrine, *kuni* was the first divine emanation, while a Sufi, Ibn Ammar, used this name to signify the perfect Houri of Paradise to whom God said: '*kuni, fa-kanat*' (Be, and she was).[26] This same word is etymologically related to 'cunt', which, in Persian love-poetry, is frequently euphemized as 'white pearl'.

The seven circumnambulations of the Ka'aba, undertaken in a state of mystical awareness, reconstitute these original forms, so Ibn Arabi discovered. For him the angelic form was nothing less than a revelation of Sophia herself. The climax of this experience gave him awareness of his diamond body.

Abu Bakr Muhammed Ibn al-'Arabi (1165–1240), known as Ibn Arabi, was a visionary of great stature. His early ability to mystically become or experience states and characters sets him apart from other mystics. His disciple, Sadruddin Quyawi wrote of him: 'Our *shaikh* Ibn Arabi had the power to meet the spirit of any Prophet or Saint departed from this world, either by making him descend to the level of this world and contemplating him in an apparitional body similar to the sensible form of his person, or by making him appear in his dreams, or by unbinding himself from his material body to rise to meet the spirit.'[27]

Ibn Arabi was the pupil of two Sufi female mystics, Yasmin of Marchena and Fatima of Cordova, who seem to have prepared the way for his particular method of theophanic prayer, whereby the simultaneous awareness of many levels of existence and significance were actualized.

At the age of 36, Ibn Arabi made his *haj* to Mecca where he fell in love with the young daughter of his Persian host. Her name was Nizam Ayn al-Shams (Harmony, Eye of the Sun), and at fourteen, she was the embodiment of physical beauty. She was Ibn Arabi's Beatrice and undoubtedly the catalyst for his experience at the

Black Stone which he encapsulated in his poem *The Interpreter of Ardent Desire*. He writes of her in this poem: 'I was unable to express so much as a part of the emotion which my soul experienced . . . or of the grace of her mind or the modesty of her bearing, since she is the object of my Quest and my hope, the Virgin Most Pure.'[28] Ibn Arabi, in this chivalric statement leaves us in no doubt of his intentions, yet he adds the disclaimer: 'Whatever name I may mention in this work, it is to her that I am alluding. Whatever the house whose elegy I sing, it is of her house that I am thinking . . . I never cease to allude to the divine inspirations, the spiritual visitations, the correspondences of our world with the world of the angelic Intelligences . . . this is because the things of the invisible world attract me more than those of actual life, and because this young girl knew perfectly what I was alluding to.'[29]

We do not know whether or not their relationship was consummated or whether, like Dante's Beatrice, she was taken from this world before her time, but Nizam is the foundation of ibn Arabi's experience at the Ka'aba. He tells how he was performing the ritual circumnambulations of the Ka'aba, when he fell into an interior state through which a verse came to his lips. Then a hand was laid on his shoulder. 'I turned round and found myself in the presence of a young girl.'[30]

The vision of Sophia did not appear in the form of Nizam, the Persian girl, but as 'a priestess, a daughter of the Greeks, without ornament, in whom you contemplate a radiant source of light.'[31] Ibn Arabi does not evoke the image of his own race, but the Classical Sophia of Greek Orthodoxy. It was she who responded to his pious ritual circling of the Ka'aba. It should be pointed out that Ibn Arabi's experience of Western culture was wide, and that he is still known as Ibn Aflatun, or 'The Son of Plato'.

His mystical dialogue with Sophia concerned the nature of the spiritual journey, the possibility of ultimate knowledge and the vulnerability of the faithful believer in Wisdom.

The juxtaposition of the two images – Nizam/Sophia and the Black Stone – gave Ibn Arabi a total theophanic vision of the transcendent and manifest images of Sophia.

A further experience of circumnambulating the Ka'aba led him to encounter an angelic being who said to him: 'I am knowledge, I am he who knows and I am what is known.'[32] It has been pointed out that these are echoes of Aristotle, 'I am Sophia, philosophy and the philosopher.'[33] Led further on, Ibn Arabi was invited to enter the Ka'aba itself. He was told: 'Enter with me into the Ka'aba of the

Hijr, for that is the Temple that rises above all veils and coverings. It is the entrance of the Gnostics.'[34] As he kissed the Black Stone, Ibn Arabi was told that he kissed God's right hand.[35]

Brought into the heart of the Sophianic presence, at one with his true nature, Ibn Arabi comprehended the mystery: that to know oneself is to know the Divine. His sevenfold circumnambulations had brought him to the heart of the shrine, the seat of the World-Soul herself.

The Goddess of Islam

The prophet Mohammed, according to Surah 53 of the *Koran*, had a vision upon Mount Hira in which he ascended through seven levels and experienced God directly. In this Surah, the reader is asked to consider Al-Lat, Al-Uzza and Menat, saying, 'They are not names which ye have named, ye and your fathers, for which Allah hath revealed no warrant. They follow but a guess and that which they themselves desire.'[36] The *Koran* uncompromisingly states, 'it is those who disbelieve in the Hereafter who name the angels with the names of females.'[37] It further says: 'Serve Allah. Ascribe no thing as partner unto Him.'[38]

This same vision is depicted in early Persian miniatures as 'The Night-Journey of the Prophet'. In this picture, the veiled Mohammed (whose face is never iconographically depicted) is seated upon a sphinx-like creature. She is Al-Buraq an-Nabi, a winged-mule with a woman's head. Like a female Garuda, she carries the Prophet between the worlds as his muse, representing in her own person the 'animal nature, human mind and angelic inspiration, spanning the rungs on the ladder of creation with ambiguous ease.'[39] The textual and iconographic paradox of Mohammed's vision presents the dichotomies submerged within our Western experience of Islam.

For the non-Moslem world, the symbol of the Goddess within Islam remains the veiled woman, her potency an unknown quantity. The power of the veil has been seen by most feminists as an empty one, symbolic of female degradation and dishonour; but this is the view of an outsider who judges Islamic women by her own social standards. It is frequently galling to Western women that their Islamic sisters regard *them* as constrained and illiberal. The veiling of both women and the Divine Feminine is of great significance for it means that, within Islam, the feminine becomes the natural medium of esoteric transformation.

Sophia is the mystical companion, the soul within each body, seeking the Divine Beloved. It is she who causes the mystic to proclaim that he belongs to no race or direction of the earth: 'My place is the placeless, my trace is the traceless. 'Tis neither body, nor soul, for I belong to the Soul of the Beloved.'[40] Certainly, the Divine Feminine is so marginalized in Islam, that one might be forgiven for believing it to be totally absent.

Both Mary and Fatima are reverenced within esoteric Islam, for they are both mothers of the Logos, the Word. Fatima inherits the role of Spenta Armaiti, within Shi'ism, for she is the mother of a lineage of imans. She is seen as symbolic of the 'supracelestial earth.'[41] She is considered to be the source of the iman's wisdom because she is *lawh mahfuz* or 'the hidden tablet; upon which God has written.'[42] One of her titles in Ismaeli Shi'ism is *Fatima Fatir*, or Fatima the Creator, which recalls the Sophia *Ergane* of *Proverbs*.[43]

Ibn Arabi states that Universal nature *(Tavi'at al-kull)* 'is the feminine or maternal side of the creative act. She is the "merciful 'breathing-out' of God" *(Nafa ar-rahman)*.'[44] We may compare Sophia as the Divine Sigh of Compassion in *Sirach*: 'I came forth from the mouth of the Most High.'[45] This breathing out has the effect of manifesting Sophia to the world, yet Sophia is also the dwelling place of God for, as Ibn Arabi says: 'Where was your Lord before creating His Creation? He was in a Cloud; there was no space either above or below.'[46]

The nature of both Black Goddess and Sophia are brought out in Islam. The exoteric fulminations about women, so similar to those found in Christianity and Judaism, are, of course, negative polarizations of the devouring Goddess, yet this exists side by side with the positive image of the Ka'aba, Islam's Black Madonna. Within Islam, the Divine Male and Female principles are typified by the Pen and the Guarded Tablet. The Pen is God writing upon the *tabula rasa* of the World-Soul, which preserves the veiled tradition of Sufism.[47]

The quotation which heads this chapter is the paradoxical foundation for Islam's veiling of the Divine Feminine. Ibn Arabi's exposition of this paradox may help us to understand it better. 'The Absolute manifested in the form of woman is an active agent because of exercising complete control over man's feminine principle, his soul. This causes man to become submissive and devoted to the Absolute as manifested in a woman. The Absolute is also passively receptive because, in as much as it appears in the form of a woman, it is under man's control and subject to his orders. Hence to contemplate the Absolute in woman is to see both aspects simultaneously, and such vision is more perfect than seeing it in all the forms in which it manifests itself. That is why woman is creative, not created. For both qualities, active and passive, belong to the Essence of the Creator, and both are manifested in woman.'[48]

This definition must be taken in its mystical context. For Moslems, the feminine principle is active, and the masculine principle is quiescent, in the manner of Christ within the womb of Mary. After proper preparation by spiritual practices, the masculine principle grows and is born. 'Once birth is given to the spirit, this (feminine) principle remains as Fatima, the Creative Feminine, the daughter of the Prophet, in a state of potentiality within the spirit reborn.'[49]

The secret veiled power of the Divine Feminine is thus actively at work within Islam. Its exoteric forms uncompromisingly address the Divine with masculine pronouns, but its esoteric qualities are all feminine.

The Goddess remains the esoteric heartbeat of Islam. She is the beloved of Sufis, 'the ultimate image of God the Beloved – the breaker of all images in the shrine of the heart. She is the form leading beyond form, the obstacle to the Way and the Way . . .'[50]

Sophia is herself the 'interpreter of ardent desires'. The mystical vision of Ibn Arabi portrays the longing of all for Sophia: 'The aspirations and desires of all seekers are attached to her, yet she is essentially unknown to them; hence they all love her, yet none blames another for loving her. Similarly, every individual soul and the adherents of every religion seek salvation, but since they do not know it, they are also ignorant of the way that leads to it, though everyone believes that he is on the right way. All strife between people of different religions and sects is about the way that leads to salvation, not about salvation itself.'[51]

But Sophia is also the reconciler of differences, for her love belongs to everyone: 'She manifests herself everywhere, like the sun; every person who beholds her deems that she is with him in her essence, so that envy and jealousy are removed from their hearts.'[52]

The image of the Black Stone which fell from heaven to become embedded within the earth, taking to itself the nature of the World-Soul, is the subject of our next chapter. We return to the semi-converted world of Europe to discover the Black Virgin.

=== 10 ===

THE BLACK VIRGIN

O happy gate of blackness! cries the adept, which art the passage
to so glorious a change!
Hermetic Philosophy and Alchemy, M. A. Attwood

The Marian Take-Over

At the onset of Christianity, the Goddess of Wisdom, who had
played a real part in Western spirituality, underwent an extraordinary series of transformations.

In 313 AD Constantine the Great (306–337 AD) issued the Edict
of Milan which gave toleration of worship to Christians. The
restrictive social and financial measures which followed his death
were sufficient to dismantle the well-established network of pagan
worship.[1] By about the 380s, Christianity had established itself as
the Roman state religion. Pockets of paganism survived where the
Goddess was still worshipped, but, all in all, the cult of pagan
deities was effectively outlawed.

Devotion to the Blessed Virgin Mary naturally replaced cults of
the Goddess; but while she attracted the worship once accorded
to the Goddess, the evidence for this is exceedingly slim. Within
canonical scripture, there is little mention of Mary; within apocryphal literature there is slightly more. Within the Church itself,
there is little or no evidence for Goddess survival in the shape
of a Mary cult. It is not until the fifth century that this began to
develop. However, Geoffrey Ashe has speculated: 'if the Church
eventually turned its Virgin into a new Isis or Cybele, the reason
was not that churchmen drifted absent-mindedly into doing so,
*but that some positive Goddess-making factor . . . was stronger than
their will not to do so.'*[2]

St Epiphanius, scourge of the Gnostics, fulminates against such
developments: 'God came down from heaven, the Word clothed
himself in flesh from a holy Virgin, not, assuredly, that the Virgin
should be adored, nor to make a goddess of her . . .'[3] He was to be
hopelessly outflanked on this issue by the subsequent cult of Mary

191

which gathered strength from the time of the Council of Ephesus, when Mary really entered the liturgical life and theological sanction of the Church for the first time, right up until the Reformation, which only refuelled the Catholic trajectory of Mary's popularity. 'The cult has an intense, mysterious life of its own – the life of the Goddess, mediated through a living daughter of Zion – which the Church has not only been powerless to control but has often submitted to.'[4] While we shall be considering the many levels of Mary's part in the Sophianic myth in subsequent chapters, here we consider her pagan and prophetic correlations.

The Mary of the scriptures is none other than Mariam of Nazareth. This name, Latinized as Maria and Englished as Mary, derives from the Hebrew *marah* or bitter (salt) sea. We will remember that Tiamat represented the bitter waters in the Babylonian creation epic. This bitterness of name is retained in Mary's liturgical title, Stilla Maris (Myrrh of the Sea), which was later replaced by Stella Maris (Star of the Sea).[5] Mary thus comprehends a gamut of archetypes from Tiamat to Isis Pelagia, though as a Hebrew woman, her origins are more humble.

Mary stands in the line of Jewish women who still look for the coming of the Messiah as prophesied: 'Behold a young woman shall bear a son and shall call his name Immanuel.'[6] Here, 'young woman' is sometimes rendered as 'virgin'. The only inviolate virgin in scripture is Wisdom herself: 'nothing defiled gains entrance into her.'[7] She is with God at the beginning of the world, as the prophet Isaiah notes,[8] and she is given the commission to be built or established upon earth after the fashion of Jerusalem or its temple.[9] In this same prophecy, God promises: 'I will give you the treasures of darkness and the hoards in secret places.'[10] So it is that the veiled and unmanifest Wisdom becomes active in the person of Mary.

Like the Gnostic Sophia, Mary carries the stigma of bearing a child whose father is unknown. St Joseph, though supporting Mary in the early part of her life as Christ's mother, soon dies, leaving Mary alone with her Son. The scriptural drama is worked out between Christ and humanity, not, as in the old mythic narratives, between the Goddess and her son. However, Mary's historical humanity was no disqualification to her receiving divine honour. With the opportunity of clerical hindsight, Mary acquires not only the Biblical adornments of Wisdom, but becomes the Daughter of Zion of Isaiah's prophecy, as well as assuming the recently_ vacated metaphors of the Goddess. And where the prophetic and mythic input for Mary's goddessly continuance is thin, apocryphal scripture makes up for this deficiency.

The *Protoevangelium* tells the story of Mary's parents, Joachim and Anna, and casts Mary in a Persephone-like task of helping to weave the temple veil. To her falls the royal and priestessly lot of weaving the red and purple wool with six other maidens.[11] This weaving image is taken up once more by Proclus, who preached the sermon on the occasion of Mary's acclamation as *Theotokos* or Mother of God in 428: she is 'the awesome loom . . . on which the garment of union was woven.'[12]

This Greek expression *Theotokos*, literally God-Bearer, was increasingly translated into Latin not as *Deipara*, but as *Dei Genitrix*, God's Mother. This doctrine was enthusiastically expounded by the same Cyril of Alexandria who had been responsible for Hypatia's death at the hands of the mob.

At the Council of Ephesus in 431, where the Goddess had ceased to be worshipped formally only a few years previously, Mary was formally declared to be *Theotokos* Mother of God or God-bearer in clear echo of the Goddess' former titles, for *Mater Dei* was truly the title of Cybele or Rhea. It is almost as if the spirit of Mary who, in apocryphal tradition, was taken by St John to Ephesus, had remained after her Dormition to reactivate the mysteries of the Goddess in person.[13] It was, after all, a city with a long history of devotion to the Divine Feminine.

The Black Virgin

The continuing cult of the Blessed Virgin Mary from the fifth century until the Middle Ages is based largely on the concept of the Black Goddess as the initiator in the cave, the miraculous Black Virgin.

Ephesus, the place of Mary's emergence as *Theotokos*, has its own Black Goddess, Diana of the Ephesians, who appears to have many breasts which, on closer examination, prove to be the testicles of bulls draped about her. This custom of offering the virility of beasts to the Goddess is evidently an ancient one. The custom of bull-fighting prevalent in Spain may indeed be a remembrance of the bull-leaping dances which were once offered in honour of the Goddess in Crete. We have noted that the giving of male virility is a prime feature of Cybele's cult and it is no wonder that Cybele and Diana were frequently conflated.

The image of Diana was said to have been erected by the Amazons. According to Pliny the image was made of ebony, although some supposed that the original statue had been an aerolith or black stone. Frequently confused with Cybele and Tellus Mater, Diana was a contributory factor to the popularity of the cult of Mary. She was, moreover, black. The Black Virgins of many regions stem from aspects of former worship of the Goddess as Isis, Diana, Cybele, Demeter Melainia. The Black Virgins of the West are true upholders of the ancient Black Goddess tradition in ways which the orthodox devotions to Mary are generally not.

Black Virgin statues are found throughout Europe, with a notable concentration in Southern France and Northern Spain, though Italy, Germany and Britain also have theirs. The question of their blackness is always rationalized as the blackening which occurs through the many votive candles burned before them, or extreme ageing of the wood. Other theories have suggested negroid origin, thus bringing the Black Virgin into an immediate racial context which is not without relevance here, for these statues have their greatest patronage from native and indigenous peoples. We may wonder how much the Black Virgins of Northern Europe owed to the iconography of Sheba or the Shulamite of *The Song of Songs* ('I am Black but Beautiful') or to pre-existent Goddess forms.

Pagan Goddesses still have their presence in many ways. Images of the Classical and Celtic Goddesses remained extant well into the Christian period. The *Matronae*, depicted as three mother goddesses with cornucopias, babies or bread upon their laps obviously prefigure the Madonna, as do statues of Isis suckling Horus. The writer of the *Libri Carolini*, representing the official policy of Charlemagne's court, denounced those who worshipped pagan images and wrote about the very real difficulty in recognizing the Virgin and Child from Venus and Aeneas.[14] Bernard of Angers in the eleventh century, was scornful of statues at all, disdaining even the much-venerated statue of St Foy at Conques 'as though it were a likeness of Venus.'[15]

A recent example of a pagan statue venerated by Christians is found in the Madonna and Child worshipped at Enna, formerly known as Castrogiovanni, in central Sicily, where, until the nineteenth century, a statue of Ceres with the infant Proserpina in her arms was worshipped with offerings of grain sheaves, flowers and soil. The statue was later authenticated, relegated to a nearby museum and replaced by a more conventional statue.[16]

The spread of Christianity throughout Europe was assisted by fervent missionaries who were often sensitive to the native beliefs they encountered. Thus, the temple of Isis at Soissons was rededicated to the Virgin in the fifth century , and the Isis temple of Paris became the site for St Germaine-des-Prés, where an Isis statue was venerated until 1514.[17] The temple of Pallas Athene in Toulouse was rededicated as the Church of La Daurade, where the present Black Virgin replaces the original statue of Athene which was dredged from a lake in 109 BC, when Consul Cepio was seeking the treasure stolen from Delphi by the Gauls.[18]

There are many stories of how Black Madonnas were miraculously discovered, and one wonders whether these were statues of previous veneration or not. Between the Gallo-Roman period when such statues would have been made and the Carolingian period when the Romanesque statues appear, it is thought that the making of momumental statuary ceased. Christian missionaries in Europe were assiduous in the removal of pagan statuary, particularly St Columban who ordered pagan images thrown into Lake Constance.[19] The iconoclast controversy of Eastern Christendom which briefly outlawed the making of any devotional images, scarcely touched the West, which was still embroiled in the basic policing of kingdoms. The second council of Nicea in 787 restored the use of icons, but art needs rich patrons and it was not until the settled reign of Charlemagne that we see a flowering of such work again.

Traditions speak of the finding of Madonnas in caves, such as the Virgin of Monserrat, discovered by shepherds in her hiding place where she had been put for safety during the Moorish incursions.[20] One wonders how many such pagan statues were so concealed, only to be renamed. The cave is undoubtedly the prime temple of the Black Goddess. Oracular caves, incubatory underground chambers and stone vaults are all associated with her worship. Orthodox icons still depict Mary giving birth in a shepherd's hill-cave, with the star of revelation shining down into the darkness both of the cave and of her womb.

There is a long-held tradition that the original Black Virgin of Chartres, Notre Dame Sous Terre (Our Lady Beneath the Earth) was of Druidic derivation. It is true that modern Chartres was once the area of the Carnutes, a Gallic tribe. We know from the writings of Caesar and Pliny that Chartres itself was one of the druidic centres of sacred assembly. The tradition states that the statue had been carved at the orders of a Gallic prince before the birth of Christ and that it was placed in a secret shrine with other pagan statues and became the focus of a prophetic cult. The statue was known always as *Virgo Paritura* (the Virgin about to give birth), despite the fact that the figure held a child in her arms. It was placed in a grotto beneath the medieval cathedral with its own well and altar. Both these features were immured in the seventeenth century when the clergy attempted to discourage the excessive piety of the faithful. The well was the *Puits des Saints Forts* (Well of the Strong Saints) and had healing qualities. The statue was subsequently unceremoniously burnt in the cathedral square on 20th December 1793 during the French Revolution.[21]

The beauty and mystery of Chartres Cathedral is realized in the notion that the cathedral itself is the cavern of the Virgin Wisdom, decorated profusely with images and symbols of her teachings. It is significant that the foundation relic given by Charles the Bald was the veil in which the Virgin had given birth to Christ.[22]

Chartres is aligned, not to the more orthodox east-west axis, but along a north-east axis, so that the midsummer sun lights up the central altar and the length of the nave. The time of greatest light is thus received by the cathedral that housed the image of the Black Mother of the Deep Earth. The Black Stones venerated in Middle Eastern tradition as symbolic of the Black Goddess were more likely to manifest as trees and caves in North European tradition. The sacred tree was a boundary and tribal omphalos, the dwelling of the deity. Black Virgins are frequently discovered roosting like black hens in trees from which they cannot be moved. Artemis is often similarly associated with trees, notably the willow and cedar.[23] The Celtic Goddess of the Grove, or Nemetona, was worshipped in sacred groves of trees, and similar rites are associated with Germanic tribal veneration of Nerthus.

Black Virgins are frequently fiercely territorial, refusing to be moved once they have found the site with which they are happy. When the Bishop of Manresa attempted to move the Virgin of Monserrat to his own cathedral he found that it could not be moved.[24] Another frequent occurence is the way in which Black Virgins see off intruders, as the Madonna of Rocamadour has done throughout her history (see plate 12).[25] She is also renowned for restoring life to unbaptized babies, along with many other European statues including the famous Madonna of Avioth who is also called La Récévresse. The name Avioth is an acrostic of the prayer, 'Hail, Virgin who bringest forth a child', or AVE   O   THeotokos Virgo.[26] During the Middle Ages, unbaptized children were not buried in consecrated ground and were destined for limbo – the state between heaven and hell. The Black Virgin's ability to resuscitate dead children therefore meant their happy reception in paradise.[27]

The stories surrounding the South of France are particularly interesting. Marseilles was the home of the Phoceans who founded it in 600 BC and spread the fame of their replica of the Artemis of Ephesus. It was here, as elsewhere in Europe, that the Isean festival of the *carrus navalis*, or carriage of the ship, took place, which celebrated the launching of Isis' ship at the inundation of the Nile. The myth of the boat – whether it be of the launching of Isis' sacred barque or of the apocryphal journey of the Magdalene[28] – is still remembered in Marseilles, where bakers still make the boat-shaped pastry called *navette* at Candlemas.[29] In French, *navette* also means shuttle, and it betokens both Kore and Neith, the weaving Goddesses. Mary is also the weaver in the *Proto-Evangelium*.[30]

Legend says that Mary Cleopas, Mary Salome, Mary Magdalene, Martha and Lazarus all fled from Palestine and landed at Ratis in France – the town where Isis Pelagia, Artemis and Cybele were worshipped. This site, now called Les-Saintes-Maries-de-la-Mer, is famous for its statue of Sarah le Kali, Black Sarah, the patroness of gypsies worldwide. Sarah was the servant of the saints who fled to Ratis. The gypsies who congregate in Gard at that time of year, annually dip her statue in the sea.[31] Sarah le Kali is not a Black Virgin at all, for her lineage comes through an ancient gypsy tradition which probably connects to India rather than to Europe. Nevertheless, the inclusion of Sarah into the legend of Mary Magdalene reinforces the Sophianic theme of the Black Goddess as the possessor of wisdom and healing.

The potency of the Black Virgin cult has its roots in the native spirituality of Europe; it has rarely sprung out of orthodox Christianity. These empowering statues call out to earthier instincts than those evoked by daily liturgies; they call out also to those who perceive the face of Sophia in the mud beneath our feet as well as to those who see her radiant as starlight. The 'official' Sophianic face of Mary is usually perceived in the *Mater Dolorosa*, a cult that has collected its own distinctive imagery. The Western convention is to view the Divine Feminine only in transcendent terms, as a loving Mother or sweet-faced Virgin. It utterly denies other expressions. Despite this, we can still see the older understandings arising, albeit unconsciously. This polarization left room for only the conventional Madonna and Child or Mater Dolorosa at the foot of the Cross,

12 *The Black Virgin* This twelfth century statue from Rocamadour in France is one of the very oldest of the original Black Madonnas of Europe. The statues of the Black Virgin depict the real potency and help which the Blessed Virgin Mary can offer, and are still highly venerated today. The often saccharine images of Mary do not inspire such confidence or veneration. Photo by Jennifer Begg.

weeping for her son. Upon Mary is polarized all the sorrow of the world, drawing upon the saying in the temple: 'Truly a sword will pierce your soul'. The sorrowful mother of Mediterranean spirituality is well-established in the sequence, *Stabat Mater*, written by Jacopone da Todi, a Franciscan of the twelfth century, which remains the epitome of liturgical sorrow. It is sung on the feast of the Seven Dolours and on Good Friday in Catholic churches.

Our Lady of Czestochowa in Poland is herself a late form of Black Virgin icon. As a miraculous image, it is reputed to have averted many disasters. She also, inadvertently and significantly, become a Sorrowful Mother by the fact that her image is marred by two sabre-strokes across her cheek, giving her a grievous aspect. She was carried into battle as the Queen of Peace by Polish troops and suffered this outrage at the hands of a Hussite trooper.[32] Her scarred face has been critical in the re-emergence of Polish identity in the last few years, especially when members of the outlawed Polish union, Solidarity, were forbidden to wear their own distinctive emblem. In retaliation, union members and Solidarity symphathisers started to wear the image of Our Lady of Czestochowa on their lapels. The election of a Polish pope, John Paul II, to the Vatican has also been influential in bringing this Black Madonna to a wider audience.

In the *Salve Regina*, the Sorrowful Mother is addressed: 'to thee do we send up our sighs, mourning and weeping in this vale of tears.'[33] But the world may be 'a vale of soul-making as well as a peril of the soul,'[34] a place to find a glorious dwelling or else a makeshift shelter. Sorrows it may have, but the potent presence of the Black Virgin gives it purpose.

Mother of the House of Wisdom

As the Shekinah became associated with the people of Israel, so did Mary become cognate with the Church as Ecclesia.

The Shepherd of Hermas, a text which was considered canonical to the early Christian scriptures, features Ecclesia for the first time. Hermas, a freed slave, had three visions on his way, significantly, to Cumae. He saw: 'a white chair of great size made of snow-white wool; and there came a woman, old and clothed in shining garments with a book in her hand, and she sat down . . . and greeted me.'[35] She read to him from her book and related, in words which echo both *Timaeus* and *Proverbs*, how God created the world and the church 'by his own wisdom and forethought'. The Greek originals are *Sophia* and *Pronoia* – the Gnostic causes of creation. Her two subsequent appearances caused Hermas some puzzlement, since she appeared successively younger each time. He was told that her appearances parelleled the state of his soul which had been 'youthened' by Christian hope. After the second vision, he enquired of an angel whether she was the Sibyl. The angel replied; '(She is) the Church . . . she was created the first of all things. For this reason is she old; and for her sake was the world established.'[36] Finally, Hermas saw Ecclesia attired as a bride. This was her final manifestation, although Hermas had many other allegorical visions to guide his Christian progress.

This text shows Ecclesia, like Wisdom, as preexistent, as an old woman. During the visions, she assumed younger manifestations until, finally, she appeared as the bride adorned for her husband. Hermas' reasonable association between his vision and the Sibyl was no mistake, since he was traveling to Cumae, the abode of the Sibylline oracle, and the author clearly intended to draw upon the reputation of the Sibyl of Cumae to support his own Ecclesia. Like a sibyl, she interpreted Hermas' visions.

As we explore the ways in which Sophia becomes attached to the Christian tradition, it is advisable to be aware that Mother Church, Ecclesia, can be a crabby old woman who likes to leave Sophia out of things if she can. 'Mother Church . . . did not much like it to be known that she divided the responsibility (of caring for the world) with her twin, though sometimes her better nature prevailed and she admitted in bursts of generous homage, that she couldn't possibly manage without Sophia.'[37]

The idea of a prior maternal figure haunts Christianity: it may be the shadow of a pagan Goddess, it may be the extra-liturgical presence of Black Virgins. Even in the symbolism of Ecclesia, we find a corresponding image of Synagogia, or Synagogue, who precedes and opposes Ecclesia, often spiking her effectiveness by insistence upon former tradition. Synagogia represented for Christians the Judaic tradition, often seen as threatening.

Throughout pre-Christian European spirituality, the Goddess was always present as the Great Mother. Cybele, Rhea and Danu reigned, among others. Medieval Christianity did not allow this role to lapse, but substituted St Anne, the mother of the Virgin. This cult did not arise until 600 AD in the East churches and until 800 in the West. It went through an amazing development in the fifteenth and sixteenth centuries. St Anne was the patron of fertile child-bearing and her status of matriarch remained unchallenged. Devotees of St Anne reported: 'She always grants him what he requires of her', and 'anyone who is in distress and calls in devotion to St Anne becomes restful and confident.'[38] She is iconographically depicted teaching the Virgin from her Book of Wisdom. She has a sovereign, primordial quality about her, which is enhanced when we realize that, if Mary is the Mother of God, St Anne is his Grandmother. St Anne has been accepted in Brittany perhaps more than in any other place, where she doubtless found fertile images in which to seed. The Bretons derive their origins from Britain where the ancient ancestress of the Gods is called Don or Danu. High places in Britain are frequently named after St Anne.

The education of the Virgin was a frequent subject for iconographic depiction, showing St Anne teaching Mary to read. When we look upon a statue of St Anne with the Virgin upon her lap we are seeing Mary Sophia seated in the lap of the Black Goddess, learning from the Book of Life. At the turn of the Christian millennia, it is now we who sit in the lap of Mary and learn to read from the Book of Wisdom.

The idea of Goddess as enclosure is at the heart of the Sophianic myth. The seven-pillared temple of *Proverbs* 9 provided the model of the Church of the Holy Spirit – a sapiential Church. Ecclesia, as the Church became familiarly represented, appears in Christian iconography as a woman of great beauty, a bride of Christ, an image developed fully by St Hildegard.

Mary is herself the Ecclesia of the Trinity, as a statue at the Musée de Cluny shows. The statue is really a three-dimensional tryptich and Mary opens up to reveal God the Father supporting the cross on which hangs God the Son, while the pendant dove-like Spirit hovers over the Crucified. Like the icons which depict Mary as Theotokos, revealing the child immanent in her womb, this statue confirms the idea of Mary as a dwelling-place or Ecclesia. She surrounds and encompasses God as easily as she assumes the concepts of Mystical Body of the Church and Christianity's World-Soul.

St Isadore of Seville (560–636) summarized Mary's role as Ecclesia: 'Mary signifies the Church who, although espoused to Christ, conceived us of the Holy Ghost and gives birth to us as a Virgin.'[39]

Ecclesia's trinitarian origins are here lauded by Gerhoch of Reichersberg: 'Glory be to the Father, who created her matter from nothing through the Word; and to the Son, who together with the Father built her from the fore-ordained matter; and to the Holy Spirit, who has already consecrated her foundations and in the end will yet consecrate her whole structure.'[40]

This theme of matter which will be redeemed into a transcendent form is echoed in the antithesis of the mourning Jerusalem and the celestial Jerusalem. Mary/Ecclesia is a two-fold structure: the geomantic guise of the Black Virgin who is the prima materia – both the heavenly Jerusalem and the bricks of its wall. Sophia is the one who proves matter with its formation, as co-creator of life, like the qabalistic hypostasis, Binah, whose magical image is Mother of Form, but who has a daughter, Malkuth, who manifests her mother's image in the world. It is so that the Black Virgin appears most often in crypts, not on the main altar, for she is the withdrawn powerhouse from which all needs are answered. The manifest answer appears more often as the transcendent Virgin of the Lady Chapel, and it is usually she who receives the thanks.

The temple of the Black Goddess is hidden beneath the church of Sophia. To find that holy house and dwell within it has been the ambition of many mystics. It is also an image which has been utlized throughout Christianity.

In her song *Columba Aspexit*, Hildegard of Bingen praises her patron saint, Maximin, in audacious masonic imagery which pictures Sophia as the nurturer in the crypt:

Inter vos fulget hic artifex	This architect shines among you,
paries templi	this temple wall,
qui desideravit alas aquile	he who longed for eagle's wings
osculando nutricem Sapientam	kissing Wisdom, his nurse,
in gloriosa fecunditate	in the glorious cincture of
Ecclesie.	Ecclesia.[41]

The holy houses of both Walsingham in Norfolk and Loreto in Ancona, said to be replicas of Mary's own house in Nazareth, are the focus of significant Marian pilgrimage. The house of Loreto is supposed to have flown from Nazareth to its present site in 1294. Walsingham is an earlier devotional site, established in 1061 by Lady Richeldis after a vision.[42]

Metaphors of Mary as temple for the Holy Spirit or for Wisdom are complex for the non-liturgical mind to grapple with. This tradition is not just a veneration of Mary because of her chastity, emptiness or receptivity: a kind of *tabula rasa* or vacant house is not intended here. Indeed, the image persists right up to our own time. The recent encyclical *Lumen Gentium* 53 says that Mary has had 'conferred upon her the highest charge and dignity, which is to be the mother of the Son of God and therefore the preferentially loved daughter of the father and the temple of the Holy Spirit'. The restatement of Mary as Theotokos, God's Seat or dwelling, enthrones the notion of humanity – of whom the Virgin is a full member – as the dwelling place of the Divine. But this mystery cannot be fully accomodated into Goddess spirituality because the Goddess of Wisdom has her own divinity and is not human, though she may choose to take human form.

Like the Shekinah, Mary as Ecclesia becomes the container of creation, a kind of World-Soul in her own right. She also takes on the throne symbolism of Isis.

The Litany of Loreto addresses the Blessed Virgin as 'Seat of Wisdom, House of Gold, and Health of the Sick.'[43] As we have seen, the Hellenic name of Isis derives from the Egyptian *Au Set*, or throne. Both Isis and Mary, despite their seeming independence, are literally the power behind the throne. Mary is said to be the throne itself. This idea of establishing power from the lap of the Goddess of Wisdom runs throughout Christian symbolism, though it is not acknowledged as such. One medieval inscription on a statue of the Virgin reads: 'In gremio Matris: resident sapientia Patris', or 'On the lap of the Mother sits the Father's wisdom'. Here, of course, Jesus represents Wisdom.

In the mid-fourth century, St Epiphanius inveighed against a set of female Thracian heretics called Collyridians, who worshipped Mary as Queen of Heaven: 'they adorn a chair or a square throne, spread a linen cloth over it, and, at a certain solemn time, place bread on it and offer it in the name of Mary; and all partake of this bread.'[44] This extra-liturgical practice seems to be an echo both of the eucharist and of earlier devotion to the Semitic Goddess Asherah, against whom the prophet Jeremiah similarly inveighed.

A distinctive form of Madonna and Child statue, called 'the Throne of Wisdom' or *sedes sapitientiae*, developed around the mid-tenth century AD. These Romanesque statues exude a hieratic stillness and innate authority which is absent from the more naturalistic Madonnas of the middle ages. The Virgin wears a tunic covered by a paenula, a full overgarment, with intricate pleating. Her head is usually mantled with this garment or separately veiled. She holds the man-like Child on her lap and has the attitude of a queen. This statue is the Western icon of the *Theotokos*, or God-bearer. She is seated upon a stool or throne which often has seven pillars about its back, in token of Wisdom's temple.

Patristic writing had early identified Mary as the throne of God, but whether or not this tradition was based on an unconscious imitation of Isis as the throne of the Pharoah is pure speculation. John of Damascus (675–749) recalled the vision of *Isaiah* 6:1 when he addressed Mary as 'Hail, throne lifted up on high in glory, living throne, representing in thyself the throne of God.'[45] Both Peter Damian (*d.* 1072) and Guibert de Nogent (*d.* 1125) both allude to the throne of Solomon described in *I Kings* 10:18–20. Peter Damian likens the ivory to Mary's virginity and after describing the gold which sheaths the throne, concludes: 'in like manner God sheathed the Virgin and was sheathed in the Virgin.'[46] This extraordinarily subtle image of containment and inspiriting evokes the idea of Mary as dwelling-place or temple.

The image of the throne was very important to Eastern iconography where it was called the *etimasia*, where it specifically represented the throne of Christ's second coming. Normally the Book and Cross were placed upon it as emblematic of Christ's action. By analogy, in the Throne of Wisdom iconography, Mary would parallel the throne of the *Etimasia* while Christ, holding the Book, is actually present. The significance of this will be discussed again in Chapter 14.

The oracular, or prophetic, chair is a reminder of an earlier Sophianic vocation, that of sibyl.

The Way of the Black Mother

The voice of the Black Goddess may have been temporarily stifled, but her actions were clear enough through the medium of the Black Virgins of Europe. It is interesting to see that, at the turn of the millennium, everyone suddenly evinced an interest in what the Black Goddess had to say. It was then that the old priestesses and sibyls were consulted, those who were still in touch with the earth and spoke her unflinching truth to fearful ears.

During the transition from Goddess to God's Mother, the Black Virgin became the voice of the people in a particular way. She answered their needs most directly by miracles of healing and material provision; and when all was lost, she was the one who received the soul at death into her warm lap. She was the intercessory Virgin who held open the doors of heaven – the Recévresse whose way was dark but welcoming.

We know thee not, nor the way of thee, O Queen!
But we bring thee what thou lovedst of old, and forever:
The white flowers of our forests and the red flowers of our
bodies!
Take them and slay not, O Slayer![47]

So writes Fiona MacLeod (William Sharp's pseudonym) in his play, *The Black Madonna*. The primeval worship offered to the Black Mother is both simple and profound. Something in the human psyche understands that while God may turn a deaf ear and the angels may be about more important tasks, the Black Virgin will always listen to them. She is near, she is a neighbour. She will aid in necessity.

With the veneration of the Black Mother goes the apophatic spirituality developed by Dionysius the Areopagite – a way of unknowing, but not of unwisdom. The Black Virgin is our Western image of Kali. She may appear as a mother and child, but her awesome power is just as dynamic.

Latterly, we have need of the Black Mother. 'When the heart of the matter is death – whether nuclear or viral – it is to the dark guardian spirit of the earth and of our true nature that we must turn. As least we in the West now have an image for her.'[48] The primal and urgent needs of our time evoke the Black Goddess among us.

We have seen how the role of the pythoness suffered diminution and was subsumed into the cult of Apollo. Similarly, the sibyls were also turned to Jewish and Christian use. The old voices of the earth did not cease to speak the plain truth.

The Christian sibylline tradition arises out of the ancient model. The influence of the Christian sibyl can be traced to Virgil's Fourth Eclogue. The sibyl still sits in her cave, to be consulted, just as the Black Virgin inhabits her crypt – the submerged, instinctual and forgotten Goddess of Wisdom.

'Foremost among the ladies of sovereign dignity are the wise sibyls, most filled with wisdom . . . (God) placed in them such a profound and advanced prophecy that what they said did not seem to be prognostications of the future but rather chronicles of past events which had already taken place, so clear and intelligible were their pronouncements and writings.'[49] So wrote Christine de Pizan. During the Middle Ages, the sibyls enjoyed a prestige which was not frequently accorded to women; that of actually fulfilling a prophetic vocation. Because of their legendary existence, the sibyls were frequently made into mouthpieces for all manner of prophetic utterances. Because the sibyl lives from before all time to the end of time she may thus utter prophetically.

The original sibyl was from Erythrae in Ionia, but her archetype was replicated many times, until many places boasted their own 'divine voice'. The voice of the sibyl has ever been a true voice of the earth, of the Black Goddess. Hers is a hard and warning voice, for she is diagnostician of the times.

The Sibylline books were kept by the Vestal Virgins, but both Jewish and Christian tradition boasted their own Sibylline books. The Christian sibyl Orphically declaims: 'The world is my origin but my soul have I drawn from the stars.'[50] These sibyls draw upon their native traditions, as well as foretelling the apocalyptic fate of the Jewish and Christian traditions. But there are other voices of the Black Goddess, in Northern Europe. These stem from the primal pre-Christian traditions.

The mouthpieces of the Black Goddess are invariably, although not always, female elders, *shamankas*, *volvas*, ancient priestesses of the old ways who guard the ancestral realm of knowledge.

In the Irish text *The Second Battle of Mag Tuiread*, the Goddess, Morrighan, was asked to proclaim the victory of the Tuatha de Danaan after they had defeated their rival gods, the Fomorians. The Morrighan is a Black Goddess, responsible, like Kali, for reeving the bodies of the slain. In this text she acted like a sibyl and Black Goddess combined. As the mediator between all worlds she proclaimed the victory 'to the royal hills of Ireland, to the armies of the *sidhe*, to the principle rivers and their estuaries. "What is the news," said the hills and rivers to her, and she replied:

> "Peace up to heaven;
> Heaven down to earth,
> Earth under heaven,
> Strength in everyone."'

Then she began prophesying the end of the world:

> "I see a world which displeases me:
> summer without flowers,
> cows without milk,
> women without modesty,
> men without courage . . .
> trees without fruit,
> sea without fish;

bad advice in elders,
evil judgement from judges . . .

A bad time:
son betrays father,
daughter betrays mother."[51]

Having given her news to the land, the Morrighan gave back
the prophecy of the land itself to the Tuatha de Danaan. The
admonitory voice of the Black Goddess makes it clear: 'You may
have triumphed briefly, but this is still to come, beware.'

The tenth century Icelandic *Voluspa* gives us a clear prophecy
about the ending and beginning of the world. Odin woke the
volva, or sibyl, from her mound to question her about forthcoming
events. She told him that the world would end in winter, rocks and
mountains would fall, volcanic eruptions would devastate the land
until only the ash would be left. 'The sun will be dark and there
will be no stars in the sky. The earth will sink into the sea.'[52] This
is the prophecy of Ragnarok, the Scandanavian *apocatastasis*.

But her prophecy was not entirely without hope: 'The earth will
rise again out of the water, fair and green. The eagle will fly over
cataracts, swoop into the thunder and catch fish under crags. Corn
will ripen in fields that were never sown.'[53] She told how some of
the gods would survive, as would two humans – Lif and Lifthrasir
(Life and Life's Desire) – who would hide themselves deep within
the world-tree, Yggdrasil. Then the gods would sit down and 'turn
by turn, they will call up such memories . . . as are known to
them alone.' Slowly everything would reconstitute itself into a
new pattern. 'Lif and Lifthrasir will have children. Their children
will bear children. There will be life and new life everywhere on
earth. That was the end; and this is the beginning.'[54]

Let us now take a brief respite from the Mediterranean and
sojourn awhile with the Sophia of the North, the matchless lady
of Celtic and Arthurian tradition, the Grail-Goddess.

═══ 11 ═══

THE GRAIL GODDESS

... and the kingdom became dead and desert, for they lost the voices of the wells and the damsels that were therein.

The Elucidation

The Race of Kundry

The traditions of Northern Europe that cherished the Black Virgins also preserved their native pagan survivals of the Goddess of Wisdom. These survivals, or heresies, acted as Sophia's safety net in this time of transition between native and Christian belief. The method of transmission was potent and popular, for Sophia took the way of the story which spoke to every heart: the quest for the empowerment of the Grail.

The Grail legends are popularly thought to derive solely from Christian apocryphal sources and the Grail itself is analogous to the Cup of the Last Supper or to the chalice in which Joseph of Arimathea caught the blood and water from Christ's side while he hung on the cross. However, although the Christian legends were later added into the Grail tradition, the Grail itself derives from much earlier, pre-Christian sources. Its guardian is none other than a Black Goddess who has the interests of the earth at heart: this Goddess of Wisdom has the ability to change into a transcendently beautiful woman. Only fleeting glimpses of this Sophianic figure remain in the Christianized legends, who have a tendency to separate her into two distinct characters, but the original Black Goddess who is also Sophia can be glimpsed in Kundry,[1] the Black Maiden,[2] and the Bald Damsel,[3] among others. The character of Kundry is familiar from Wagner's opera based on Wolfram von Eschenbach's Grail-text, *Parzival*. Wagner, in the tradition of the German romantic movement, was guilty of diminishing her power and enslaving her to the evil Klingsor. This is something which has bedevilled most appearances of the Black Goddess, who is relegated to the service of evil, the Devil, acquainted with malignant witchcraft and so on.

Kundry appears as the Dark Woman of Knowledge in Northern mythology, a figure of skilful wisdom. She is the Grail-messenger, dark-faced and mysterious, who admonishes the Grail seekers and finally comes in her white wimple decorated with golden doves – the Sophianic sign of the Grail's achievement – and is hailed as a delivering Goddess.[4] She is based on one of the most ancient European Goddesses, the Cailleach (pronounced 'Kal'yak'). This Scottish Gaelic word is about the only respectful term meaning 'old woman' which does not have the derogatory emphasis of 'hag' 'crone' etc.

The Cailleach is the Black Goddess. St Adamnan's *Life of St Columba* relates that the river Lochaidh in Lochaber, Scotland was sacred to the *Nigra Dea*, the Black Goddess.[5] Rites were performed in her honour until very recently: 'at the well of St Declan, Ardmore, County Waterford, about a century ago masses of people assembled annually on December 22nd, crawled beneath a hollowed stone and then drank of the well. It was surmounted by the image of a female figure which is described as being *like the pictures of Callee (Kali), the black goddess of Hindostan*. The Catholic priests actually whipped the folk away from the spot, but to no purpose.'[6] 'There shall always be some great Cailleach among them' is said of the people of the Corco Duibhne in West Kerry. It is a true saying among the people of North-West Europe, for the Cailleach is the grandmother of the European native tradition – the experienced matriarch who initiates her grandchildren into wisdom.

The Cailleach is an established character within Celtic folk tradition – sometimes a hag, sometimes an admonitory maiden – she is a teacher and instructor in wisdom. She is but one aspect of the Goddess of the Land who, in the Grail legend, is manifest as the Wasteland. The land is nearly always called after a Goddess. The Romans consistently recognized the genius loci and accorded respect to Britannia, perceived as the Goddess of the Land. This figure, attired in the attributes of Minerva, graces the British fifty pence coin. The Goddess of the Land, or Sovereignty as she is called, literally empowers the one who will aid the land and accept it exactly as it appears. Hence, Sovereignty always appears first in her challenging and often judgemental Cailleach aspect, although she may also change into the transcendently lovely Grail-Keeper whom most of the Grail seekers would seek to marry, in the old marriage of the land scenario.

The Black Goddess shows her changing faces in the Celtic Goddess of the Land. The Cailleach transforms into the beautiful

209

13 *The Grail Goddess* The native British Goddess of the Land is shown here as the guardian of the Grail. In Celtic tradition, empowering cups and cauldrons of rebirth are commonplace manifestations of the Goddess's power. Misuse of the earth creates a wasteland. In Christian tradition, the Grail became associated with the Cup of the Last Supper, itself a redemptive cup. The two traditions were interwoven to create the Arthurian way of wisdom: the Grail Quest. Picture entitled *Goddess of Sovereignty* by Stuart Littlejohn.

maiden as Sovereignty. She has the secret of the well of youth, which she keeps guarded near Loch Ba on Mull, which keeps her endlessly young. As the Cailleach has lived many centuries, she has hundreds of children. She usually manifests at wells, which she guards, not allowing any to drink until they have given her a kiss. Of course, most refuse. But the man who kisses her receives the accolade – not of knighthood – but of the Goddess of Sovereignty herself, the Grail-Keeper, the Queen of the Hallows.[7]

Marriage to the Cailleach underlies most Celtic quest stories. *The Marriage of Gawain and Ragnall* is a later medieval variant of the story which is now well-known. In protecting Arthur's honour, Gawain undertook to marry the hag, Ragnall, who answered the question of 'what women most desire'. On their wedding night, he embraced her and she turned into a beautiful maiden. Gawain was given the choice of having her fair by day and foul by night, or foul by night and fair by day. With the intuition of a Goddess initiate, he bade *her* choose: this is the answer to the question, for women desire sovereignty over men.[8]

The ancient analogue of this story is the sacred marriage of the Celtic king to the land, a theme which is found from India to Ireland in different tales. The candidate king is ttested in a forest and encounters a hag guarding a well. He desires water with the urgency of one parched, but she will not permit him one drop until he offers to kiss or lie with her. If he does so, she will change her Cailleach face into that of a radiant maiden who, as the Goddess of Sovereignty, bestows the land's guardianship into his care. The king must accept the land as it really is, with all its imperfections and problems; his contract with the land through the medium of the Goddess of Sovereignty is sealed in the water from the well which she guards, itself an analogue of the Grail.[9]

This question is a very important one for our time. 'What do women most desire?' Has the answer changed in our age? One of the most important questions of the Grail quest, is 'Whom does the Grail serve?' Whoever can answer that question is usually the Grail-winner. However, the juxtaposition of the two questions is significant here. The Grail does not serve the self-server: neither are women available on the demand of men. The energy which is available from both Grail and Woman must be freely and honourably offered *in an appropriate way*. It cannot be stolen or appropriated or won by trickery. The answer lies in the nature of the exchange. The Grail, like Sophia herself, cannot remain in the presence of injustice and hatred. Women do not usually have Sophia's option of disappearing. The conditions under which they can fulfil their desires *must first be prefaced by freedom to act for themselves*. When this is granted, then the answer to both questions can be seen as 'love'. The medieval story of *Gawain and Ragnall* looks back to the old Celtic king-making stories in its answer of 'sovereignty over men'. This answer can only truly be given by the Goddess herself, unless women are prepared to enter into a manipulative and 'power-over' contract with men similar to the one under which they have suffered at male hands. The 'sovereignty' of Ragnall's answer is the basic freedom of independence.

We may compare this experience with that of Tannhauser at Venusberg, the place where the Norse Holda, or Hel, became associated with the Classical Venus – the hidden Goddess in the mountain who knows everything and whose embrace confers the transmission of knowledge.[10] The hidden Goddess, similarly, lies dormant in our society, waiting for seekers who will learn from her wisdom. This is why so many Celtic kingly candidates had to embrace the Cailleach.[11] And if they did not actually lie with her, there were other challenges to face.

The Black Goddess was one of the original Grail-Keepers, when the Grail was still a cauldron. She was a queen of the Underworld who had to be encountered in a battle of knowledge and motherwit. The successful initiate became the new knowledge-holder for that generation. The prime figure associated with this myth is the British Goddess Ceridwen who brewed a cauldron of knowledge to give to her ugly son, Afagddu. She set Little Gwion to tend it, but some of the hot liquor splashed out onto his thumb so that he put it into his mouth to cool it, consequently receiving all knowledge. The story tells of his transformations into many animal shapes until he finally became a grain of wheat and was devoured by the furious Ceridwen who had taken the form of a black hen. Nine months later, Gwion was reborn of her womb as the seer-poet, Taliesin.[12]

This myth is an allegory of initiation into wisdom. The empowering draught which Gwion imbibed from the cauldron is like that fleeting sip of the Grail achieved by Grail seekers. In both instances, the vessel was withdrawn or its contents rendered worthless, as in the case of Ceridwen's cauldron where the remaining contents become poisonous. Ceridwen is shown as the initiatory Mistress of Life, Sheila na Gig, the hag with the cauldron whose womb became a tomb for Gwion and a womb for Taliesin, whose cauldron became the cup of rebirth and enlightenment.

The notion of a vessel of redemption runs throughout esoteric thought. The Gnostic *krater* or spirit-filled bowl of Poimandres,[13] and the alchemical *vas* are both analogues of the Grail and the cauldron: all are wombs wherein rebirth takes place.

The Cailleach takes her name from the *caille*, or veil, which also typified the later Celtic priestess, the nun, whose prophetic duty remained to observe the rites, to keep the fire burning. On the Celtic wheel of the year, the Cailleach cedes place at Imbolc (Candlemas) to another aspect of the Goddess of the Land who represents the Celtic face of Wisdom.[14]

The Irish Goddess, Brighid, as both Goddess and saint, links the pagan Celtic and medieval Christian traditions in much the same way as the Celto-Arthurian stories of the wisdom-bearing cauldron and the Grail. Brighid acts as the bridge between Celtic and Christian cultures, and is shared by each as a common metaphor for the Goddess of Wisdom.

Brighid was the patron of healing, poetry and smithcraft. These triple aspects associate her with both practical and inspired wisdom: she was the healing in the draught, the inspiration in poetry and the warmth of the smith's fire. Brighid had many aspects. As warrior-maiden she is still nationally venerated as a symbol of justice and authority in Britain. In Northern Britain, Brighid was worshipped as Brigantia. A Romano-British statue from Birrens, Northumberland, shows her with the attributes of Minerva – the shield, spear and *gorgoneion*, crowned with the mural crown of Cybele.[15] This image was assimilated into British tradition as Brittania, the Roman personification of Britain, still present upon British coinage.

The Romans fused Minerva with another British Goddess at Aquae Sulis, modern Bath, where the hot healing mineral waters of the Celtic Goddess Sulis rise to feed the Roman baths. Sulis Minerva and Brighid have a lot in common. The Classical writer, Solinus, writes of the 'hot baths, finely kept to the use of men, the sovereign of which baths is that of the Goddess Minerva (Sul), in whose chapel the fire burneth continually, and the coals do never turn into ashes, but as soon as the embers are dead, it is turned into balls of stone.'[16] Minerva, or Athene, was patron of women, weaving and spinning. Her peplum or mantle was exhibited as an object of veneration at the Acropolis. Brighid is invariably also called the Mistress of the Mantle, a palladium garment which is invoked frequently in Celtic prayers.

Perpetual fire is a symbol of the Northern Sophia. To be a fire-keeper is still an honoured title among native clans and was a role which usually fell to women. There are many rituals concerning the making and keeping of fires in Celtic tradition: in all of them, Brighid is invoked to help this procedure. Brighid's fires continued to be fed at Kildare, the monastic city of St Brigit, where the sacred fire was enclosed by a thorn hedge which could not be penetrated by men. Gerald of Wales, in his *Itinerary of Ireland* speaks of the sacred fire which was kept at Kildare and had not been extinguished since the saint's day. The fire was tended by nineteen nuns and on the twentieth night the last one would say: 'Brigit, guard your fire. This is your night'. Brigit was then responsible for keeping the fire enclosed and alight.[17]

The continuous occupation of the site by a strong abbess who was believed to be mystically attuned to the Goddess/Saint remained until 1132 when an Abbess of Kildare was raped by the troops of Dermot MacMurrough. Dermot wanted one of his own kinswomen to take over Brigit's position, and the rape was perpetrated in order to disqualify the reigning abbess. The ordination of Brighit had caused a stir in orthodox circles and ever after empowered her abbatical daughters; after the twelfth century rape, Kildare lost much of its power.[18] The fires were at last quenched by Henry VIII's men during the Reformation.

St Brigit's shrine at Kildare is probably a Christian survival of an older college of native vestal priestesses, many of whom were scattered about the land as guardians of sacred wells, hills, caves and trees in much the same way that the Greeks had sibyls and priestesses dedicated to the numens of the land. There are many such sisterhoods in British traditions, usually ninefold in number, like the sisterhood of the cauldron of the underworld, Annwn, who blow at it to cool it with their breath. There are also the Nine Witches of Gloucester who give Peredur, the Celtic Perceval, his weapon-training.[19] The Avalonian sisterhood of Morgen (later called Morgan le Fay) and her eight sisters is also part of this tradition.[20]

The sibyls and pprophets of Christian tradition are paralleled by the Celtic tradition of *bansidhe* and *filidh*: the Woman of the Fairy Hills and the Seer-poets. These mystical sisterhoods and brother-hoods preserve the poetic function of the Goddess Brighid. By their prophetic storytelling and fire-keeping, by their remembrance of the words, songs and actions of ancient tradition they keep alive the Sophianic lore of North-West Europe. Like Plato's daemons, they inhabit the realms between the worlds, sometimes numinously overlying certain places in our world wherein we can hear the initiatory story of Wisdom, told over and over without end in the perpetual choir of their chanting.

The Grail Maidens

If we are looking for the hidden face of Sophia, there can be no better place to find it than in this dense, covert story which was, nonetheless, one of the most important and popular stories of the Middle Ages. The Church, while giving no sanction as such to the Grail tradition, nevertheless never banned it. Its storytellers were too skilful for the tale of the wandering Grail to die.

The twelfth century renaissance polarized the crystal clarity of rational thought against the 'dense symbolic undergrowth of Arthurian romance.'[21] In this forest scenario, the *Celtica terra* of the cosmologist poet Bernardus Silvestris, many extraordinary scenes are enacted. The druidic groves of Britain and Gaul become the places of Arthurian empowerment, the Grail quest.

The Grail legends arise out of the oral tradition of storytelling and spirituality of the great forests of North-West Europe, whose greatest exponents lived within the Celtic countries. Here the spoken word had a currency and immediacy which the written word was not to achieve until the era of mass literacy.[22]

One of these myths is retained in the mysterious medieval Grail text *L'Elucidation*.[23] It concerns the Damsels of the Wells who, in a time prior to King Arthur, would emerge from the wells and offer food and a drink from their golden cups and so minister to travellers. However, King Amangons raped one of the damsels and his men followed his example by raping the others, so that no well-maidens would issue forth as before. They also stole away the golden cups for their own service. From this time, the land was laid waste and desolate and no-one could find the Court of the Rich Fisherman, or earthly paradise. At this time also 'the voices of the wells' were lost, which represented the voice of the Goddess of Land.

After Arthur had instituted the Round Table, the story of Amangons' outrage came to the ears of the Knights of the Round Table. They swore that they would not rest until they had avenged the Damsels of the Wells and erased the kin of Amangons from the earth. Despite their good intentions, they could neither hear the voices of the wells nor see any damsels. They set off in quest of the evil knights and eventually came upon a mysterious company wandering in the forest, comprised of knights and maidens. Capturing one of their number, the Round Table knights listened to their story. The mysterious company were the descendants of the Damsels of the Wells and of King Amangons and his men. They were fated to wander the earth until the Court of Joy was found, where the Grail should be achieved.

The knights then realized the fruitlessness of their vengeance quest: to kill Amangons' kin was to kill the children of the Damsels also. They thereupon decided to quest for the Court of the Rich Fisherman and to find the Joy which was prophesied. One knight finally managed to win through to that hallowed place and asked the Grail question correctly, whereupon the wasteland was restored to its former fruitfulness.

This profoundly moving story serves as the pre-Christian prequel to the medieval Grail legend as we know it. The Damsels of the Wells are the sibylline 'voices of the wells', voices of Sophia in her aspect of World-Soul. This inability to hear what the earth is saying has typified our own century. Only now are a few ecologists and mystics listening hard to hear what she says, and to win through to the Court of Joy, so saving us from Wasteland.

The descendants of the Damsels and Amangons can only wander and tell their story, until others are inspired to act. In this way, they represent the voices of the wells but, because of their mixed ancestry, they are powerless to bring the Grail to manifestation and heal the wasteland, as they are only messengers who are themselves in need.

The Damsels of the Wells are the original Grail-guardians and their nourishment is freely available. Dwelling in wells and rivers, they were the sisters of Tiamat. After their rape, not only were their spiritual services no longer available, but the rivers of the land dried up and all became the barren Wasteland. These watery damsels, familiar to us as Ladies of the Lake, korrighans or Melusines, are the signature of water: as Wolfram remarks: 'We see by means of water.'[24] The visionary ability of the Goddess to help us communicate with what really matters is desperately lacking from our world, which is without the assuaging waters of imagination and insight: qualities which are needed for the task of restoration. It is only by an initial kenosis of suffering and loss, the experience of Wasteland, that we can gain the satisfaction of the Grail's plerosis.

The Grail and its Celtic analogues frequently appears as the assuager of physical need and hunger. It serves the food which one most desires; if food for one is put into Gwyddno's cauldron, food for a hundred will be taken out of it; no coward can eat of the cauldron of Diwrnach. This simple answering of bodily needs is the task of the Grail-Goddess, who disdains duality: if something is good for the body, it is also good for the soul. The object of the Grail quest is not the possession of a physical cup which can then be displayed in a museum, it is a more subtle, less definable quest. If we look deeper into the earlier Grail legends, we find that the object of the quest was not the physical cup but the cup's bearer: that the Grail and the Grail Maiden were able to give the same experience, in a non-dual sense. Parzival's pagan half-brother, Feirfitz, seated at the banquet which celebrated the Grail's achievement, could not see the Grail at all, only Repanse de Schoy, the Grail-bearer.[25] Similarly, Peredur, the Celtic Perceval, fell into a revery upon seeing the blood of a wild duck lying in the snow as a raven feasted on the body. The combination of the red, black and white put him in mind of 'the lady he loves best'; since he was a virgin, he must have been thinking of the Grail-Goddess, to whom he became contracted in the person of the Empress his wife.[26]

We trivialize the Grail-quest if we think of it only in terms of a spiritual attainment. It is nothing other than Sophia's sign of wholeness, where duality is restored to unity, where the fragmentations of the Fall are mended.

The Christian paradigm of the Fall surrounds the fruit of the Tree of the Knowledge of Good and Evil. In Celtic tradition, there is no such duality. The apple is rather the gift of the Blessed Islands of the West, of Avalonian healing. Wisdom must be acquired first hand – it must be tasted – and it is so that both Fionn Mac Cumhaill, the Irish hero, and Taliesin, the poetic protegé of the British Goddess, Ceridwen, both acquired their prodigious wisdom by means of tasting. Both Peredur and Feirfitz ended up marrying the Grail-bearer, tasting their Grail at first hand, in the manner of the Celtic sacred marriage. It is only the later Grail legends which stress the attainment of a heavenly vessel which gives healing to the wasteland and, in the case of Galahad, a nirvanic attainment in the Otherworldly city of Sarras. The necessity of sexual experience for knowledge still underlies the earliest myths: it is a pre-Christian Celtic response of people unacquainted with sin, who believed that, in the Blessed Otherworldly Islands, worldly visitants and faery people coupled without guilt.

The loss of Paradise and the absence of Wisdom's empowerment are the twin themes underlying the Grail quest. Loss of paradise betokens a fall into dualism. The achievement of the Grail is the reassimilation of humanity into creation in a loving bond of kinship. Consequently, the themes of spiritual and blood kinship are strong within the Grail legends. Those who have supped from Ceridwen's cauldron or from the Grail are knitted together by ties stronger than those of blood kinship – they are brothers and sisters of the cauldron or the Grail Family, kindred of Sophia.

These analogues are blended into the later medieval Christian Grail legends, which symbolize the Grail as the physical cup used by Jesus. We should mention here the Mary Magdalene and Joseph of Arimathea traditions; these saints are the joint bearers of relics of Jesus' crucifixion which, according to apocryphyal traditions, were brought to the South of France and Britain, respectively. Joseph brought to Glastonbury the two cruets in which he collected the blood and water from the body of Christ. These two substances, anciently symbolic of the basis of all life, are blended more subtly into the myth of the Magdalene, who is said to be a living Grail, her womb nurturing the child of Jesus.[27]

This myth is represented by Sara le Kali, Black Sara, the patroness of gypsies, who apparently stems from the race of Kundry. Supposedly the servant of the two Maries – Magdalene and Cleopas – she is venerated in rituals all of her own at Les-Saintes-Maries-de-la-Mer in Gard, France, where gypsies come from all over Europe to worship. The nomadic gypsy, like Sophia and the Shekinah, does not settle anywhere for long. The incorporation of Sara le Kali into a Catholic pilgrimage church is but one stopping place on the way to enlightenment. Perhaps the Romany clan is kin to the company of knights and damsels wandering in the forest, always looking for its spiritual mother?

In *Parzival*, 'maidens are sent openly, men secretly' to serve the Grail and mediate its call. We notice the immediate reversal of the veiled Sophia of the East here. In Celtic tradition, women are openly given in marriage that the Grail tradition may be furthered. Men retain the withdrawn role in Northern tradition, whereas women perform the practical and manifest role of the Grail. Together they form the Grail Family which is the extended family of Sophia's lovers. It is so that the Goddess is seeded in all of us, to be rediscovered and activated after a long winter of the spirit. The simultaneity of images involved in the Grail's appearance – as cup, woman, Goddess, cauldron – is as confusing as its sudden withdrawal; for as soon as the Grail-seekers of that time manifested it for their generation, it forthwith disappeared or was said to be guarded between the worlds. The Grail's withdrawal is like Sophia's retirement to her place of waiting.

The effect of the Grail is therapeutic, by its achievement both king and wasteland are simultaneously healed and the marriage contract between king and land is complete. The Grail is not achieved for the benefit of one person, but for all people of that time. Its reoccurence in the cycles of time is like the reappearance of Sophia who may come as radiant initiator into bliss, or else she may choose to take the guise of a sorrowful widow upon the road. Her features may be discerned in the faces of all who suffer injustice, famine and oppression; they are seen in every polluted stream, each barren field, each diseased tree, as well as within each hopeless human face.

The Grail represents the presence of the healing Goddess of Wisdom who comes to make all things right. While injustice and greed prevail, the land reflects the inner state of the Goddess – it becomes a wasteland, the healing power of the Grail is withdrawn and the Black Goddess, in the form of Kundry, the Black Maiden and others, travels the land in solitary pilgrimage to exhort all people of good heart to seek for the Grail and display it in their lives. The Goddess of the Grail roams the earth in many guises, ever seeking to manifest her healing. It is an indictment on our times that all we behold is the face of the Black Goddess when we look towards the earth. However, the prophecy of the Grail Goddess's return also recurs in our age.

The Celtic spirit remains firmly rooted in the Divine Feminine, ever looking towards a manifestation and restatement of Sophia. Gaelic tradition says that St Brigit is the foster-mother of Christ and the midwife-companion of Mary. She certainly upholds this role of midwife to the rebirth of Sophia among us, as Fiona MacLeod wrote in the early years of this century about a prophecy current upon Iona: 'which foretells, now as the Bride of Christ, now as the Daughter of God, now as the Divine Spirit embodied through mortal birth in a Woman . . . the coming of a new Presence and Power . . . I believe that though the Reign of Peace may be yet a long way off, it is drawing near: and that Who shall save us anew shall come divinely as a Woman . . .'[28]

Speaking further about this prophecy that the Holy Spirit would come as Woman, MacLeod wrote: 'She would rise suddenly in many hearts, and have her habitation among dreams and hopes.'[29] It is so that Sophia arises in many hearts now, in fulfilment of the propphecy.

The Grail is a prime symbol of Sophia; it is ever virgin like inviolable Wisdom, for the distillation of all Wisdom's experience lies only in the first sip which confers knowledge and empowerment.

The guardianship of this tradition remains within the native European tradition as well as within mystical Christianity. From these former roots rise the clans of the ancient craft of paganism which is still operative today. The radiant spirituality of the Grail is here transposed to the green spirituality of the cauldron, wherein Nature is Goddess. This earthy corrective to the often unearthed concepts of orthodox spirituality has never been a Christian heresy but a true survival of the native tradition.

The sisterhoods of the cauldron did not suddenly cease to be. The skills of healing, divination and prophecy continued to be taught and inculcated, as well as born as a gift in many people. The Clan of the ancient spiritual crafts had descendants who are still among us today. Despite the often phony claims of modern Wiccan revivalists to be the continuators of the old pagan crafts, there are still some who live according to the wisdom of their ancestors.[30] This clan is not a single blood-linked family now, of course. It is as fragmented as the offspring of King Amangons and the Damsels of the Wells. Yet it continues to offer the nourishment of those ancient wells and it listens still for the voice of the Goddess of the Land.

The pagans who are kin to Wisdom – as she prefers to be known in the North – are often those who have reawoken from the spell of sleep to resume an ancestral occupation. Few are literally descendants of the old clan. Wisdom kindles in them by exposure to the old places of holiness, where the earth speaks clearly. They are the modern prophets and sibyls of ancient Wisdom traditions.

The Grail is still guarded by wise ones who listen to the Damsels of the Wells and hear the voice of the Grail Goddess in every land.

═══ **12** ═══

VIRGO VIRIDITAS

O most noble Greenness, rooted in the sun,
shining forth in streaming splendour upon the wheel of Earth.
No earthly sense of being can comprehend you.
You are encircled by the very arms of Divine mysteries.
You are radiant like the red of dawn!
You glow like the incandescence of the sun.
Item de Virginibus, Hildegard of Bingen's song

And it thus appears that the entire world is like a single
mirror full of lights presenting the divine wisdom, or as
charcoal emitting light.
Collationes in Hexaemeron II:27, St Bonaventure

Woman, Fall and Nature

If the paradigm of failure in the Grail legends is the Wasteland,
then for Christian mystics it is the Fall. The mythic story of the
Adam and Eve's expulsion from the garden underlies the Christian
understanding of creation. Because Eve was seen as ultimately
responsible for the Fall, so women were viewed accordingly.

The theophanic vision of the Christian mystic deals in prime
qualities – wholeness and order – ways of restructuring that which
is broken; the instinct of the mystic is to heal, to bring together that
which is divided, to assent to the message of Sophia. However,
because the story of the Fall lies behind the Christian ethic, mystics
have a great problem. Is Woman ultimately responsible for the Fall?
How should she be viewed? Can any good come out of Woman?
In the Litany of Loreto, the Virgin is addressed as 'Morning Star'.
This innocent title has a mystical counterpoise, for this is also given
to the Prince of Darkness before he fell. Lucifer is thus opposed
to Mary just as the Woman Clothed with the Sun is the eternal
opponent of the Beast with seven heads in *Revelations* 12. The
mythic necessity for an adversary who polarizes demonic evil
with Deity's good has generally taken the line of least resistance
in the West and this role has been assigned to Woman. The real

221

counterpoise of Christian life is between Eve and the Woman Clothed with the Sun who, in the Bible, represent the two female images at the beginning and end of time respectively. These dual metaphors of the Divine Feminine represent the integrity of Sophia, for she is the unheeded herald of unification and resacralization of life. However, this is not, historically, how she has been seen, for the enemy of creation is understood to be Woman, she who is a receptacle for evil.

Christianity has chosen to polarize the Divine Feminine with Eve as the marring Black Goddess, and Mary as the mending Sophia. The Gnostic descent of Sophia has here been transposed into Eve's Fall from Grace, while the associated Return to Grace has been attached to Mary who, though she transcends her humanity, is not yet a Goddess. However, it is centrally important to the Christian mythos that, if humanity caused the Fall, then it should also have the opportunity to make amends, a task which Mary undertakes on behalf of all. Reversing the story of the Damsels of the Wells, we find that for the 'people of the Book' their progenetrix and mother of physical life and spiritual death is Eve.

In the medieval imagination, Eve was the prime image of Woman, seen as Pandora who had opened the box of tricks and let loose havoc upon the world. The effect of the Fall was generation and sexuality, and Eve was the gateway of generation.

Eve's fall was seen, in medieval terms, as a sexual failing; her fallen condition is emphasised by God's dictum 'in pain shall you bring forth'. Mary's motherhood is free of such taints, even to the creation of a new theological concept to cope with this. Mary remains a physical virgin. Sometimes, she is seen to conceive through her ear rather than by conventional methods; even Hildegard of Bingen speculated that Mary gave birth through her side, rather as Buddha's mother is said to have done. These procedures circumvent the earthly gateway of the Black Goddess in favour of mystical virginity and its preservation. This avoidance is a feature of Western creation mythology: Eve is created from Adam's rib in *Genesis*, Athena is born of Zeus' head, and Sophia comes from the mouth of God. The reversion of the birthing procedure to the male body, while not completely unknown in the animal kingdom, is bizarre when applied to humanity, however metaphysically we view this.

In the myth of Pandora, the famous box which she opened was originally a large storage jar – the kind which the Greeks used to store wine or as a funerary vessel. *Pithos*, a jar was mistakenly translated *pyxis*, a box, by Erasmus. This jar, like the cauldron of Ceridwen, was the womb of the Goddess herself – giver of life and receiver of the dead.[1] The pre-Hesiodic myth may thus be seen in a different light. Pandora does not inflict evils upon humanity by her curiosity, rather she opens the womb of the Goddess and gives birth to many possibilities.

But did the Christian Fall have a similar beneficial purpose? Medieval speculation could not remain aloof from the problem of evil. As we have seen, the abduction of Kore and the tasks of Psyche can be seen as productive, learning experiences. Rather ignoring Eve's contribution to this process, the Easter liturgy triumphantly proclaims: 'O *Felix Culpa* (O Happy fault of Adam!)' The Fall provides an opportunity for growth, reassimilation and learning which Creation did not supply, since everything was in its completion. This theme is taken up by the mystic, Julian of Norwich, whose vision of the Christly Wisdom concluded that 'love was his meaning'[2] and that 'in falling and in rising we are preciously kept in the same love.'[3]

Does this not suggest the presence of the guiding hand of Sophia, she who leads us on tortuous paths until we see and manifest wisdom in our lives? We have already seen how Eve's eating of the apple was interpreted by the Gnostics in another light, so that the whole Fall became a Sophianic triumph. The orthodox Christian interpretation, in common with the Jewish and Islamic view, is that Eve is little better than the serpent who tempted her.

Eve's name is interesting. When she and Adam leave Paradise, he called her *Hawwah*, which has been usually intepreted as meaning 'Mother of All Living'. However, *hiwya* in Aramaic means 'serpent'.[4] Islamic legend credits Eve with being fashioned from the feet of the serpent.[5] The serpent may be seen as the voice of the Black Goddess, the voice of earth's motherwit, Eve's daemon, not her demon.

Eve, like Pandora, is the Mother of the Desire to Know. Of all the trees in Paradise, only the Tree of the Knowledge of Good and Evil was forbidden. Perhaps God, knowing human nature, purposely forbade its consumption? The serpent's beguilement pivots on the temptation 'you will be like God, knowing good and evil.'[6] And Eve saw 'that the tree was to be desired to make one wise.'[7] Like Sophia, Eve wanted to know, and in order to do that she first had to experience.

The threefold punishment of God itemizes the ills of humanity: the serpent should go on its belly and be the enemy of Woman's descendants; Eve and all women would suffer childbirth pains and be subject to Man; Adam and all men were condemned to toil all their days.[8] This passage has been vindicated historically because it has been taken as divine sanction for the sublimation of Woman. Even in our own irreligious age, that sanction still has potency. Loss of paradise has meant work and not play. The Sophianic freedom to play has been denied us. The Gnostic conception of the Demiurge or craftsman, the Divine Technician condemning creation to a world of work, is in strict contrast to that of Sophia, the Creative Imagination, which liberates us to a world where work becomes play. The world of childhood, the paradisal state of innocence, is a time of play. But the Fall is about loss of paradise: it is about acquiring consciousness of good and evil. Only human beings have this blessed/cursed understanding, for animals inhabit a consciousness which *is* paradisal and thus they stand apart from our eternally dual perspective. It is for this reason that many native spiritual traditions lay so much stress on the healing powers and otherworldly mediation of totem animals. The concept of guilt has no part in native spirituality but, as in North America, was introduced to tribal society by missionaries.

The Christian disdain for the Divine Feminine was reflected upon Nature also, since most images of Nature were feminine. Nature, once epitomized as Demeter, Ceres, Rhea, Isis or Cybele, the focus of spectacular cults towards the end of the pagan era, faded into folk-memory. The Church father, Lactantius, inveighed against the pagan conception of Nature as mother of all: 'Nature, removed from divine providence and power, is absolutely nothing.'[9] Nature becomes creature, not creator in Christian orthodoxy. It is not until we come to the allegorical goddesses of medieval writing that Nature comes again to sing her *planctus*.

Wendell Berry has written: 'Perhaps the great disaster of human history . . . is the conceptual division between the holy and the world, the excerpting of the Creator from the creation.'[10] The perceived inferiority of the natural world, like the status of women, made it ripe for exploitation: a disdainful rapine which now threatens our very existence and for which we need a corrective creative theology, which may well be offered by Sophia.

Sophia's connection with Nature is continually restated within medieval writing, as though loss of the Divine Feminine created unconscious craving. As we have seen, Sophia has her practical manifestation, and just as women share the fate of the Goddess, so too do nature and the created world. We have seen how

Sophia comes from the All for the all, she enters the experience of matter as the inspiriting soul. The roots of Sophia's association with Nature go back to the creation, through the Classical and Orphic schools whereby Persephone is the Weaver of the Web.

In the West, Nature is conceptually seen as chaotic, requiring the ordered reasoning of Spirit. Women are metaphorically seen as earthy and creative, not in control of their biological functions. Men stand aloof from these processes and are therefore associated metaphorically with the world of the Spirit.

The Sheila na Gig, the Creating Goddess, is the *fons et origo* of pagan culture, and the devil's gateway, according to misogynist theologians. The medieval duality about creation was echoed even in allegorical depictions of Venus who was understood to be present in two manifestations. 'We read there are two Venuses, a legitimate goddess and a goddess of lechery. We say that the legitimate Venus is . . . the equal proportion of worldly things, which some call Astraea and others natural justice. For she is in the elements, in the stars, in times, in animate things. But the shameful Venus, the goddess of sensuality, we call concupiscence of the flesh because she is the mother of all fornication.'[11] This statement recalls the Gnostic Sophia Prunikos. Set against the shameful Eve was the chaste Mary, the Second Eve.

The Green Virgin

The hopeful feminine metaphor of Christians is Mary, for she redeems Eve's mistake.

O Maria, Redemptoris	O Mary of creaturely kind,
Creatura, Creatoris.	who created our Redeemer.

wrote Adam of St Victor (*d*. 1180). The dichotomy of that statement sums up Mary's predicament in our world today: neither Goddess nor ordinary woman, she inhabits a limbo with Eve, polarizing a set of characteristics which have been the playthings of theologians. Eve is disobedient; she conceives her children in sorrow after listening to the words of the serpent, she loses Paradise and brings death. Mary, by contrast, is obedient; she conceives after hearing the word of the angel, she reopens paradise and the gates of eternal life. The monastic and ecclesiastical structure

225

was such that even mystics of forthright integrity were able to side-step, explain away or else skirt round the problem of woman. Theologically, the Virgin had saved what Eve had marred. As a Portuguese *cantiga* goes: *Entre Ave et Eva gran departiment et.* Between Ave (as in Ave Maria – Hail Mary) and Eva, there's a world of difference.

This famous antithesis echoes those we have already discovered: Ecclesia and Synagogia, Sophia Stellarum and Sophia Nigrans. Mary is the achieved archetype from which Eve has fallen; Eve loses, Mary restores paradise. Mary as Second Eve is an idea introduced by Justin Martyr in 155 which has informed Christianity at all levels. Between Fall and Redemption, at its very heart, is the theology of the Incarnation. God became man that man might become God, runs the Athanasian creed. Mary is therefore venerated because she is the Mother of her Creator. This concept was little different from the Classical mystery schools, wherein the mother begot a saviour son. In Mary's case there is one distinct and unique feature: Mary, however many myths and associations she acquired, was a *human* creature. This uniqueness is linked to the other unique feature of Christianity: that its saviour becomes a human being and dies, before resurrecting. Within the mysteries, the protagonists of the salvific story are almost always gods, though the stories of Psyche and Lucius Apuleius depict the human quest. Mary's humanity is the most important feature which she bequeaths to her son, enabling him to take part in the divine drama. She gives him human birth, and thereby gives him the ability to die: a solely mortal ability.

The Sophianic role is to penetrate to the heart of matter, to accompany creation on its journey. Mary's *fiat* – her assent to become Christ's mother – is a harmonic of Eve's action, by which she wished to be wise as a god: it is almost a natural corollary that Christ should subsequently taste death, enter into the underworld and burst the locks of its gates. The concept of divinity entering mortality to the extent of experiencing death is an important initiation for Western human consciousness. It means that divinity has interpenetrated humanity and points to the possibility of humanity interpenetrating divinity. This last scene in the Christian drama is played out in the Assumption of the Virgin into heaven, where Mary enters, body and soul, into heaven to become the bride of God, the representative of humanity, the Church personified.

The fourth century father, Methodius of Patara, wrote: 'Out of His bones and flesh the Church was born; . . . indeed for her sake the Logos left His Father in heaven and came down, to cleave to His Wife; and . . . he slept in the ecstasy of His passion, choosing to die for her that He Himself might cleanse her in the bath and present her to Himself a Church glorious and without blemish.'[12] St Augustine saw this restoration happening in 'the bridal chamber, that is in the womb of the Virgin, (where) divine Nature united itself to human nature when the Word became flesh for us.'[13]

Hildegard of Bingen's *Scivias* II:6, depicts Ecclesia holding a chalice in which to catch Christ's blood at the crucifixion. This redemptive blood does not fall upon the earth, therefore, but is reserved sacramentally for all baptized Christians. Initiation into the pagan mystery schools was usually reserved for people of established status: Christianity might be professed even by a slave. Mary, by giving birth to the Logos who will redeem the world, is seen as the Mother of All and we are all kindred of Mary.

The loss of paradise was keenly felt by medievals. In compensation for this, their writings abounded in figures depicting or representing the fructifying and eternally innocent nature of creation. These paradigms and archetypes are clearly figured within the Grail literature. Within the writings of Hildegard we see the fertile waters of Sophianic grace irrigating the ground of the spirit, to bring forth a vision of the Green Virgin.

Hildegard of Bingen (1098–1179) was one of the most extraordinary polymaths of the Middle Ages: a mystic and visionary whose unusually detailed and creative theology is outstanding. She is one who lived under the 'shadow of the living light' of Sophia's radiance. The great abbess's works show a bewildering multiplicity of luminous images of the Divine Feminine: Caritas, Sapientia, Ecclesia, Scientia Dei (Knowledge of God), etc. While Hildegard shows a great flexibility in the use of these diverse images, she nevertheless rarely strays far from the orthodoxies of her age. Hers is the allowable diversity of the artist or mystic, whose individual vision is coloured by poetic perception which is not quantifiably orthodox.

Her images of the Divine Feminine are always co-workers with the Divine Masculine, with the Father, Son and Holy Spirit. They are sometimes complimentary qualities, or else they are hypostatizations of the Divine Masculine. She frequently presents them as subservient to God. However, the images are strong, passionate and visionary.

Significantly, Hildegard's mystical work comes through most strongly in her songs. She believed that 'singing of words reveals their true meaning directly to the soul through bodily vibration.'[14] The peregrinatory modes and wild leaps of cadence of her music present Hildegard's vision more clearly than words can. Wisdom appears in many places in Hildegard's work, but no better portrait is given than in *Scivias*.[15] Wisdom is crowned, dressed in a gold tunic, girded with gems. 'She has been joined in God and to God in the sweetest embrace in a religious dance of burning love . . . This beautiful image was looking into the world for people. This is because she loves people greatly. As a result, she always guides and protects with her own protection those who wish to follow her and to stand firm with her . . . Her hand had been placed reverently upon her breast, (because) she directs her work in such a way that no one is able to resist her work with any other prudence or power . . . Her secrets are naked and manifest to God alone.'[16] This description clearly refers back to Wisdom calling aloud in the street and looking for her lovers. It is also typical of Hildegard to recognize the nuptial relationship of God with his Wisdom, to whom she is joined in a cosmic dance. She sees Wisdom as the bride of God: 'Let my Word be a bride to you for the restoration of my people. You may be their mother, regenerating their souls through the salvation of the spirit and water.'[17]

The nuptial imagery of Hildegard appears in her portrait of Caritas, who says; 'I am the most loving consort of the throne of God, and God hides no counsel from me. I keep the royal marriage bed, and all that is God's is mine as well.'[18] In the same work, *Liber Vitae Meritorum*, Hildegard called Sapientia 'a most loving mistress in [God's] lovely embrace.'[19]

Hildegard's songs express the full virility of Wisdom's power. In *O virtus sapientia*, she conceives Wisdom as a three-winged entity simultaneously interpenetrating the heavens, the earth and all places. Sophia encompasses the cosmos, just as Wisdom does in *Sirach* 24:5–6. Wisdom is pervasive, inspiriting and a giver of vitality.

This brings us to consideration of Hildegard's extraordinary vision of spirituality bringing greenness (*viriditas*) to the soul.[20] We now speak of greening the earth, but the equally urgent task is that of greening the soul, allowing the deep compassion of Sophia to arise within us; without this, Nature is laid waste. This spiritual greenness allows Sophia to appear as the Red Queen, with the dynamic and elemental vitality of the Goddess.

Hildegard's elemental awareness refreshingly rises above the medieval disdain for the flesh. Caritas says: 'With wisdom I have rightly put the universe in order. I, the fiery life of divine essence, am aflame beyond the beauty of the meadows. I gleam in the waters, and I burn in the sun, moon and stars. With every breeze, as with invisible life that contains everything, I awaken everything to life. The air lives by turning green and being in blood. The waters flow as if they were alive . . . And thus I remain hidden in every kind of reality as a fiery power . . .. I breathe life into everything so that nothing is mortal in respect to its species. For I am life.'[21]

This paean of self-praise is scarcely distinguishable from the boast of Wisdom[22] or from Isis' speech in Apuleius. *The Book of Divine Works* further speaks of how: 'Creation was, so to speak, Wisdom's garment because Wisdom clothes her own achievement in the same way as we human beings are aware that we are wearing clothes.'[23]

Hildegard's view of Mary is a mixture of conventional theology and an idiosyncratically mystical lyricism. She is described in terms of a saviour Goddess in Hildegard's song *O Virga ac Diadema*, where Mary is conceived of in terms of Isis collecting the dismembered remains of Osiris.

Unde, o salvatrix	O female Saviour who pours out
que novum lumen	a new light
humano generi protulisti	upon the human race,
colligi membra filii tua	gather the members of your Son
ad celestem armoniam.	into heaven's harmony.[24]

Yet sometimes the garment is soiled. For as the soul is clothed in the flesh which may sin, so may the garments of Wisdom, or Ecclesia. Sapientia washes her garments clean in the blood of the lamb.[25] Ecclesia has no such recourse, save through the urgings of the visionary Hildegard who acts as her mouthpiece in a letter to the priest, Werner of Kircheim. Denouncing the simony and greed of certain clergy, and decrying other acts which defiled the sacraments, Hildegard describes her vision of a beautifully radiant woman in gorgeous robes: 'But her face was smudged with dust and her dress was torn on the right side. Her cloak too, had lost its exquisite beauty and the tops of her shoes were soiled. She cried to high heaven with a loud, plaintive voice . . . Hear me, O heaven, for my countenance is sullied. Mourn, O Earth, for my robe is torn. Tremble, O abyss, for my shoes are soiled. The foxes have their holes and the birds of the sky have their nests, but I have no helper, no consoler . . .'[26]

These images, suggestive as they are of Boethius' Lady Philosophy, whose garments are likewise rent by philosophic dissention, remind us of the blackened primal face of Wisdom who reappears in unlikely places as the Black Virgin, the despised corner-stone of alchemy, the prima materia, whose wisdom remains veiled. Ecclesia's cry is also Sophia's lament.

The darkness of Sophia is represented in Synagogia, whom Hildegard understands as a precursor of Ecclesia who completes the work of wisdom. Hildegard has a vision of Synagogia, whose image is frequently set up in opposition to that of Ecclesia in medieval tradition: 'She came into existence from the beginning when her sons were coming to their full strength. And she foresaw the mysteries of God in darkness. But she did not appear fully'[27]. This might well prove prophetic in the light of Goddess spirituality today, which is uncovering a wealth of insights into the Divine Feminine as the veil slips from the head of Sophia.

Hildegard makes prolonged parallels between Sophia and Mary:

> O form of woman, sister of Wisdom,
> how great is your glory.
> For in you there rose a life unquenchable
> that death shall never stifle.
> Wisdom exalted you to make
> all creatures fairer in your beauty
> than they were when the world was born.[28]

Here the motherhood of Mary is the fulfilment and culmination of creation. Just as Wisdom created the world with God, so, with the inspiriting seed of God, Mary recreates it for salvation. The text echoes *Proverbs* 7:4 'Say to wisdom: "You are my sister," and call insight your intimate friend.'

Hildegard calls upon the warrant of the sapiential books to furnish a pre-existent Divine Feminine principle. As the *Speculum Virginum*, a manual for nuns states: 'If all things existed in the Wisdom of the Word of God, waiting to be unfolded in their different species according to their preordained nature, manner, and order, how could the Mother not preexist with the Son, whose conception and birth opened the way for the whole rational creation to be sancitified, unified and restored to peace? How could she be absent, in whom an eternal decree had laid the foundation of an eternal building, the celestial Jeruslem?'[29]

Here Wisdom as Mary, is seen as preexistant with her Son. This concept is based on a reading of Wisdom as co-creatrix, with an understanding of Mary as a type of Wisdom. It is a staggering statement which comprends the beginning and end of creation in which Mary, as the New Jerusalem, has fulfilled the promise of Wisdom, rather as Hildegard conceives the fulfilment of Synagogia by Ecclesia.

Hildegard's exegesis of the Fall in the Garden of Eden is related to the fact that in both Hebrew (*hokmah*) and Latin (*sapere, sapientia*) the word for wisdom means 'to taste'.[30] This 'tasting' of Wisdom, whether it be Eve with her apple, or Taliesin with the draught from Ceridwen's cauldron, is essential to our knowledge. The first thing a young child does with a proffered object is to put it into the mouth. If it is not food, then it immediately becomes a plaything, something which stimulates the creative and wise centres of the body. The Green Virgin can thus be seen as the playful Wisdom who allows us to experience life, as Mary allowed her son to experience death and transformation, as Eve with the apple – the unappreciated ancestress who gave us knowledge of wisdom.

Lady Philosophy, Lady of the Wheel

The medieval opinion of the Divine Feminine was subject to the paradoxical changes which life, Nature and Goddess presented. Death, destruction and violent change were neatly polarized either upon the devil or upon Eve, and woman as her representative. It was unthinkable to accord these functions to God, source of all good. These dichotomies were occasionally explored in safe allegorical forms by the philosophical and mystical schools of the Middle Ages.

All texts and stories about Sophia testify to her fundamental unity with the stuff of creation. She is the *prima materia* from which life emerges. Yet she is also the creator or co-creator and is thus as one with the Divine. Can Sophia be simultaneously creator and deconstructor of creation?

The Irish philosopher, John Scotus Erigena (*c.* 810–877) attempted to answer this question in his *Periphyseon* which includes a fourfold division of Nature:

1 Nature which is not created but which creates – the Deity.

2   Nature which is created and which creates – the world
    of Platonic forms. ('The angelic nature was established
    before every other creature, not in time but in status.')[31]
3   Nature which is created and does not create – the things
    perceivable by the senses.
4   Nature which neither creates nor is created – the Deity to
    whom all things must return.

All is Nature; all is natural. In this wholistic fourfold division
of creation, the Deity has a creative and destructive persona. It
also partakes in the imaginatively creative realms of angelic and
daemonic appearances as well as in the created species of the world.
This may perhaps be helpful to bear in mind as we trace the track of
Sophia through the complex theologies and philosophies in which
she has been trussed up.

The medieval period saw many literary and allegorical flow-
erings of the Goddess of Wisdom. She appeared in the guise
of Natura and Philosophia. In a world which lacked a Divine
Feminine principle, Sophia was a legitimate feminine archetype
who helped to eke out the sparse dramatis personae of the poet,
playwright and mystical theologian: Boethius' Lady Philosophy,
Prudentius's Queen Sapientia (in *Psychomachia*), the *Marriage of
Philology and Mercury* by Martinanus Capella, etc. Personifications of the Divine Feminine during the Middle Ages served to
make accessible abstract concepts, making it difficult to separate
philosophical and poetic personifications.[32] Wisdom retained her
feminine guise, appearing iconographically, poetically, and theologically individual herself.

The patron of philosophers and virgins, Katherine of Alexandria,
was martyred during the reign of Maxentius by being broken
on a wheel which subsequently also broke. She was thereafter
beheaded. She had refused to marry the Emperor because she
was 'a bride of Christ'. She became the patron of all craftspeople
who used the wheel, such as millers, wheelwrights, but most
especially, of spinsters. This is a fascinating turn of events, for
Katherine resonates to the spindle of necessity in Plato's *Myth of
Er*. The Classical idea of *heimarmene*, or fate, is transcended by
the wise figure of Katherine.

Katherine's wheel, now more familiar at firework displays, is
like the wheel of Fortuna – a figure who exercised the medieval
imagination a great deal. Fortuna was directly derived from the
Roman Goddess who we now call Lady Luck. The changing

fortunes of humanity were represented iconographically by the turning of her wheel, upon which the great were elevated to be eventually demoted. This wheel was none other than the round of existence itself, whirled by the Goddess: those who are upon it must expect the cyclity of the wheel to affect them. To have 'flown out of the weary wheel' was the ambition of the Orphics: to break forever the cycle of existences. By triumphing over torture and philosophical debate, Katherine overcame the wheel of Fortuna to become a patron of wisdom.

However, the one continual plaint against the Goddess throughout time is her mutability, her changeablity. This quality has been perceived as dubious rather than helpfully cyclic. Any attempt to spike her wheel from turning obviates the purpose of life. Whoever wishes to stop Fortune's wheel, pinions the wings of Sophia.

The virgin integrity of St Katherine refused a spouse and so she was martyred. Her death is a triumph not a defeat, but it is nevertheless a rather final way out. Similarly, women are said to be changeable, ever changing their minds ('which is their female privilege'). To realise the cyclicity of our access to knowledge is wisdom. To be without wisdom is to be disempowered. But it is only in emptiness that wisdom grows in us. Katherine's wheel turns round and another part of our potential understanding is stimulated.

Katherine's historically attested pagan counterpart, the Neo-Platonic philosopher, Hypatia (375–415), was also martyred, rather more messily, at the hands of an Alexandrian mob. On the suspicion that she had inflamed the Alexandrian prefect against the Christians, the mob tore her from her chariot, stripped her naked and scraped off her flesh with oyster shells, in an attack as vicious as any Christian martyrdom.[33] Both Katherine and Hypatia represent the learned woman whose practical wisdom is to communicate her skills with the efficacy of Athene.

In Anicius Boethius's (c. 480–524) *The Consolations of Philosophy*, Philosophia appears as the opponant of Fortuna. Written during his imprisonment, *The Consolations* owes more to Stoicism and Platonism than to the Christianity which Boethius professed. Lady Philosophy herself appeared to comfort him in his cell. She was of mature years and very tall, so that she seemed to reach the sky. 'Her clothes were made of imperishable material, of the finest thread woven with the most delicate skill. (Later she told me that she had made them with her own hands.)'[34] Embroidered near the hem was the letter Pi from which rose a ladder terminating in the letter Theta; the Greek characters indicated her patronage of both philosophy and theology. Her garment was torn and she told Boethius that on the death of Socrates, mobs of Epicureans and Stoics tried to seize the inheritance of wisdom. 'In the fight, the robe was torn which I had woven with my own hands. They tore off little pieces from it and went away in the fond belief that they had obtained the whole of philosophy. The sight of traces of my clothing on them gained them the reputation among the ignorant of being my familiars.'[35]

This allegory of Philosophia is one which might well be transferred to the Goddess herself, scraps of whose greatness were apportioned or abandoned during the very time in which Boethius was writing. Philosophia's struggle with the false philosophers is reminiscent of the terrible death of Hypatia. Philosophia came as a nurse to physic Boethius and gave him medicine for his soul. She warned against trusting in the Goddess Fortune whose wheel casts one down, while raising another up. Philosophia tartly pointed out: 'You have discovered the changing faces of the random goddess. To others she still veils herself, but to you she has revealed herself to the full. If you are satisfied with her ways, you must accept them and not complain.'[36]

Boethius was anxious to demonstrate God's benevolent government of the universe and its essential unity under the divine will, and so Philosophia appears as a mouthpiece, not an actress in this drama, despite the orthodox depictions of Wisdom in the Bible which might have served as models. It is not until the twelfth century that the writers of the School of Chartres brought the Goddess back in the form of many allegorical figures.

The mutability of the Goddess had little place in the Middle Ages. It was time for Sophia to make a number of orderly scheduled appearances, to become the mistress of scholasticism, the Goddess of education.

The Seven Pillars of Wisdom

In *Proverbs* 9, Wisdom sends out her handmaids to invite everyone to her feast of wisdom. These seven virgins, inherited perhaps from Manichaean cosmology, are the assessors of Wisdom. The Middle Ages transformed them into the daughters of Sophia, the Sophianic examining board of the Seven Liberal Arts. It was the English cleric Alcuin (735–804) who associated Wisdom's house with seven pillars as analogous to the Seven Liberal Arts. These consisted of the *trivium*: Rhetoric; Dialectic (logical thought) and Grammar, and the *quadrivium*; Music; Arithmetic; Astronomy and Geometry. These formed the basis for Western academic education up until the sixteenth century. These handmaidens of Sophia are depicted on the right hand doorway of the *Portail Royal* at Chartres. The central image is of the Black Virgin, copied from the original pagan statue in the crypt, for according to Albert the Great (1200–1280), Mary herself was the possessor of the Seven Liberal Arts. As Black Virgin of Wisdom, Mary is surrounded by seven female figures representing the Liberal Arts who are accompanied by seven historical exponents of each art:

The liberal arts	Their exponents	Planetary sphere
Grammar	Donatus	Moon
Dialectic	Aristotle	Mercury
Rhetoric	Cicero	Venus
Music	Pythagoras	Sun
Arithmetic	Pythagorus	Mars
Geometry	Euclid	Jupiter
Astronomy	Ptolemy	Saturn

This is the Classical *Klimax Heptapulos*, the seven-fold ladder which underlay the Mysteries of Mithras, and the many Gnostic sects, elements of which passed into alchemical usage.[37] The purification of the soul through the seven planetary experiences was common to many cultures and traditions. This spiritual journey became a mundane study; an ascent through the seven academic studies necessary for complete wisdom.

John Erigena defined the Seven Liberal Arts as the organs of wisdom:

Grammar is the art which protects and controls articulate speech.

Rhetoric is the art which carries out a full and elaborate examination of a set topic under the headings of person, matter, occasion, quality, place, time and opportunity, and can be briefly defined: rhetoric is the art which deals accutely and fully with a topic defined by its seven circumstances.

Dialectic is the art which diligently investigates the rational common concepts of the mind.

Arithmetic is the reasoned and pure art of the numbers which come under the contemplations of the mind.

235

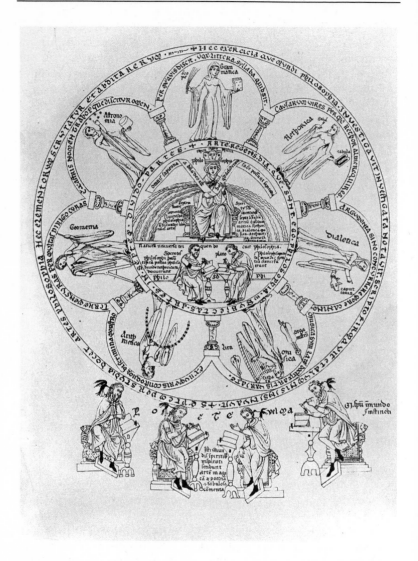

14 *Philosophia* Sophia is shown here, crowned with the three-faced Trinity, while streams of nourishing wisdom flow from her breast. Below her, Socrates and Plato sit upon the bench of philosophy. About Sophia, as though standing in the colonade formed by her seven-pillared temple, are the seven liberal arts: Grammar, Rhetoric, Dialectic, Music, Arithemetic, Geometry and Astronomy. According to the conventions of Medieval education, the Liberal Arts are the true daughters of Sophia. From twelfth century ms, *Hortus Deliciarum*, of Herrad of Landsberg. Formerly in Bib. Nat., Strasburg, destroyed 1870.

236

Geometry is the art which considers by the mind's acute observation the intervals and surfaces of plane and solid figures.

Music is the art which by the light of reason kindles the harmony of all things that are in motion. It is knowable by natural proportions.

Astronomy is the art which investigates the dimensions of the heavenly bodies and their motions and their returnings at fixed times.[38]

These seven handmaids of Sophia, like carytids on Greek temples, supported the structure of the academy.

The seven planetary powers of pagan tradition become the seven gifts of the Spirit in Christianity: Wisdom, Understanding, Counsel, Fortitude, Knowledge, Piety, the Fear of God. These qualities are also to be found on the qabalistic Tree of Life. Christianity manifests them through the seven sacraments: baptism; confirmation; confession; marriage; communion; ordination and anointing – the seven gateways through which Christian initiates enter the Church.

The seven pillars of Wisdom's temple make their appearance in another guise within Christian mystical tradition, becoming the seven swords which pierce the heart of the Virgin in her aspect of Mother of Sorrows. Devotion to Our Lady of Dolours was widespread and constitutes a continuation of the cult to the Black Madonna.

The Seven Liberal Arts are somewhat less liberal in our own day and are subject to more fragmentation. Some have forgotten that they are the handmaids of Wisdom, and have attempted to become dictators. As the many fields of science and art gravitate more and more towards their own cliquey centralizations, so the traditional arts and sciences no longer appear as sisters so much as rivals, each shrieking defiance at the other and further destroying the fabric of Nature.

In an era when the Goddess appeared 'by kind permission of the management', the academics of the School of Chartres show a tendency to break through the wall of silence surrounding the Divine Feminine and present Nature or the World-Soul in sympathetic terms.

The Chartres School

The Middle Ages tend to be categorized as a stultifying period of restrictive mentality. When we look at the school of Chartres which had its flowering in the early twelfth century, we may be astounded at the complexity and beauty of its vision.

The underlying principle of the Chartres School was the *opus sapientiae*, the work of wisdom, which related the physical world and the sacred realms in mysterious kinship; and while its members frequently resorted to over-detailed summations of theoretical knowledge, this was mostly redeemed by the great works which derived from its impetus – the sacred architecture of the great cathedrals, music, scientific speculation and a wise nurturing of all the arts were the result.

Plato's *Timaeus* and Boethius's *Consolations of Philosophy* were both key works for the Chartres School. Both, in turn, influenced new generations, infecting them with a veneration of Wisdom. Hugh de St Victor, in his *Didascalion*, defines philosophy in a very Platonic way as: 'the love of that Wisdom which . . . is the living Mind and the sole primordial Idea or Pattern of things.'[39] Boethius's great prayer, *O Qui Perpetua*,[40] asks to see into the heart of things and know their nature and implicit order. This spark of knowledge is our motherwit, the kindling spirit at the heart of every enterprise, and it reveals itself in the guise of the Platonic World-Soul or as the Holy Spirit within the Chartres School. Within many of the writers of this movement, a kind of syncretic ellision of the two occurs.

The *Timaeus* provided the seedbed and warrant for the Chartres School to engage in virtual unlimited scientific speculation, since God the Creator was envisaged as the creator of matter and the sustainer of the creation's vital energy. The Platonic World-Soul was perceived as the providential goodness of God itself, while the *archetypus mundi* (image of the earth) was seen as the divine wisdom. 'When divine power and wisdom and goodness are beheld in the creation of things we fear one so powerful, worship one so wise and love one so benevolent', wrote Guillaume of Conches in his gloss on *Timaeus*. This philosophy associated three aspects of God as *opifex, archetypus* and *anima* (the Efficient, Formal and Final Cause) with the persons of the Trinity. It was by this means that the elision of World-Soul and the Holy Spirit came about.

The Chartrian's interest in the World-Soul can be seen as a natural curiosity about creation. Certainly it stands poised midway between philosophy and theology as a being of uncertain character and was, as such, incorporated in the works of Bernardus Silvestris and Alain de Lille as Natura and Genius.

Bernardus Silvestris' *Cosmographia* is one of the complex and beautiful testaments to Sophia and her indwelling spirit within the Chartres school. It is mythologized creation narrative in which God is absent. Creation stems from the Goddesses who, though they are subject to God's will, act in a seemingly independent way. In surpassing beauty and delicacy of image, *Cosmographia* unfolds the chain of being. In the first book, called *Megacosmos*, or macrocosm, Nature makes complaint to Noys that Silva, or Hyle, the prime matter, is in a confused state and deserves to be more finely ordered. Noys, who stands, Minerva-like, for Divine Providence, is the most Sophianic figure in this text. She immediately separates the elements, creates the nine hierarchies of angels after the fashion of Dionysius the Areopagite, arranges the stars, the Zodiac, the seven planets and the winds, before creating life itself from the rocks to the vegetation. The second book, called *Microcosmos*, deals with the preparation for Silva's final ordering – the creation of humanity. Noys sets Nature to search for Urania, Queen of the Stars, and Physis, the Mistress of Earthly Life. Nature treks from the highest heavens to the deepest earth to find these two Goddesses, and Physis forms humanity.[41]

Nature begs Noys to know her true Sophianic function, and is told: 'Quicken what is inert, govern what moves at random, impose shape and bestow splendour.'[42] Bernardus manifests the twin poles of Sophia very clearly: the transcendent Noys is set against the disorganized Achamoth-like Silva; the transcendent Urania is polarized with her earthly counterpart, Physis, and the power of Noys with the weakness of Endelechia, who is the soul in matter.

Bernardus' Wisdom is Noys who is described as 'the intellect of supreme and all-powerful God, a nature born of His divinity', though in his narrative, the deity does not appear as a named character. Noys is the mediator of God's will and she brings forth Endelechia who, as the World-Soul, is described in very Platonic terms as a sphere of vast size, perceivable only by the intellect. The true affinity of Endelechia is with the stars and so, hidden in matter, she is often sluggish and less powerful than in the celestial realms. She continually labours to repair her dwelling place, says Bernardus and, using an extraordinary image, he says, 'the rites of hospitality were maintained, but she would neither cooperate with nor suffer willingly any unbidden intruder within her tabernacle.'[43] Bernardus seems to imply that Endelechia is the temple of humanity, but that her innate virginity cannot be sullied. The inviolability of Sophia and her ability to find a temporary dwelling place is a feature of her myth, as when the Temple of Jerusalem was destroyed and the Shekinah took up her dwelling in the hearts of all her faithful. 'The life and well-being of the universe depend on sovereign and ancient causes: spirit, sentience, a source of motivation, and a source of order. Noys and the divine exemplars live eternal; without their life the visible creation would not live everlastingly.'[44] 'For as Noys is forever pregnant of the divine will, she in turn informs Endelechia with the images she conceives of the eternal patterns, Endelechia impresses them upon Nature, and Nature imparts to Imarmene (Fate) what the well-being of the universe demands.'[45]

Noys bestowed three gifts upon her daughter Goddesses. Urania received the Mirror of Providence in which resides 'the intellect which is the creator and destroyer of all things.'[46] Nature received the Table of Destiny in which is 'the sequence of those things which come to pass by the decrees of fate'. And Physis received the Book of Memory in which 'the combined workings of Providence and fate could be deduced.'[47] With the help of these gifts, the three Goddesses were enabled to fashion humanity. The gifts acted like mirrors in which the nature of humanity was foretold, circumscribed and ordered.

The work ends with Physis making limbs 'of which the universe has no need: eyes to keep watch in the head, ears for sound, feet to bear him and all-capable hands.'[48] Here humanity received, as it were, the organs of motherwit. Bernardus conceives of the universe as an animal, after the manner of Plato's *Timaeus* in which 'one may not detect the substance of animal life apart from the soul', but where 'animal understanding and awareness thrive, and draw nourishment from their antecedent principles', by which Bernardus means the Goddesses of his creation narrative.

In Alain de Lille's *De Planctu Naturae*, we hear of the lament of Nature for humankind's abandonment of her law. Alain's *Natura* is described as a Goddess, her crown set with zodiacal and planetary jewels, her garment embroidered with the variety of life-forms, yet, like Boethius' Philosophia, her robe is rent where humanity is stitched. Although *Natura* is not given sacramental powers of restoration within this poem, she nevertheless points out the divorce of humanity from Nature as a token of the Fall. Alain's ethic is informed by a virile Ovidian response to sexuality. *Natura* is the vicar of God but Natura makes Venus her sub-vicar, with Hymen and Cupid, who together regulate the renewal of the human species by generation. Alain attempts an imaginative reconstruction of the nature of human sexuality before the Fall in which Hymen is attended by the virtues, including *Largitas* (Liberality) whom Natura addresses thus: 'O maiden through whose noble architecture the human mind is made a palace for the Virtues . . . through whom the far off times of the Golden Age live anew, through whom men align themselves by the bond of heartfelt affection . . . such a binding conformity unites our minds in trusting peace that not only does our love seek to vest itself with the appearance of unity but indeed . . . it aspires to an identity of essence.'[49] *Largitas* is thus seen as a deep emanation of Nature herself, the bond by which the effect of the Fall may be overset.

Alain uses an image pertinent to Sophia's creative action. He describes how *Veritas* (Truth) was begotten of Natura and Genius, 'not by the carnal passion of Aphrodite, but by the loving kiss of Natura and Genius at the moment the eternal idea greeted matter: while meditating on the mirror of forms, the idea kissed matter through the intermediary image.'[50] Truth is thus the daughter of Nature in this text and Wisdom is transmitted by the cosmic kiss of Nature and Genius who, in this text, governs the idea.

In the same way that Eve and Mary were compared, so too are Nature and Mary – both being virgins who brought forth abundantly according to their nature: the multiplicity of forms stems from Nature while Mary brings forth the summation and completion of the human species.

The idea of Nature as God's deputy or vicar is manifest in Chaucer's *The Physician's Tale*, where Nature says of herself:

> For he that is the former principal
> hath maked me his vicaire general,
> To forme and peynten erthely creaturis
> Right as me list, and ech thing in my cure is
> Under the mone, that may wane and waxe,
> And for my werk right no-thing wol I axe.[51]

The creative skills of Nature were stressed by Jean de Hanville in his *Architrenius*. He also brought out her mutable and indiscriminate qualities: ' Whatever you behold is Nature: she labours at her forge, an omnifarious artisan and creates anything at a nod, and spreads abroad a miraculous array of new events. She has power to alter the moral course of events; prodigal, she litters the world with huge and monstrous shapes. She is ever changing the manner of her conception and with fantastic fertility gives shape to abnormal beings by a fearful labour.'[52] Here Nature is seen as a prodigious work-woman, but without the grace of Wisdom in *Proverbs*, laboriously churning out factory goods in an indiscriminate way.

Alain de Lille, recalling the reflective nature of Wisdom in his *Anticlaudianus*, speaks of the activity of *Ratio* (Reckoning) and the mirror in which she perceives: 'how divine idea begets terrestial form, transcribes formlessness into human progeny, and sends into exile those forms which it destines for the world; how the offspring become degenerate and put off the likeness of the father, grown forgetful of the countenance of their ancient parent; how in the universe a 'phantasm' of the idea is reflected, and its unsullied splendour is perceptible in this shadowy reflection; how the stream which descends from the fountain of form loses its original radiance in the tide of material existence.'[53]

In contemplating the tapestry which she weaves, Proserpina, in *De Raptu Proserpina* by Claudian (*c.* 370–404), depicts how Mother Nature made order out of the primordial chaos: 'In this cloth she embroidered with her needle the concourse of atoms and the dwelling of the Father of the gods, and pictured how mother Nature ordered elemental chaos and how the first principles of things sprang apart, each to his proper place.'[54]

The image of Wisdom as a weaver and Goddess of Justice is awoken here, for the raiment of Nature is ripped by human frailty, and so the veil of the Temple is torn in two so that the ages may be rewoven.

In the last analysis, the School of Chartres shows that by a reunion with Nature, humanity may return to God. By the observation of natural laws, by balancing our own ecology with wisdom, so too our planet may afford us a world fit to live in and bring us to an experience of primordial spirituality.

In both Alain de Lille's *De Planctu Naturae* and Bernard's *Cosmographia*, Nature is seen as complaining, either of humanity, or else of the disorganized state of matter. She attempts to reconcile the Black Goddess with the Transcendent Goddess by means of evoking pity and compassion. This *planctus* is echoed throughout medieval literature, and occurs in the medieval poem *Quia Amore Langueo* where the Virgin complains to God of humanity's misfortune. Here, Mary shows herself as the *Virgo Viriditas*, the Green Virgin, the mother and mediatrix of creation, whose Ave is the Christian antithesis to the Fallen Eva. The poem's chorus recalls verse 5 of *Song of Songs*, 'I am sick with love'.

> I seek thee in weel and wrechedness,
> I seek thee in riches and poverty;
> Thou man behold where thy mother is,
> Why lovest me not, since I love thee?
> Sinful or sorry, however thou be,
> So welcome to me there are no more;
> I am thy sister, right trust on me,
> *Quia amore langueo.*[55]

Mary, as Sophianic advocate, stands as in her first iconographic depictions, hands raised *orante*, mediating the needs of creation to the Divine Nature. Her song has not ceased in our time, her voice now reminding us that she cannot sustain her appearance as *Virgo Viriditas* without our help. And she turns, *orante*, towards the earth and pleads:

> Now man, have mind on me forever,
> Look on thy love thus languishing;
> Let us never from other dissever,
> Mine help's thine own, creep under my wing;
> Thy sister's a queen, thy brother a king,
> This line's entailed, soon come thereto,
> Take me for wife and learn to sing:
> *Quia amore langueo.*[56]

Part Three

THE RED QUEEN

══ 13 ══

THE VEILED GODDESS

Symbols . . . are merely veils of light rendering visible
the 'Divine Dark'.
Anna Kingsford in her introduction to *Kore Kosmou*

Lady of the Perfect Black

Sophia will lodge with any who will receive her with a good heart.
We should, therefore, not be surprised to find her within the very
depths of magic, hermeticism and alchemy. Here the moonlit
Diana of the pagans associates with the Black Isis of alchemy,
and meets the green Venus of the Rosicrucians.

The Goddess has always been a way-shower of the Mysteries,
leading to spiritual illumination. As her image was subsumed
in orthodox spirituality, so it became enhanced within the off-
shoots of Classical mystery schools of the ancient world, who
bequeathed their esoteric legacy to hermeticism, alchemy and
ceremonial magic. Here Sophia has found a permanent lodging.

There has been a fragmentation of the esoteric and mystical traditions within the West: orthodox spiritualities have usually retained
the mystical content for themselves and rejected the esoteric or
magical content as inappropriate. But they are a unified whole
which cannot be split apart. Effective mysticism *is* esotericism.[1]

Magic is often understood to mean cheap spells, illusions and
deception. The true magician is a *theurgist* – literally 'god-worker'
– who mediates the operation of the divine in human affairs
with the selflessness of the mystic. Theurgy is the term used by
Iamblicus to describe magic, for by this means the qualities and
powers of the Gods are archetypally applied to the realms and
actions of humanity. In this respect, the magician acts solely as a
burning-glass or focus for the Gods to effect a phenomenal action.
This very process is, in the context of spirituality, identical to that
of a priest and congregation at prayer for one intention.

At the end of every magical action, the energy is sent to the
required end, perhaps to the healing of a person or situation. It

is common practice to send the remaining energy of the ritual to any in need throughout the world, often by means of invoking the World-Soul, Nature or the Goddess, depending on the philosophy of the assembled group. Sometimes a female practitioner is allotted the task of personifying the World-Soul or Angel of the Planet Earth, that she may mediate the work more thoroughly. That this is the purpose of magic may surprise some, whose ideas are confused by occult practices as reported in the popular press. Unless the observer of a ritual is also experiencing these things, it is impossible to gain a clear impression of what is going on – hence the confusion.

Esotericism is primarily about the harmony between the seen and unseen realms, the Great Above and the Great Below, Heaven and Earth. Because it operates by means of symbolic language, it is also called occult or hidden, like the veiled Sophia.

The work of completion or perfection is the work of Sophia. In one form or another, she is the creator or co-creator in the major Western cosmologies; she is also the mistress of creation's restoration or completion. As we will see below, the planetary gods, so important to hermetic philosophy, omit the Goddess of Wisdom from their canon. The sevenfold schema of planets, shown here with their corresponding Greek deities, represent the sevenfold ladder of experience, so often associated with the Sophianic myth:

Sun	Helios/Apollo
Moon	Artemis/Selene
Mars	Ares
Mercury	Hermes
Jupiter	Zeus
Venus	Aphrodite
Saturn	Kronos

The secret of magical work is the completion and perfection of creation. Like the notes of a scale, these sevenfold qualities are unresolved. The leading note causes us to listen for the completion of the octave – this is resolved by Sophia who is both the ground note of earth and the transcendent note of heaven. To this list, then, we may add Athene-Sophia as the octave of resolution, for she crowns the Great Work. Sophia is the companion of the soul who, like Psyche, passes through the experiences represented by these planetary qualities. These symbolic correspondences are the signatures of the earth. 'The Earth is a loom in which the planets weave their vibrations. The vibrations may be through or as musical notes that become concretized in the loom, transmutation is thus a changing of the planetary note.'[2]

Magicians and hermeticists have always been tuned to this sevenfold resonance, ever seeking the accompanying wisdom of Sophia in their work. The prayer of Giordano Bruno, (1548–1600) the hermetic monk who suffered the orthodox penalty for esoteric dissent, must remain that of all esotericists. 'The divine Sophia have I loved and sought from my youth; I have desired her to be my spouse. Ever have I loved her beauteous, radiant form. Ever have I prayed that she might be sent to abide with me, that she might work with me to the end that I might know what I lacked and what in me God would find acceptable. And since she had ever known and understood, had guided me in all my life's activity, I am persuaded that even after death she will ever keep me safe, wrapped securely in her watchful, constant love.'[3]

Because of the revival of the texts known as the *Corpus Hermeticum* during the fifteenth century, we see a rediscovery of and interest in things Egyptian, in pagan mystical thought. The impulse to reappraise these texts came for the first time after the sacking of Constantinople by the Turks in 1453. Manuscripts which had been housed in Byzantine libraries and scriptoriums, the remnants of undesirable paganism consigned to dusty shelves, flooded into the West. After the long bread and water fast of Christian doctrine, the early Renaissance sustained itself upon the meatier fare of the Classical philosophers and syncretic mystics.

The *Corpus Hermeticum* is considerable, possibly originating from as early as the third century BC within Egypt. Manetho, an Hellenic Egyptian historian, preserved the tradition that Thoth-Hermes had imparted a heritage of teachings in his own family.[4] The *Hermetica* belies traces of Egyptian myth, Platonizing philosophy, and Gnostic beliefs. The present corpus dates from about the first three centuries of the first millennium AD, but was edited in Byzantium in about the eleventh century before emerging in the West after the fall of Constantinople.

The *Hermetica* explains the old mystery teaching, which we will meet again in Eastern Orthodoxy: 'This is the goal, the aim of those who have Gnosis: *to become God.*'[5]

The purpose of hermeticism is gnosis or knowledge. In many ways, it restates the Gnostic principle, yet usually outside the orthodox structures of the Church. 'First you must tear up the garment you are wearing, the fabric of ignorance, the base of evil, the bond of corruption, the dark wall, the living death.'[6] However, although it sometimes uses the language of dualism inadvertently, hermeticism does not despise matter.

God works through Nature, says Trismegistus to his student Asclepius,[7] and through her He is the maker of all things, so that while 'Nature fell along with Adam and Eve, as her guardian we perform the Great Work to lift her up again – to free the *Anima Mundi* from her incarceration in matter.'[8] The hermeticist who makes this his or her work is told by Hermes:

> You are holy who did not blacken Nature.
> You are holy who has become the image of all Nature.[9]

It is here that Sophia met herself again. The fully-developed and radiant mother of the philosophers rediscovered her Egyptian persona in Isis, the queen of the alchemical process. The function of Isis as wonder-working Goddess survived into the Christian era when she became subsumed in the Hermetic texts. 'I have discovered and carved with chisels the secret hieroglyphs of inventive Hermes, engraving for my initiates the awe-inspiring Sacred Word.'[10] In this role, Isis takes on the teachings of Thoth, the great Logos of Egyptian tradition, and Hermanubis – a fusion of Hermes and Anubis as messengers of esoteric wisdom. Isis is an initiator. She was called *Mystis* or Lady of the Mysteries, which recalls *Wisdom* 8:4 where Sophia is called 'an initiate in the mysteries of God's knowledge'.

Isis was regarded as the vessel of creation, who provides the forms and matter of creation. As a divine womb or alembic, she becomes Alchymia, Lady Alchemy, the Queen of the Great Work, in subsequent alchemical literature. She is the Black Goddess incarnate, in whom the radiant Sophia waits to be rediscovered. A magical papyrus calls upon Isis 'pure virgin, give me a sign of the fulfilling of the charm, lift the sacred mantle, shake thy black destiny.'[11] Another papyrus text says of Isis: 'Thy kingdom resides in that which is utterly black.'[12] Initiated by Hermes into 'the rite of the Black (Perfection)', she is queen of the land of Chem, queen of the utmost black, mistress of the alchemical process.[13]

The Hermetic Corpus is arranged as a series of dialogues between a teacher and pupil. In one of these texts, *Kore Kosmou*, (The Virgin of the World), Isis instructs her son, Horus, about the ordering of the world. She describes how the demiurge created nature; 'and there came forth from his voice a Being in woman's form, right lovely, at the sight of whom the gods were smitten with amazement . . . he conferred on nature the government of all things in the world below . . . and God filled his august hands with the abundance of seeds which Nature supplied, and gripping the handfuls firmly said: "Take them, thou holy Earth, take them, all-honoured one, thou that art destined to be mother of all things.'[14] God then blended his breath with fire and created the different kinds of souls; each kind occupies one grade of the great round heaven, in a similar manner to the spindle of Ananke. The gods then created the limitations of the creation, which would guard and limit it from excess. Each deity gave something: the Sun gave light by day and the Moon light by night, as well as bearing Silence and Sleep. Cronos gave Diké (Justice) and Ananke (Necessity). Zeus gave Peace. Ares gave Struggle, Anger and Strife. Aphrodite gave Love, Pleasure and Laughter. Hermes gave Wisdom. 'To those same stars is assigned the race of men; and we have in us Moon, Zeus, Ares, the Lady of Paphos, Kronos, Sun and Hermes. Wherefore it is our lot to draw in from the aetherial life-breath tears, laughter, wrath, birth, speech, sleep and desire.'[15] This is a hermetic way of understanding personal astrology, and indeed modern astrology works in a similar psychological way to this, following the old Gnostic method of overcoming the rulers of the personal horoscope.

Thus the seven planetary powers bestowed their qualities upon humankind and the whole of creation. Just before human souls were embodied, they were told: 'The destruction of your bodies then will be the starting point for a rebirth, and their dissolution, a renewal of your former happiness. But your minds will be blinded, so that you will think the contrary, will regard the punishment as a boon.'[16] Here we encounter the theme which closely pursues the Sophianic myth – that involution, the fall into matter, is not misfortune, but an opportunity for experience.

The Elements then complained to God because they were polluted by humankind, but God told them that a great one would come 'who shall keep holy watch on men's deeds. He shall be judge of the living . . . and a terrible king of the dead.'[17] This is none other than Osiris who, with Isis, would bring divine worship to earth and who, to avoid the pollution of the elements with corpses, would teach the art of mummification.

Isis describes how the land of Egypt is superior to other realms by explaining how the Earth 'lies in the middle of the universe, stretched on her back, as a human being might lie, facing towards

251

heaven . . . her head lies towards the South of the universe, her right shoulder toward the East and her left shoulder toward the West; her feet lie beneath the Great Bear, and her thighs are situated in the regions which follow next to the South of the Bear.'[18] Likening both the earth and the dwelling place of the soul to herself she says, 'the right holy land of our ancestors lies in the middle of the earth; and the middle of the human body is the sanctuary of the heart . . . headquarters of the soul.'[19]

The *Kore Kosmou* is related entirely by Isis who describes the creation with the eye of one who was present, just as Sophia is present in *Proverbs* 8. Her skilful relation is like a verbal tapestry, not unlike that of Persephone's weaving.

Whether Isis was also responsible for the promulgation of the Emerald Tablet, attributed to Hermes Trismagistos, is not known. This alchemical Rosetta Stone has virtually been the sole basis of all hermetic work:

1 In truth certainly and without doubt, whatever is below is like that which is above, and whatever is above is like that which is below, to accomplish the miracles of one thing.

2 Just as all things proceed from one alone by meditation on one alone, so also they are born from this one thing by adaptation.

3 Its father is the sun and its mother is the moon. The wind has born it in its body, its nurse is the earth.

4 It is the parent of every miraculous work in the whole world.

5 Its power is perfect if it is converted into earth.

6 Separate the earth from the fire and the subtle from the gross, softly and with great prudence.

7 It rises from earth to heaven and comes down again from heaven to earth and thus acquires the power of the realities below. In this way you will acquire the glory of the whole world, and all darkness will leave you.

8 This is the power of all powers, for it conquers everything subtle and penetrates everything solid.

9 Thus the little world is created according to the prototype of the great world.

10 From this and in this way, marvellous applications are made.

11 For this reason I am called Hermes Trismagistos, for I
    possess the three parts of Wisdom of the whole world.
12 Perfect is what I have said of the work of the sun.[20]

This 'work of the sun', of transmutation, is taken by all hermeticists
as the Great Work, whatever their chosen field of operation. It may
also stand as a compressed myth of Sophia and the Black Goddess,
the Gnostic passion of Sophia reworked as the history of matter,
the myth of Psyche's quest for her Eros. Clauses 7 and 8 of the
above represent the central core of Sophia's own myth. The work
of the sun is nothing other than the realisation of Sophia as the
Red Queen, winged and radiant as the sun.

The chief protagonist of the hermetic and alchemical work is
Hermes himself, the subtle Mercurius, whom alchemists defined
as both the soul and the spirit. Like the wind-borne Holy Spirit or
Eros, he gives quicksilver swiftness and enthusiasm for the work.
He is even identified with the World-Soul by Avicenna: 'He is the
spirit of the Lord which fills the whole world and in the beginning
swam upon the waters. They call him also the spirit of Truth which
is hidden from the world.'[21] This quality of Hermes/Mercurius is
that of Sophia herself, in her guise as androgyne, the daemonic
messenger of the soul.

In his *Twelve Keys*, Basil Valentine identified the Soul or Spirit of
the World with *'an earth-spirit which is life itself*, endowing all created
things with strength, yet itself intangible and invisible . . . as the
reflection in a mirror. It is of course found in "our earth" – the
prima materia – and is the "root of all bodies", or substances.'[22]

The Lady of the Perfect Black in Christian tradition is, of course,
Mary. Not only are many of her images black, but she is herself
a human creature, the prima materia of the redemption. It is as
Stella Matutina, Star of the Morning, that she rises in the heavens
with all the promise of restored creation at the summit of her
Assumption.

When the influence of the Goddess has been submerged in
everyday life, hermeticism has acted as an esoteric safety-valve.
The Northern Protestant world of the post-Reformation produced an esoteric order, the Rosicrucians, whose focus was upon
the initiatory experiences of their mystical founder, Christian
Rosenkreutz, a Christly figure who gained the 'treasures of
darkness' and secreted them in his vault. One of the prime
Rosicrucian texts examples how Rosenkreutz took the initiation
of Venus, who represents the subsumed and sleeping Goddess in

the allegorical world of the Rosicrucians. Probably drawing on the Renaissance text, *The Dream of Porphilo, The Chemical Wedding of Christian Rosenkreutz* is about the awakening of the adept through the planetary agency of Venus as mistress of love. The *Chemical Wedding* derives part of its myth from that of Venusberg, the place where the Germanic Goddess, Holda/Hel, appears as Venus. Here, Tannhauser wishes to remain forever, like Arthur with his Avalonian consort, Morgan.[23]

The Chemical Wedding, written in the early seventeenth century by an anonymous Rosicrucian writer, is an allegorical myth concerning the progress of an ideal adept, personified by Christian Rosenkreutz, through the Great Work.[24] Significantly, the psychopomp of this drama is a dynamic virgin, Alchymia, who conducts Rosenkreutz throughout his adventures which cover seven days, each one assigned to one of the planetary qualities. On the fifth day, the hero is vouchsafed the privilege of entering the chamber where the naked Lady Venus lies sleeping. He uncovers her, thus enacting the thing which initiates are strictly warned not to do – to unveil the Goddess. In this act, Rosenkreutz, whose name means Rose-Cross, is revealed as an adept of high degree: those who look upon the Goddess unveiled are stricken with death, madness or transformatory wisdom.

Venus is the mistress of love and desire, the one who gives life its impetus. This aspect of the Goddess has been so over-emphasised in our own time that the cult of beauty has turned upon itself and gone sour. Ugliness terrifies us, but beauty also has become indistinguishable from mediocrity. The veiled Goddess is an image of the Black Goddess – she who cannot be looked upon. But when her veil is drawn, the Goddess reveals herself to be beautiful. This vision does not provoke sexual desire, although that lies at the root of all longing, but an intense and profound understanding of beauty as wholeness and perfection. The veiled Venus stands for the undivided beauty of archetypal origin, the potential Pleromic experience of Sophia.

In this text, Venus lies sleeping in the depths of a castle. Here truly is the submerged Goddess whom every magician and esotericist must encounter, for she is the initiatrix of the Great Work. Rosenkreutz's reward/punishment for this act of uncovering the mystery of the Goddess is to become the porter of the castle, taking on the role of the current porter, Atlas, who previously uncovered the Goddess. Here lies one of the great truths of esoteric work – that whoever penetrates to the heart of the mystery thereafter becomes its guardian. It is by this means that all esotericists are sons and daughters of the Goddess, the guardians of her mysteries, taking conscious responsibility for Nature. In every generation the torch of the initiator passes from hand to hand, that the mysteries of Sophia may be guarded and transmitted until the time when human guardianship is no longer needed, when the Rose of the World shall bloom upon the cross of the elements, when the Mistress of Life shall lead us home.

Lady Alchymia

Alchemy is the proper craft of Sophia, for she transforms one thing into another, allowing the true gold of creation to shine through the prima materia. 'Sophia is, will be, and has always been the elixir of life; the philosopher's gold, the oneness and essence of the physical world-self, the Quinta Essentia.'[25]

Alchemy is an art which seeks to realize the eternal perfection which constitutes creation: the Mistress who redeems creation is Sophia.

The purpose of alchemy is the reconstitution of nature into its primal and holy state. The physical chemistry of alchemy may indeed produce gold from lead, but that is not the prime purpose of alchemy, whatever traditions have arisen as a result of that myth. The production of gross gold is merely a by-product of what is really a spiritual process, rather as the miraculous feats of mystics, such as levitation, healing and bi-location are the result of the mystic's union with the divine.

The practice of alchemy is established in many cultures. Considering our earlier look at the Islamic toe-holds of Sophia, it is not insignificant that many alchemical processes and indeed, much of medieval science, was preserved and transmitted by Islamic tradition. Within Islam, science is viewed in the light of the divine, and is considered a holy art: this is in stark contrast to the practice of science in the West.

The transubstantiation of the natural species of bread and wine into the Body and Blood of Christ is the alchemy of the Mass within Catholicism. The transubstantiation of base matter into pure gold is the preoccupation of the alchemist. From the point of view of Wisdom, Sophia strives to be recognized in all creation and her alchemy is worked within the soul itself. For all people this has meant finding a foundation in the Mysteries themselves.

255

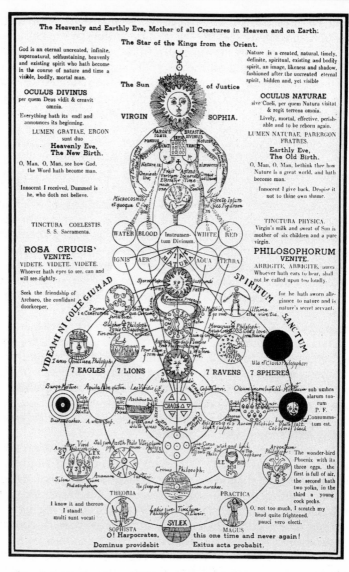

15 *Alchemical Virgin* Here Sophia is represented as the inspiration of the alchemical Great Work. Her body represents Nature while God, in the form of Jesus as the Sun of Justice, is her head. Sophia provides the four vehicles of the alchemical process – the elements. As the instrument of the Divine Will, she presides over the sevenfold working out of all matter from the roots of Chaos upwards. Combining the natural and divine approaches, she shows herself a common path of wisdom. Time and eternity wait in her womb. Taken from the *Secret Symbols of the Rosicrucians*.

To make the sun shine at midnight was the initiation of the Mystery Schools. To make light shine in darkness, or to draw light from darkness is the initiation of alchemy. It is the gift of the perfect black.

Just as the knight or candidate king embraced the ugliness of the Cailleach at the well, thus allowing her the freedom of transmutation in the Grail Quest, so also, we embrace the work of the *prima materia* that the gold may shine forth.

Gnosticism had its own alchemy. 'No matter what we eat, whether meat, vegetable, bread or anything else, we are doing a favor to created things by collecting souls from all things and transporting it with us to the above.'[26]

The approaches to alchemy are indeed forbidding. Like an unscalable cliff-face, it offers no hand-holds to the uninitiated. The veiling of the alchemical processes is analogous to the veiled Neith or Isis. Alchemy was protected from the profane by the simple expedient of pied and symbolic language, the whole proliferation of technical jargon guarded it well.

Modern chemistry does indeed evolve out of alchemy, but the purposes of the two are quite variant. 'Whereas chemistry deals with scientifically verifiable phenomena . . . alchemy pertains to a hidden reality of the highest order which constitutes the underlying essence of all truths and all religions.'[27] It would be true to call alchemy the skilful ecumenism of spiritual sciences.

Paracelsus, perhaps one of the most straightforward commentators on natural sciences and one who used his knowledge for healing, had little time for those who muddied the clear stream of wisdom. 'That Greek Satan has sown in the philosophic field of true wisdom, tares and his own false seed, to wit, Arissttoteles, Albertus, Avicenna, Rhasis, and that kind of men, enemies to the light of God and Nature, who have perverted the whole of physical science, since the time when they transmuted the name of Sophia into Philosophy.'[28]

Again and again we come back to Sophia's association with the mystic seven – from ancient times, the *Klimax Heptapolous*, the Seven-Gated Stair was the way of Wisdom. By purification of the seven levels of created life – perceived of variously as the seven planetary qualities and metals – the initiate of the mysteries attained to interior wisdom and effective action. We have seen how the Gnostics utilized this understanding. It is truly an alchemical process which finalizes and completes the soul.

In an anonymous alchemical book, *The Book of Thirty Chapters*, we read about an alchemist who dreams of a guide. 'I rose up and went off with this person. Soon we arrived before Seven Gates so fine that I had never seen the like. "Here," my guide said to me, "are found the treasures of the science you seek." "Thank you," I replied. "Now guide me so that I may penetrate into these dwellings where you say are found the treasures of the universe." "You will never penetrate there," he answered, "unless you have in your power the keys of those doors." '[29]

Each of these doors is associated with the seven metals; by working alchemically with each of these, the alchemist accordingly unlocks the nature and mystery of each of the seven planets. Why is this so? Because there is the same correspondence between astrology and alchemy as between heaven and earth, as between the despised and the transcendent Sophia. These mystical associations have become conventionalized through esoteric practice, because they observe the law of the Emerald Tablet: 'That which is below is like that which is above'. The correspondences of planets with metals are conventionally given thus:

Metal	Gold	Silver	Quicksilver	Copper	Iron	Tin	Lead
Planet	Sun	Moon	Mercury	Venus	Mars	Jupiter	Saturn

Each subtle vibration of the planet affects its corresponding metal. In dealing with the seven metals, alchemists were undergoing the same spiritual initiation as Mithraists, Gnostics, Orphics and followers of Sophia.

What lies beyond these seven doors of the treasure-palace of the alchemical work? One alchemical work says that a divine mirror is discovered. 'When a man looks at himself and sees himself in this, he turns away from everything that bears the name of gods or demons, and, by uniting himself with the Holy Spirit, becomes a perfect man. He sees God within himself . . . This mirror is set up beyond seven doors . . . which correspond to the seven heavens, beyond the sensual world, beyond the twelve mansions.'[30]

The stages of the alchemical process are variously and confusingly described as being three, four, seven, eight or twelve in number. The lack of information and the purposeful occultation of these processes makes commentary difficult. Bald statements such as 'alchemy consists of the extraction of pure Sulphur, Mercury and Salt from the raw material; the fusing of these materials into a new and unknown substance called 'the Philosopher's Stone,'[31]

258

seem initially helpful. Certainly Sulphur, the hot, active spirit of alchemy and Quicksilver (mercury), the receptive and passive soul, were indeed considered central to the alchemical process. Salt corresponded to the basic constituents of the body.

'Wherever there is metal, there are Sulphur, Quicksilver, and Salt – spirit, soul and body,' says Basil Valentinus.[32] It is by the marriage of Sulphur and Quicksilver, conceived of metaphorically as male and female, king and queen, that the alchemical process is concluded.

Whatever the physical or chemical structure to be submitted to the alchemical process, it first had to be reduced to the *prima materia*. By analogy, we may say that this corresponds to finding the basic common denominator of matter – that which is common to all creation. This recognition is the first step in reconnecting the chain of existence. Without this realisation, we may not proceed.

The links of Wisdom's chain are forged through each of the alchemical processes. It is an interior process also, as Basil Valentinus' acrostic for the alchemical Vitriol suggests: *'Visita interiora terrae; rectificando invenies occultum lapidem* (Visit the inner earth; through purification you shall find the hidden stone).' The alchemical process returns us immediately to the original state.

The major stages of the alchemical work are *nigredo* (blackening), *albedo* (whitening) and *rubedo* (reddening). Sometimes, between the *albedo* and *rubedo* a change of colour is inserted – the *cauda pavonis*, (the peacock's tail). We have here again the three sacred colours of the Goddess, typifying her major phases. According to the Hindu teachings on the *gunas* (fundamental tendencies), which also reproduce these colours, black corresponds to *tamas*, the downward movement which 'flees the luminous Origin', white (*sattva*) represents the upward aspiration towards the Origin, and red (*rajas*) represents the tendency to 'expansion in the plane of manifestation.'[33]

If we consider the three main alchemical processes, we may virtually posit an alchemical mythos of Sophia:

Nigredo (Blackness)   Sophia falls from her original condition into the gross matter of earth and water. She falls to earth and her tears make the earth fertile.
Albedo (Whiteness)   Sophia's struggle to return is typified by air. She becomes like the wind, and is blown about invisibly.
Rubedo (Redness)   Sophia is established in fire, her original state. This is the inner fire which warms and inspirits us all.

However many sequences are involved in the alchemical work, they are repetitions of the purificatory processes. When expressed in a sevenfold sequence, the alchemical processes are like the myth of Sophia.

1 *Calcination* The purgation of the material into powder. Sophia is subject to material existence.
2 *Sublimation* The removal of spirit from matter. Sophia is divided into Sophia Nigrans and Sophia Stellarum.
3 *Solution* The matter is dissolved into a water that does not wet the hand. Sophia's power is extracted in a primary way.
4 *Putrefaction* The matter is subjected to vigorous disintegration by heat. Sophia is unconsciously subsumed into many ideologies.
5 *Distillation* The heated matter gives off vapours which are condensed and reabsorbed in the vessel. Sophia's power works through many ideologies and is reabsorbed by them.
6 *Coagulation* The matter is deprived of humidity and forms a solid. Sophia begins to be consciously perceived by many people.
7 *Tincture* The matter is transformed into its holy and primal state. Sophia is understood by many to be of one holy blood and kinship with humankind.

This alchemical sequence is offered as a means of exploring the Sophianic myth, for there is no doubt that, taking the alchemical initiation of the planet earth as a whole, we are living in the time of the tincture. This sequence may be taken to represent the return of Sophia through the seven planetary or alchemical experiences, or it may be personally applied to the individual spirit. A similar mode of experience may be paralleled by the seven sacraments of the Church, which are seven means of purifying the soul. The seven chakras of the subtle body are likewise gates of entry to Sophia, and this is the work of many Eastern disciplines and spiritualities. The tincture, or Elixir, produced at the end of the alchemical process has the ability to turn the gross human body into 'an incorruptible body of light.'[34] The purification and realignment of the chakras is solely to alter our subtle body, sometimes called the astral body, so that it takes on a crystalline or diamond form, filled with sparks that run through our physical body like those that run through carbon-based charcoal. The diamond, or *varja*, body is the aim of Varjayana Buddhism.

But before that body of light can be attained, the adept has to work to reconcile and integrate the elements which are missing from the individual and cosmic spirit. This work is then nothing less than the resacralization of matter, the integration of the feminine and masculine, the craft of Sophianic restoration.

Aurora Consurgens

Aurora Consurgens is an alchemical manuscript attributed to St Thomas Aquinas, but more likely the product of an anonymous cleric working sometime between the thirteenth and fifteenth centuries. It is a strange fusion of theology, sapiential quotation and alchemical lore. Consider the beginning where Wisdom calls aloud, as in Proverbs: 'Nought is more base in appearance than she, and nought is more precious in nature than she, and God also hath appointed her to be bought for a price.'[35] This is a description of the Black Goddess herself in her form of *prima materia* of the alchemical work. She is likened to a firestone, alluding to the *ignis noster*, or fire of the soul, which kindles the Great Work within the breast of each alchemist. Wisdom is called, 'a gift and sacrament of God and a divine matter.'[36]

'Divine matter' may seem an odd juxtaposition, given that throughout history, matter has been seen as lacking in divinity. The text identifies Wisdom 'with the soul of the dark earth, the impure prima materia. Alchemy, accordingly, lays upon man the task, and confers upon him the dignity, of rescuing the hidden, feminine aspect of God from imprisonment in matter by his opus, and of reuniting her with the manifest, masculine deity', concludes von Franz in her commentary on the *Aurora*.[37]

Throughout the text, Wisdom speaks of herself as the basis of the alchemical process, to be treated and recognized in many ways. It is indeed by the ascent of the alchemical ladder that Sophia resumes her former appearance.

The *Aurora* speaks of seven women, exiled and imprisoned together, who yearn after one husband. These are fragmentations of the composite Sophia, the spouses of the seven planets which are fallen. They await the seven gifts of the Holy Spirit, by which we may understand the alchemical processes.

But it is as Mistress of the Elements that she is accorded first place in this text: 'Let him hear what the spirit of the doctrine saith to the sons of the discipline concerning the earthly and the heavenly Adam . . . When thou hast water from earth, air from water, fire from air, earth from fire, then shalt thou fully and perfectly possess our art.'[38] This part of the text refers symbolically to the doctrine of the elements: air and fire are, according to Aristotelian thought, the higher elements; water and earth are lower elements and are, needless to say, associated with the female. Figured in this text is a hint at the admixture of the elements, of male with female, of Christ, the Second Adam, entering into union with his Wisdom. The alchemical riddle may run thuswise:

> *water from earth* = dew, distilled from the female alone – the moist matrix of life.
> *air from water* = steam, distilled from the female by the male – the energy of creation.
> *fire from air* = gas, distilled from the male alone – the life-giving breath.
> *earth from fire* = a forged metal or fired mould, wrought by the female from the male – the child or offspring of union.

In token of this understanding Wisdom says of herself: 'I am the mediatrix of the elements, making one to agree with another; that which is warm I make cold, and the reverse; that which is dry I make moist, and the reverse; that which is hard I soften, and the reverse. I am the end and my beloved is the beginning. I am the whole work and all science is hidden in me.'[39]

Aurora Consurgens gives into our hands the keys of the mystery: that Sophia is the matrix of life, the end of which is to understand and balance the elements – whether it be in the alchemical process ('the work' mentioned above), in the creation of a child, or in the birth of an idea. Here Sophia appears as *Athene Ergane*, the work-woman who is not only the mediatrix of life but also of our understanding of it.

The Nuptials of the Womb

That which is continually hinted at and prefigured in Gnostic, Qabalistic and esoteric texts – the nuptials of God and Sophia – is actually depicted in the alchemical process, whose images show the cohabitation and conjoining of alchemical king and queen.

Many spiritual disciplines require that the operator be assisted by a partner. In the Tibetan tradition, the *terton* – the finder of wisdom-bestowing caches hidden in the earth by divine beings – must be accompanied by his yogini or consort.[40] Simiarly, Judaism regards as unbalanced any man who attempts qabalistic work without a wife. Again, the inner tantric tradition of the West, enshrined within alchemy, requires an alchemist to have his *soror mystica*, or mystical sister. The complete degradation of this tradition is seen in the conjuror's attractive assistant whose sole duty is to hold hoops and strike admiring attitudes. The union of the practitioner and consort is very important, for between them they produce a third and special thing. In the case of alchemy it is nothing other than the Son of the Philosophers – *filius philosophorum*.

The protagonists of the alchemical sacred marriage are Sol and Luna, the emblems who represent the spiritual and metallic qualities of the alchemical process, as well as many other dualities – heaven and earth, male and female, etc. Their meeting results in a series of relationships which are both painful and proving. Finally they conjoin to bring about the last phase of the work, which is nothing less than the rebirth of the world itself, the remaking of creation.

In the sixteenth century text, *Rosarium Philosophorum*, the penultimate alchemical stage is represented by the Coronation of the Virgin, wherein Mary is brought into heaven and honoured by the Trinity and the last stage is represented by Christ rising triumphantly from the tomb. The Christian analogues of the alchemical work are dealt with in more detail in Chapter 17, but we may note here that Christ and Mary enter the wedding chamber of heaven, as the Hindu Shiva and Shakti embrace, to end creation that it might be remade.

Vladimir Soloviev wrote of the *coniunctio* of the syzygies thus: 'Only in this . . . chemical union of two beings which are of the same species, of equal worth and yet completely dissimilar in form, is the creation of a new person possible (both in the natural order as well as in the spiritual order) . . . Such a union we find in sexual love, and therefore we grant it an exclusive significance as *the requisite and irreplaceable basis of all future perfection*.'[41]

Corbin, in his assessment of Jung's *Answer to Job* sees the descent of Jerusalem, as 'an equivalent to Sophia: she has cosmic attributes making her the Anima Mundi, the primordial female Anthropos and male Anthropos, *Heaven above, heaven below* . . . The vision is a part of and an anticipation of the *hieros gamos* of which a divine child is the fruit. It announces the union of opposites, the reconciliation of nature and spirit. The divine child, the *filius Sapientiae*, begotten by Sophia in this heavenly marriage, is also a *complexio oppositorum*.'[42] 'The *filius Sapientiae* is the one through whom the Holy Spirit brings about the divine anthropomorphosis, a God of love into a man of gentleness. He is begotten by an 'unknown father' and by the Sophia-Sapientia.'[43] Sophia's task is to reconceive us, giving us spiritual rebirth.

The tikkun, or apocatastasis of alchemy is the *coniunctio*, the transmutation of all things and their final union. Rumi wrote a fitting invitation to the wedding chamber of the alembic:

> Dearly beloved!
> Let us go toward Union.
> And if we find the road
> That leads to separation,
> We will destroy separation.
> Let us go hand in hand.
> Let us enter the presence of Truth.
> Let it be our judge
> And imprint its seal upon our union
> For ever.[44]

The image of the Alchemical King and Queen in congress is the highest human conception of union. We return to our pivotal word 'knowledge' once more, where sexual union and sacred knowledge are one and the same. The mystic's union with God, the alchemist's production of the Elixir or Living Stone, are symbols of this union. The Islamic alchemist Sheikh Ahmad Ahsa'i, bids us to contemplate 'the living stone' of the alchemical process: 'Meditate and understand this Sign . . . for such a body is precisely the Sign of the dwellers in Paradise, "for they have bodies in which exist all the attributes, laws, and actions of bodies, but such bodies enact the actions of Spirits and pure Intelligences; they perceive what the celestial Souls and angelic Intelligences perceive, just as the latter perceive through their own essence what Souls and bodies perceive."'[45]

This is nothing less than a description of the production of the diamond body of light, into which the physical body is transfigured by the study and practice of the Mysteries. The alchemical way is one method of knowing what the angels know, or of being married to Sophia. The end of the work is the production of the

Philosopher's Stone which is an alchemical reprise of the Black Stone sacred to the Lady of the Cubic Stone herself, Cybele, the Ka'aba, the Black Virgin transformed to fiery gold. 'Alchemy is the soul-price of the cosmos: it teaches us to relate the infinite to the mundane, to find the presence of the divine in the daily circle of being. The process is a spiritual code used . . . by those who seek the Stone.'[46]

Alchemy is the process which reverses the Fall. The soul's descent into matter is a wise journey where much is learned; alchemy is the soul's return journey, in a state of knowledge where the Red Queen is encountered.

Rending the Veil

Sophia stood for many centuries upon her pedestal, the darling of philosophers and theologians. In the ideological débacle of the Reformation, the complicated scaffolding of medieval theology was thrown down. Throughout Europe powerful factions stated their case: there was no point in venerating the Mother of Christ, she was merely a creature. The Black Virgins were thrown upon pyres, the shrines of the Virgin's healing and counsel were destroyed, the kind customs and comforting prayers were abolished. So passed the spirit of Sophia out of the world, exiled once again.

As the spiritual consequence of this dethroning, humankind found other ways of limiting the power of the Divine Feminine. The object of this assault was Nature herself. Yielding Nature, Dame Kind, whose body endlessly produced that we might live, was to be vivisected by the new science. Thus began the rape of Nature.

The Hermetic dictum, 'Nature takes delight in Nature, Nature contains Nature, and Nature can overcome Nature,'[47] was drastically reinterpreted by Cartesian science. Francis Bacon spoke of Nature as 'a common harlot', as a fertile female slave, a subservient creature which could be exploited by mankind.[48] Hermetically, Nature was Uroborus, the serpent which bites its own tail: the material realization of this image hovers near us as we enter the twenty-first century and find the serpent of scientific temptation already waiting in the garden, willing us to explore the manipulation of matter. Adam and Eve were made the stewards of creation before they were evicted from Eden. The question before us now is, 'quis cusodit custodes' – who guards the guardians?

Vladimir Soloviev wrote: 'It is time men realized their oneness with Mother Earth and rescued her from lifelessness so they also can save themselves from death. But what oneness can we have with the earth, when we have no such oneness, no such moral relationships among ourselves?'[49]

This alienation of Nature permeates the latter days of our history. It has gone hand in hand with a distrust of femaleness and the exploitation of all forms of creation, from the rape of world mineral and tree resources to the vivisection of animals and the attempt to recreate human life in laboratories. The loss of our sense of the sacred has thus inflicted sufferings on the four kingdoms which constitute our created world: mineral, vegetable, animal and human. Regardless of the so-called benefits of *in vitro* fertilization, there is something deeply repugnant in this tampering with the stuff of life. It seems to be a truly black alchemy, whatever 'beneficial' by-products it may have for infertile couples.

The manipulation of matter will not necessarily give us access to the roots of wisdom. There may be wiser routes, as Rupert Sheldrake's theory of morphic fields has observed. His thesis is 'that memory is inherent in nature.'[50] It is clear that certain natural organisms have habituated into certain repetitive patterns which determine their individuality as a species but which are nevertheless crucial in keeping that species in touch with all its members past and present.

If we may put this metaphysically, wherever Sophia has walked, the path of Wisdom is found. And, as everyone knows, it is easier to walk along an existing path than to make a new one. These chreodes, as Sheldrake calls the pathways of evolving change within morphic fields, exist in all life forms. This presents us with a staggering new concept: that the indwelling soul of earth, the *anima mundi* is not immutable, lodged eternally in the mind of God, but open to evolutionary creativity. Therefore manipulation may not be necessary, the changes we seek may already be unfolding within Nature.

'Environmental changes, like genetic mutations, impose new necessities on organisms. Necessity is the mother of invention: but the inventions themselves are made by organisms.'[51] Ananke, or Necessity, is the mistress of the Fates, they who spin, weave and cut the thread of DNA within each of us. The adaptation of the planet earth itself, metaphored as Gaia, the Greek Earth Goddess, is the basis of James Lovelock's theory. Gaia, he says, is an independent organism with the power to adapt to necessity.

The Black Goddess is the regulator of life on earth. Let us hope that Sophia will give us the wisdom to adapt to the necessary changes which lie ahead of us; the *volva* of Scandinavian tradition reminds us that life renews itself endlessly, in ever widening spirals. Although the theory of morphic fields is essentially about the law of physics, it is a theory which holds good also for metaphysics. Indeed we can see immediately how morphic fields give us a view of Sophia in Nature. If the collective memories of every species were pooled, we would arrive at the totality of Wisdom. This is the true body of the Black Goddess, signed in the patternings of our skin, woven into the cortex of our brain, twisted into every strand of DNA. The wisdom of Sophia is present in every spark of inspiration that leaps to conflagration within us. The kindling of that wisdom occurs when a morphic resonance is stimulated.

What lies at the heart of the earth itself but the secret fire which warms our planet in maternal love? It is the volcanic fiery heart which keeps us alive, sometimes manifesting in unusual ways which we have symbolized as dragon, serpent and fiery lights.

We saw how Christian Rosenkreutz lifted the veil of the Goddess and lived; but shall the initiates of science lift the veil of Persephone and behold the naked universe with both reverence and responsibility? The aim of alchemy had been to transmute everything to true gold, just as the aim of religion had been to purify the soul to its innate integrity – these intrinsic values are the eternal currency of Sophia who is the presence which connects both heaven and earth, the Divine and Nature.

We pass from the world of alchemy to the Age of Reason, which was determined to view the world in a material light. There were no gods or spirits. The definition of inert elements into absurd metaphorical images had to stop. However, while science was gearing itself for the progressive strides of the Industrial Revolution, other fields began to sense the beauties of Nature, the loss of the Divine Feminine in their concerns. The very products of the Age of Reason turned their backs upon its materialist concerns and began to speak out in prophetic, poetic and revolutionary ways. And so the spark of Sophia was kindled once more.

=== 14 ===

THE WOMAN CLOTHED
WITH THE SUN

I have no pen to describe the Heavenly Kingdom; neither can I
express it, for the earthly tongue is much too insufficient to do
it. We will defer it until we come into the bosom of the Maiden.
Three Principles, Boehme

The Mirror of Nature

At the Reformation, the cult of Mary lost its impetus. Its trajectory
remained ghetto-like in the southern Catholic countries of Europe,
while Northern Europe gloried in the cleaner lines of scriptural
wisdom. For the Goddess of Wisdom, the Reformation might have
seemed a hard blow to recover from. Mary was, after all, almost her
only representative in an embattled realm. The Protestant return
to scriptural sources brought Sophia stage centre, focalizing the
Goddessly power of Mary.

But after the long extravagance of the Renaissance, and the
contra-blows of the Counter-Reformation, a new simplicity reigned.
Wisdom took off her masquing gown and went attired in a
dove-grey mantle. Her gifts of wisdom never ceased to flow.
We see them coming a few steps nearer to the human condition,
her voice manifesting through women themselves.

Wisdom is free and unconfined by traditions. In the dismantling
of the Catholic tradition by the Protestants was a careful nurture
of the mystical concept of Wisdom. The Protestant and Non-
conformist traditions have nurtured the mystical and prophetic
lines of Sophia. The bridging figure of this time is Jacob Boehme
(1575–1624), who was born in German Silesia, the son of poor
peasants. As a shepherd boy he had his first visionary experience:
he climbed to the top of the Landes Krone, a local mountain,
and there saw 'a vaulted entrance of four red stones leading

into a cavern.'[1] Inside the cave was a vessel full of money. In panic he fled and was subsequently unable to find the place again. This vision was a prefiguring of the treasures he was to uncover. He became a shoemaker, married and had four sons. In 1600, he fell into a trance upon looking into a burnished pewter plate which reflected the sun. In his ecstasy he saw into the very heart of nature itself, feeling totally in harmony with creation.

He went on to write many books and treatises and suffered considerable persecution, for his natural philosophy seemed at variance with the Christianity of his day. This persecution however also brought him many friends and patrons, who helped support him and gave him access to hitherto undreamed of knowledge. It was while struggling with his deficiencies in ancient languages that he made another breakthrough. He found he was able to spontaneously intuit the meaning of unknown words. Dr Kober, a student of Paracelsus' doctrine of signatures, tested him, Boehme divining from the form and colour of plants their hidden properties. One such intuition set him off on his search for Wisdom. When he heard the Greek word for *idea* he exclaimed: 'I see a pure and heavenly maiden!'[2] This was the foundation for his acquaintance with Sophia.

Boehme practiced a form of theosophy – a natural knowledge of God. Boehme's theosophy was not identical to Theosophical principles as practiced today, which incorporate Eastern philosophy. Rather, Boehme's theosophy was based on observance of the natural world, a deep intuition for the medieval and qabalistic concepts of theology. He remained a devout Lutheran throughout his life; his theosophy was supra-confessional. It was blended of qabalistic understanding, with neo-Platonism, Gnosticism, magic, alchemy and the mystical theology of Thomas Aquinas. Any attempt to simplify Boehme's thought is doomed to failure, since his concept was as complex as the systems which informed it.

For Boehme, Sophia is the mirror of God's will. 'There is nothing in heaven or earth which did not, at the beginning, become manifest in this mirror.'[3] For him, Sophia is a maiden because she does not engender, merely receive and reflect. She is the 'visibility' of God, in which the Trinity of Father, Son and Spirit ever behold and discover themselves.

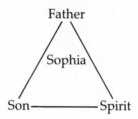

The Father's energies are concentrated in the Son, but Spirit breathes them forth. The Divine Visibility, as Boehme calls Sophia, unifies the three energies and plays with them in an infinitude of ways.

Boehme's response to the hypostases of the Trinity (who theologically comprises three persons but is indivisible) is to create a quarternity, in much the same way that Jung was called to do. Again and again, we will see the problems which this realization has caused among orthodox theology. Sophia is the *doxa*, or Glory of God, almost appearing as the Platonic 'beauty' of the 'Good'. She sits in the heart of the Temple, the virgin priestess of the seven lamps of Fire burning eternally before the Throne, which are the 'seven Spirits of God.'[4] The Maiden Wisdom stands before God 'as if in a vision, a morning-dream of Eternity, which prophetically reveals to Him what He can become, what he can make Himself.'[5]

In this way, Sophia represents the creative faculty, summoning the uncreated into creation. It is this vision which William Blake shared with Boehme which focuses the understanding that 'all effective magic depends upon desire and imagination.'[6] For Boehme, Nature was hidden within God and was enabled to manifest through desire and imagination.

Wisdom is described as a fertile mirror: 'The Wisdom is the true Divine Chaos, wherein all things lie, i.e. a Divine Imagination in which the ideas of angels and souls have been seen from Eternity in a Divine type and resemblance, yet not then as creatures, but in resemblance, as when a man beholds his face in a glass.'[7] Wisdom, like Tiamat, provides the form, God the matter from his eternal Nature.

In his commentary upon *Genesis*, *Mysterium Magnum*, Boehme follows the alchemical schema in speaking about Creation. The seven forms of Nature are represented by the seven planetary qualities.

The energies hidden within God were sevenfold: these correspond to the seven planets and the seven associated stages of the alchemical work. These sevenfold spirits are those sevenfold gifts of the Holy Spirit:[8] Wisdom, Understanding, Counsel, Knowledge, Fortitude, Piety and Fear of the Lord. They are also the seven pillars of Wisdom's temple.

Within God are also the two centres of Nature: the dark or Desire centre and the light or Imaginative centre. The dark centre is in potentia within God, the light centre is manifest. We need to turn to Ezekiel's vision in order to come at the basis of Boehme's meaning – that major source for qabalistic thought. In *Ezekiel* fire comes out of darkness, and light out of fire.

This realization of his vision gave Boehme endless trouble and sent him into depression – that God contained duality. However, this seeming duality arose out of the same realization as that which underlies *The Cosmic Doctrine* by the esotericist, Dion Fortune,[9] that there is positive and negative good. These qualities are complimentary and contrasting in effect, but they are not contradictory and combative. The condition of darkness does not necessarily mean evil – though our society has taken it to be so. It can also posit potential light and be a condition of spiritual fallowness and finding of treasure. It is in such darkness that the Black Goddess of potential wisdom is discovered. The mysteries uttered in the night become new suns, new stars.

This non-dualistic means of expressing the Godhead is manifest in the qabala, wherein the two pillars of the Tree of Life are 'mercy and severity'.

Boehme held that that before the Fall Adam and Eve were each androgynous virgins. When the Fall took place, the Virgin Sophia left them. Mary's *fiat* brought hope for Adam and Eve's restoration: 'The Eternal Word passed into her flesh and blood, together with the heavenly Virgin Sophia, by the power of the Holy Ghost; and the Divine Fiat stood in her womb . . . The Word was in the heavenly Maiden and drew Mary's essences to Itself and arrayed Itself in her flesh.'[10]

'Christ is thus, in a double sense, the Son of the Virgin. He is the Son of the earthly Virgin Mary,and He is the Son of the heavenly Virgin Sophia, who united herself with Mary . . . the heavenly Virgin is wedded to Him . . . She is the same heavenly Virgin or Idea who departed from Adam when he became unfaithful to her . . . This heavenly Idea has absolutely entered into the Second Adam, who is to restore her to us.'[11]

Boehme himself relates a mystical experience of his own marriage to Sophia: 'I will go through thorns and thistles . . . until I find again my Fatherland, where my Virgin dwells. I rely upon her faithful promise, when she appeared to me, that she would turn all my mournings into great joy; when I lay upon the mountain at midnight, so that all the trees fell upon me, and all the storms and wings beat upon me, and the Anti-Christ gaped at me with open jaws to devour me, then she came and comforted me, and married herself to me.'[12]

The hermetic and natural theosophy of Boehme gives insight into the nature of Wisdom. The profound influence of his writings was to pass beyond Germany into Russia (cf. Chapter 15) and westwards into Britain where it became the basis for a reawakened spirituality – a non-conformist Sophiology with a hermetic dynamic.

The Wonder Woman

Boehme's work was first presented in the English language in 1662 and became the study of Dr. John Pordage (1607–81) who gathered around him a community who, it was popularly reported, 'pretend to hold visible and sensible Communion with Angels . . .'[13] This community studied Boehme's theosophy in a non-conformist Christian way and called themselves the Philadelphians, after the church in *Revelations* 3:7–13 which is commended for its faithfulness. They are sometimes also known as 'the Behmenists'. With Pordage's first wife, Mary, 'Cloathed all in White Lawne, from the crown of the Head to the Sole of the Foot, and White rod in her hand', and hailed as 'Prophetess', the group held ecstatic sessions in his parish at Bradfield.[14] Pordage said of Sophia: 'She is my divine, eternal, essential self-sufficiency. She is my wheel within my wheel.'[15] Pordage was also an alchemist.

The secretary of the Philadelphians was an extraordinary woman called Jane Leade (1623–1704) whose revelations of Sophia give us a startling picture of female mysticism. While dancing as a girl of fifteen at a Christmas Eve party, she heard a spiritual voice: 'Cease from this, I have another Dance to lead thee in, for this is vanity.'[16] There followed a period of spiritual crisis during which her parents tried to force her into marriage with a suitable husband. Jane felt herself to be a bride of Christ and, in another society, would doubtless have entered a monastery as a nun. However, she eventually married her relative William Leade and had four daughters. Following her husband's death in February 1670, she had a vision of Sophia in April which exhorted her to live thereafter a virgin life. For some years, Jane had been meditating upon the spiritual principles underlying Boehme's work. While walking one day, she was óvershadowed by a bright cloud wherein stood a woman dressed in gold, with long hair: 'Behold I am God's eternal Virgin-Wisdom, who thou hast been enquiring after.'[17] Thereafter, Jane received three further visions of Sophia who told her,'I shall now cease to appear in a Visible Figure unto thee, but I will not fail to transfigure myself in thy mind and therefore open the Spring of Wisdom and Understanding.'[18]

A succession of books flowed from her pen, as her revelations revealed themselves steadily. Because she was a woman and had the potential to be a strong mystical leader, she aroused opposition among the entrenched, including the German Behmenist, Gichtel, against whom her son-in-law, Francis Lee, defended her and her inspired sources: 'it is true she pretends not to any visible Schechinah, such as was accommodated to the infant state of the Jews, but she pretends to . . . a Schechinah that is substantial and permanent, even to the real inhabitation of the Holy Ghost as in his Temple . . .'[19]

An indefatigible pamphleteer and writer in an era which not only penalized non-conformists but which also denied the right of women to speak of their spiritual experience, Jane is a shining light. She kept a series of diaries, *A Fountain of Gardens*, in which to record these experiences, being told by Christ to 'Keep in record the Journal of the new raised Life.'[20] Her individual style shows a woman who entered into 'the birthright-Blessing' of Sophia. This blessing was, according to Jane Leade nothing less than the ability to enter into 'one's own Native Country and original Virginity.'[21]

Jane exhorted her readers to meditation: 'Draw into thy Centre-deep . . . thy Heavens within . . . because the Virgin . . . there will first appear . . . Dive into your own Celestiality, and see with what manner of spirits you are endued; for in them the Powers do entirely lie for Transformation.'[22]

Jane Leade experienced Wisdom in the cyclicity of her life: 'I have learned to observe her Times and Seasons, I witness her opening as in the Twinkling of an Eye, a pure, bright, subtil, swift Spirit, a working motion, a Circling Fire, a penetrating Oil.'[23] She was certainly in no doubt about the stature of Sophia, saying that the name 'eternal Goddess' was the worthiest title which could be accorded to her.[24] As many of her Sophianic visions appeared as the Woman Clothed with the Sun, Jane sometimes called this aspect 'The Wonder Woman'.[25] She was sensible of the exile of most people from Wisdom as her moving prayer expresses:

> Oh, great Goddess and Queen of all worlds! wilt thou, after so long a time of desertion, once appear again! Who is it that hath entreated thy favour, and gained a promise from thee, of a visit . . . because nothing now will satisfy, unless thou bestow thyself, with all thy divine senses, as a co-deified life, to show that thou art not prevailed upon, to . . . restore thy own virginity, where thou findest humility and importunity in that personality which is all beloved of the highest Wisdom, and only Spouse of God; know and remember us who are brought to thy feet, and have been under thy severe discipline; therefore allot thy self to be our garland and crown.[26]

The Philadelphian's historian Richard Roach remarked on the amenability of the female soul to the spirit of Sophia, that the Virgin Wisom 'standing in the Female Denomination . . . will in an Extraordinary Manner Excite and Animate that sex whereby She is represented; and Endow them with her Peculiar Graces and Gifts, in such Degrees, that they shall Out-run and Exceed the Males themselves.'[27] This may well stand as Jane Leade's epitaph. Thirty-two years after her death, the spirit of Sophia was again incarnated, this time in another extraordinary woman, called Ann Lee.

The Simple Gifts

Mother Ann Lee was the founder and spiritual mother of the Shaker movement which arose out of Quakerism. The mode of worship favoured by the Society of Friends was one of quiet waiting on the Lord in silent meetings. The Shakers were formed out of those whose reaction to the movements of the Spirit were less silent. Many felt moved to sing, speak in tongues, to dance and tremble – hence their name 'Shaking Quakers'.[28]

Ann Lee was born the poor daughter of a Manchester blacksmith in 1736. She was frequently jailed for her enthusiastic Shaking Quaker activities and in the loneliness of her cell, she received revelations which strengthened her spirit and gave her to believe that the Parousia, the Second Coming, was present within each person. It was her role as messenger of this revelation which led to her becoming a spiritual mother, associated and frequently identified with Wisdom herself. The Shaker precept of celibacy was based on I *Corinthians* 7:29–31 which said that the time is too short to begin family life. This would give more time for the recognition among believers that the Body of Christ was present in the fraternity of peace, the practical sharing of life's good things, and the equality of women and men.

After violent attacks upon her, Ann Lee sailed to America to Albany, New York, in August 1774. Many converts were drawn to her community but, as Catholic families objected to Catharism, many Christians with families saw the Shaker precept of celibacy as threatening. Mother Ann was flogged and driven out, eventually suffering being tied to a wagon by her heels and dragged several miles. She died in 1784 but her movement continued, and she became revered as an inner mother. Father Joseph led the Shakers for the next few years, regularizing the Shaker worship and tradition, but not insisting on rules so much as 'Waymarks such as a forester uses to mark out a path for the guidance of others if they walk the same way.'[29]

A succession of male and female elders guided the Shakers through history. Their work was responsibly millennial and inspired for they founded interracial communities and were opposed to economic and sexual slavery.

Questions of propriety arose about the Shaker veneration of their spiritual mother. 'Having been *Idolators* – worshipping *Jesus* as *God* – are they not tempted to worship *Ann* as *Goddess*?' This query is answered in *The Shaker* in 1872 about the role of Mother Ann. 'When . . . the Shakers tell you that Christ has made His second appearance *in a Woman*, they mean that the Gospel which was revealed in and by Jesus, the Christ, after having been lost, has been revealed a second time through a woman . . . (It was Mother Ann who) came forth in the same power of the Spirit . . . as it was the special mission of Jesus to reveal the *Fatherhood* in God, so it was the special mission of Ann to reveal the *Motherhood* in God.'[30]

Mother Ann was associated with the Woman Clothed with the Sun in *Revelations* and her redemptive role interpreted as being 'the *first born of many sisters*, and the true MOTHER *of all living* in the new creation.'[31]

The Shaker concept of Godhead is further expounded in *Summary View* by Calvin Green. 'The Almighty is manifested as proceeding from everlasting as the *first Source* of power, and the *fountain* of all good, the *Creator* of all good beings, and is the ETERNAL FATHER: and the Holy Spirit of Wisdom, who was the *Co-Worker* with him, from everlasting, is the ETERNAL MOTHER, the *bearing Spirit* of all the works of God.'[32]

As God had sent his only begotten Son, so too, 'God, the Eternal father and Mother, sent forth into the world their beloved Daughter in the chosen *one prepared* . . . she was the true representative of the Daughter, the Mother Spouse in Christ, the *"express image and likeness of her Eternal Mother."*'[33]

This cult of personality subsumed into Deity is typical of many similar spiritual traditions, yet Shakerism has somehow retained the pristine simplicity of Mother Ann's original message in a way that the revelation is more prominent than the personality.

The gifts of the Spirit animate the whole Shaker tradition. It is this very freedom to create which aligns Shakerism with the purpose of Wisdom. 'The Shaker Way is one of gift, *charism*, beginning and ending with what is ultimately the Only Gift, God Himself, but including all the myriads of great and small gifts which flow ceaselessly into lives lived in the Spirit.'[34]

The many gifts of the Spirit were welcomed by the Shakers, especially as these were manifest in ritual enactments, singing and dancing. The most famous of Shaker songs, made familiar by Aaron Copland's *Appalachian Spring*, says it all:

> Tis the gift to be simple, tis the gift to be free,
> tis the gift to come down where we ought to be.
> And when we find ourselves in the place just right,
> 'twill be in the valley of love and delight.
> When true simplicity is gain'd,
> to bow and to bend we shan't be ashamed.
> To turn, turn will be our delight,
> 'til by turning, turning we come round right.[35]

This song might indeed be the anthem of Wisdom, attuned as it is to her cyclity and simplicity.

Mediumship was a sensitively used gift among the Shakers, many of whom were cognizant of Native American spirits whom they welcomed into their community, some perfectly channeling long-dead native people, singing their songs and dancing their dances.

The work of Wisdom was recognized in a Shaker ceremonial, enacted annually for eight years after 1842. 'The Midnight City' was an anamnesis of the visitation of Wisdom. 'Led by two mediums carrying lighted lamps, a company of six male and six female instruments marched through every room in every building, a work occupying nearly two weeks.'[36] Rousing families to worship, they continued to sing for an hour each night. Possibly one of the songs they sang then was this stirring dance song:

> Oh, I love Mother, I love her power,
> I know 'twill help me in ev'ry trying hour.
> Help me to shake off, help me to break off,
> Help me to shake off ev'ry bond and fetter.[37]

Nearly all the Shaker communities are closed now, while the remnant contemplate their committment to sending out their gifts into the world. In Shakerism, Sophia appears in her most simple guise like a little girl playing before God, but with a practical wisdom and ability to create virtually unparalleled.

Jerusalem

The British poet William Blake (1757–1827) was primarily a prophet of Sophia's creativity – the degradation of which he never ceased to decry. Having inherited some of the keys of knowledge from Boehme, Blake's idea of Sophia resided in the figure of Jerusalem herself. She appears as the Emanation or spiritual spouse of Albion or England, yet she is also, paradoxically, the Bride of the Lamb. She represents Inspiration and Liberty. In Blake's poetic commentary on the loss of inspiration, Jerusalem's children are enslaved by the Daughters of Albion.[38]

His full portrait of Jerusalem occurs in the gargantuan poem of that name. It is a long and prophetically obfuscated work, made further confusing by the reworking which it underwent. Its time-scales are unclear and Blake's use of his own symbolic figures and characters render it difficult to the casual reader. Nevertheless, it contains Blake's understanding of the Sophianic conflict, framed in the stanzas of his own spiritual struggle and set against a cosmology which seems arcane and nationalistic. As in much visionary writing, Blake is the main actor in this drama and its action is played out in his own land, with Lambeth – his own dwelling place – as the place where Albion fell.

Jerusalem concerns Albion, a titanic figure who represents England and derives partially from Adam Kadmon and Swedenbourg's

Great Man. Albion's primary Emanation or female counterpart is Britannia, who later divides to become Jerusalem and Vala. He determines to keep Jerusalem from her heavenly bridegroom: 'My mountains are my own, and I will keep them to myself,'[39] and in selfish jealousy he hides Jerusalem, his emanation, in his bosom, embracing instead the bride whom the Lamb gave him – Vala, the natural world. By so doing, he commits himself to the materialism of 'Vala's Veil', a concept similar to that of the Eastern Mara. He thus chooses moral law rather than liberty: the necessity of Nature rather than the freedom of Wisdom. It is when Albion tries to draw his emanation into his bosom that Britannia's dragon wings reveal Vala and Jerusalem.

Albion's fall results in the sundering of Jerusalem and Vala who hitherto existed in innocent harmony. Together, Albion's spouses utter a lamentation which is like that of Eve and Lilith over Adam, as the numberless sorrows of the human condition fall upon their offspring.[40]

Albion determines to reject Jerusalem, while retaining her essential form within his own bosom. To all intents and purposes, Jerusalem is scattered, like the Shekinah. With an image coined from *Exodus*, Blake writes, 'Jerusalem is scatter'd abroad like a cloud of smoke thro' non-entity.'[41] Her fate, like that of Sophia herself, is to become the matter for theoretical philosophy: Jerusalem drifts towards the Starry Wheels of Abstract Philosophy. She is eventually received among the mourning Daughters of Beulah in Erin, who are Blake's muses.

Meanwhile, Albion has died, having been cast from the tower of Golgonooza, the foursquare city of 'Art and Manufacture', by his own Spectre, the destructive rational faculty which divides Albion from his essential self.

In a colloquy between Jesus and Jerusalem, Albion's erstwhile emanation mourns:

> I am an outcast: Albion is dead;
> I am left to the trampling foot and the spurning heel:
> A Harlot I am call'd: I am sold from street to street:
> I am defaced with blows and with the dirt of the Prison.[42]

Los, the representative of Poetry and the Creative Imagination, has a vision of Jerusalem, wherein she is seen as hovering over the sleeping Albion like the celestial Egyptian Goddess, Nuit, over the Earth-God, Geb. Over the cold body of Albion, Britannia awakes –

278

seemingly reunited from her severed halves. She mourns his death and her voice summons his spirit, breath is granted him by Divine means.

In the mighty culmination of the poem, Albion, like Adam Kadmon, calls forth his assembled powers, emanations, coadjutors, as Jesus came to call Jerusalem to him in imitation of the *Song of Songs*:

> Awake, Awake, Jerusalem! O lovely Emanation of Albion,
> Awake and overspread all Nations as in Ancient Time;
> For lo! the Night of Death is past and the eternal day
> Appears upon our Hills. Awake, Jerusalem, and come away![43]

Blake's vision here is equal in prophetic spirit to that of Ezekiel, even down to the fiery chariots which are 'Sexual Threefold' (the Orphanim) and the Fourfold Vision where the elements, cardinal directions, inhabitants of Golgonooza and the Gates of Paradise assemble, as Jerusalem is summoned.

> All Human Forms identified, even tree, Metal, Earth and Stone:
> All Human Forms identified, living, going forth and returning wearied
> Into the Planetary lives of Years, Months, Days and Hours; reposing,
> And then Awaking into his Bosom in the Life of Immortality.
> And I heard the Name of their Emanations: they are named Jerusalem.[44]

Here Blake describes the *apocatastasis*, the calling together of all things at the last day, the rolling-up of creation into the heavenly Jerusalem. Yet it is clear that he intends us to understand, as Mother Ann Lee revealed, that every living soul already had the seeds of the Parousia within them – for *they are all named Jerusalem.*

Sophia's role in *Jerusalem* is indeed tangled and confused, yet ultimately triumphant. Blake's obsession with the divisions of duality: sexual, spiritual and moral, render him extremely sensitive to the Sophianic struggle. In *The Marriage of Heaven and Hell*, Blake conceives of the Eternal Female whose groans are heard all over the Earth. Certainly she never groaned so greatly as at this time. What she has to say is the message of Sophia: 'Every thing that lives is Holy.'[45]

Albion's Fall is a prophetic counterpoint to Adam's. He falls under the yoke of necessity, or Ananke, having to observe the severe rules of the system he has chosen, rather than the spiritual freedom which is offered by Jerusalem in her role as Sophia.

Blake bids us cleanse the doors of perception, to listen to the evidence of the five senses. Sophia is about experience, connection and interconnection. She makes sense of physical experience. As Black Goddess, she is the guardian of the motherwit – that subtle combination of all our senses. She bids us feel the texture, taste the flavour, hear the music, see the glory, smell the scent, with true discrimation and appreciation.

Blake, above all, recognized the powers of Sophia in liberation. He knew that she cannot operate when confined. Images from Blake's early poetry of the innocent child, the worm and the butterfly remain with the reader long after *Jerusalem* has fallen from memory.

> He who binds to himself a joy,
> Does a winged life destroy,
> He who kisses the joy as its flies,
> Lives in eternity's sunrise.[46]

To reawaken that joyful innocence within the breasts of her children, Sophia once more took the route of storytelling.

The Sophianic Fable

At the same time as Blake was writing, a new school of romanticism was opening up in Germany. Among its proponents were Goethe, Novalis and the philosopher, Fichte. Their work bears traces of Sophia, enshrined in a literary or poetic form.

Johan Wolfgang von Goethe (1749–1832) is perhaps best known for his poem, *Faust*, which retells the medieval story of Georg Faust, a German magician, who sold his soul to the devil in exchange for great power. This concept has gone down in the history of the world, for it is the subtext of Job's own problem. When God debates with Satan as to the possession of Job's soul, Satan replies: 'Skin for skin! All that a man has he will give for his life.'[47] It is a theme taken up again by Jung in his *Answer to Job*.

At the beginning of *Faust*, God gives Mephistopheles leave to tempt Faust, just as Lucifer tempts Job. Faust is in a prime situation for such a descent. His great wisdom, acquired in a cell of books, has not given him happiness or satisfaction. He evokes *Anima Mundi* in an attempt to conquer world-weariness. She comes with her eternal message: 'I flow this way and that. I am birth and the grave, an eternal ocean, a changeful weaving, a glowing life. And thus I work at the humming loom of time, and fashion the earth, God's living garment.'[48]

Faust concludes that all his study is for nothing. 'You can't pluck nature's veil, she stays a mystery in full daylight. What she doesn't choose to reveal you can't force out of her with screws and levers.'[49] Even though he hears the Easter chorus of the Maries who laid Christ in the tomb, he fails to rally his drooping spirit. Enter Mephistopheles who is the 'part of the darkness that gave birth to light. Light that in its arrogance challenges Mother Night and claims the possession of space.'[50] So Faust sells himself to darkness in exchange for his desire's fulfilment in the currency of Nature herself, the very life-blood of his own veins.

Faust's desire falls upon Gretchen, the epitome of innocence, the gentle daughter who falls into despair. Her prayer for assistance is significantly addressed to the Mater Dolorosa. Under the influence of Mephistopheles, Faust seduces Gretchen who bears him a child. In panic, she drowns it and is condemned to death.

Faust then enters the service of the Emperor, whom he diverts with masquerades and magical displays. He promises to show the Emperor Helen and Paris from Classical times. Mephistopheles who has until now aided and abetted all Faust's plots, now retires from the action. Helen and Paris are to be found in the realm of the Mothers who maintain the pagan's hell, he says. 'The Mothers,' cries Faust. 'Does it give you the shivers?' asks Mephistopheles 'Queer it is. Goddesses unknown to mortal men, hardly to be named by them. You'll need to dig deep to reach them.'[51] And he gives Faust a key to their realm. After many adventures, Faust gains Helen as his own mistress and they have a son, Euphorion, whose vaunting immoderation tempts him to leave Arcadia whereupon, like Icarus, hs falls dead. Helen expires, leaving Faust to return alone. Eventually, Faust realises the extent of his folly in attempting to control Nature by magical ploys and the foolishness of compact with Mephistopheles. He realizes that our achievements, if 'not safe from every hazard' are 'safe enough.'[52] He knows the truth of the philosophy: 'This is the farthest human wisdom goes: The man who earns his freedom every day, alone deserves it, and no other does. And in this sense, with dangers at our door, we all, young folk and old, shall live our lives.'[53] He expires while wishing to savour the beauty of the passing moment.

Mephistopheles is, however, robbed of his expected reward of Faust's soul, which is taken to heaven. The scene of Gretchen's prayer to the Mater Dolorosa is transformed. Now she kneels before the Mater Gloriosa as a penitent, praying for Faust's soul. Gretchen begs to be allowed to become Faust's teacher. The poem ends with the Chorus Mystica singing: 'Transitory things are symbolical only. Here the inadequate finds its fulfilment. The not expressible is here made manifest. The eternal in woman is the gleam we follow.'[54]

This hymn to the Eternal Feminine brings us to the realization that Gretchen and Mephistopheles are the Venus and Lucifer of Faust's existence. The dilution of the Sophianic mythos has already happened within this work. Gretchen, like the fallen Sophia, languishes in a multitude of emotions but the Eternal Feminine, idealized as the Virgin, can be construed as the transcendent Sophia who draws the instincts of humanity to higher ends. The fall of Faustus and the degradation of Gretchen may be seen as a restatement of the Sophianic myth. The influence of Goethe's Eternal Feminine has permeated the aesthetic and theological worlds right into our era, preparing the way for Sophia to manifest.

Novalis, the pseudonym of Friedrich Philipp von Hardenberg (1772–1801), was firmly of the German Romantic school and much influenced by Goethe. Novalis was engaged to be married to young Sophie von Kühn who died before their wedding could take place. His awareness of the mystical presence of Sophia never left him, and he subsequently translated her into a figure of innocent wisdom.

His book *Henry von Ofterdingen*, described as a novel, is really an episodic string of faery-stories and allegorical visions, the last of which is called 'Klingsohr's Fairy Tale'. It depicts a mythological scene set at the end of time. It opens with Arcturus, King of the North, bereft of Sophia, who has descended to the realm of humankind. Arcturus' daughter, Freya, represents the harmonious concord which should be between opposites, yet she, like an enchanted princess, cannot function in the unremitting Northern cold. Iron, an ancient hero, hurls his sword into the world where its shards will form a pathway for the coming of the liberating prince who will help Freya.

The scene shifts to the earth where Father Mind, Mother Heart, and their child Eros live with Ginnistan, or Imagination. Ginnistan and Mind also have a child, Fable. Two other guests grace the house: Sophia, Eternal Wisdom, and the Scribe, who represents Reason. Mind occasionally shares his thoughts with the Scribe, who writes them down and passes them to Sophia who dips the leaves into a bowl of water, thus causing most of the ink to run off. If any script remains, she passes them back to the Scribe who grumblingly binds them into his book. Sophia also showers drops of water from this bowl onto Eros and Ginnistan, whereupon the drops turn into myriads of images. If any drops by chance hit the Scribe, then they turn into numbers and geometric figures which he then threads about his neck.

A shard of Iron's sword falls into the yard, causing the occupants of the house to have many reactions: the Scribe immediately catalogues it as of Northern origin; Ginnistan causes it to assume a snake-like appearance, until it bites its own tail; Eros seizes the snake and immediately assumes the stature of a young man and begins to feel drawn towards a quest in the North. In the confusion, little Fable starts writing with the Scribe's pen; thinking that the same thing will happen to Fable's script as to his, the Scribe passes it to Sophia who dips the pages in the water, yet they remain unchanged.

Eros returns attired in armour and takes Sophia's advice to take Ginnistan with him on his journey, only Imagination must wear the form of his mother, Heart. Ginnistan leads him first to her father, King Moon. His presence in the realm of phantasmagorical images causes Eros to be confused and uplifted at once. He embraces Ginnistan who omits to remind him about the water which Sophia gave them for the journey, which might have kept him from temptation.

Meanwhile, at home, the Scribe has imprisoned both Mind and Heart, and has designs on both Fable and Sophia, neither of whom can be found. Fable has disappeared through a secret door behind the altar of Wisdom, and descends to meet strange adventures. She first of all has a dialogue with the Sphinx who guards the portal. She utters the passwords, 'Sophia and love', and is enabled to pass through. She then enters the cave of the Parcae (the Fates) and begs to be allowed to spin. It is here that the Scribe catches up with her. He sends Fable on a Psyche-like errand to fetch tarantulas to render into oil, but she escapes, ascending a ladder which emerges into the throne-room of Arcturus. She greets him prophetically:

> A speedy return of Wisdom! (Sophia)
> An eternal awakening to peace! (Freya)
> Repose to restless love! (Eros)
> Transfiguration for the heart! (Heart)[55]

Fable returns to earth with the gift of the Lyre of the heavens. She meets her mother, Ginnistan, who recounts how Eros has become ungovernably wild and lost his innocence. He has grown long wings as a result of their union, which has brought forth a host of winged children. Fable's lyre causes them to fall into slumber. She then sees the flame of a funeral pyre with the blue veil of Sophia floating over it in the air. It is the pyre of her mother who has been immolated by the Scribe. Fable's lyre overcomes the Scribe and his minions who fall into a web of tarantulas which cause them to fall to dancing. Fable again gives the correct password to the Sphinx and brings the tarantulas to the Parcae who are bitten by them until they also fall to dancing. Fable liberates Atlas before returning home where she finds Sophia at the newly rebuilt altar. Fable finds Mind's body, which is sleeping in a vivifying bath, while a chain is put about Ginnistan's neck. It touches the waters of the bath, awakening Mind, and the chain turns into a mirror. Sophia bids them look therein, for the mirror reflects everything in its true form, and destroys all illusion. She takes the ashes of Heart, mixing them in her bowl, and bids everyone drink.

'They all noticed what they had been lacking, and the room now became an abode of the blessed. Sophia said, "The great mystery is revealed to all and remains unfathomable forever. The new world is born of pain, and in tears the ashes are dissolved into a drink of eternal life. In everyone dwells the heavenly mother in order to give birth to each child forever."'[56]

So liberated, Eros is bidden to go with Fable on his appointed quest, to rescue Freya. Eros and Freya become the new king and queen and everyone is reunited, fulfilling Fable's earlier prophecy to Arcturus. Sophia finally says: 'Mother is among us, her presence will bless us forever. Follow us into our dwelling; in the temple there we shall dwell forever and guard the secret of the world.'[57] Fable sings the final song:

> The kingdom of eternity is founded,
> By love and peace all strife has been impounded,
> The dreams of pain are gone, to plague us never,
> Sophia is priestess of all hearts forever.[58]

This allegorical story traces the influence of Sophia in an archetypal manner. Arcturus is the great Northern king, whose realm is icy without the touch of Love and Wisdom. Like God the Father without his Wise Daughter, he is powerless. On earth, Reason desires to control Mind, Heart, Love, Story, Imagination and Wisdom. Sophia disdains to give him more than a fragment of wisdom for his book, though Fable's print remains unsullied by the Sophianic waters. Fable, as story and as child, has the advantage over the Scribe. The German romantic tradition recognized the place of the story, or Fable, as a didactic device which had as much authority as other more literary or philosophic forms. Fable can penetrate states and conditions which grander archetypes cannot infiltrate, so her power is stronger than Reason's. Reason can only garner Sophia's leavings. Sophia, although a guest in a human household, remains aloof from the action, retaining her transcendent function. It is Heart who represents Sophia's manifest workings. When she dies on Reason's pyre, everyone has communion of her ashes in Sophia's water. Sophia thus brings about the reconciliation of lost and separated souls, ideas and people, because she gives them of the Mother or Heart.

This naive, yet complex, allegory bears the burden of the book. In explaining the work to Friedrich Schlegel, acknowledged as the leading light of the German Romantics, Novalis wrote: 'The antipathy between Light and Shadow, the yearning for clear, hot penetrating aether, the Unknown-Holy, *the Vesta in Sophia* . . . this is the way to look upon my Fairy Tale.'[59]

The fire of Sophia's presence glows in this story, the more so because it is a story. Stripped of her philosophical honours, Sophia is free to operate as a Goddess. Everyone becomes clothed in her robe of glorious light, all life is renewed and even the flowers and trees 'greened mightily'. She is shown as the renewer of souls and Nature.

The New Isis

Among others, Goethe was to exercise considerable influence over Rudolph Steiner (1861–1925) when he came to found his school of Anthroposophy in the early twentieth century. Anthroposophy literally means 'the wisdom of man' and the movement is dedicated to the understanding of the human spiritual nature.

Steiner's background in philosophy and science brought him to a tacit agreement with the tenets of Theosophy, a movement of which he was a member for many years, before breaking away to found his own movement. There is no space to delineate the internal patterns of Anthroposophy, though we may draw a vast parallel between Steiner's concept and that of Soloviev's God-manhood. There is much in Steiner's philosophy which is vague and impossible to substantiate. Where Soloviev was working from the friction of Orthodoxy, Steiner's thrust-block was esotericism.

His Christmas lectures, delivered at Dornach in 1920, included an interesting observation. In speaking of the sacrifice of Christ, he alluded to the legend of Osiris: 'My dear friends, it is not the Osiris, but the Isis legend that has to be fulfilled in our time. We cannot lose the Christ . . . but we can lose, and we have lost that which we see portrayed by the side of Osiris – Isis, the Mother of the Saviour, the Divine Wisdom, Sophia . . .'[60] He bade his listeners to find and renew the Isis legend, and suggested a mythic route to that quest: 'Lucifer carried the Isis-Being, the divine wisdom whom he had killed, out into the world's spaces; he sunk her into the world's ocean. When we look out into this ocean and see the stars moving only according to mathematical lines, then we see the grave of the world's spiritual essence; for the divine Sophia, the successor of Isis, is dead.'[61]

This becomes an urgent request: *We must give form to this legend, for it sets forth the truth of our times*. We must speak of the dead and lost Isis, the divine Sophia . . . We must set out in search of the dead body of the New Isis, the dead body of the divine Sophia.'[62] He bade us open the coffin of Isis which is hidden in the depths of 'luciferic science' and find within it 'that which natural science gives us, something which stimulates us inwards towards Imagination, Inspiration and Intuition.'[63]

He concluded this insightful lecture with a typically Anthroposophical poem reflecting its own esoteric brand of Christianity:

> Isis-Sophia
> Wisdom of God:
> Lucifer has slain her,
> And on the wings of the world-wide Forces
> Carried her hence into Cosmic space.
> Christ-will
> Working in man:
> Shall wrest from Lucifer

And on the boats of Spirit-knowledge
Call to new life in souls of man
Isis-Sophia,
Wisdom of God.[64]

Sophia as the New Isis is dispersed throughout creation, await-ing the great *apocatastasis*. The process of her emergence takes place whenever such stories and myths are woven. The submerged image begins to rise to the surface of consciousness when such stories are read.

When she rises on vulture's wings from the swamp of her suffering as the avenging Isis, the once and future Woman Clothed with the Sun, will show herself as an Apocalyptic Virgin in truth, fierce to triumph over her enemies, terrible in glory. But this is to anticipate the unfolding myth. The Revelatory Virgin safeguards the childhood of the future, she stands forth as Sophia, Mary, Isis, protecting her children from the dangers which threaten them. Before we uncover these dangers, let us pass further eastwards and discover the deep mother country of Sophia.

=== 15 ===

SAINT SOPHIA

Let it be Known; today the Eternal Feminine
In an incorruptible body is descending to earth.
In the unfading light of the new goddess,
Heaven has become one with the deeps.
The Eternal Feminine, Vladimir Soloviev

Mother Russia

Sophia has always been at home in Russia. Perhaps one of the reasons for this is the almost continuous veneration of the concept of Moist Mother Earth (*Mat' syra zemlia*), or Mokosha, as she is sometimes known.

'The mother earth is identical in popular (Russian) belief with the mother of God, with Sophia. "The Holy Spirit lives in the earth" an old Russian proverb has it, or "You should not lie, the earth hears it." Here Wisdom, Spirit and the Great Mother are still cosmic powers which are not incorporated under any patriarchal common denominator.'[1] Until the early twentieth century, peasants still observed the custom of asking the earth's forgiveness before they died.[2]

Countries are metaphorically designated as fatherlands or motherlands: Russia is a motherland where the concept of Divine Motherhood is irreversibly ingrained. Indeed it is not entirely clear whether Mother Russia has yet given birth to her children, who are still intimately associated with their motherland as infants within the womb, or like a series of *matryoska* dolls, one inside the other. The spirit of the Goddess of the Land in Russia is devouring and possessive, in the way of the Black Goddess. In Russian legend, Mother Earth complained to the Almighty about the pain which humanity was wreaking upon her. 'Do not cry, for in the end you will eat them all,' replied God.[3] This image is still reflected in the frighteningly efficient superwomen of modern Russia who, though complaining of *peregruzhennoit*, or 'over-burdening', in their lives, still fulfill the proverb: 'Women can do everything, men can do the rest.'[4]

Prime among the many images of the Black Goddess in Russia is Baba Yaga who propels herself by means of her pestle and mortar, like the Cailleachs of Celtic tradition, the old woman tossed up in a basket whose duty is to scour the sky and our souls. Baba Yaga may appear as a witch, yet she is often a helpful one within folk tradition, for she aids heroes to find weapons, simplifying tasks and quests when she is treated with courtesy. Her transposed reflection is none other than Vasilisa the fair – the young, just maiden who defeats her opposite aspect by truth and integrity. The folk story which preserves this interaction of the Russian Black Goddess and Sophia is called *Vasilisa the Fair*.

Vasilisa's mother died when she was young. In order to watch over her, her mother gave Vasilisa a doll which her daughter had to keep hidden, feed and consult. Vasilisa's father remarried a woman who had two daughters who despised and tormented her. By consulting and feeding her doll, Vasilisa was able to perform the many arduous tasks which they set her. Her doll bade her rest and magically fulfilled the tasks.

One day when her father was away, Vasilisa and her step-sisters were sewing by the light of one candle which went out. Since their task was unfinished, the stepsisters sent Vasilisa to Baba Yaga's house nearby to fetch another light. As Vasilisa proceeded through the forest, she was passed by a horseman in white at dawn, a horseman in red at midday and a horseman in black as twilight fell. Baba Yaga's house was surrounded by skulls on poles, whose eyes gleamed in the darkness. Vasilisa begged to serve Baba Yaga in exchange for light and was set various tasks, which her doll fulfilled. At Vasilisa's fears the doll remarked: 'Fear not. Eat your supper, say your prayers and go to sleep; the morning is wiser than the evening.'[5]

Vasilisa was emboldened to ask the identity of the three horsemen. Baba Yaga replied that the white horseman was her bright day, the red horseman her red sun and the black horseman her dark night, 'And all of them are my faithful servants.'[6] In return Baba Yaga demanded to know how the girl fulfilled all her tasks so easily. Without disclosing her doll, Vasilisa said, 'I am helped by the blessing of my mother.'[7] Baba Yaga then cast her out, because she could not have anything blessed in her house, but she gave Vasilisa a stick with an illumined skull stuck upon it.

She was about to throw it away as she neared home, when the skull bade her take the stick in to her stepmother. She was amazed at how kind everyone was to her. It transpired that, in her absence, they had been unable to kindle any fire or light in the house. The skull was accordingly set up, but its eyes followed the stepmother and her daughters everywhere so that, by morning, they were burned to ash. Vasilisa interred the skull, then lodged with a poor old grandmother and sustained them both by her spinning and weaving. So fine was her work that Vasilisa met the Tsar who eventually married her.

Within the simple limits of a folk-story, the interaction of Sophia (Vasilisa) and the Black Goddess (Baba Yaga) are demonstrated. Here, Vasilisa was exiled from her family home, but the spirit of her mother accompanied her in the form of the doll. The stepmother and stepsisters caused Vasilisa to suffer for the first time all the exigencies of the poor. To be sent to Baba Yaga was tantamount to being sent to one's death, but Vasilisa was actually helped by Baba Yaga. By facing her worst fear – that of death itself – Vasilisa was liberated from her former situation. Like Psyche, she received from the hands of death the light which she needed. She returned from the house of the dead with the flaming skull, thus not only perfectly fulfilling the conditions set by necessity but also overcoming them. By never disclosing her strength – the doll in the pocket of her apron – Vasilisa was never overcome and finally triumphed.

Russians have rarely let it be known that they have the blessed image of Sophia hidden in their breast, but she has been their sure support just as much as the earth beneath their feet.

Byzantium in Exile

The juxtaposition of Orthodoxy and the primal Russian spirit can never cease to thrill the observer. Here liturgy is full-blooded, a celestial banquet indeed. To those used to the milk-sop liturgies of the West, with their ill-sung, apologetic and sloppy vernacularisms, Russian Orthodoxy may sometimes shock with its power. This is what true worship is supposed to do – shock us into awareness. As the Orthodox liturgy proceeds, it is frequently punctuated by the deacon's exhortation to the faithful: 'Wisdom, let us attend!' Being mindful of such Wisdom is the work of religion.

Perhaps here the extreme patristic spirit of Orthodoxy is partnered by an equally strong matristic spirit of ancient religion. Here heaven and earth embrace in a spirit of reconciliation and support.

This is particularly true of the doctrine of God-manhood and theosis. God becomes a man, in the person of Christ. Humanity has within it the ability to strive towards deity or theosis – literally, God-becoming. This state is not achieved on earth, though it is sought after in every act of the faithful.

The interpenetration of the holy and the profane, the exalted and the humble, is profoundly visible in the Russian spirit. The Orthodox wedding service preserves a vestige of the early Sacred Marriage in that it places crowns upon the heads of husband and wife during the marriage ceremony, in token of the joy of union and the self-sacrifice which care of each other brings with it.

An examination of the Orthodox liturgy should be accompanied by attending at an Orthodox rite – the incandescent luminosity of the liturgy is a true doxophony of Sophia. Icons surround the worshipper – true windows into heaven – the chant swells, borne up by the human voice alone. Here ecstasy is not pietistic posturing. Here *Ecclesia orans* stands revealed in every worshipper. Here one can believe in Christ's saying: 'I am come to bring fire upon the earth.' In Orthodoxy, the wings of the Holy Spirit have scarcely ceased beating since the first Pentecost. Tongues of fire descend upon the unbidden spirit, even the body is responsive to the reverberant chant. The eucharistic liturgy is a true anamnesis of Sophia's agape within her seven-pillared temple.

The newly-minted seal of the Holy Trinity is set upon the lips of all who chant the Trisagion: 'Holy God, Holy Strong, Holy Immortal One, have mercy upon us.'

The Russian spirit is naturally that of Sophia. There is a great reverence for both her manifestations as Mother of the Black Earth (*Miru Mir*) and for the Virgin as the spirit of Sophia. One twelfth century apocryphal text, *Descent of the Virgin into Hell*, describes how the Virgin wished to see the torment of the souls in hell and was conducted thence by the archangel Michael. She met various groups of sinners and said: 'They deserve this for their sins.' Immediately a fiery wave broke over the damned and engulfed them in flames. In pity and horror, the Virgin said: 'I have only one request. Let me also enter, that I may suffer together with the Christians, for they have called themselves the children of my Son.' Then she called upon the company of heaven to petition her Son to have pity upon them. Jesus then descended from his throne and judged that, from Good Thursday to Pentecost, the damned should be given rest and a chance to praise God.[8] This response is typical of the Russian spirit: unfortunates and sufferers are not another class of being to pious Russians who identify themselves with the sinner.

The Mantle of Mary is venerated as *Pokrov Presvyatyya Borogorditsy*, 'Mantle of the Very Holy Mother of God', just as Athene's peplum and Brighid's mantle were venerated.[9] The idea of the Virgin as a defence, or palladium wall, is the very *zone*, or belt, of Sophia, which girdles her virgin integrity.

Sophia Enthroned

Sophia, Holy Wisdom, came into the Russian soul never to leave it. She is deeply associated with the native images of Vasilisa and others. When the cathedral of St Sophia was erected at Kiev, 'the Byzantine builders . . . are said to have painted above the altar an immense image of a woman with hands raised, in order to suggest to the pagan Slavs the association of the Christian feminine deities, Mary and Sophia, with the pagan Great Mother whose image with uplifted arms adorned folk art.'[10] This image is still sustained in icons which depict Mary as the Apocalyptic Woman, clothed in the sun.[11] It is also the subject of much Russian embroidery which enshrines the image of the early Goddess of the Earth as a woman with uplifted hands flanked by horsemen.[12] It is also, more usually, considered to be the Holy Virgin herself, as *Mary Orans*.

Many Russians never gave up their pagan beliefs but practiced *dvoeverie*, or 'double faith', switching effortlessly between paganism and Christianity as it suited them. The incorporation of Christian elements thus deepened their native practice and vice versa. A similar arrangement is found in Japan where, according to a religious survey, 90% of Japanese are Shinto, but 90% are simultaneously Buddhist.

We can look to the Altaic and shamanic traditions of early Russia for the native myth of Sophia. The Cheremis story about God's daughter is highly reminiscent of the Gnostic myth. This pagan story tells how God's daughter came down to earth to look for grass for her cattle, there being none in heaven. Moreover she was alone and unpartnered. She met a young man and took him as her husband, but she did not wish to let her father know about this, so she left her dress upon the ground. God came to search for his lost dautghter and, seeing the dress, assumed her dead. After two years of exile, the daughter returned with her husband

16 *Wisdom Enthroned* Here Wisdom appears as a crowned angel, her feet upon a cushion which represents the world. She is flanked by Mary and St John the Baptist, who are theologically considered to be the forerunners of Christ. Above Sophia appears God the Father in a cloud of glory, while above him is an empty throne and the Gospels. The iconographer intends us to understand that the glory of God has descended in the person of Christ. The red-robed Sophia has golden wings which represent her as a mediator between the heavenly and earthly realms. Icon of Novgorod School.

and God gave a feast to celebrate his newfound relationship with humanity.[13]

Eastern Orthodoxy boasts several Sophias. The female martyr who is commemorated on September 17th, and who is the mother of Faith, Hope and Charity, is frequently confused with Divine

Wisdom, to whom the great cathedrals of Kiev, Novgorod and Contantinople are dedicated.

'In dedicating its most ancient temples to Saint Sophia, the substantial Wisdom of God, (the Russian people) have given to this idea a new expression which is unknown to the Greeks . . . By intimately linking Saint Sophia to the Mother of God and to Jesus Christ, the religious art of our ancestors distinguished her manifestly from one and the other, but representing her in the features of a particular divine being. It was for them . . . the luminous spirit of regenerated humanity, the guardian Angel of Earth, the future and definitive appearance of the Godhead.'[14]

The few icons of Sophia may suggest that she is a separate entity from the Trinity. Despite this, Orthodoxy proclaims that Christ alone is the true Wisdom and the true Word. 'The icon is a theology in lines and colours' writes Evdokimov.[15] Icons are windows into heaven. To gaze at one with understanding is to cleanse the sight.

Icons of Sophia are rare and very unusual in their depiction of a female entity. The icon shown on page 101 shows a pictorial representation of Wisdom from *Proverbs* 9, slaughtering her beasts, pouring her wine and inviting all to come to her table. The seven sections at the top of the icon show not only the seven pillars of her temple, but also the seven ecumenical councils which regulate Orthodox belief. Holding a staff in her right hand, Wisdom sits on a throne surrounded by the five circles of heaven. The red circle shows the vision of Ezekiel.

The other icon shown in this book (page 293) is that of Wisdom as the Angel of the Lord. The face and hands of the angel are bright fiery red, as are the wings. With feet upon a cushion, representing the earth itself, the Sophianic angel sits on a throne of four legs which also has seven pillars descending from it. The angel has an eight-fold nimbus, or *slava*, behind her head. This is often called 'the sign of Wisdom',[16] and recalls the ogdoadic perfection of Sophia who descends through seven spheres or levels and ascends to the completion of all things. The brilliant fiery colour of this icon has caused Evgeni Trubetskoi to write that 'it is the red of God's dawn emerging from the night of nonbeing: it is the eternal sun rising over all living things. Sophia is what precedes the *days* of creation.'[17] Above the angel is a starry band which recalls the very end of creation. 'And all the host of heaven shall be dissolved, and the heavens shall be rolled together as a scroll and all their host shall fall down, as the leaf falleth off from the vein, and as a falling fig from the fig tree.'[18] The parallels between this image and that of the Woman Clothed with the Sun are close but not identical: they may well be a purposeful iconographic superimposition of each image.

The fiery wings of the iconic Sophia remind us of the mediating love of Cupid, the bearer of Eros. These same incandescent images appear in icons of the Midsummer Saint, John the Baptist, and of the prophet Elijah who ascends heavenwards like Helios and his quadrigal-chariot of the sun. Both Apocalyptic Virgin and Sophia appear as angels, glowing with incandescent power like the sun.

Prophet of Wisdom

In the last 150 years, Sophia has acquired a quorum of followers who have carried her message throughout the world. Vladimir Soloviev (1853–1900) was a mystic philosopher in the true sense. His life was marked by three 'meetings' with Sophia who first came to him when he was attending the liturgy of the Ascension as a boy of nine years. The second meeting occured while he was studying Gnostic texts in the British Museum in 1875. Sophia appeared and instructed him to 'meet her in Egypt', where his last meeting took place. He wrote a poem, *Three Meetings*, to commemorate these sacred encounters.[19]

In formulating his theology of Sophia, Soloviev consciously drew upon the writings of Paracelsus, Boehme, and Swedenbourg as well as resorting to the Gnostics. His aim in so doing was the revitalization of the spiritual tradition which he envisaged in three successive developments: the monotheistic Hebrew tradition, followed by the Christic dimension of God, to be concluded by the marriage of God and humanity.[20]

Soloviev fully recognized the dual appearance of Sophia through the persons of Jesus and Mary as a joint expression.[21] The following diagram shows the shape of his conception in three triplicities which may be considered as harmonic resonances of each other:

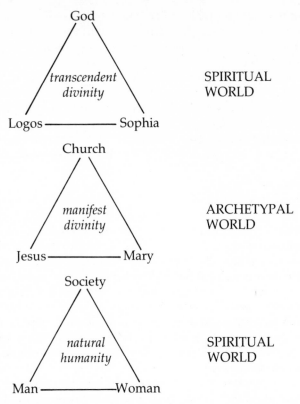

Sophia plays 'by evoking before God the innumerable possibilities of all the extra-divine existences and by absorbing them anew
into this omnipotence, his absolute truth and his infinite grace.'[22]
For Soloviev, Sophia is 'the potential and future Mother of the
extra-divine world (which) corresponds as an ideal complement
to the eternally actual Father of the Godhead.'[23] She is both
World-Soul and bride of the Logos, 'the guardian angel of the
world covering with her wings all the creatures in order to elevate
them gradually to true being just as a bird covers its young. She is
the substance of the Holy Spirit who is borne over the shadowy
deeps of the nascent world.'[24]

Soloviev's relationship with Sophia was both personal and passionate. His prayer to her is some indication of his dedication.
'Most holy Divine Sophia . . . I beg of thee: descend into the
prison of the soul, fill our gloom with thy brilliance, with the fire
of thy love having melted the shackles of our spirit, present unto us

light and freedom, in a visible and substantial way manifest thyself unto us, incarnate thyself in us and in the world, resurrecting the fullness of the ages, that the deeps may be encompassed and that god may be all in all.'[25] His writing is nothing less than a profound prophecy of Sophia's return among humanity.

In the light of the dangers threatening our world, Soloviev wished to encourage all who were terrified of this spectre to become absorbed in Sophia and let her creatively work out the solution, manifesting through many illuminated souls.[26]

The Wise Heresy

Throughout this book we have seen how Sophia has insinuated herself back into religious traditions from which the Goddess was believed to have been excised. Very few mystics have fought very hard for her official acceptance, but to this steadfast band we must add the name of Pavel Florensky. As a Russian Orthodox priest, he attempted the impossible – the vindication and acceptance of Sophia into the Trinity. Of Sophia he writes: 'This Great Being, both royal and feminine, who being neither God, nor the Eternal Son of God, neither angel nor saint, receives the veneration of one who accomplishes the Old Testament as well as of one who is the Begetter of the New: who is she then, if not the truest humanity, the purest and most whole of beings, the macrocosmic whole, the living soul of Nature and of the universe eternally united and uniting in the process of time with the Divine and uniting with Her all that is.'[27]

This view might indeed be upheld aesthetically, if not doctrinally, by a lay person, but for an Orthodox priest to account for the presence of Sophia, some special arguments were going to be necessary: 'The novelty of Sophia from the point of view of traditional Christian theology – whether Eastern or Western – is the setting up of Sophia as the fourth person in the hypostases of the Divine.'[28] This was an insuperable problem and final stumbling block of Florensky's argument, for Sophia cannot be held as consubstantial (of one being) with the Trinity. Florensky states: 'She is admitted to the depth of the Trinity by the humility of God.'[29] This would suggest that God, not content with becoming human, accepted into His own realm a created being in order to learn from her. This is by no means a new theory – that God learns from us. In considering Florensky's point, we must remember that Orthodoxy does not endorse as doctrine the apochryphal accounts of the Virgin's Assumption into Heaven in the same way that Catholicism does.

How is Florensky able to prove that Sophia has a special relationship with the Trinity? He takes the following Behemist view and expresses the action of the Trinity through the burning glass of Sophia. The Father is expressed through Sophia as the ideal being, the foundation of creation, which enhances the power and strength of her own being. The Son is expressed through Sophia as the meaning of creation, its intelligence, truth and justification. The Holy Spirit is expressed through Sophia as the spirituality of creation, its holiness, purity and its immaculate aspect.[30] Sophia becomes for him 'the light shining in darkness',[31] the natural glory or adornment of both creation and the Church, manifest in the Blessed Virgin.[32]

Father Sergei Bulgakov (1871–1944) was a torch-bearer for what was coming to be called Sophiology. His spiritual conversion happened when he was 25 and travelling on the southern steppe of Russia. Looking upon the vastness of the desert which he had been taught to accept as lifeless, he realized that 'nature was not death, but life.'[33] From this awakening to Nature he was given insight into the divine and he subsequently found solace in the contemplation of the Blessed Virgin. His championship of Sophia was clearly an attempt to revitalize Orthodoxy and to re-establish the spirit of the Divine Feminine so that the Church did not remain off-balanced by its Christocentric view.

He believed fervently that 'the future of a living Christianity rests with a sophianic interpretation of the world and of its destiny . . . Sophiology is a theology of *crisis*, not of disintegration, but of salvation.'[34] Bulgakov urged that we should struggle 'with the world out of love for the world', bringing about the necessary changes 'through a sophianic perception of the world in the Wisdom of God.'[35]

Bulgakov's theory was that 'God discloses himself from the standpoint of eternity as Wisdom which, in turn, represents itself in the two hypostases of Son and Spirit. The Son is an archetype of men, and the Spirit, as 'daughter of God', serves as the archetype of women.[36]

Bulgakov did considerably more work on the relationship between Sophia and the Blessed Virgin than Soloviev, relating to the Holy Spirit which was itself a hypostatis of maternity. In Sophia, the Divine and Earthly natures of Christ are founded.

His theories came under investigation by the Church in 1922 when he was accused of promulgating the doctrine of an androgynous

Christ and his sophiology 'which, under the influence of Palamism and Cabala, regarded God as androgynous and characterized him equally as "Father" and as "Mother".'[37]

Undaunted, Bulgakov continued to write about Sophia, producing a mature thealogy which attempted to loosen the constraints of patriarchal philosophy but which nevertheless strove to remain within the boundaries of Orthodoxy. He reconciled the dualisms implicit in Soloviev's work and posited not a fallen Sophia like that of the Gnostics, but an earthly Sophia who, in the shape of the World-Soul, became dark because humanity lost its sovereignty over Nature.[38] It was that very forsaken Black Goddess that Bulgakov upheld and restored to rights once more.

Virgin of Peace

Nicholas Roerich (1874–1947), the Russian artist and philosopher, was another of the Russian ambassadors of Sophia. His interest was in cultural inter-connection and although he went to live in America, he ended his life in India, having explored Tibet. This gave him interesting insights into the nature of the common symbologies of different countries. His work is haunted by the Divine Feminine. He observed: 'Throughout the entire East and in the entire West there lives the Image of the Mother of the World, and deeply significant salutations are dedicated to this High Entity.'[39] To what extent the Russian Orthodox experience of Sophia influenced him is hard to say.

As a result of the Russian Revolution and the European hostilities resultant from the First World War, his major preoccupation became the preservation of cultural institutions and monuments in times of war. He accordingly proposed the Roerich Pact, for which he was nominated for the Nobel Peace Prize in 1929. His intention was that all such cultural institutions and art collections be deemed neutral, to be protected and respected by both sets of combatants.

To this end, he designed a flag to be known as the 'Banner of Peace', which was to identify such neutral cultural collections. It consisted of three red spheres within a red circle, on a white field. 'The design has been interpreted as symbolizing religion, art, and science encompassed by the circle of culture, or, as the past, present and future achievements of humanity guarded within the circle of eternity.'[40] The symbols on the Banner of Peace are common to many cultures including the Three Treasures of Tibet,

17 *Madonna Oriflamma* Here the maiden Sophia holds the 'Banner of Peace', depicted as three spheres within a circle upon a white field. This symbolic device was the vision of Nicholas Roerich, the Russian mystical painter. He intended it to symbolize the treasures of wisdom and culture as an international sign of Sophianic inviolability. Nicholas Roerich Museum, New York.

in India as the Chintamani, or Sign of Happiness, and in medieval art on the breast of Christ in Memling's *The Adoration of Christ*.

'Because of its universality and agelessness, Roerich believed that no symbol was more appropriate for the preservation of the world's treasures.'[41] The banner was to symbolize universal protection of humankind's achievements in the same way that the Red Cross or Crescent represents the protection of life.

He depicted this banner of peace in many paintings, the most striking of which is the *Madonna Oriflamma* (1932), which shows the golden-haloed Madonna, dressed in purple to signify her links with Wisdom, holding up the banner of peace in much the same way that, in medieval art, St Veronica shows the vernicle with the icon of the agonized Christ upon it. This is truly a depiction of Sophia with her banner of peace, revealing her to be the guardian of our cultural treasures (see page 300).

The three spheres in Buddhist iconography signify the Buddha, the Dharma and the Sanga with which each Buddhist aligns when he or she takes the protection, or, in more general terms, aligns him/herself with Divinity, the Wisdom of Divinity and with the faithful ones who have, do and will practice this wisdom.

Roerich's sense of the Goddess of Wisdom reveals itself in several of his paintings. His philosophy was a subtle blend of Western and Eastern spirituality, fuelled by his Russian and Scandinavian roots. The picture, *The Mother of the World* (see page 311), reveals a virgin veiled in crystalline light, sitting on a throne very similar to that of the icon of Sophia. Of this figure, he writes: ' The Great Features of the Face are often covered and under the folds of this veil, glowing with the squares of perfection, may one not see the One Great Unifying Aspect, common to Them All!'[42]

Roerich believed that women were the natural guardians of earth's treasures. 'Ancient legends actually attribute to woman the role of the guardian of sacred knowledge. Therefore, may she now also remember her defamed ancestress, Eve, and again hearken to the voice of her intuition in not only eating of but also planting as many trees bearing the fruits of the knowledge of good and evil as possible.'[43] He prophesied: 'Women, indeed you will weave and unfold the Banner of Peace.'[44] He wrote: 'To both East and West, the images of the Great Mother – womanhood – is the bridge of ultimate unification.'[45]

This understanding is extraordinarily consistent within the Russian character. Whether we look at Madame Blavatsky's *Isis Unveiled*, Soloviev's championship of Sophia or Bulgakov's attempt to incorporate the Divine Feminine into Orthodox Trinitarian understanding, the Goddess of Wisdom emerges as a dynamic source of inspiration and strength.

This vision of Sophia is Russia's gift to the West, a bridge by which we may restore and reunite the divided halves of our being. Paul Evdokimov, the theologian, writes 'the Wisdom of God is pre-existent to the formation of mankind, and every man carries within him "a guiding image", his own Sophia or Wisdom, he is thus God's living project. He must decode this image, in the process decoding himself, freely conquering his own intelligence, and making his own destiny.'[46]

This is of course the pursuit of all spirituality – finding in oneself the image of the divine. Sophia is the divine pattern, imaging herself within the whole of creation and when it is called together and recognized, then creation itself will realize perfection and completion.

It has been frequently prophesied that something wonderful will come out of Russia. Nicholas Berdyaev writes: 'It is imperative to bear in mind that human creativity is not a claim or a right on the part of humanity, but God's claim on and call to humanity. God awaits humanity's creative act, which is the response to the creative act of God.'[47] In other words, we must recognize the Sophianic potential within each of us and give it expression.

As I write this chapter, Communism is being wiped off the slate in Russia: an unprecedented event in the lives of generations of people. Roerich's own words may stand as prophetic testament to the work which lies ahead: 'Verily, the hour of the affirming of beauty in life is come! It came in the travail of the spirits of the peoples . . . Each living rational being, may receive . . . the living raiment of beauty, and cast away from him that ridiculous fear which whispers: "This is not for you" . . . All is for you if you manifest the wish from a pure source.'[48]

The great heritage of Russia lies untapped, its treasures still accessible and within living memory. But 'holy Russia demands holy work!'[49] The Russian people have served a long apprenticeship in the chicken-legged house of Baba Yaga; now they are invited to leave it. Let us pray that Fair Vasilisa can lead them into possession of their own homeland with the image of Sophia borne ever before her as talisman and touchstone.

APOCALYPTIC VIRGINS

> Who is this that looks forth like the dawn,
> fair as the moon, bright as the sun,
> terrible as an army with banners?
>
> *Song of Solomon* 6:10

The Eternal female groan'd! it was heard over all the Earth
The Marriage of Heaven and Hell, William Blake

The Parousia

Every religion has its projected 'end-time'. For Jews, it is the *tikkun*; for Gnostics, the *apocatastasis*; for Zoroastrians, the *Fravarti*; for Christians, it is the *Parousia*. Time was, time is, time shall be no more. The millennial spirit is running strongly at this time, only ten years before the new millennium which is alternatively viewed as the New Age of Aquarius or else as Armageddon.

The return of the Holy Spirit as the Risen Christ has been long expected in Christian eschatology. However, whether the presence winging its way across our skies is to be that of doves or of missile-headed jets has been doubtful. As we approach the end of the second millennium after Christ, afficionados of both peace and destruction seem to reign supreme. As ever at such times, the mere threat of the last days has sent the faithful to the *Book of the Apocalypse* and everyone else to the consultation of divinatory means, including the perhaps aptly named, Nostradamus, whose prophecies expire at 1999. Sophia, so familiarly imaged by the dove of peace, might seem ill at ease in this millennial scenario, yet she draws upon her aspect of Black Goddess to deliver warnings and to bring the kenosis of war and conflict to those with no peace in their hearts.

The Woman Clothed with the Sun stands forth in *Revelations* as a continual reminder of the struggle of Sophia, to emerge from her embattled guise. Whether we see her as Isis or Mary, for this book has both images within it, the presence of Sophia is strongly upheld here.

Revelations 12 tells of John's vision of a woman 'clothed with the sun, with the moon under her feet and on her head a crown of twelve stars,'[1] who was with child. A seven-headed dragon came to devour the child as it was born. War in heaven ensued, and Michael and his angels cast the dragon down to earth. The dragon still pursued the woman who was given two wings like those of an eagle to fly into the wilderness, there to abide for three and half years. One of the dragon's heads spewed forth a flood of water, but 'the earth came to the help of the woman', and swallowed it up.[2] Who is the woman? In the historical context, she is the Church, Ecclesia, who can be identified also as Mary. Yet there are elements in this chapter highly reminiscent of Isis' flight from Set, her bearing of Horus in the marshes where she nourished him as a mother-vulture with great wings. Also reminiscent is Leto's flight from the python and her giving birth to Apollo and Artemis on the island of Ortygia.[3]

The adversary of Mary/Ecclesia is none other than the Devil and so the ancient curse upon women uttered by God in *Genesis* 3: 15 'I will put enmity between you and the woman, and between your seed and her seed; he shall bruise your head and you shall bruise his heel', was finally fulfilled as the serpent was overthrown.

Mary assumes the burden of the World-Soul in *Revelations* – clothed with the sun, she encompasses the solar-system; she has put the sublunary and illusory realm under her feet and defeated the dragonish chaos of the earth. In Sophianic terms, she subsumed the Tiamat power into herself. She had on her head the crown of the zodiac. These are the cosmic attributes of Sophia herself. The *Beatus Apocalypse* picture of this scene, see page 58, shows her glorious sun-illumined self and her veiled, hidden self, in flight from the dragon.

This vision is one of the constellation Virgo, the place of Astraea's retirement, from which, says Virgil, the Virgin will descend and give birth to a son. For her sake, the earth itself will co-operate in her escape from the evils of the dragon. That this should be so is not strange, since the Black Goddess and Sophia are one being, as the Gnostics held: 'they call the Divine Wisdom both Holy Spirit and Earth, and also Mother as well as Jerusalem.'[4]

The prime image of *Revelations* is the restoration of the heavenly city. Jerusalem, as we have seen, has been a consistent image of Sophia throughout scripture: she is the widow-woman, the raped virgin, the despoiled temple. Jerusalem is the earthly locus and meeting place for the heavenly Jerusalem. Anyone looking over that city today at the miseries caused there in the name of three different faiths, may indeed envision the rejected Sophia who wisely orders all things, if only she was allowed. Her torn garment, ripped away in *Song of Songs* 5:7 and despoiled in *Consolations of Philosophy* (cf. page 222) is restored in *Revelations*: 'his Bride has made herself ready; it was granted her to be clothed with fine linen, bright and pure.'[5]

The city of Jerusalem is a microcosm of the earth itself which can be transformed and filled with light. Many deny the possibility of this transfiguration within temporal occurence. *Revelations* is like an icon which shows us the eternal possiblity of change. The earth, like woman, has been imaged as the Whore of Babylon: a destructive and vicious bitch from whom we should extract all that we can. That she can be imaged as the Glorious Sun-Woman, shedding her own radiance and waiting to emerge as Queen of Creation, rarely occurs in our desacralized society.

Mary is not often considered as an agent of the apocalypse, yet Gnostic tradition gives many stories which show her in this dynamic stance. Mary appears in the Apocryphal *Gospel of Bartholomew* where she described her Annunciation to the disciples as she lay near to death. When she was in the temple she was accustomed to receive her food from an angel who came daily with a cup and some bread. However, one day another angel came and the veil of the temple was riven in two. A cloud of dew fell from heaven, enveloping her and the angel wiped her with his robe and said: '"Hail, thou that art highly favoured, the chosen vessel, grace inexhaustible." And he smote his garment upon the right hand and there came a very great loaf and he set it upon the altar of the temple and did eat of it first himself, and gave unto me also. And again he smote his garment upon the left hand and there came a very great cup full of wine: and he set it upon the altar of the temple and did drink of it first himself, and gave also unto me. And I beheld and saw the bread and the cup whole as they were.'[6] The Apostles begged her to tell them how she became Theotokos: she warned them not to aask. However, as she told of her Annunciation, fire began to issue from her mouth. 'And the world was at the point to come to an end: but Jesus appeared quickly and laid his hand upon her mouth and said unto Mary: "Utter not this mystery, or this day my whole creation will come to an end."'[7] Here Mary is almost the prime mover of the Apocatastasis by telling of her conception of God's seed.

Revelations speaks of war and final peace. Yet the descent of the dove, as Charles Williams called it, has been long in coming.[8] The medieval prophet, Joachim of Fiore, spoke of the age of the Holy Spirit as one of tranquility.[9] Before the Parousia, the Apocalyptic Virgin must appear as the dazzling Red Queen and give her admonitory call to change.

Virgo Potens

The eleventh century Byzantine thinker Psellus said: 'When thou seest a most holy formless Fire shining and bounding throughout the depths of the whole cosmos, give ear to the Voice of the Fire.'[10] He may have been prophesying the return of Sophia as the Woman Clothed with the Sun who, with a voice of fire, has been appearing over the last two hundred years in the form of the Blessed Virgin Mary.

One of the impressive features of the many sightings of Mary is perahelion – the spectacle of the sun dancing – an unusual but natural phenomenon in which the sun appears to dance, actually oscillating slightly in its course. That perahelion should accompany the apparitions is very interesting for the Woman Clothed with the Sun should indeed make her appearances with heliacal phenomena.

The apparitions of the Virgin present Mary as the *Virgo Potens*, the strong Virgin who, like a Christian Athena, represents the justice of the earth and the integrity of its spirit. She admonishes and recalls people to metanoia. Like Maat and Astraea, she returns to awaken us. She brings us back to the potent virginity of clear thought and radical action, in focusing upon the wasteland of both land and spirit. Into the sleep of *bios* – that genetic life which we all lead – she injects the dream of *zoe* – that inspirational life which we might potentially live.[11]

Isidore Glabas, a fourteenth century Greek theologian, reverted to the Astraea myth to describe the first descent of Mary. He posited that she was the image of Wisdom, a creature above both human and angelic power, who had no reason to leave her place next to God. However, when humanity grew corrupt, she descended in order to make God incarnate through herself and so save them.[12] In her second descent as Apocalyptic Virgin, it would seem that Mary reverts also to the Goddess Anath or Ishtar in her role as Queen of Battle.

George Herbert's riddle:

How well her name an army doth present,
In whom the Lord of Hosts did pitch His tent.[13]

gives an anagram of Mary as Army, based on the *Song of Songs* 6:10 which heads this chapter. Mary's militant face usually only appears in times of danger. Her image as the Virgin has long been borne into battle; the Emperor Heraclitus (*c.* 575–641) marched into battle with her banner, as did later Byzantine emperors until Constantinople fell.[14] King Arthur himself bore 'the image of holy Mary, the everlasting Virgin on his shield, and the heathen were put to flight.'[15] One of the strongest Catholic sodalities, the Legion of Mary, presents this militant face of the Virgin, but it is one which the Virgin manifests without help.

Since 1830, the Virgin Mary has been appearing all over Europe. These appearances have one thing in common – they look towards the end of time and they issue the call to *metanoia*. Pope Pius XII stated that 'the human race is today involved in a supreme crisis, which will end in its salvation by Christ, or in its dire destruction.'[16] Certainly this statement sets the tone of the second half of the twentieth century. The appearance of the Virgin to two young children at La Salette in 1846 was the beginning of many apocalyptic messages which have continued unchecked ever since.

Do we hear the voice of Sophia in these manifestations? Certainly, the ancestral voice of the earth sounds through Mary who is, after all, the kinswoman of all people, since she is a human being who became the Mother of God. It is within Catholic tradition that Mary has been most usually pied with Sophia. Sapiential images pepper the liturgies and devotions to Mary in such a way that outsiders might well be forgiven for assuming that one was the other.

Mary is accorded *hyperdulia* – reverence a little higher than that accorded the angels – but not the *latria* which is accorded to God alone. Despite this mealy-mouthed definition, the faithful have always gone directly to Mary in their troubles, treating her as the true ear and effective troubleshooter of the Divine Family. A Catholic bishop is reported to have said: 'Do not overburden your Saviour with your request, for He is very busy; better address your prayers to the Holy Mother. She will pass your prayers on to whomever is necessary.'[17] On the one hand, this makes Mary seem no more than a secretary for God, but this accords well with the apocryphal medieval legends which assign her a more active role. While St Peter is forbidding access to the Pearly Gates, Mary lets in lost souls by the back-gate, according to a medieval apochryphal tale. Similarly, Mary is no regarder of ecclesial authority today: she appears, admonishes and establishes pilgrimage centres without permission from the Church. The passive Madonna of the Lady Chapel has leapt out of her niche and is about the world inciting the faithful to political agitation. It is often asked whether Mary may be considered in the light of a Goddess since she is, after all, only a human creature. I believe it purist to eject Mary from the realms of the Divine Feminine just because she is merely the last in a long line of women who have achieved semi-divine status among her followers. We live in an age which is making its own myths. Within the twentieth century, the Assumption of Mary into heaven has been officially accepted as a Catholic doctrine. The Virgin is appearing spontaneously to many Christians, just as the Goddess is appearing to many non-Christians. This is not a well-documented phenomenon, but I believe we must see the Marian apparitions as part of a total manifestation of the Divine Feminine and not split them up. I will be detailing instances of the Goddess's reanimation of spirituality in the next chapter.

One feature of the apparitions often overlooked is that the seers often call their vision 'the Lady' and that it is often *after* the event that the apparitions are identified as the Virgin. Bernadette Soubirous, for example, called her Lady 'Aquerò', the local patois for 'that one' or 'her'.[18] Aquerò appeared as a girl of about 14 years, a fact which has been totally ignored by the Lourdes populizers. Bernadette's response to the Lourdes statue, which depicts a thirty-year old woman, was alternately scathing and politely tight-lipped: it clearly did not portray Aquerò at all. 'The figure does not seem young enough and does not smile enough.'[19]

Lucia, one of the seers at the Portuguese apparition site in Fatima in 1917, was distressed when she heard her brother boast that they had seen the Virgin. 'I don't know if it was Our Lady. It was a very pretty little woman.'[20]

What does the Virgin do and say when she comes? She very often institutes a pilgrimage cult associated with prayer or healing, just as Demeter did at Eleusis. She sometimes asks her followers to wear a medal or scapular as a talismanic emblem of their devotion, such as the Miraculous Medal struck in 1830 after the visions of St Catherine Labouré.

308

The Lourdes apparition is interesting in that it corresponds to the usual pattern of Black Madonna sightings. The Virgin appeared in a grotto which, though the area around it had been used as a rubbish-tip by the peasants for years, proved to have been the source of healing waters. Aquerò bade Bernadette to dig near the rock and to drink. Three times she dug and brought up nothing but mud; the fourth time it turned to pure water.[21] The water, which has no spectacular mineral properties, used in faith, healed many and so a pilgrimage cult was born which still attracts millions of visitors each year.

The apparition of the Virgin at Fatima instructed the seer children to make her Immaculate Heart better known and loved, and that they pray the rosary.[22] The saying of the rosary has been standard Christian practice from early times. It is a method of counting and saying prayers while meditating on the images contained therein or on mysteries associated with them. The rosary is a familiar personal and family devotion. It has been called 'Our Lady's lifeline' with good reason for the repetition of the many *Aves* (Hail Marys) creates a chain of of petitions which connects the pray-er with the object of prayer. The 'weapon' of the Apocalyptic Virgin is usually the rosary, by which the faithful will bring about changes. It is a particularly appropriate prayer for the apocalyptic messages which often accompany the apparitions, for it specifically asks Mary to guard the soul at the moment of death. Standard Catholic meditation before bed is a consideration of the 'four last things' – death, hell, judgement and heaven – so that each night becomes a preparation for either a new day or else death.

The message of Fatima was to consecrate the whole world to the Immaculate Heart of Mary, something which was eventually done by Pope Pius XII in 1942. Along with this devotion, the faithful were exhorted to recite the rosary daily and to amend their lives. The prayer of Fatima is dedicated to world peace. 'O Queen of the Rosary, sweet Virgin of Fatima, we beg of thee to watch over our dear homeland and assure its moral and spiritual revival. Bring back peace to all nations of the world, so that all and our own nation in particular, may be happy to call thee their Queen and the Queen of Peace.'[23]

Lucia, the chief seer of Fatima, received certain secrets which were recorded and deposited in the Vatican where they were not to be opened until 1960. They are still there, presumably. The 'message of Fatima' has been frequently construed as a divine blast against Communism. Certainly, the apparition on May 13th 1917 could not have been more timely, if this was indeed the Virgin's purpose, since the Russian Revolution occured six months later that year.

Apparitions of the Virgin have also been witnessed by Muslims when, in Zeitoun in Egypt, a few men noticed a figure in white perched on a Coptic Church roof. Many thousand witnesses saw the spectacle. While the apparition did not speak, many 'doves of light' were seen moving at high speed about her. Mary is considered to be the mother of the Prophet Jesus, within Islam and so her appearance to Muslims should be taken as particularly unusual. Zeitoun is the place, in legend, where the Virgin rested under a sycamore tree during the Flight into Egypt.[24]

In Amsterdam in 1951, the Virgin appeared as Our Lady of all Nations. She inaugurated a prayer to be said which echoes the words of Sophia as Christian World-Soul:

Lord Jesus Christ, Son of the Father,
Send now your Spirit over the earth.
Let the Holy Spirit live in the hearts of all peoples,
That they may be preserved from degeneration, disaster and war.
May the Lady of All Nations, who once was Mary,
Be our advocate. Amen.[25]

Are we to understand these apparitions of the Virgin as an expression of the Goddess? The evidence of seers is usually open to normal cultural interpretation. The apparition is female and it is understood to be the Virgin. The apparition at Knock, Ireland, in 1879, reported not a figure but a 'large globe of golden light' which moved up and down.[26] These apparitions in the vicinity of a high mountain may bear another interpretation.

The earth produces many anomalous yet natural phenomena, such as ball-lightning, will of the wisp and earthquake lights. These latter frequently appear along fault-lines, near mountain ranges, etc. The phenomenon of 'earth-lights' has been investigated by Paul Devereux. These phenomena are frequently described as ghostly apparitions, UFOs and other such. Devereux, himself a seer of earth-lights, suggests that it is possible that such natural phenomena 'can respond to witness movement and *thought*.' He witnessed such earth-lights over Bromley Common where they rearranged themselves into a clear form: 'the shape of a figure with its arms outspread. Perhaps because of my Catholic upbringing I associated this with an angel or Christ figure.'[27] In his objective scientific research, Devereux considers the possibility that 'we are

18 *Mother of the World* Sophia, like the statue of the Egyptian Goddess, Neith, is veiled: 'I am all that was, and is and shall be, and no man has lifted my veil'. Wisdom's mysterious ways are intentionally pursued by men and women the world over: we call such people mystics, philosophers, esotericists. In this painting by Nicholas Roerich, the veiled Sophia is surrounded by star-like disincarnate avatars of her wisdom, while below upon the earth, a pair of male and female mystics invoke her influence. This is a true representation of the World-Soul and of the transcendent appearance of Sophia Stellarum. Nicholas Roerich Museum, New York.

dealing with a very sensitive energy form.' Might the World-Soul be manifesting in this way, able to take on whatever image it wishes? For where once people saw deities in the sky, they now see UFOs. Within the history of the Goddess's manifestations, such a thing is not impossible: that the World-Soul might appear in the desired image. The power of the earth may manifest by such means as earth-lights, just as it does through volcanic activity. The symbol of the earth's energy field is universally represented by the dragon.

Whatever our standpoint, whether we see these appearances as the folk-soul of Catholics stating what is not being stated in the Church, or whether we take the Virgin's appearances at face-value, they have had effect. Wherever the Virgin has appeared, the faithful follow. 'As long as there is a cult devoted to Her, there will be people who speak with the Goddess face to face.'[28]

Mary is coming in the role of Sophianic Mother to warn and encourage. In her latest appearances at Medjugorje in Yugoslavia, which started in Midsummer 1981, the Virgin has come as Queen of Peace. This message from her own lips was reinforced by a supernatural light in the dark sky which read MIR or peace. This unmistakable sign would have been comprehensible to any astrologer for it is none other than the zodiacal sign of Virgo: MR♍.[29] The winged Virgin Sophia comes to us in visions. Meanwhile, the earth itself is groaning.

The Groaning of the Earth

The Apocalyptic Virgins represent a call to faith which calls into question Adam and Eve's stewardship of the paradisal garden and, latterly, of the earth itself; they proclaim a call to greater responsibility in our use of earth's resources; they bring us face up against the nature of the Fall.

The force of Nature herself has manifested in some spectacular and, to human viewpoints, disastrous ways. The old relationship between the Goddess of the Land and humankind has had its *ketubah* (marriage contract) cancelled and renewed several times this century alone. While we conciliate one part of the earth, another part is visited with hurricanes, droughts, famines and earthquakes.

Always aware of the danger of the Black Goddess, humanity has striven, like Perseus, to look at the head of Medusa only in the reflected image of Athene's shield. That palladium will not hold forever. The time has come to look the Black Goddess squarely in the face. Athene says: 'The veil upon My shield is beginning to wear thin, and the glory of the Rays of Medusa become apparent to earthly gaze. The inner power of the atom has been violently exposed, and reduces the physical body to the shadow which in verity it is. . .'[30]

When the earth itself cries out, then we may be sure that the World-Soul is agitated. This feature of pathetic fallacy is as resonant within Christianity as among other spiritualities. When Christ rode in triumph into Jerusalem, the pharisees told him to rebuke the people's hosannas. He answered: 'I tell you, if these were silent, the very stones would cry out.'[31] And if the stones cry out in joy, how much more so in terror? 'We know that the whole creation has been groaning in travail together until now; and not only the creation, but we ourselves, who have the first fruits of the Spirit, groan loudly as we wait for adoption as (children), the redemption of our bodies.'[32] This earth-cry is echoed within ourselves for Wisdom 'dwells with all flesh'[33] and, as indwelling spirit, cries out within us.[34]

The Goddess has been reappearing in many ways – normally through her familiar faces of the Virgin – though not always. Sometimes the ancient Goddesses re-emerge in surprising ways. In February 1940, an old woman mounted a bus between Athens and Corinth. As she had no money for her fare, she was put off at the next stop which happened to be Eleusis – the very place that Demeter stopped by the well in her mourning search for Persephone. The bus refused to start and the passengers chipped in to pay her fare. As she got back on, the old woman said: 'You ought to have done it sooner but you are egotists, and since I am among you, I will tell you something else: you will be punished for the way you live, you will be deprived even of plants and water!' No-one remembered her getting off, but there seemed little doubt that Demeter had manifested among them once more, with an ancient, yet contemporary, relevant prophecy.[35]

The voice of the Black Goddess is still with us. It speaks to us now in unpredictable metereorological patterns: rain in the desert, drought in formerly fertile places, rising sea-levels, global warming, the dispersing of the earth's resources – these are the new wastelands predicted by the sibyls of ancient time. Both outwardly in the world, and internally in the soul, wasteland is now a familiar condition.

'If you broke the rules of the old Goddess you were zapped,' said Lovelock,'strangely the Gaia theory says much the same thing. You can make models that demonstrate this. They show that any species that adversely affects its environment is eliminated. If we continue to corrupt, pollute and rip the skin off the Earth by deforestation, then we may be eliminated, but of course, life will go on.'[36]

The Sibyl of the Rhine, St Hildegard of Bingen, wrote about the earth and our treatment of it. 'The earth should not be injured, the earth should not be destroyed. As often as the elements of the world are violated by ill-treatment, so God will cleanse them. God will cleanse them through the sufferings, through the hardships of humankind. All of creation God gives to humankind to use. But if this privilege is misused, God's justice permits creation to punish humanity.'[37]

Sophia, as the Virgin Astraea, or as an enraged Athene, will defend her own. When Christ lamented with the voice of Sophia over the people of Jerusalem, he said: 'Behold, your house is forsaken.'[38] The temple of Wisdom was empty and Wisdom had nowhere to lay her head. Christ's action of blasting the infertile fig-tree is seen as an instance of Messianic paranoia by some,[39] yet that fig-tree which Christ encountered when he entered Jerusalem betokens our unpreparedness of spirit. The fig-tree, which should be fertile of its nature and which is the harbinger of the warm season,[40] was uncharacteristically barren as he entered the holy city.

The wasteland of the spirit is represented by fundamentalism which offers one of the greatest challenges to our age. It arises within all religions, though seldom within the native spiritualities. 'Because these fundamental movements always lack the integrality of justice, deep violence lurks just beneath their sentimentalisms.'[41] They attempt to seduce people from rich, creative lives into narrow restatements of exoteric practice. Fundamentalism is a spirituality content to live on the margins, as though the power of Sophia were rationed. As Matthew Fox has commented: 'paranoid people believe there is a conspiracy in the universe against them, mystics believe there is a conspiracy in the universe on their behalf.'[42] Fundamentalism is usually a denial of Sophia on all levels.

It accepts the end of the world as a desirable thing, because all the chosen will be saved and all disagreeable things and people swept away into hell. This millennialist doom and gloom afflicts the spirit in an invidious way. It promotes contempt for the earth and all creation as expendable. It views the body as an unfortunate evil which heaven will allow us to dispense with.

Those with no spirituality and therefore no comprehension of other states of being may indeed be afflicted with millennialism themselves, ever fearful of what the future will bring, cautious of giving love in case the object of that love is suddenly torn from them. Typical modern examples of this are the survivalists who pile up caches of food and supplies against the day of disaster when nuclear war may strike.

Possibly as a reaction to hell-fire and predetermination, the question of evil is generally overlooked in our society. The issues raised in *Revelations* – the punishment of the wicked and the suffering of the innocent – are there resolved by the second coming of Christ and his union with Mary/Ecclesia/Sophia. In a post-Christian and New Age society, we no longer see things in terms of sin or Fall, although we are aware of our social divisions and inequities and still yearn for a wholistic restoration. For modern Western society, the only redemption which can be countenanced is a total one, not one which rescues only 'the chosen' and consigns the rest to punishment.

How do we enter the synergy of Sophia and creation, the marriage of heaven and earth? It may be that we must continue upon the road with the Black Goddess who will help us encounter and challenge all that impedes this synergy from operating effectively. Or it may be that we each become the synergic touchstone for Sophia's operation, that we become again as little children and find the spark of creativity within each of us that will be the blast to wither wickedness.

Immaculate Conception

One common feature of most apparitions of the Virgin is the youth of those to whom the vision appeared. 'Wisdom opened the mouth of the dumb and made the tongues of babes speak clearly.'[43] The clarity and truth of youthful observation has been one of the channels of Sophia's integrity and justice among humankind. The focus of the innocent is unmuddied by sophisticated human concerns, uncoloured by thought of personal gain or fame.

In the Gnostic *Thunder Perfect Intellect*, Sophia exhorts her faithful to 'draw near to childhood, and do not despise it because it is small and paltry.'[44]

When Bernadette asked her 'Lady' who she was, the apparition replied 'Que soy era Immaculada Councepciou.'[45] Bernadette, a simple shepherdess, could not know the theological implication of this reply: 'I am the Immaculate Conception.' This doctrine defines that Mary, alone of all women, was conceived without original sin – it was necessary to define this doctrine because of the dualism of Augustine's concept of original sin which would necessarily make Mary the transmitter of the sin of the Fall to her son.

The Feast of the Immaculate Conception has been celebrated since 1476, but it was not defined as a Catholic doctrine until 1854, four years before Bernadette's vision. 'Had Valentinus been looking down on this cosmos from his place in the pleroma on December 8, 1854, then he must not have been able to resist a bemused smile. For on that day Pius IX decreed, in full *Ineffabilis Deus* that Mary by a special act of grace had been made utterly sinless from the moment of her conception. Thus even the *psychikoi* of the Roman Church had finally come to acknowledge what Valentinus had known all along: that salvation could come into this fallen world only though a perfect Virgin Mother who without intercourse conceived the Savior and without loss of virginity gave him birth. A tortuous road to Sophia! Still, better gnosis late than gnosis never,' concludes Paula Fredriksen in her essay *A Response to Vitiated Seeds and Holy Vessels.*[46]

Feminists have not responded happily to this doctrine since it mythologizes Mary and leaves Woman just where she was. However, though the doctrine of the Immaculate Conception is applied solely to Mary, it may be possible to apply it in a wider context which may help our world-view immensely. If Mary is taken as a representative of the human race, of creation, of matter itself, then truly all that is made is immaculate. Everything is truly without sin in its deepest essence, in the heart of its integrity. This heretical view goes hand in hand with the concept of the Incarnation of Christ.

Mary is Mother of the Incarnation. Thousands of Catholics pray to the Angelus daily in remembrance of her *fiat* – 'let it be' - the response which she made to the angel when invited to be the mother of Christ. This prayer is an acknowledgement, not only of the Incarnation of Christ, but also of our own Sophianic ability to change our material state into a spiritually empowered gift. The dove descends onto the stone and it becomes purest gold in an alchemy which is irresistibly appropriate to all people, whether Christian or not.

The Immaculate Conception is truly the state of innocent awareness within us all which is our kinship with Wisdom and her inviolability.[47] 'God leads the child God has called in wonderful ways. God takes the soul to a secret place, for God alone will play with it in a game of which the body knows nothing. God says: "I am your playmate! Your childhood was a companion of my Holy Spirit,"'[48] wrote Mechtild of Magdeburg.

There have been many hidden messengers of Sophia's urgent call, those who have vaunted her justice above their own lives or who have lived as secretly as Sophia herself. They speak of the little way, of spiritual childhood. St Thérèse of Lisieux was one such. The dynamism in this consumptive Carmelite nun propelled the message of Sophia beyond the cloister walls to a world embattled in the First World War, where mothers' sons slew other mothers' sons. Her way of spiritual childhood has often been presented as a soft option or as a sickly and sentimental bourgeois response to God; rather it is a call to live dangerously and truly to 'become as little children.'[49]

On a very different social level to that of Thérèse, Alice Miller spoke in the eighties about the state of childhood: 'Someday we will regard our children not as creatures to manipulate or to change but rather as messengers from a world we once deeply knew, but which we have long since forgotten, who can reveal to us more about the true secrets of life, than our parents were ever able to do.'[50]

It has been in the shape of a child, as a maiden barely out of girlhood, that Sophia has chosen to make her appearances in the Christian world. As the image of the abused child is making headlines in the West, we are drawn to our sacred guardianship of the body once again. As we said in Chapter 2, the rape of children is on the increase, possibly as a direct result of more and more women actively taking their power so that they are increasingly being seen as less vulnerable. The degradation of the weak and innocent does not stop, it merely victimizes another, weaker section of society.

Of all the evils perpetrated by Western society, this is one against which the Goddess of Wisdom speaks out most strongly. The Christian call to purity remains an abstraction for most, as does the Pagan call to honour the earth. Both are united on this point: our bodies are sacred temples in which the indwelling Spirit is alive. The rape of that Spirit evokes the rage of the Virgin, terrible as any army, as devastating as Tiamat struggling to birth the world.

317

The message of the Apocalyptic Virgins may seem to reinforce millennialist fears. Indeed, for some parts of our creation, it may already be too late, as species and habitats have been and are being destroyed. However, the seed of Sophia is within us all, waiting for the opportunity to manifest her skilful wisdom in the world. Hers is the greatest gift – the liberation of the mind from oppressive concepts which keep us enslaved. It is in this spirit that we must see the manifestations of Mary in our world.

Mary has been rejected by many feminists as a role model because of the often simplistic manner in which she is presented as a perfect wife and mother – roles which women reasonably reject as hidebound and unhelpful. That Mary might help to rediscover the power of Woman is pointed in an apocryphal text, *The Gospel of Bartholomew*, where Mary says: 'In me was he contained that I might recover the strength of the female.'[51] Is this the intended trajectory of Sophia, which Christianity has generally failed to address? If it is then Mary does not need re-investing with potency, she already has it: maybe feminism will vaunt it and celebrate her power. Even as I write, views of Mary are changing.

In a modern poetic restatement of the Magnificat by Kurt Marti, *Und Maria*, we read of Mary's humility and effective action in the human realms:

> And Mary could hardly read
> and Mary could hardly write
> and Mary was not allowed to sing
> or speak in the Jewish House of Prayer
> where men serve the man-god
> that is why she sang to her oldest son
> that is why she sang
> to daughters of other sons
> of the great grace and her
> holy overthrowing . . .[52]

And after looking on askance as the prelates knelt to her, she walked:

> out of the pictures
> and climbed
> down from the altars . . .
> and she was
> burnt as a witch
> a million times over
> in a false god's honour . . .

and she was
the lion Madonna naked
on the lion's back
riding for her Indians
and she was and she is
many bodied many-voiced
the subversive hope
of her song.[53]

This poem expresses the way that the Divine Feminine, whether seen as Goddess or Virgin Mother of God, finds her effective level of action. She embodies the hopes of all people, enshrined in their hearts. Whether she is persecuted as a witch, as a woman who has presumed to take her power, or whether she is repressed in the third-world in economic and political slavery, her song of hope wells up. *Virgo Potens* has left her niche, no longer *sedes sapientiae*, but vibrantly manifest at all the ancient earth-honouring places where the communion of the Goddess can still be experienced. The song of Sophia is the true liberation thealogy, for she has suffered everything which humankind has suffered. She has made the descent of the seven levels.

The ancient model of Wisdom's temple with seven pillars is restated in Mary's role as Mother of Sorrows, Mater Dolorosa, her heart pierced iconographically with seven swords. These seven sorrows were the subject of medieval devotion and they may now be taken to stand for the seven inevitable sorrows which strike to the heart of our lives: folly; incomprehension; lack of help; weakness; ignorance; spiritual disease and desacralization. To these wounds the medicine of the Seven Gifts of the Holy Spirit of Sophia can be applied: wisdom; understanding; counsel; strength; knowledge; spiritual health and respect for life. In ancient Egypt, the oldest hieroglyph for the soul (*ka*) was a pair of upstretched arms. These are those very arms and hands which shelter us, sometimes raised to admonish or warn. They are also the hands which were depicted on the basilica of St Sophia in Kiev, in likeness of the Earth Mother. They are the advocatory hands of Mary *Orante*. They are the pleading hands of the Sophia within us, lifted upwards for assistance and mercy. Let us hope that our prayer and Sophia's warning are sufficient to avert danger from our earth and bring us safely home.

═══ 17 ═══

THE SOPHIANIC MILLENNIUM

And I came for a second time, in the manner of a woman; and I
spoke with them,
And I shall instruct them about the coming end of the realm.
And I shall instruct them about the beginning of the coming
realm, which does not experience change, and in which our
appearance shall change.
  Prophecy of Sophia from *Trimorphic Protennoia*, Gnostic Text

A Sophianic Consciousness

We have seen how the Goddess has been marginalized, denied
and ignored throughout history but also how she nevertheless
finds her way of surviving in the most restrictive ideologies.
Sophia's task as a between, or bridging, Goddess, has been a
difficult one. She links us to the ancient Goddesses through the
shared symbolisms of Isis and Mary, as well to the native creation
Goddesses of Europe. Present in the apocryphal incident, in song
and story, in the visions of mystics and philosophers, disguised
in both transcendent and earthy images, Sophia comes into our
lives and bids us follow her into the Sophianic millennium when
the Divine Feminine will no longer be so veiled.

Sophia has been inching her way into popular consciousness
throughout the latter half of the twentieth century. The two world
wars and the increasing population of the world have forced
great changes upon Western society. The dismantling of orthodox
spirituality has put in question long-held certainties, soul-loss has
been followed by spiritual quest. Those born in this century are
now prospective citizens of the New Age, an era where spiritual
orthodoxy will be replaced by spiritual adventure, where a greater
responsibility for personal behaviour and environmental awareness will be paramount. It is an era where the Divine Feminine
will lead the way and where women will rediscover and enter
their power. One of the major factors which have paved the
way for the New Age is the work of C. G. Jung (1875–1961). In

many ways, Jung stands to our society as Plato once stood in relation to Western philosophy: a dealer in archetypal and Platonic forms. Jung's thought, so influential and far-reaching, has made it possible for us to identify our personal myth and actively work with it in the world. For those who deal in the world of spirituality, it is now almost impossible not to speak of 'archetypes' rather than deities. Jung's comprehensive gnosis stretched from Classical mythology through to Gnosticism and Alchemy.

In an early television interview, Jung was asked whether he believed in God. He hesitated and then replied, 'I do not believe, I know!' Thus, he proved himself to be a gnostic in the broadest sense of that word. Jung studied the extant Gnostic material between 1916–26, feeling that this would prove fertile ground for his study of the unconscious. He wrote to Freud that the Gnostic conception of Sophia was, in his opinion, 'a reembodiment of an ancient wisdom that might appear once again in modern psychoanalysis.'[1] But he laid aside this work, feeling that the Gnostics were too remote from today. This was before the Nag Hammadi finds and before his own researches in alchemy brought him the connections that he had always hoped to find.[2] The first major finds of Gnostic scriptures in the 1940s at Nag Hammadi were followed with interest by Jung, after whom one of its main manuscripts was later called the *Jung Codex*. These significant finds have helped re-evaluate the Sophianic myth and have created a new dwelling for her.

Jung made his realizations about the Divine Feminine in a world which was still marginalizing the feminine on every level. He fully realised that 'an avowedly biological or coarse-minded attitude to women produces an excessively lofty valuation of femininity in the unconscious, where it is pleased to take the form of Sophia or of the Virgin.'[3] But he was never afraid to vaunt the spiritual and psychic importance of the Goddess within, nor was he slow in making that image manifest in the world. He pointed out the Sophianic role of Mary in a new way in *Answer to Job*. As Geoffrey Ashe has said, devotion to Mary 'should, on Jung's showing, activate the archetype (of Wisdom) and help unlock the treasury of the psychical depths.'[4] Jung's insights on the Divine Feminine are timelessly accurate and have provided a springboard for many seekers of Sophia to find an effective approach to the Goddess – a task which many women have made their own.

Jung identified four interrelated aspects of the Divine Feminine, each drawn from the cultural background of the West: Hawwah

(Eve); Helen of Troy; Mary and Sophia.[5] These four archetypes accord with the unfolding of the Goddess in consciousness.

Hawwah   the biological woman, the earth, the fertile mother.
Helen   the erotic woman, the romanticized earth, the inspirer.
Mary   the spiritual woman, the willing earth, the virgin mother.
Sophia   the wise woman, the World-Soul, the initiator and completor.

Sophia, like Isis and Mary before her, subsumes all these roles into herself: identifying strongly with the earth and with the role of women, as well as reflecting the most appropriate contemporary image of the Goddess at any time. She can be a creative inspirer, a virginal whore, a fertile virgin, a mother who takes life back into her womb. The dichotomies which the Gnostics perceived within Sophia are all actively present in our society. At this time of spiritual and ecological crisis Sophia comes as a mediator to represent the possibilities of change.

The process of Jungian individuation is nothing other than the personal recognition of the indwelling spark of Sophia: a realization that enables the individual to act in a self-aware but unselfish manner.[6]

Jung has helped us understand the Western myth within each of us. This process, once the major feature of the native and Classical mysteries, is available again. The application of deistic metaphor to the human psyche is a potent poultice which Sophia uses to open the old sores which civilization has dealt our consciousness. By painful rediscovery of these wounds, we become aware, able to be helped and healed by the Divine Feminine. Not everyone understands this process psychologically, but may be working through the metaphor of Sophia's passion by religious, magical or therapeutic means. All are valid paths of exploration. The ubiquity of Sophia in all traditions renders humankind susceptible to her healing wisdom and awakening.

Sophia is the Grail-Goddess and her healing is essential in our post-Hiroshima, post-Holocaust age which already dreams of its own Armageddon. Suffering is caused by dualism and fragmentation: it is healed by integration and wholeness. Jung made a deep investigation of the problems of suffering in his *Answer to Job*. It is a book which confronts the dichotomy of evil in the presence of the Divine Mercy and of the integration of the Goddess in the form of Mary into heaven. Henri Corbin's comment on this book sums up Jung's findings: 'It is not only the *Anamnesis* of Sophia . . . but her reign and her exaltation with her work of *mediation* . . . that is the answer to Job.'[7] The idea of the Saviour Goddess had re-emerged into twentieth century consciousness, bringing new hope. Sophia can help us disassociate ourselves from the delusions of duality. 'It is not the incarnate Sophia's role to bind or reconnect us to the earth but to help us recognize that our understanding of ourselves as separate from the earth is a delusion.'[8] This idea is one with which our society is coming to terms.

Assumption of the World-Soul

The major Sophianic dogma proclaimed by the Church during the twentieth century was the Assumption of the Virgin into heaven. This dogma defined that Mary was assumed body and soul into heaven, a view which had been unofficially held by the Church for many centuries, but whose definition within this century shows that the popular view of Mary as a Sophianic mediator has been acknowledged officially. It represents the marriage of Mary to Jesus, Ecclesia to God, Logos to Sophia, humanity to Creator.

The Book of Wisdom says: 'Wisdom I loved; I sought her out when I was young and longed to win her for my bride, and I fell in love with her beauty . . . So I determined to bring her home to live with me, knowing that she would be my counsellor in prosperity and my comfort in anxiety and grief.'[9] These words, spoken by the seeker after wisdom, may be applied in divine terms for, within the Christian context, they are also spoken by Christ. The German medieval mystic, Mechtild of Magdeburg, puts the following words into the mouth of Mary. 'When our father's joy was darkened by Adam's fall, so that He was endangered, the everlasting wisdom of Almighty God was provoked. Then the father chose me as a bride that he might have something to love; because His noble bride the soul was dead. Then the son chose me as mother and the Holy Spirit received me as friend. Then was I alone the bride of the Holy Trinity.'[10]

Mary is the mystical spouse of Christ, for she is believed to be Ecclesia and the representative of the whole human race. Mary is thus raised, as Christians believe all humanity shall be, to the level of God's bride. As with all mythologems, the incestuous factor does not enter into consideration here, although Mary is Jesus' mother. As Sophia, she becomes the sister-spouse of Christ in the manner of Isis with Osiris when, at the Assumption, she was elevated as his *paredros*.

It may be argued that Mary's role within the Church does not reflect equal status with that of Christ. Indeed, the failure of the Church to define Mary as co-redemptrix, by which she would be seen as equal partner with Christ, has been put down to its fear of upsetting the ecumenical applecart. Protestant theology already has enough problems with accepting Mary as a spiritual entity, it seems, without being asked to take her as a Saviour Goddess. The reality of co-redemption is wider, however. Mary is co-redemptrix because of her *fiat*. As representative of the human race, she assents to be a vehicle of Sophianic grace; she is 'the worthy co-operator in the accomplishment of the mysteries of salvation.'[11] It is a role to which all may aspire, for if we exercise free will under the guidance of Sophia, we also assent to cooperate in the resacralization of nature.

Why should the Assumption doctrine be so important, and does it mean anything in terms of the Goddess? It demonstrates a willingness to refresh Marian metaphors and has, for Catholics, secured the notion that Mary alone of humanity is in heaven,[12] a promise that wholeness is possible. For the rest of the world, it restores the actuality of a Saviour Goddess and it prefigures the resacralization of the *corporality* of creation. Theology has been mostly concerned with the redemption of the soul or spirit, not of its vehicle, the body. Mary's Assumption is the first step towards the ecological restoration of the earth as well as the redemption of the human spirit. This will enable us to go beyond the end-point of the *apocatastasis*, beyond the punishment of the flesh in hell, and look towards 'a new heaven and a new earth'.

Mary is assumed into the divine condition in a true theosis. Ignorance of the divine nature was at the basis of the Fall and is still at the heart of our own dilemma. Unless we can find the means to theosis, we remain ignorant. Mary is the only gnostic in heaven. Because she was born Immaculate – with all graces and without sin – and was assumed bodily and spiritually into heaven, she is, in effect, a completely transformed human being, exempt from human heredity and human death. The true alchemy here is that Jesus takes both these qualities of Mary's being. The interpenetration of the divine and human is complete in this action. This is the true sacred marriage of heaven and earth, the divine and human, the resacralization of humanity and the humanization of the divine.

Sophia is the sign of divine and human partnership, and Mary is her representative in the scenario of the Assumption. Our participation in the nature of Sophia wakens us to the needs of our creation. It enables us to look beyond the prevalent Christian response to creation as a convenience shop for humanity; it takes us beyond the reservation of spiritual quest and vocation as a solely human pursuit, and helps extend our sights and kinship to the greater family of other species. As Sophia has come to humanity, so humanity now turns to the mineral, plant and animal kingdoms in a redemptive and resacralizing way.

In Mary's Assumption, we may comprehend the assumption of Sophia as the World-Soul, the recognition of the earth and of creation as divine. The reaction to the Church's new dogma was not universally well received. For Teilhard de Chardin (1881–1955), the French theologian and scientist, the dogma of the Assumption was 'somewhat of a challenge to physics and biology'.[13] Nevertheless, Teilhard's vision approved of the mystical correlatives of the dogma. '"He who descended is he who also ascended far above all the heavens that he might fill all things." We cannot say of Mary, as we do of Christ, that she descended. But we can say that she "ascended, that she might fill all things". And because Mary has ascended, to be with Christ, like him she is "universal", and with him she "fills all things".'[14]

For Teilhard, Mary and the Feminine is the Eternal Feminine. His *Hymn to Matter*[15] praises the stuff of matter which will one day be restored at the *apocatastasis*: 'Blessed be you, universal matter, immeasurable time, boundless ether, triple abyss of stars and atoms and generations: you who by overflowing and dissolving our narrow standards or measurement reveal to us the dimensions of God.' In a hymn inspired by *Proverbs*, Teilhard put these words into the mouth of Sophia:

> When the world was born, I came into being,
> Before the centuries were made,
> I issued from the hand of God . . .
> I am the beauty running through the world,
> To make it associate in ordered groups:
> The ideal held up before the world
> To make it ascend.
> I am the essential Feminine.[16]

Teilhard's attempt not only to incorporate the findings of modern science, but also to find a more secure place for the Divine Feminine within Catholicism, served him ill. After his official silencing, he wrote quietly, sequestered like Sophia, in a place which the disapproving authorities had made for him. In this prison of silence he died and, though his works have enjoyed a remarkable popularity, he has not been officially rehabilitated within the Church.

Christianity'sss failure to cope with corporality, with the intrinsic divinity of creation and of the body, has left Ecclesia in a very ugly condition. It is now for us to recognize and acknowledge the Black Goddess among us and transform her. For those who stand outside the Christian arena, the urgent and overwhelming heritage of this neglect is grossly visible in the fabric of our planet.

The imperialist school of interference with Nature seems finally to be crumbling, but until every created being is capable of honouring the earth, we shall doubtless see many more horrors perpetrated upon the body of the planet.

The scientist James Lovelock, at the suggestion of William Golding, called the earth Gaia. This simple metaphor, with all its associations with the Greek Earth Goddess, has had a remarkable impact by helping many to re-envisage the earth as a living being once more. Although many scientists disdain the use of metaphor because it muddies the scientific stream with philosophic and mystical ambiguity, the idea of Gaia has inspired many to reform their lifestyle in accordance with the ecological implications of consumer society upon our continued existence. Gaia is the World-Soul re-personified as Goddess. Her groans are now clearly audible in even the most intractible conscience.

Our exile has not only been from the Goddess, but also from Nature. It is not surprising, considering that most Westerners live apart from their environment, protected by concrete roadways, consuming machine-processed foods and filled with media information to the detriment of the experience of our own senses. The seasons go by unnoticed, we seldom touch the earth, eat fresh food or observe the world personally – media input and journalism provide our informational diet. The sacred is a forgotten dimension in our society which we ignore at our peril.

Earth-honouring is an integral part of the native traditional religions, who have never deviated from a vision of the whole of creation as sacred. As we begin slowly – perhaps too slowly – to reassess this primal nurture, we realize that the native traditions have much wisdom to teach us, and this may, in turn, stimulate our own.

Maybe the return of the Goddess among us heralds the marriage of humanity with Nature, the necessary resacralization which must precede any marriage between humanity and the Divine.

> She is rising, she is rising . . .
> Inanna is ascending . . .[17]

The seven powers of Inanna are being slowly restored to her as our image of Nature is redeemed, but the work of its resacralization must now hasten, aided by every living soul.

The current ecological trend has alarmed many traditionalists who see it as endangering the real business of spirituality – that of saving the soul. Let them be assured: global restatement of the earth's holiness can only enhance the human spiritual vocation.

The native spiritualities of the world point the way in which we might approach our earth-honouring and make relations of the whole creation. In 1890, 153 native Americans gathered together to perform a Ghost Dance to gain a vision of a world healed of the evil works of white civilization. Their massacre is remembered by white Westerners as the Battle of Wounded Knee. One hundred years later, a group of white people of assorted spiritual allegiance gathered outside the U.S. Embassy in Grosvenor Square, London, to re-enact the Lakota ceremony of 'Making of Relatives', in memory of Wounded Knee. At the ceremony's heart was this invocation:

> Grandmother Earth, hear us! The two-legged, the four-legged, the winged and all that move upon You are Your children. With all beings and all things we shall be relatives; just as we are related to You, O Mother, so we shall make a peace with one another and shall be related to them. May we walk with love and mercy upon that path which is holy! O Grandmother and Mother, help us in making relatives and a lasting peace here![18]

This is truly the work of the New Isis – the Sophianic re-assembling of earth-wisdom, scraps of whose garment blow about the world in rags and tatters of glory. We may be privileged to live through this time and see, if not Sophia unveiled, a glimpse of her *doxa*. The native earth traditions teach us that without a whole view of the world, we can be both presumptuous and stupid – the complete reverse of wise.

Why do we follow Sophia, what is her attraction for us? The fact that she has made the descent into the seven levels of hell, that she knows and shares our pain and exile? Or do we follow her because she goes to prepare a home for us in her temple of seven pillars? Many of us find her here and now, practically and skillfully using the seven gifts of the Spirit to transform our lives alchemically.

There will always be those who look towards the endtime, the *apocatastasis*, just as there will always be those who want to know how to live effectively right now. Between Sophia and Black Goddess there is a wide choice.

Theology or Thealogy?

While orthodox Christian theologians may have set the tone for the twentieth century, they certainly will not end it in tune with the times. For if the excerpting of the Creator from the creation has been a problem in the West, it is equally true that women have been excerpted from the divine. The feminist theologians of the late twentieth century stand ready to make a mercy dash into Christianty and deliver the Sophianic fragments to a safer abode.

The Apocalyptic Virgins who have been appearing over the last century and a half, admonitory and sibylline in their utterances, have heralded a corresponding upsurge of feminist reaction from the long yoke of subjection. What with revelatory appearances of the Blessed Virgin over the firmament and the awkward polemical challenges of amazons and furies upon earth, it is clear even to the most hidebound theologians that something important is going on. What is the divine weather forecast for our coming century? Is it possible to tell, living as we do in the supernova of Ecclesia and the foreglow of Sophia's radiant wings?

Many sibyls and prognosticators have attempted projections of how the world will develop. These seldom take into account more than a small portion of the total picture. Feminists select 'the world as it appears to Woman', theologians take various views of 'the world from the Trinitarian angle', politicians usually see 'the world according to economic projection'. Sophiologists must regard the full spectrum of created life which includes gender, culture, ecology, spirituality, social-relations, education and economics. They must not discount the unknown quantities of such countries as

Russia and China, and the massively discounted impact which Africa will have upon the world in a future age.

Christian feminists have a vast struggle ahead of them: to bring the submerged feminine, both human and Divine, into the consciousness of a patriarchal Ecclesia. Does Woman remain spiritually in hiding, as coy as the Sabbath bride peering through the lattice, or does she come forth and assume her spiritual ministry openly? This question does not only raise the question of the ordination of Woman into the Christian church or the Jewish synagogue; it challenges the nature of Woman's spirituality which has ever been questing for a real home and which has always been overlooked as a social issue.

What role shall Woman adopt in the Church? Prophetess, healer, mediator, counsellor? In the spirit of Sophia, Woman could doubt-less take up such roles with great verve and resource if the ortho-dox barriers could admit the annexing of the ecclesial sanctuary where only men may celebrate the eucharist. What sacramental action could women best minister from? Would new sacraments be devised? Would Woman as Christian priestess administer the rites of healing, reconciliation, death-counselling, therapy of the mentally tormented? This would indeed manifest the compassion of Sophia.

The priest George Tavard concludes that 'all ecclesiastical disa-bilities of women should now be raised, that women should be admitted to all sacraments and to all positions of authority, ministry and service.'[19] It is clear that unless the Church acknowledges the spiritual capacity of Woman, she is going to vote with her feet and set up shop elsewhere – the classic solution of Sophia. This is not to say that she will never come back for, like Sophia, Woman may seek to arbitrate, persuade and show compassion for those whose hearts are hard, but that will not stop her radical and effective activity elsewhere.

New liturgies are required to help us understand and cope with the problems of our own age. Liturgy and ritual are merely effective ways in which Wisdom can be manifest, where Maat can bring her order and open the way for the love of Sophia to function. Rose-mary Ruether has already collected many Christian feminist litur-gies for healing a rape-victim, acknowledging a divorce, recovering from incest, dedicating a house after a burglary etc.[20] Where are these rites in our churches, synagogues and mosques? The parents of a miscarried child are still as bereaved as though their child had come to term, yet for them where is the relief of a funeral service?

Ruether's *Woman Church* envisages a method for reinvesting the Church with nourishment for women, with space and acceptance for the realities of life. It also considers the feminist exodus community – the many Christian women who will not conform to the accepted norms of the Church, like the exclusion of women from ordination, until change comes about. These women are clear about their importance: 'the Church is in exile with us, awaiting with us a wholeness that we are in process of revealing.'[21] Again, women lead the way, with Sophia as a pillar of fire by night, guiding them this time into a new millennium.

The millennial prophecies of St Malachy and Nostradamus predict only two more popes at the time of writing. This has been construed as meaning the termination of the universe. But consider another possibility: what if these prophets were true seers and that the reason for this cessation of popes was so extraordinary that they felt duty bound to remain tactfully silent? The Church has all the signs of going supernova. What if the next pope after those predicted was a woman?

Sophia seems the perfect solution for women who are sympathetic to the Divine Feminine, yet who wish to remain within Christianity and Judaism without compromising their beliefs. It may be that Sophia is about to be discerned in much the same way as she was in first century Alexandria: as a beacon to Christians, Jews, Gnostics and Pagans alike.

For those who remain within the confines of orthodox spirituality there are problems, as Paula Landes points out: 'For those feminists concerned with the religious dimensions of life, the absence of any spiritual tradition which resonates with their experience and which grounds women in a religious cosmos is one of the most insidious aspects of Western culture. To submit to the guidance of traditional religion is to become subjected to a kind of spiritual rape; to reject it is to fall prey to a powerful spiritual loneliness.'[22] The action of Sophia cannot be confined within the boundaries of orthodoxy. Even the Bible speaks of wisdom as being poured out upon all as a free gift. To pretend otherwise is to deny the very spirit of Wisdom herself; denial of Wisdom is the real sin against the Holy Spirit.

The new feminist theologians come from a variety of perspectives and look to be in similar straits as the philosophers of past ages. Many reject the Goddess model as impossibly antique, naïvely ineffectual. Speaking from within Christianity, Susan Cady boldly asserts, 'We must find a way to mainstream the goddess into the universe within which women are actually living their lives,' and wonders, 'or perhaps it is simply a question of recognizing that she has been there all along?'[23] Many feminists have already made an exodus from such ground into actual Goddess spirituality, as we shall see.

And yet there are still arguments against the adoption of Sophia as a positive feminist model. It is argued that Sophia has never been an autonomous Goddess-figure but has always been dependent upon God for her existence, being a mere hypostasis rather than a co-equal like, for example, Isis and Osiris. Many women are doubtful about Sophia because, like many other refugees, she comes clothed in the raiment of the enemy. But there are still other trends within Christian feminism: 'Many Christian feminists have begun, without much fanfare, to speak of the Sophia God of Jesus and of Jesus-Sophia,'[24] which takes us back to the divine syzygy of Gnosticism.

The appeal of Gnosticism as a model for modern feminist spirituality has been challenged by the feminist theologian, Elizabeth Schuessler Fiorenza. 'Salvation in the radically dualistic gnostic system requires the annihilation and destruction of the female or the "feminine principle". In the moderately dualistic systems, salvation means the reunification of the male and female principle, while the male principle stands for the heavenly realms: Christ, God and Spirit. The female principle is secondary, since it stands for that part of the divine that became involved in the created world and history. Gnostic dualism shares in the patriarchal paradigm of Western culture. It makes the first principle male and defines femaleness relative to maleness. Maleness is the subject, the divine, the absolute; femaleness is the opposite or the complementary opposite.'[25] However, Sophia frequently exemplifies this quality of complementarity and we must ask how suitable is Sophia for women as a role model?

For women, Sophia is a powerful archetype for identification on many levels. She is every woman ever raped, denied her creativity, kept isolated, abandoned or exiled. She is also potentially within all women who wish to discover their creativity, maintain their integrity, and support justice in the world and in themselves. She is the strong woman who survives in the face of adversity and rescues her treasures, to display them at a more suitable time. As Sophia emerges further into consciousness, so will the image of the empowered woman become apparent in the world.

Sophia supports the cyclic rhythms of the female spiritual experience: women, generally speaking, do not have an innate linear sense of spiritual progress. Their acknowledgement of the turning seasons of nature and the female life cycle give a profoundly different sense of spiritual presence – one in which the *kenosis* and *plerosis* of the Black Goddess and Sophia are happening periodically.

It is critically important to women in the West that Deity should have a female face for they need the comfort, strength, and spiritual support which only the Divine Feminine can give.

The Goddess has restored to women their innate pride in themselves. No need, as in the case of Hildegard, for example, to apologize for being 'a weak woman' – the standard apologia for all female mystics from Hildegard to Thérèse of Lisieux. Rather there is the renewed confidence to speak out in the voice of Sophia who 'speaks her own praises, in the midst of her people she glories in herself.'[26]

Such statements, taken at their face value, have been demonstrably helpful. Sophia is a practical craftswoman, busy about her affairs. Her way is not to sit about theorizing, but to achieve an effect. The legitimate participation in our own femininity has been extended into the affirmation of our own spirituality also. Feminine patience, like a steady drip of water, wears away the rock of resistence.

But not all women are as sympathetic to the feminist cause. The writer, Barbara Newman's, plaint against the feminist approach to the Divine Feminine is that, 'the feminine is somehow problematic; being neglected, undervalued, or wrongly understood within a patriarchal culture, it needs to be perpetually redefined, revalued, and relocated in the general worldview.'[27] She seems impatient that, 'the feminine rather than the masculine is to be singled out for special attention, as if the meaning of maleness were self-evident whereas the meaning of femaleness were in continual need of discovery.'[28]

Yet this is the very crux of the problem: the restatement of the feminine, both human and divine, is critical to our spiritual survival. Nothing is going to delay the Goddess's second coming, whether in the guise of Sophia or under any other form. As she emerges so the imbalances of our culture will inevitably iron themselves out.

Sophia brings insight into the gender muddle of Western society. Speaking about the popular feminist paradigm of the matriarchy – a prehistoric era when women were alledged to have been dominant – Marie-Louise Janssen-Jurreit asked, 'What use is it for women if they console themselves over the oppression which has now lasted for millennia with the notion that at the beginning of human history they dominated men?'[29] For answer, Sophia arises with all the equity of Maat or Astraea.

The metaphorical shape of future beliefs will be determined by the needs of the people who live in that future. We are working towards better integration of the sexes and that cannot come about until the spiritual values are given justice. Sophia's androgeneity and her extensive repertoire of metaphors exemplifies her availability to both men and women; for she symbolically reconciles the left and right halves of the brain – the intellectual and intuitive sides which have been seen as masculine and feminine. She is both ordered and chaotic, active and receptive, sequential and simultaneous, defined and diffused – endlessly reconciling the dualistic factors which polarise our human existence in her own person.

The manner in which Supreme Deity has been imaged as male in Judaism, Christianity and Islam, has definitely marginalized women. It has also rendered humanity collectively female for, in the Divine partnership, God is husband and humanity the beloved wife. Veneration and identification with Sophia will help to stablize the balance of gender, for she arises almost as the prime representative of created life; like dew she rises from the earth, distilled from so many yearning hearts who long for justice and freedom.

The answer to the gender-divinity problem is to acknowledge the metaphor of divinity for what it is – a metaphor, not a confirmation that God is either male or female which thus gives men or women sole rights in the world. The Divine and the human are different: we must be careful how we apply our metaphors. So it is that Sophia is not a Goddess for women *or* men exclusively. She will give us a totality of wisdom, if we accept her for both the practical earth wisdom of the Black Goddess and the transcendent cosmic wisdom of the World-Soul which are equally available to us.

The Second Coming of the Goddess

But for many people the old orthodoxies have been proved hollow and impotent. Many are no longer interested in inhabiting the ramshackle dwellings of their immediate foremothers and fathers who had to shelter under whatever roof they could find during the exile of the Divine Feminine. Such people require the full-blooded assumption of power which only the Goddess can bring. These are spiritually undernourished people who must gorge themselves on the riches of the past. But is the diet of past ages still a sustaining diet for today? So much has changed, ourselves and our society not least. Where do we go for spiritual nourishment?[30]

The ways are as various as the men and women who are seeking the ways. Contact with the Divine Feminine occurs at the level of the sacred and the imaginal. When a woman has once assented to the Goddess in her life, it can never be the same afterwards. She is eternally committed to a truthful manifestation of her creative powers. It is by this means that the Goddess comes again. She arises as spontaneous metaphor within the soul and psyche, through poetry, dance, music, art and ritual. Life becomes a cyclic round wherein Sophia finds her true dance floor.

It is within the feminine psyche that the Goddess comes again, producing some astonishing priestesses and mediators who are the voice of the Goddess incarnate.[31] For, if it is allowable that orthodox spiritualities have their holy ones, why not also among us?

Instead of feminist theology, Goddess religion has established a *thealogy* where the practice of the Goddess is personally experienced. Thealogy needs hands to work it out and manifest it, like Wisdom the craftswoman of creation. Thealogy is a way of wisdom which involves all arts and crafts, domestically and publicly. Wisdom is the craft of life itself, not the preserve of experts. We need a network of philo-sophias, fedéles d'amore, friends of Wisdom to help co-create this work.

The challenge of our time is to create a Goddess thealogy which can work realistically. It cannot, as we have seen happen so often, merely stress the beneficial, spiritual, loving and nurturing side of the Goddess; it must also demonstrate the wrathful, physical, sexual and independent nature of the Black Goddess. How else can we overcome the errors of the past, which have ignored the Divine Feminine so shamefully?

The unfolding of a Goddess thealogy is happening as I write. The only difference between this and orthodox theologies is that Goddess spirituality spurns hierarchy, dogma and doctrine. Within the fluid and simple lines of Sophia's dance are the future steps of practical spiritual manifestation. The priests and priestesses of the Goddess of Wisdom address the need directly, not by thinking twice of giving their time and effort to effect a sophianic solution, but by passing beyond the boundaries of impossibility and taking the problem to Sophia's lap.

What makes this development so interesting is that there are also priests of Sophia who are very aware that it is through Woman that the Goddess is now speaking. This may go some way to balance the inequity of the past two millennia.

However, we need a thealogy with a compassionate womb and courageous guts, which will squarely address the nature of evil. 'Wisdom renders us invulnerable from attack' only if we acknowledge her in our lives, it does not mean that we shall never be challenged or attacked ourselves. The cosy thealogy of 'the Goddess is on earth and all will be right with the world' cannot be indulged at the cost of creation's suffering.

The search for spiritual consciousness – a common ground from which worship of the Divine Feminine arises – is a problem which is being immediately redressed. The making of rituals, liturgies and spontaneous devotions typifies the expression of the Goddess amongst us. Homes are temples, shelves become shrines, gardens are places given over to circle dancing, earth-altars, places of meeting and devotion.

These spontaneous liturgies, celebrations and devotional practices most often arise from outside conventional religious traditions. They come from feminist and pagan standpoints, arising out of a wellhead of creative genius. This movement is by no means isolated but is sparking off new manifestations of the Goddess throughout the world. Such conscious acts of devotion make real the veiled reality of Sophia among us.

We stand on the threshold of a Goddess religion which, by virtue of its membership and its aim, is non-hierarchical, decentralised, locally-manifest, in many and various ways. Goddess spirituality addresses directly the problems of our own world now. Its work of healing, blessing, celebration will never become fixed because of the spontaneous presence of Sophia in its midst. The liturgies and practices of orthodox religions which offer children stones instead of bread, or serpents in place of fish,[32] will find themselves rapidly displaced unless they invite the invigorating presence of Sophia within them.

The institution of loose, informal networks and associations such as the *Fellowship of Isis* and the *Covenant of the Goddess*,[33] each of which has thousands of members, show the slow beginnings of a trend towards a re-assimilation of Goddess-based spirituality among us.

The presence of a Goddess spirituality is discounted by governmental and religious hierarchies because of its refusal to be pigeon-holed, or perhaps one should say, dove-cotted! That it will be a power to reckon with, we can have no doubt. Those animated by the Goddess, in her many forms, are concerned with all world problems: economy; justice; racial, sexual and species equality; education; ecological balance and many other concerns. To acknowledge the Goddess is to open up immediately to issues which threaten our total existence. For we cannot deny our common heritage of life which the Goddess safeguards.

To encompass the change of spirit necessary to safeguard and appreciate all that the Goddess offers us, many have reverted to ancient modes of spirituality, reframed in modern ways. The rapid growth of Wiccan and Pagan circles which causes such alarm among fundamentalists is nothing less than a restatement of ancient native traditional values of spirituality, where Deity can be expressed as validly in female as in male terminology. The sacred character of Nature is upheld by Pagans and Goddess-venerators, and the sustenance of the Black Goddess's wisdom makes them stern judges of modern society's materialism.[34] The face of the Goddess is being restored to us in many forms, not least that of Sophia, the Goddess of Wisdom, who has preserved and sustained the Goddess' ancient love for the creation. She is not *just* the planet earth or Nature, though some see her so; she also is the Lady of our physical, creative and spiritual life.

The New Gnostics

Sophia has ever been the Goddess of the Hidden Way, a Kindler of Interior Wisdom. While many individuals and movements have been accompanied by her, the late twentieth century has seen an upsurge in the rare veneration of Sophia for her own sake.

The Holy Order of Wisdom in Santa Cruz, founded by Aurora Terrenus, is dedicated to communicating the idea and spirit of Sophia, 'for the enlightenment, enrichment, peace and prosperity of all.'[35] Aurora Terrenus is the pseudonym of a visionary and poet who received a mystical vision of Sophia in the New Forest in England some twenty years ago. *The School of Holy Wisdom* is also part of the Order, offering free workshops and lectures. Also part of the Order is the *Hagia Sophia, Ecclesia Spiritualis*, a non-denominational church which offers ordination to seekers from all spiritual paths. The publications which are released from its press, *Celestial Communications*, stress the guiding and peace-giving aspects of Sophia, frequently referring to the Sapiential books. The following poem expresses the vocational call which *The Holy Order of Wisdom* issues to all members:

> O Gnostic,
> O Knower
> of the unity of Love and Wisdom,
> the androgyny of Heaven and Earth,
> and of Nature and Spirit.
>
> O Knower
> of The Great Goddess,
> The Great Mother,
> who calls herself
> Sophia.
> Holy is her name,
> Sophia,
> co-creator of all things,
> earthly and divine.
>
> Divine Love
> lives with Eternal Wisdom,
> together as one,
> as a child in its mother's womb.
>
> Sophia
> gathers all of her children.
>
> O Gnostic,
> to you she calls
> to fulfill the prophecy,
> to manifest the vision
> of Peace on Earth.[36]

The Holy Order of Wisdom communicates the love of Sophia in an ecstactic and immediate way, thus ensuring that Sophia will receive a wider audience.

Meanwhile, across the Atlantic, *The Order of Sancta Sophia* has recently been founded in North Wales. This is a contemplative and healing Lay order of loosely associated Christians. Its emphasis is upon the restoration of the role of the feminine within the Divine and upon the encouragement of the healing and creative arts. Its motto is a summation of Sophia's creative and wholistic role: 'Be healthy, be whole, be holy.'[37] The interweaving of the contemplative and secular life is enhanced by the practice of pilgrimage and a practical opportunity to help peace and justice in the Middle East. The most interesting feature of *The Order of Sancta Sophia* is its committment to Celtic spirituality which, like the Eastern Orthodox tradition, does not vaunt the spiritual role of the religious above the layperson. Thus, any seeker may find the Grail as long as she is on pilgrimage in the spirit of Sophia.

This celebration of Sophia also derives its impetus from a reawakened interest in the Gnostic *Nag Hammadi* texts, whose finding at the start of the New Age itself cannot be insignificant. Apart from these named orders and associations, there are countless other groups who are passing through the veil of Sophia into the uncharted realms of the spirit. The foundation of a Gnostic church, the *Ecclesia Gnostica Mysteriorum*, is but one expression of the diversity and enthusiasm of the spiritual tradition of Sophia. Founded in 1978, this church takes its spiritual authority from Wisdom herself. It boasts the first female Gnostic bishop since Classical times, Tau Rosamonde Miller, who maintains a loving guardianship of Sophia's pathways. Ordained to the priesthood via the traditional masculine lines of apostolic succession in 1974, she became bishop in 1981. Within the *Ecclesia*, she is a tradition-holder and spiritual head of the *Holy Order of Mary Magdalene* – a tradition of gnosis not recognized by orthodox Christianity, since it derives its lineage of succession from Mary Magdalene herself. This secret tradition has, it is claimed, been maintained (until recently when Tau Rosamonde Miller began to ordain men) by a female priesthood. This was for reasons of security, not sexist exclusivity, for it is a well-known fact that women are the guardians of the spiritual fire especially in times of persecution.

This remarkable woman is reticent about herself, preferring to remain centred in her work. 'Since my earliest recollections, the awareness of a Presence, a Love so pervading, so utterly fulfilling, so completely and extraordinarily present has been with me at my every breath. Neither the pleasure nor the pain that I have experienced has ever been able to touch That. Dare I call it God? It is beyond names.'[38]

The tenets of the *Ecclesia Gnostica Mysteriorum* itself are not a slavish following of historical Gnostic doctrines, but a pursuit of *gnosis*, drawing on all levels of the perennial wisdom of the Western tradition. It encourages all people to find their personal path and rejects doctrine, theology or dogma, preferring the mythic and allegorical traditions of the salvific story. This

19 *Tau Rosamonde Miller* Tau Rosamonde Miller of the *Ecclesia Gnostica Mysteriorum* is shown here in contemplation during the celebration of the Eucharist. She is the first female Gnostic bishop (or Tau) since the early centuries of the first millennium AD. The physical impact of a woman celebrating the sacraments at the altar has a profound effect upon those for whom the Divine Feminine is a veiled or esoteric truth which seldom becomes manifest. The way of gnosis re-emerges in the twentieth century as each individual seeks to reclaim her spirituality.

tradition of storytelling is a venerable one in the transmission of wisdom.

The *Ecclesia* teaches that 'gnosis cannot be given or passed on. We can only teach the individual to reach the state in which gnosis can be made manifest.'[39]

Participation in the *Ecclesia*'s communion is extended to all people of good-will, not only to its self-professed members. It maintains the seven sacraments as the ritual basis of its work, but it does not marginalize these life-giving streams of Wisdom as many churches do. 'These Sacraments are administered through a priesthood that admits both men and women who are trained for many years in accordance with the Mystery School tradition.'[40] Moreover, 'the mystery of the Eucharist is celebrated as a *hieros gamos*, a sacred marriage, of the Sophia, radiant Mother of the World, and her consort, the Christ.'[41] Its liturgy draws freely upon many Gnostic and mystical sources, as well as upon Biblical and liturgical ones. The *Ecclesia*'s literature betrays a healthy sense of humour which is notably lacking from many such traditions. One feels that Sophia is truly at home here. It cannot be at many altars that the faithful ones of love are sent forth with this blessing: 'May that glorious Mystery of the Two-in-One, the eternal and boundless love of Christ and Sophia, fill your hearts and minds that ye may carry into the world the sweet fragrance of Life Eternal.'[42]

The *Ecclesia Gnostica Mysteriorum* is an example of gnosis in action today. Without the hierarchical and dogmatic bases of orthodox Christianity, it is unlikely that it will ever be part of mainstream Christian spirituality. However, it does offer a broad pathway to the discovery of gnosis in the Western tradition. It speaks to the soul which, like Sophia, is lost in a confusion of spiritual pathways: 'And the Logos said: "They say I came for all, but in truth I came for Her Who came for all. For it had come to pass that there were those who had lost their way and, lacking in spark, could not return into the Fullness; seeing this, She came unto them, giving Her life to the depths of matter. And in truth She did suffer and become blind. But our Father, sensing Her anguish, sent Me forth, being of Him, so that She might see and We be as One again. Though they see it not, it is She, the tender Mother of Mercy, Who is the great redeemer."'[43]

The Saviour Goddess is among us once more, approachable by those who wish to remain within orthodox spirituality as well as by those who are using Sophia's practical wisdom to open new spiritual pathways.

Sophia Supreme

The divine spirit within each of us is the receptacle and transmitter of wisdom. As we enter the Sophianic millennium, the time for finding, appreciating and using our spiritual treasures has come. Sophia, as the Goddess of Transformation and Connections, will help us access our treasures.

The metaphors of deity are shifting – perhaps irretrievably. Deity can no longer be symbolized only as a masculine image, nor solely as feminine either. Creative channels have been opened to allow new life to our spirituality. One of the most important considerations that faces us is that if the Goddess is not to become a restrictive symbol, as imprisoning as those which we have left behind, then Sophia must be free to go where she will. She cannot be restrained by orthodoxies of any kind. She is a trickster, making us fall into our own dogmatic traps where we fall prey to her aspect of the Black Goddess. Between them, they will show us the way of effective spirituality, one that is not concerned with theories but with skilful actions.

We are no longer bound by the constraints of custom and culture into believing only one orthodox creed. The coal of the divine self can only be kindled by the burning glass which most clearly allows the Divine Light to pass through it. If we persist in holding up burning glasses which are obscure or opaque to our spiritual understanding, our divine self will remain unkindled. The incandescent thealogy of Sophia is to bring fire to all souls and she will assume the form which each person can understand. She comes as the Holy Spirit to Christians, as the Pillar of Fire to Jews, as the Goddess to Goddess worshippers: her form does not matter.

Every living being must listen for the voice of Sophia on every street corner, for she still cries aloud for those who can hear her. She is seeded in all, to be found by all. It behoves us all to cultivate the seed-ground of the soul. Her word is simple: 'Obey me willingly, trust me completely and love me absolutely.'[44] Obedience is not a word which we relish in this age, but it is one request which the Black Goddess makes, and she needs our free assent. Trust requires the faith to act 'as if' the Divine Feminine were a reality to our imaginations. Love can only come through true gnosis, for by knowledge we are able to give the *fiat* of Mary which is, after all, no more than the obedience requested by the Black Goddess, and which is the virginal response of Sophia herself to the whole of creation.

Orthodox religions are having to learn that the jettisoning of their mystical traditions has caused many to leave their ranks. Practical alternatives to orthodox spirituality are now sought in the native, earth traditions of our planet.

We are learning to love the earth and its creation, to reconstitute the four divisions of Nature into a single vision. We begin to understand that there is no division between the energy which creates, the potentiality of creation, the created and the uncreated – they are all one. The Lady Wisdom returns to our hearts, ennobling the commonplace, enlivening the stalemate. With the resacralization of Nature we must also acknowledge the dimension of the sacred and the imaginal, for Sophia is the mistress of all creativity. The maintenance of a basic daily existence is not the sum of life's purpose: without the sparkle of Sophia we are zombies. She inspires us to extract the last ounce of fun out of life, to learn to play at living, rather than dourly traipsing from place to place.

More and more people, within many spiritual traditions, are awakening to this realization. 'The Shalom of the Holy; the disclosure of the gracious Shekinah; Divine Wisdom; the empowering Matrix; She, in whom we live and move and have our being – She comes; She is here.'[45]

The prophets of Sophia's coming among us speak ardently of her reintegration, which is nothing less than the re-assembling of the original Goddess mirror. 'And since then I have learned and do see, that not only prophecies and hopes, and desires unclothed yet in word or thought foretell her coming but already a multitude of spirits are in the gardens of the soul, and are sowing seed and calling upon the wind of the south; and that everywhere are watching eyes and uplifted hands, and signs which cannot be mistaken, in many lands, in many peoples, in many minds; and in the heaven itself, that the soul sees the surpassing signature' of Sophia.[46]

The cumulative identity of created life is Sophia. She descends in order to have the initiation of human existence. She is a sharer in our work, she is a teacher of primal playfulness and creativity. We all bear her seal and signature, not as her possessions, but as sharers in the prima materia of DNA itself. The secret of that fragile double helix is life itself. Sophia is the companion of every soul; she is the Goddess's mirror, and within us lie the divine reflective shards.

The recognition of the divinity of created matter, the marriage of humanity to the divine, are the Sophianic initiations on offer in the coming millennium. The voice of the Black Goddess as the Apocalyptic Virgin and as Gaia awakens us to unity with the earth while the return of the Goddess to our ideological metaphor restores us to a new octave of spiritual wisdom.

The transcendent Sophia of the Stars returns once more to hear what her earthly counterpart is saying. The Black Goddess speaks to us urgently, warning us to take responsibility for our neglected environment. The Sophia in us answers with true, just

20 *Reclaiming Ritual* Diké or Astraea, the Goddess of Justice, left the earth in the Age of Bronze, disgusted at the strife which humanity brought to the planet. Aratus, the Greek writer, told how she left earth and became associated with the constellation of Virgo. In this reclaiming ritual, from the sequence *See For Yourself: Pilgrimage to a Neolithic Goddess Cave,* enacted and photographed by the feminist artist Mary Beth Edelson, we see the return of the Goddess of Justice in the person of her priestess. The cave is frequently associated with initiation into the mysteries of the Goddess. Here the constellation Virgo decends into the darkness of the cave, bringing with it a new initiation for the earth.

and compassionate response: where our treasure is bestowed, there also is our heart.[47]

Open your heart, walk within and find Sophia.

APPENDIX

Glossary of Specialist Terms

In dealing with the subject of Wisdom I have had to use particular terms which have exact values and meanings but which have no direct equivalents in English. Often transliterated from the original languages they are unfamiliar to the reader. This glossary is an attempt to elucidate such words and expressions with the minimum of fuss. Each may have wider definitions than I have indicated here.

analepsis   the art of remembering past events by accessing the back brain.

anamnesis   the act of remembering in the sense of re-enacting; ritualized remembrance.

ananke   'necessity'. She is depicted as the Goddess of the Spindle in Plato's *Myth of Er*.

anastasis   the immortality, literally 'undyingness', of Christ.

anima mundi   the World-Soul.

apocatastasis   originally a theory of Origen's that, at the end of time, all creatures, including the damned and demons, shall be brought into the divine embrace. In Gnostic parlance, the end of time when the fulness of the Pleroma shall be opened.

apophatic   apophatic theology is the knowledge of Deity through complete ignorance and darkness. Thus, one cannot say 'God is good or perfect', one can only say what God is not. The mysticism of midnight illumination.

aretalogy   self-praises. Both Isis and Wisdom utter a series of aretalogies about their own virtues and abilities.

demiurge   craftsman or technician. Plato called the Creator of the world the demiurge. Valentinus also used the term to designate the son of Sophia who created the phenomenal world.

Divine Feminine   this term throughout signifies the feminine appearances of deity.

doxa   glory.

doxophony   the manifestation of Sophia's glory.

dunameis   powers, daemonic agencies or angelic forces.

Dyad   in Platonism, the Dyad stemmed from the **Monad**, and was usually symbolised as female or Mother.

ergane   'work-woman'. This is one of the titles of Athene, which may be given also to Wisdom in *Proverbs* 8 where she helps in the creation.

gnostic   knowledgeable, one who 'knows' or is an initiate of the **Mysteries**.

Gnostic one of myriad branches of Gnosticism, a blend of Christian, Judaic, Near Eastern Paganism and Mediterranean mystery religion.

hebdomad the sevenfold levels of creation, each usually represented by a planet.

heimarmene fate. The late Classical world believed that everyone was subject to the **ananke** of *heimarmene*, and was fated.

hypostasis an intermediary being or quasi-personification of certain attributes proper to the Divine, but which is mid-way between a personality and an abstract being; alternatively, that which is of one substance with God, e.g. Sophia is frequently called 'a hypostasis of God' from *The Wisdom of Solomon* to the works of Bulgakov.

kataphatic affirmative knowledge of the Divine, through sure and certain knowledge; the mysticism of daylight.

kenosis the emptying of the self, the spiritual experience of the Black Goddess.

klimax heptapulos 'the sevenfold stairway'. This name was adopted by both Orphic and Mithraic cults to signify the passage of the initiate through the sevenfold planetary experiences.

Logos literally 'word'. It is a term which is adopted by some aspects of the Divine Masculine, especially Jesus Christ.

meta-history the progression of spiritual events which have their reflection in history.

metanoia change of heart.

Monad In Platonism, the Monad is the originator, or the One. This archetype was seen as male or Father.

Mysteries, the the core rites into which individuals were initiated, e.g. The Eleusinian Mysteries, the Mithraic or Christian Mysteries. That which is incommunicable save to those with direct personal experience or communion with the Divine.

native tradition the wisdom of aboriginal societies, coresponding to our contemporary sense of 'religion'.

ogdoad literally, 'the eighth'. The eighth level of creation is the place where Gnostic Sophia sits, between the **hebdomad** and the **pleroma**.

paredros the throne-companion or assessor of God.

parousia 'the presence'. Used to denote the Second Coming of Christ. The chief protagonist of the parousia is Sophia as the Holy Spirit.

pleroma the fulness of heaven in Gnostic thought.

plerosis the filling of the self, the spiritual experience of Sophia.

shamanka female shaman.

synergy the action of Sophia, by which all things work together.

syzygy In Valentinian Gnosis particularly, the pair of cosmological opposites, usually male and female, twins of one quality or function, e.g. Sophia and Logos.

thalamus bridal chamber.

theosis Deification, spiritualization, the penetration of the human being by divine energies.

Theotokos 'God-Bearer'. Title of the Blessed Virgin Mary.
volva Scandinavian sibyl or pythoness.
World-Soul the **anima mundi**, or soul of the planetary world of earth, became the abstracted metaphor of the Goddess of the Earth.

Notes

Prologue (pages 5–12)
1 p. 283 Lewis
2 p. 185 Blake
3 Griffiths

Chapter 1 The Black Goddess (pages 15–33)

1 p. 164 R. Graves 1962
2 p. 164–5 ibid
3 *Isaiah* 45:34
4 p. 290 Vaughan, *The Night*
5 p. 246 Vaughan, *They are all gone into the world of light*
6 p. 517 Sjöö
7 p. 58 Clarke
8 p. ix Gribben
9 p. 74 Sandars
10 p. 80 ibid
11 p. 82 ibid
12 p. 90 ibid
13 p. 94 ibid
14 p. 95 ibid
15 pp. 39–43 C. Matthews, *Elements of the Goddess*
16 pp. 20–2 Kerenyi, 1951
17 p. 737 *Jerusalem Bible*, *Job* 26
18 pp. 240ff. C. Matthews, *Arthur and the Sovereignty of Britain*
19 pp. 151–2 Kerenyi, 1951
20 p. 28 Sandars
21 p. 86 Sjöö
22 p. 154 Gimbutas
23 p. 212 Lovelock
24 p. 256 Fontenrose
25 p. 47 ibid
26 p. 14–6 Vermaseren
27 p. 12 ibid
28 p. 24 ibid
29 p. 22 ibid
30 p. 83 ibid
31 pp. 445–9 Emperor Julian
32 p. 50 Vermaseren
33 pp. 82–3 ibid
34 p. 93 Carroll
35 p. 28 Kramer
36 p. 49 Vermaseren
37 p. 234 Nicholson
38 p. 232–39 ibid
39 *Sovereignty's Song* by C. Matthews

Chapter 2 The Sacred Marriage (pages 34–57)

1 pp. 198–9 Springborg
2 p. 182 Blake
3 p. 95 Moltmann-Wendell, 1986
4 p. 173 Fox
5 p. 106 Lang
6 p. 105 d'Alviella
7 p. 268 ibid
8 p. 549 Ringgren
9 p. 137 ibid
10 p. 41 Kramer
11 p. 60 Lang
12 p. 19 Perera
13 p. 60 Wolkstein
14 pp. 52–89 ibid, and pp. 108–21 Kramer
15 p. 89 Wolkstein
16 p. 115 Sandars
17 p. 84 Kramer
18 *St Matthew* 12:42

19 p. 109ff. Pritchard
20 p. 97 ibid
21 *Glorious Koran*, Surah 27
22 p. 122 Pritchard
23 pp. 222–35 *Quest of the Holy Grail*
24 p. 110 Pritchard
25 p. 136 ibid
26 p. 72 Kane
27 p. 183 Patai
28 p. 194 ibid
29 p. 303 Jung, *Alchemical Studies*
30 p. 17 Thompson
31 p. 991 *Jerusalem Bible*
32 p. 19 Pope
33 *Song of Songs* 1:2
34 ibid 3:1
35 ibid 5:7
36 p. 527 Pope
37 *Song of Songs* 8:2
38 p. 78 Kramer
39 p. 42 Pope
40 sonnet by Lord Herbert of Cherbourg, quoted in Pope p. 311
41 p. 606 Pope
42 p. 35 Winston
43 pp. 45–6 Ringgren
44 p. 48 ibid
45 p. 46 ibid
46 p. 103 Winston
47 p. 9 Hesiod
48 p. 103 Winston
49 p. 17 Hesiod
50 pp. 256ff. Hesiod
51 pp. 215–17 Aratus
52 p. 284 Heraclitus
53 p. 61 *Book of Enoch*
54 p. 103 Winston
55 p. 332 Maclean Todd
56 *St Matthew* 3:37–9
57 p. 37 *Other Bible*
58 p. 399–400 Pope and pp. 184–90 Grigson
59 pp. 359–417 Diodorus
60 *Leviticus* 12
61 p. 443 Fontenrose
62 p. 88 James
63 p. 85 Kane
64 p. 150 Feild
65 p. 100 Kerenyi, 1974
66 p. 162 O'Brien
67 p. 90–1 Kane
68 p. 159 O'Brien
69 p. 272 Wynne-Tyson

Chapter 3 The Saviour Goddess (pages 58–74)

1 p. 289–303 Hesiod
2 p. 402 Taylor
3 ibid
4 p. 476 Pausanius
5 p. xxviii Kingsford
6 p. xx ibid
7 p. 387 Taylor
8 p. xxvi Kingsford
9 p. 113 Apuleius
10 p. 97–133 ibid
11 *I Timothy* 6:16
12 p. 97 Kane, my itals
13 *Deuteronomy* 37:27
14 pp. 132–3 Grant
15 p. 129 ibid
16 pp. 46–53 Witt
17 p. 74 Lurker
18 p. 493–4 Scott
19 p. 181 Plutarch
20 p. 129 ibid
21 p. 236 Robinson
22 p. 63 Witt
23 p. 335 Layton
24 p. 18 *Akathist Hymn*
25 p. 109 Winston
26 pp. 177–93 Fontenrose
27 p. 41 Mead 1964, vol I
28 p. 42 ibid
29 p. 43 ibid
30 p. 305 Taylor
31 p. 228 Apuleius
32 p. 229 ibid
33 p. 241 ibid
34 p. 9 Plutarch

Chapter 4 Wisdom Among the Philosophers (pages 77–96)
1 *Wisdom* 8.17
2 p. 47 Robinson, 1975
3 p. 96 Begg, 1984
4 p. 141 Kinsley, 1989
5 p. 126 Kerenyi, 1951
6 p. 453 Hesiod
7 pp. 118–19 Kerenyi, 1951
8 p. 123 ibid
9 p. 56 Kerenyi, 1978
10 p. 32 ibid
11 p. 33 ibid
12 p. 42 ibid
13 p. 616 *Other Bible*
14 p. 127 Graves, 1958
15 p. 109 Downing
16 p. 160 Kinsley
17 p. 164 ibid
18 p. 1106 Plato *Philebus*, 29c
19 p. 1183 ibid *Timaeus*, 30d
20 p. 1165 ibid *Timaeus* 34b, my itals
21 Julian of Norwich and Blake
22 p. 143 von Franz, 1975
23 p. 45–6 Dillon
24 p. 203 ibid
25 p. 394 ibid
26 p. 25 ibid
27 p. 205 ibid
28 p. 194 Witt
29 p. 34 Wilken
30 p. 287 Dillon
31 p. 80 Wili
32 p. 57–60 Hopkins
33 p. 81 Wili
34 p. 625 Plotinus
35 p. 28 Winston
36 p. 38–9 King
37 p. 623 Plotinus
38 p. 301 Taylor
39 p. 320 ibid
40 p. 305 ibid
41 p. 549 Plato, 197b
42 p. 140 Lang
43 p. 95 Winston
44 p. 172 Pope
45 p. 164 Dillon

Chapter 5 Wisdom Builds her House (pages 97–110)
1 p. 931 *Jerusalem Bible*
2 *Proverbs* 1:20–1
3 ibid 1:24
4 ibid 1:28
5 ibid 8:17
6 ibid 8:2–3
7 ibid 8:22–31
8 p. 122 Ringgren
9 p. 123 ibid
10 *Proverbs* 9:1–9
11 p. 310 Winston
12 *Proverbs* 24:3–4
13 p. 310 Winston
14 *Proverbs* 31:26
15 ibid 31:25
16 ibid 4:11
17 ibid 5:5
18 ibid 7:4, and 7:10–13
19 ibid 9:1–6, and 9:13–18
20 ibid 14:1
21 ibid 31:31
22 *Wisdom* 6:20
23 ibid 6:22
24 ibid 7:11–12
25 ibid 7:25
26 ibid 1:6–7, 9, 12
27 ibid 7:26
28 p. 6 Reese
29 *Wisdom* 7:29–30
30 ibid 7:22–23
31 ibid 7:25
32 p. 186 Winston
33 *Wisdom* 7:26
34 *Genesis* 1:2
35 *Wisdom* 7:24
36 p. 125–6 Fox
37 *Wisdom* 8:3
38 p. 194 Winston
39 ibid
40 *Wisdom* 8:4
41 ibid 7:27
42 ibid 8:17
43 ibid 9:10
44 ibid 8:4

45 Pindar *Olympia* 8:22
46 *Wisdom* 10:14
47 ibid 18:3
48 ibid 18:15
49 p. 7 Reese
50 *Sirach* 1:9–10
51 ibid 1:14
52 ibid 4:17–18

53 ibid 6:20–22
54 ibid 6:29–31
55 ibid 14:23
56 ibid 24 3–7
57 ibid 24:9–12
58 ibid 24:28
59 ibid 24:34
60 ibid 38:34

Chapter 6   The Cloud on the Sanctuary   (pages 111–31)

1 p. 190 Jacobs
2 p. 295 Anon
3 p. 15 *Other Bible*
4 ibid
5 *Deuteronomy* 16:21
6 *2 Kings* 23
7 *Jeremiah* 44:17
8 p. 163 Ringgren
9 p. 159 Pope
10 *Deuteronomy* 33:27
11 p. 109 *Jerusalem Bible*
12 p. 155 Pope
13 p. 322 von Franz, 1966
14 p. 74 Patai
15 p. 106 ibid
16 p. 54 ibn Yusuf
17 p. 55 ibid
18 *Isaiah* 54:2–7
19 ibid 55:13
20 *Wisdom* 10:13–4
21 p. 117 Patai
22 p. 156 Ringgren
23 *Sirach* 24:13–17
24 *Exodus* 36:1
25 p. 169 Hauke
26 p. 713 *Other Bible*
27 p. 81 Jacobs
28 p. 94 ibid
29 p. 86 ibid
30 *Ezekiel* 1
31 p. 171–2 Patai
32 pp. 172–3 ibid
33 p. 55 Mead, 1979
34 pp. 75–6 Goldstein
35 p. 321 Pope

36 p. 140 Patai
37 p. 180ff. ibid
38 p. 173 Pope
39 pp. 62–3 Harding
40 p. 63 ibid
41 p. 240 Patai
42 p. 244 ibid
43 p. 305–6 Scholem
44 p. 307 ibid
45 p. 71 Goldstein
46 p. 100 Jacobs
47 p. 101 ibid
48 p. 114 ibid
49 p. 57 ibn Yusuf
50 p. 55 ibid
51 pp. 55–61 Nahman
52 p. 218 Jacobs
53 Martin Buber, *For the Sake of Heaven*, New York, 1945; c.f. p. 318–9 O'Brien
54 p. 47 Epstein
55 pp. 39–41 Eisenberg, song as arranged by C. Matthews in her Sophia workshops
56 p. 22 Bronstein
57 pp. 29–30 Phillips
58 p. 25 interview 'The Spiritual Dance', ed. Dixie Tracy-Kinney, *Gnosis* vol 4 Spring/Summer 1987
59 p. 37 Scholem
60 p. 58 ibn Yusuf
61 p. 211 Nicholson
62 p. 420 O'Brien
63 p. 419 ibid

Chapter 7 The Divine Androgyne (pages 132-49)

1   pp. 16–17 Kerenyi, 1951
2   *Galatians* 4:28
3   p. 254 Kerenyi, 1951
4   p. 287 Diodorus vol II and
    St John 1
5   *St John* 6:35–86
6   p. 33 Erigena vol 7
7   p. 39 ibid
8   p. 47 ibid
9   *St Matthew* 3:16
10 p. 207 Evdokimov
11 p. 84 ibid
j12 p. 128 King
13 p. 116 Jung 1954
14 *Sirach* 15:2; *Wisdom* 8:3,
    8:2–9, 9:4
15 p. 293 Hauke
16 p. 286 ibid
17 p. 293 Hauke
18 p. 332 Layton
19 p. 65 Semmelroth
20 p. 752 Charlesworth
21 p. 293 Hauke
22 *1 Corinthians* 2:6–8 and p.
    38 Cady
23 p. 95 Zolla, 1971
24 p. 217 *Nag Hammadi Library*
25 p. 15 Dart
26 pp. 85–6 Robinson, 1975
27 p. 7 ibid
28 *St Matthew* 23:37–8
29 p. 14 Robinson, 1975
30 *St Luke* 10:24
31 *St Matthew* 5:3–13
32 p. 61 Evdokimov, my trans
33 *Hebrews* 1:1–5
34 *St John* 1:14 *Jerusalem Bible*
35 *St Matthew* 2:18
36 ibid 18:5,10
37 p. 118 King
38 *Revelations* 22:17
39 *St Matthew* 25:40
40 p. 335 Layton (the square
    brackets indicate where text
    is missing or damaged)
41 p. 80 ibid
42 *St Mark* 9:1–8
43 *St John* 15:17 and *1 Corinthians*
    11:24
44 *St. John* 14:18,26
45 *St Matthew* 27:51
46 *St John* 19:23
47 *Jonah* 2:7, *Jerusalem Bible*
48 p. 283 C. Matthews, *The
    Rosicrucian Vault*
49 *Sirach* 24:45
50 p. 12 Knight
51 *Acts* 2:3
52 *Acts* 1:11
53 p. 5 Moltmann-Wendell, 1986
54 p. 243 Hauke
55 pp. 170–1 Julian of Norwich
56 *2 Corinthians* 3:18
57 pp. 56–7 Jung 1970, my trans
58 *Wisdom* 7:27
59 *St Luke* 7:35

Chapter 8 The Bride of God (pages 150–78)

1   p. 260 Layton
2   p. 232 *Oxford Dictionary of
    the Church*
3   *St Matthew* 13:33
4   p. 293 Layton
5   p. 28 Robinson
6   p. 99 *Nag Hammadi Library*
7   p. 111 ibid
8   p. 112 ibid
9   p. 267 Layton
10 p. 308 ibid
11 p. 394 Dillon
12 pp. 294–5 Layton
13 pp. 272–3 *Nag Hammadi
    Library*
14 p. 34 Olson
15 p. 753 Charlesworth
16 p. 246 *Nag Hammadi Library*
17 pp. 121–40 Layton
18 p. 164 King
19 p. 300 Layton
20 p. 359 King
21 p. 661 *Other Bible*
22 ibid

23 p. 616 ibid
24 p. 204 Layton
25 p. 205 ibid
26 p. 180 *Nag Hammadi Library*
27 p. 184 ibid
28 p. 353 King
29 p. 349 ibid
30 p. 308ff. *Nag Hammadi Library*
31 p. 357 King
32 p. 94 King
33 p. 63 Tavard
34 p. 413 King
35 p. 346 King
36 p. 366 Sjöö
37 p. 114 King
38 p. 15 Tavard
39 p. 25 ibid
40 p. 71 Layton
41 p. 72 ibid
42 p. 270 King
43 p. 204 Layton
44 *Sirach* 24:28–9
45 p. 80 ibid
46 *Joshua* 2:18
47 p. 186 *Nag Hammadi Library*
48 p. 607 *Other Bible*
49 p. 26 Mead, 1979
50 p. 607 *Other Bible*
51 ibid
52 p. 34 Olson
53 Baigent
54 p. 64 Moltmann-Wendel, 1980
55 *St John* 20:13–17
56 *St Luke* 8:43–8
57 *St John* 20:24–9

58 p. 287 Layton
59 p. 339 Layton
60 p. 20 Mead, 1974
61 p. 103 ibid
62 p. 135 ibid
63 p. 193 ibid
64 p. 103 ibid
65 pp. 300–2 Layton
66 p. 67 Tavard
67 p. 557 Plato: Symp 205d
68 *St John* 3:29
69 p. 63 Mead, 1974
70 p. 180 Layton
71 p. 664 *Other Bible*
72 p. 151 *Nag Hammadi Library*
73 p. 343 Layton
74 ibid
75 p. 294 ibid
76 p. 295 Layton
77 p. 281 Anon
78 p. 37 Davis
79 p. 38 ibid
80 p. 85 Robinson
81 p. 51 Mead, 1974, my itals
82 p. 369 King
83 p. 371 ibid
84 p. 408 King
85 p. 376 James
86 p. 378 ibid
87 p. 196 Layton
88 p. 129 ibid
89 p. 291 ibid
90 *Proverbs* 8:3
91 p. 764 Charlesworth

Chapter 9 The Virgin of Light (pages 179–90)

1 p. 55 Cragg
2 p. 21 Bakhtiar
3 p. 38 Wilson, *Scandal*
4 p. 22 Corbin, 1985
5 *Deuteronomy* 6:4
6 p. 46. *Glorious Koran*, Surah 112
7 p. 7 Bakhtiar
8 p. 303 Eliade, 1979
9 p. 15 Corbin, 1977
10 p. 21 ibid

11 p. 47 Corbin, 1986
12 p. 22 Corbin, 1985
13 p. 103 Corbin, 1977
14 p. 303 Zaehner
15 p. 304 ibid
16 p. 49 Corbin, 1977
17 p. 121 Wilson, *Drunken Universe*
18 p. 10 Monaghan
19 p. 41 Harding
20 p. x *Glorious Koran*

21 p. 38 Begg, 1985
22 p. xvii *Glorious Koran*
23 pp. 183–262 Corbin, 1977
24 p. 220 Corbin, 1986
25 pp. 237–8 ibid
26 p. 345 Corbin, 1969
27 p. 224 ibid
28 p. 137 ibid
29 p. 138 ibid
30 p. 140 ibid
31 p. 326 ibid
32 p. 279 ibid
33 p. 385 ibid
34 p. 388 ibid
35 p. 162 Meier
36 p. 700 *Glorious Koran*
37 p. 701 ibid

38 p. 105 ibid
39 p. 176 Wilson, *Scandal*
40 p. 74 Cragg
41 p. 63 Corbin, 1977
42 p. 65 ibid
43 p. 66 ibid
44 p. 116 Burkhardt
45 *Sirach* 24:3
46 p. 185 Corbin, 1969
47 p. 28 Bakhtiar
48 p. 22 Bakhtiar
49 p. 23 ibid
50 letter of Ya'qub ibn Yusuf, *Gnosis* vol 5, p. 5, Fall 1987
51 p. 81 Wilson, *Scandal*
52 ibid

Chapter 10 The Black Virgin (pages 191–207)

1   pp. 76–7 Carroll
2   p. 145 Ashe, my itals
3   p. 151 ibid
4   p. 229 ibid
5   p. 48 ibid
6   *Isaiah* 7:14
7   *Wisdom* 7:25 and *Sirach* 24:28–9
8   *Isaiah* 44:24
9   ibid 44:26–8
10 ibid 45:3
11 p. 43 James
12 p. 188 Ashe
13 p. 144 Metford
14 p. 63 Forsyth
15 p. 63 ibid
16 p. 61 Preston
17 pp. 20, 66 Begg, 1985
18 p. 229 ibid
19 p. 65 Forsyth
20 p. 21 Begg, 1985
21 p. 105ff. Forsyth
22 p. 36 Querido
23 p. 54–5 Begg, 1985
24 p. 257 ibid
25 p. 216 ibid
26 p. 171–2 ibid
27 pp. 170ff. St Hilare, *Ardennes Mystérieux*

28 p. 74 St Hilaire, *Bruxelles Mystérieux*
29 p. 43–4 Begg, 1985
30 James
31 p. 220–1 Begg, 1985
32 p. 57 Preston
33 P. 6 *Simple Prayer Book*
34 p. 45 Begg, 1984
35 p. 11 Lake
36 p. 25 ibid
37 p. 10 Haughton
38 pp. 186–7 Moltmann-Wendell, 1986
39 p. 45 Semmelroth
40 p. 199 Newman
41 Hildegard of Bingen, *A Feather on the Breath of God*, my trans
42 pp. 166, 242 Begg, 1985
43 p. 15 *Simple Prayer Book*
44 p. 150 Ashe
45 p. 24 Forsyth
46 p. 25 ibid
47 p. 96 Sharp, 1912
48 letter of Ean Begg, *Gnosis*, vol 4, p. 5 Spring/Summer 1987
49 pp. 99–100 de Pizan
50 p. 565 *Other Bible*

51 trans. C. Matthews from *Goddess Icon*, forthcoming
52 p. 175 Crossley-Holland
53 ibid
54 p. 176 ibid

Chapter 11 The Grail Goddess (pages 208–20)
1 p. 163 Wolfram
2 p. 281 *Mabinogion*
3 p. 34 Bryant
4 C. Matthews, *Sophia, Companion on the Quest*
5 p. 155 MacKenzie
6 p. 37 Spence
7 P. 200–4 C. Matthews, *Arthur and the Sovereignty of Britain*
8 p. 160ff. J. Matthews, *Gawain*
9 pp. 23–4 C. Matthews, op cit
10 p. 541 Fontenrose
11 pp. 13–19 C. Matthews, op cit
12 J. Matthews, *Taliesin*
13 p. 227 Jung *Memories, Dreams and Reflections*
14 pp. 242–5 C. Matthews, op cit
15 p. 455 Ross
16 p. 57 Condren
17 p. 82 Gerald
18 p. 107 Condren
19 p. 307 C. Matthews, op cit
20 Matthews, J. and C. *Ladies of the Lake*
21 p. 16 Wetherbee
22 C. Matthews, *Voices of the Wells*
23 p. 250–2 C. Matthews, *Arthur and the Sovereignty*
24 p. 406 Wolfram
25 p. 202 C. Matthews, op cit
26 p. 202 ibid
27 p. 247 ibid and p. 319 Baigent
28 p. 100 MacLeod
29 p. 102 ibid
30 Jones

Chapter 12 Virgo Viriditas (pages 221–43)
1 pp. 17–21 Phillips
2 p. 209 Julian of Norwich, chap 86
3 p. 205 ibid chap 82
4 p. 41 Phillips
5 p. 42 ibid
6 *Genesis* 3:5
7 ibid 3:6
8 ibid 3:14–19
9 p. 59 Economou
10 unable to trace original source
11 p. 85 Economou
12 p. 211–12 Newman
13 p. 83 Semmelroth
14 p. 110 Fox
15 p. 312ff. Hildegard, 1986
16 p 312–3 ibid
17 ibid
18 p. 49 Newman
19 ibid
20 Hildegard *Ordo Virtutam*, recording, 1982
21 pp. 9–10 Hildegard, 1987
22 *Sirach* 24
23 p. 219 Hildegard, op cit
24 p. 27, Newman, my trans
25 p. 220 Hildegard, op cit
26 p. 329 ibid
27 p. 59 Hildegard, 1986
28 p. 165 Newman
29 p. 62 ibid
30 p. 26 Fox
31 p. 45 *Erigena* vol I
32 p. 38 Economou
33 p. 684 *Oxford Dictionary of the Christian Church*
34 p. 36 Boethius
35 p. 39 ibid
36 p. 55 ibid
37 pp. 176–7 Mead, 1965
38 pp. 111–13 *Erigena* vol I

39   p. 27 Wetherbee
40   p. 97 Boethius
41   Wetherbee
42   p. 68 ibid
43   p. 75 ibid
44   p. 88 ibid
45   p. 90 ibid
46   p. 115 ibid
47   p. 116 ibid
48   p. 127 ibid

49   p. 201 ibid
50   p. 91 Economou
51   p. 265 Chaucer
52   p. 244 Wetherbee
53   p. 213 ibid
54   p. 46 Economou
55   p. 235 Brown, medieval
      English modernized
56   p. 237 ibid

Chapter 13   The Veiled Goddess   (pages 247–67)

1   pp. 84–5 C. and J. Matthews, 1985
2   p. 24 Devereux, *Earthmind*
3   pp. 334–5 Allen
4   p. 447 Layton
5   p. 573 *Other Bible*, my itals
6   p. 39 Davis
7   p. 298 Scott, vol 2,12–17
8   p. 322 Harpur
9   p. 573 *Other Bible*
10 p. 108 Witt
11 p. 219 Springborg
12 p. 193 Witt
13 p. 198 Anon
14 pp. 463–5 Scott, vol I
15 p. 533 ibid
16 pp. 479–81 ibid
17 p. 491 ibid
18 p. 301–2 ibid
19 ibid
20 pp. 127–8 C. and J. Matthews, 1985
21 p. 208 von Franz
22 p. 305 Harpur
23 C. Matthews, *The Rosicrucian Vault*
24 pp. 108–9 Knight
25 letter of Kathy Fletcher, *Gnosis* vol 4, p. 5 Spring/Summer 1987

26 p. 210 Layton
27 p. 7 Klossowski
28 p. 24 Grossinger
29 p. 46 Gilchrist
30 p. 55–6 Burkhardt
31 p. 227 Grossinger
32 p. 147 Burkhardt
33 pp. 182–3 ibid
34 p. 8 Klossowski
35 p. 33–5 von Franz, 1966
36 p. 43 ibid
37 p. 242 ibid
38 p. 131 ibid
39 p. 143 ibid
40 p. 82–3 Tulku Thondup
41 p. 31 Cioran, my itals
42 p. 18 Corbin, 1985
43 ibid
44 p. 175 Corbin, 1969
45 p. 101 Corbin, 1977
46 pp. 207 C. and J. Matthews, 1985, vol 2
47 p. 129 Burkhardt
48 p. 18 Faricy
49 p. 243 Allen
50 from introduction, Sheldrake
51 p. 318 ibid

Chapter 14   The Woman Clothed With the Sun   (pages 268–87)

1   p. 4 Martensen
2   p. 7 ibid
3   p. 41 ibid
4   *Revelations* 4:5

5   pp. 42–3 ibid
6   p. 43 ibid
7   p. 112 ibid
8   *Isaiah* 11:2

9   p. 17 Fortune
10 pp. 155–6 Martensen
11 p. 156 ibid
12 p. 157 ibid
13 p. 15 Thune
14 p. 5 Gilbert
15 p. 297 Jung, 1954
16 p. 1 Leade
17 p. 3 ibid
18 ibid
19 p. 171 Hirst
20 p. 14 Gilbert
21 p. 14 ibid
22 p. 9 ibid
23 p. 3 ibid
24 p. 56 Leade
25 p. 17 Gilbert
26 p. 58 Leade
27 p. 8 Gilbert
28 p. 9 Whitson
29 p. 18 ibid
30 p. 82 ibid
31 p. 226 ibid
32 p. 214–15 ibid
33 p. 232 ibid
34 p. 2 ibid
35 p. 136 Andrews
36 p. 31 ibid

37 p. 110 ibid
38 p. 269 Blake, *Four Zoas* II:63
39 Blake, 'Jerusalem' 4:28
40 ibid 20
41 ibid 5:13
42 ibid 62:2–5
43 ibid 97:1–4
44 ibid 99:1–5
45 p. 192 Blake
46 p. 99 ibid
47 *Job* 2:4
48 p. 10 Goethe
49 p. 12 ibid
50 p. 21 ibid
51 p. 106 ibid
52 p. 196 ibid
53 pp. 196–7 ibid
54 p. 203 ibid
55 pp. 135–6 Novalis, 1982
56 p. 144–5 ibid
57 p. 148 ibid
58 ibid
59 p. xiii Novalis, 1960
60 p. 19 Steiner
61 p. 21 ibid
62 p. 21 ibid, my itals
63 ibid
64 p. 27 ibid

Chapter 15   Saint Sophia   (pages 288–302)
1   p. 107 Moltman-Wendell,
    1986
2   p. 15 Ivanits
3   p. 132 Preston
4   de Plessix Gray, Francine,
    'Reflections: Soviet Women',
    New Yorker, 19.2.90
5   p. 442 Afanasiev
6   p. 444 ibid
7   ibid
8   pp. 153–60 Zenkovsky
9   p. 281 Anon
10 p. 131 Preston
11 p. 471 Fiene
12 p. 16 Ivanits
13 pp. 50–1 Graves, C.
14 p. 35 Cioran
15 p. 225 Evdokimov

16 p. 459 Fiene
17 p. 466 ibid
18 *Isaiah* 34:4
19 p. 345 Allen
20 p. 17 Cioran
21 p. 60 Zolla
22 p. 23 Ciroan
23 p. 25 ibid
24 p. 35 ibid
25 p. 52 ibid
26 p. 92 ibid
27 p. 109 *Le Combat, Pour L'Ame
    du Monde*, my trans
28 p. 111 ibid
29 ibid
30 ibid
31 *St John* 1:5
32 pp. 249–50 Cioran

33 p. 10 Bukgakov
34 p. 252–3 Cioran
35 pp. 152 Bulgakov
36 p. 294 Hauke
37 p. 269 ibid
38 pp. 37–8 Graves, C.
39 p. 287 Roerich
40 p. 132 Decter
41 ibid

42 p. 287 Roerich
43 pp. 193–4 Decter
44 p. 190 ibid
45 p. 159 ibid
46 p. 47, Evdokimov, my trans
47 p. 211 Fox
48 p. 265 Roerich
49 p. 189 Allen

Chapter 16   Apocalyptic Virgin   (pages 303-19)
1   *Revelations* 12:1
2   ibid 12:12
3   p. 55 R. Graves, 1958
4   p. 79 Quispel
5   *Revelations* 19:8
6   p. 172 James
7   ibid
8   Williams
9   P. 21 Reeves
10 p. 70 Mead, 1965
11 p. 277–8 Anon
12 p. 215 Ashe
13 p. 576 Pope
14 p. 175 Patai
15 p. 35 Nennius
16 p. 150 Preston
17 p. 285 Roerich
18 p. 156 Carroll
19 p. 118 Laurentin
20 p. 177 Carroll
21 p. 60 Laurentin
22 p. 177 Carroll
23 prayer card in author's
    possession
24 p. 213–6 Carroll
25 p. 280 Anon
26 p. 205 Carroll

27 p. 217 Devereux, 1989
28 p. 244 Carroll
29 p. 8 Ashton, and p. 139 Begg
30 p. 30 Robertson, *Pantheia*
31 *St Luke* 19:39
32 *Romans* 8:23
33 *Sirach* 1:10
34 *Galatians* 4:6
35 p. 416 Eliade, 1982
36 pp. 153–4 Devereux, 1990
37 p. 144 Fox
38 *St Luke* 13:35
39 *St Matthew* 21:18
40 *St Mark* 13:28
41 p. 45 Fox
42 p. 52 ibid
43 *Wisdom* 10:21
44 p. 82 Layton
45 p. 82 Laurentin
46 p. 408–9 King
47 *Wisdom* 7:25
48 p. 195 Fox
49 *St Matthew* 18:3
50 p. 186 Fox
51 p. 173 James
52 p. 259 Kinsley
53 p. 259–60 ibid

Chapter 17   The Sophianic Millennium   (pages 320–44)
1   p. 16 Hoeller
2   p. 32 Dart
3   p. 178 Jung, 1970
4   p. 235 Ashe
5   p. 174 Jung, 1954
6   p. 414 Jung, *Memories, Dreams
    and Reflections*
7   p. 18 Corbin, 1985

8   p. 82 Cady
9   p. 65 Hodgson
10 p. 365 Heiler
11 p. 78 Semmelroth
12 p. 161 ibid
13 p. 64 Faricy
14 p. 65 ibid
15 p. 75 de Chardin

16 p. 155–6 Lang
17 p. 1 Robertson *Urania*
18 p. 9 *Moonshine* No 21, Spring 1990 (498 Bristol Rd, Selly Oak, Birmingham)
19 p. 218 Tavard
20 pp. 108–282 Ruether, 1985
21 p. 69 ibid
22 p. 170 Phillips
23 p. 10 Cady
24 p. 14 ibid
25 p. 169 Phillips
26 *Sirach* 24:1–6
27 p. 266–7 Newman
28 p. 266 ibid
29 p. 53 Moltman-Wendell, 1986
30 pp. 16–19 C. Matthews, *Elements of the Goddess*
31 pp. 19–25 C. Matthews, *Voices of the Goddess*
32 *St Matthew* 7:9–10
33 *The Fellowship of Isis*, Clonegal Castle, Enniscorthy, Eire; *The Covenant of the Goddess*, Box 1226, Berkeley, CA 9470434 USA.
34 p. 33–39 Jones & Matthews
35 publicity leaflet of *The Holy Order of Wisdom*
36 from *Wisdom Works: a metanousical letter*, The Holy Order of Wisdom, PO Box 7084, Santa Cruz, CA 95061 USA
37 from leaflet of *Order of Sancta Sophia*, entitled *Celtic Enrichment*, Offrwm, The Rectory, Pennal, Machynlleth, Powys SY20 9JS, Wales
38 private communication to author, Feb 1990
39 publicity leaflet from *Ecclesia Gnostica Mysteriorum*
40 ibid
41 p. 17 Singer
42 p. 10 Miller
43 p. 5 ibid
44 private letter from the *Order of Sancta Sophia*, April 1990
45 p. 266 Ruether, 1983
46 p. 103 Macleod
47 *St Matthew* 6:21

BIBLIOGRAPHY

(Unless otherwise stated, all books published in London)

Afansaiev, A., *Russian Fairy Tales*, trans. N. Guterman, New York, Pantheon Books, 1945

The Akathist Hymn and Little Compline, Faith Press, n.d.

Allen, P. M., *Vladimir Soloviev: Russian Mystic*, New York, Rudolf Steiner Publications, 1978

Andrews, E. D., *The Gift to be Simple*, New York, Dover Publications, 1940

Anonymous, *Meditations on the Tarot: A Journey into Christian Hermeticism*, New York, Amity House, 1987

Apuleius, L., *The Golden Ass*, trans. R. Graves, Harmondsworth, Penguin, 1950

Aratus, 'The Phaenomena', trans. G. R. Mair in *Callimiachus Hymns and Epigrams*, William Heinemann Ltd, 1960

Ashe, G., *The Virgin*, Routledge & Kegan Paul, 1976

Ashton, J., *Mother of Nations*, Basingstoke, The Lamp Press, 1988

Aurora Terrenus, *The Shroud of Sophia*, Santa Cruz, Celestial Communications, 1988

Aurora Terrenus, *Sophia and the Bible*, Santa Cruz, Celestial Communications, 1988

Baigent, M., Leigh, R. and Lincoln, H., *The Holy Blood and the Holy Grail*, Jonathan Cape, 1982

Bakhtiar, L. *Sufi: Expressions of the Mystic Quest*, Thames & Hudson, 1976

Begg, E., *The Cult of the Black Virgin*, Arkana, 1985

Begg, E., *Myth and Today's Consciousness*, Coventure, 1984

Bernard Silvestris, *The Cosmographia*, trans. Wetherbee, W., New York, Columbia Univ. Press, 1973

Berry, W., *A Continuous Harmony*, New York, Harcourt Brace Jovanovitch, 1972

Bible, The, Revised Standard Version, Nelson, 1966

Blake, W., *Poetry and Prose*, Nonesuch Library, 1975

Boethius, *The Consolations of Philosophy*, trans. Watts, V. E., Harmondsworth, Penguin, 1969

Book of Enoch, trans. R. H. Charles, SPCK, 1982

Bronstein, H. (ed.), *A Passover Haggadah*, Harmondsworth, Penguin, 1975

Brown, C. (ed.), *Religious Lyrics of the 14th Century*, Oxford Univ. Press, 1952

Bryant, N., *The High Book of the Grail*, Cambridge, D. S. Brewer, 1978

Bulgakov, S., *A Bulgakov Anthology*, ed. Pain, J. and Zernov, N., SPCK, 1976

Bulgakov, S., *The Wisdom of God*, Williams & Norgate, 1937

Burkhardt, T., *Alchemy*, Shaftesbury, Element Books, 1986

Cady, S., Ronan, M. and Taussig, H., *Sophia: the Future of Feminist Spirituality*, New York, Harper & Row, 1986

Carmichael, A., *Carmina Gadelica*, 6 vols, Edinburgh, Scottish Academic Press, 1972

Carroll, M. P., *The Cult of the Virgin Mary*, Princeton, Princeton Univ. Press, 1986

Charlesworth, J. (ed.), *The Old Testament Pseudepigrapha*, 2 vols, Darton, Longman & Todd, 1983

Chaucer, G., *The Canterbury Tales*, London, Oxford Univ. Press, 1947

Cioran, S., *Vladimir Solov'iev and the Knighthood of the Divine Sophia*, Ontario, Wilfrid Laurier Univ. Press, 1977

Clarke, L., *The Chymical Wedding*, Jonathan Cape, 1989

Le Combat pour L'Ame du Monde: Urgence de la Sophiologie, Cahiers de L'Université St Jean de Jérusalem, no. 6, Paris, Berg International, 1980

Condren, M., *The Serpent and the Goddess*, San Francisco, Harper & Row, 1989

Connaughton, L., *A-Z of the Catholic Church*, Leigh-on-Sea, Kevin Mayhew, 1980

Corbin, H., *Creative Imagination in the Sufism of Ibn Arabi*, trans. Mannheim, R., Princeton, Princeton Univ. Press, 1969

Corbin, H. 'The Eternal Sophia', trans. Tuby, M., in *Harvest*, vol 31, pp. 7–23, London, 1985

Corbin, H., *Spiritual Body and Celestial Earth*, trans. Pearson, N., Princeton, Princeton Univ. Press, 1977

Corbin, H., *Temple and Contemplation*, trans. Sherrard, P. and L., KPI, 1986

Cragg, K., *The Wisdom of the Sufis*, Sheldon Press, 1976

Crossley-Holland, K., *The Norse Myths*, André Deutch, 1980

D'Aviella, G., *The Mysteries of Eleusis*, Wellingborough, Aquarian Press, 1981

Dart, J., *The Laughing Savior*, New York, Harper & Row, 1976

Davis, E., 'The Dark Mind of Gnosis', in *Gnosis* vol 14, pp. 34–41, Winter 1990

de Chardin, T., *The Heart of Matter*, Collins, 1978

Decter, J., *Nicholas Roerich: the Life and Art of a Russian Master*, Thames & Hudson, 1989

de Pizan, C., *The Book of the City of Ladies*, Picador, 1983

Devereux, P., *Earth Lights Revelation*, Blandford, 1989

Devereux, P., Steel, J. and Kubrin, D., *Earthmind: Tuning into GAIA Theory*, New York, Harper & Row, 1990

Diodorus Siculus, *Complete Works, Books One & Two* (2 vols) trans. Oldfather, C. H., Heinemann, 1967 and 1968

Dillon, J., *The Middle Platonists*, Duckworth, 1977

Downing, C., *The Goddess: Mythological Images of the Feminine*, New York, Crossroad Books, 1981

Economou, G. D., *The Goddess Natura in Medieval Literature*, Cambridge, Mass., Harvard Univ. Press, 1972

Eisenberg, A. and Globe, L. A., *The Secret Weapon*, Soncino Press, 1966

Eliade, M. (ed.), *The Encyclopedia of Religion*, New York, Macmillan, 1987

Eliade, M., *A History of Religious Ideas* (vol 1): *From the Stone Age to the Eleusinian Mysteries*, Collins, 1979

Eliade, M., *A History of Religious Ideas* (vol 2): *From Gautama Buddha to the Triumph of Christianity*, Chicago, Univ. of Chicago Press, 1982

Epstein, O., *Kabbalah: the Way of the Jewish Mystic*, New York, Samuel Weiser, 1979

Erigena, J. S., *Periphyseon*, ed. Sheldon-Williams, I. P., Dublin, Dublin Institute for Advanced Studies, 1972

Evdokimov, P., *La Femme et le Salut du Monde*, Tournai, Casterman, 1958

Faricy, R., *The Lord's Dealing*, New York, Paulist Press, 1988

Farmer, D. H., *The Oxford Dictionary of Saints*, Oxford, Oxford Univ. Press, 1978

Feild, R., *Steps to Freedom*, Putney, Vermont, Threshold Books, 1983

Fiene, D. M., 'What is the Appearance of Divine Sophia?' *Slavic Review* 48, no. 3, pp. 449–476, Fall 1989

Fontenrose, J., *Python: a Study of Delphic Myth and its Origins*, Berkeley, Univ. of California Press, 1959

Forms of Prayer for Jewish Worship, Reform Synagogues of Great Britain, n.d.

Forsyth, I. H., *The Throne of Wisdom: Wood Sculptures of the Madonna in Romanesque France*, Princeton, Princeton Univ. Press, 1972

Fortune, D., *The Cosmic Doctrine*, Welliingborough, Aquarian Press, 1976

Fox, M., *The Coming of the Cosmic Christ*, San Francisco, Harper & Row, 1988

Gerald of Wales, *The History and Topography of Ireland*, trans. O'Meara, J. J., Harmondsworth, Penguin, 1982

Gilbert, S. M. and Gubar, S., *Shakespeare's Sisters*, Bloomington, Indiana Univ. Press, 1979

Gilchrist, C., *Alchemy: The Great Work*, Wellingborough, Aquarian Press, 1984

Gimbutas, M., *The Language of the Goddess*, San Francisco, Harper & Row, 1989

The Glorious Koran, trans. Pickthall, M., Allen & Unwin, 1976

Goethe, *Faust*, trans. Fairley, B., Toronto, Univ. of Toronto Press, 1970

Goldstein, D., 'On Translating God's Name', in *The Translator's Art: Essays in Honour of Betty Radice*, ed. Radice, W. and Reynolds, B., Harmondsworth, Penguin, 1988

Grant, F. C., *Hellenistic Religions*, Indianapolis, Bobbs-Merrill, 1953

Graves, C., *Altaic Elements in the Sophiology of Sergius Bulgakov*, privately printed, Corsier, Geneva, Switzerland, 1246

Graves, R., *Greek Myths*, Cassell, 1958

Graves, R., *Mammon and the Black Goddess*, Cassel, 1962

Graves, R., *The White Goddess*, Faber, 1961

Gribben, J. and Rees, M., *The Stuff of the Universe: Dark Matter, Mankind and the Coincidences of Cosmology*, Heinmann, 1990

Griffiths, B., *Christianity in the Light of the East*, The Hibbert Trust, 14 Gordon Sq., London WC1H OAG, 1989

Grigson, G., *The Goddess of Love*, Constable, 1976

Grossinger, R. (ed.), *Alchemy: Pre-Egyptian Legacy, Millennial Promise*, Richmond, CA., North Atlantic Books, 1979

Harding, M. E., *Women's Mysteries*, New York. Harper & Row, 1976

Harpur, P., *Mercurius: the Marriage of Heaven and Earth*, Macmillan, 1990

Haughton, R., *The Catholic Thing*, Dublin, Villa Books, 1979

Hauke, M., *Women in the Priesthood? a Systematic Analysis in the Light of the Order of Creation and Redemption*, San Francisco, Ignatius Press, 1986

Heiler, F., *The Madonna as Religious Symbol*, Princeton, Princeton Univ. Press, 1968

Heraclitus, *The Cosmic Fragments*, ed. Kirk, G. S., Cambridge, Cambridge Univ, Press, 1970

Hesiod, *The Homeric Hymns*, trans. Evelyn-White, H. G., Heinemann, 1964

Heyob, S. K., *The Cult of Isis Among Women in the Graeco-Roman World*, Leiden, E. J. Brill, 1975

Hildegard of Bingen, *Book of Divine Works*, ed. Fox, M., Santa Fe, Bear & Co, 1987

Hildegard of Bingen, *Scivias*, trans. Hozelski, B., Santa Fe, Bear & Co, 1986

Hildegard of Bingen, *Sequences and Hymns*, ed. Page, C., Newton Abbot, Antico Church Music MCMI, 1982 (musical score)

Hirst, D., *Hidden Riches: Traditional Symbolism From the Renaissance to Blake*, Eyre & Spottiswoode, 1964

Hodgeson, R., *The Way*, Cambridge, James Clarke, 1984

Hoeller, S. A., *The Gnostic Jung and the Seven Sermons to the Dead*, Wheaton, Ill., Theosophical Publishing Hse, 1982

Hopkins, G. M., *Selected Poems*, Heinemann, 1953

Howell, A. O., *The Dove in the Stone*, Wheaton Ill., Quest Books, 1988

Ibn Yusuf, Y., *The Redemption of the Shekinah*, pp. 52–58, in *Gnosis* vol 14, Winter 1990

Ivanits, L., *Russian Folk Belief*, Armok, NY, M. E. Sharpe Inc, 1989

Jacobs, L., *Jewish Mystical Testimonies*, New York, Schoken Books, 1976

James, M. R., *The Apocryphal New Testament*, Oxford, Clarendon Press, 1924

The Jerusalem Bible, Darton, Longman & Todd, 1966

Jones, P. and Matthews, C., *Voices From the Circle: The Heritage of Western Paganism*, Wellingborough, Aquarian Press, 1990

Julian, *The Works of the Emperor Julian* (vol 1) trans. Wright, W. C., Heinemann, 1980

Julian of Norwich, *The Revelations of Divine Love*, trans. Walsh, J., Wheathampstead, Anthony Clarke, 1961

Jung, C. G., *Alchemical Studies*, trans. Hull, R. E. F., Routledge & Kegan Paul, 1967

Jung, C. G., *Answer to Job*, Routledge & Kegan Paul, 1954

Jung, C. G., *Memories, Dreams and Reflections*, Collins, 1967

Jung, C. G., *Mysterium Coniunctionis*, trans. Hull, R. E. F., Routledge & Kegan Paul, 1970

Jung, C. G., *The Practice of Psychotherapy*, trans. Hull, R. E. F., Routledge & Kegan Paul, 1954

Kane, E., *Recovering from Incest: Imagination and the Healing Process*, Boston, Sigo Press, 1989

Kerenyi, C., *Athene*, Zurich, Spring Publications, 1978

Kerenyi, C., *The Gods of the Greeks*, Thames & Hudson, 1951

Kerenyi, C., *The Heroes of the Greeks*, Thames & Hudson, 1974

King, K. L. (ed.), *Images of the Feminine in Gnosticism*, Philadelphia, Fortress Press, 1988

Kingsford, A. and Maitland, E., *The Virgin of the World*, Minneapolis, Wizards Book Shelf, 1977

Kinsley, D., *The Goddesses' Mirror*, Albany, State Univ. of New York Press, 1989

Klossowski de Rola, S., *The Secret Art of Alchemy*, Thames & Hudson, 1973

Knight, G. and McLean, A., *Commentary on the Chymical Wedding of Christian Rosenkreutz*, Edinburgh, Hermetic Sourceworks, 1984

Kramer, S. N., *The Sacred Marriage Rite*, Bloomington, Indiana Univ. Press, 1969

Lake, K., *The Apostolic Fathers* (vol I), William Heinemann, 1976

Lambspring, A., *Book of Lambspring and the Golden Tripod*, Preface, Bryce, D., Llanerch, Llanerch Enterprises, 1987

Lang, B., *Wisdom and the Book of Proverbs*, New York, Pilgrim Press, 1986

Laurentin, R., *Bernadette of Lourdes*, Darton, Longman and Todd, 1979

Layton, B., trans., *The Gnostic Scriptures*, SCM Press Ltd, 1987

Lewis, C. S., *Till We Have Faces*, Collins, 1979

Leade, J., *The Revelation of Revelations*, Edinburgh, Magnum Opus Sourceworks, 1981

Lindsay, J., *The Origins of Alchemy in Graeco-Roman Egypt*, Frederick Muller, 1970

Lossky, V., *The Mystical Theology of the Eastern Church*, Cambridge, James Clarke, 1957

Lovelock, J., *The Ages of Gaia: a Biography of Our Living Earth*, Oxford, Oxford Univ. Press, 1988

Lurker, M., *The Gods and Symbols of Ancient Egypt*, Thames & Hudson, 1980

The Mabinogion, trans. Lady Charlotte Guest, Ballantyne Press, 1910

Mackenzie, D. A., *Scottish Folk Lore and Folk Life*, Blackie & Son, 1935

Maclean Todd, J. and J., *Voices From the Past*, Reader's Union, 1956

Macleod, F., *The Divine Adventure: Iona: Studies in Spiritual History*, W. H. Heinemann, 1927

Martensen, H. L., *Jacob Boehme*, trans. Rhys Evans, T., Rockliff, 1949

Martini, C.-M., *The Woman Among Her People: A Spiritual Journey into the 'Planet Woman'*, Slough, St Paul Publication, 1989

Matthews, C., *Arthur and the Sovereignty of Britain: King and Goddess in the Mabinogion*, Arkana, 1989

Matthews, C., *The Elements of Celtic Tradition*, Shaftesbury, Element Books, 1989

Matthews, C., *The Elements of the Goddess*, Shaftesbury, Element Books, 1989

Matthews, C., *Mabon and the Mysteries of Britain: An Exploration of the Mabinogion*, Arkana, 1987

Matthews, C., 'The Rosicrucian Vault as Sepulchre and Wedding Chamber' in *The Underworld Initiation*, Stewart, R. J., Wellingborough, Aquarian Press, 1989

Matthews, C., 'Sophia, Companion on the Quest' in·*At the Table of the Grail*, ed. Matthews, J., Arkana, 1987

Matthews, C., 'Sophia: Goddess of Wisdom', in *Gnosis* vol 13, pp. 20–26, Fall 1989

Matthews, C. (ed.), *Voices of the Goddess: A Chorus of Sibyls*, Aquarian Press, 1990

Matthews, C., 'The Voices of the Wells' in *Household of the Grail*, ed. Matthews, J., Wellingborough, Aquarian Press, 1990

Matthews, C. and J., *The Arthurian Tarot: A Hallowquest*, Wellingborough, Aquarian Press, 1990

Matthews, C. and J., *Hallowquest: Tarot Magic and the Arthurian Mysteries*, Wellingborough, Aquarian Press, 1990

Matthews, C. and J., *The Western Way* (2 vols) Arkana, 1985 and 1986.

Matthews, J., *Gawain, Knight of the Goddess*, Wellingbourgh, Aquarian Press, 1990

Matthews, J. and C., *Ladies of the Lake*, Aquarian Press, 1991

Matthews, J., with additional material by Matthews, C., *Taliesin: Shamanism and the Bardic Mysteries in Britain and Ireland*, Unwin Hyman, 1991

Mead, G. R. S., *Pistis Sophia*, Secaucus, NJ., University Books Inc, 1974

Mead, G. R. S., *Simon Magus*, Chicago, Ares Publishers, 1979

Mead, G. R. S., *Thrice Greatest Hermes* (3 vols), John M. Watkins, 1964

Meier, F., 'The Mystery of the Ka'ba: Symbol and Reality in Islamic Mysticism' in *The Mysteries*, Princeton, NJ, Princeton Univ. Press, 1955

Metford, J. C. J., *Dictionary of Christian Lore and Legend*, Thames & Hudson, 1983

Miller, Tau R., *The Gnostic Holy Eucharist*, Sanctuary of the Holy Shekinah, 3437 Alma Street, Suite 23, Alma Plaza Shopping Center, Palo Alto, CA. 94306, n.d.

Moltmann-Wendel, E., *A Land Flowing with Milk and Honey*, SCM Press, 1986

Moltmann-Wendel, E., *The Women Around Jesus*, SCM Press, 1982

Monaghan, P., *Women in Myth and Legend*, Junction Books, 1981

Munificentissimus Deus, Derby, N.Y., Daughters of St Paul, 1950

Nag Hammadi Library, The, trans. Members of the Coptic Gnostic Library Project of the Inst. for Antiquity & Christianity, Dir. J. M. Robinson, Leiden, E. J. Brill, 1977

Nahman of Blatislav, *The Tales*, trans. Band, A. J., New York, Paulist Press, 1978

Nennius, *British History and the Welsh Annals*, trans. Morris, J., Phillimore & Co Ltd, 1980

Newman, B., *Sister of Wisdom: St Hildegard's Theology of the Feminine*, Aldershot, Scholar Press, 1987

Nicholson, S. (ed.), *The Goddess Re-Awakening*, Wheaton, Ill., Theosophical Publishing House, 1989

Novalis, *Henry von Ofterdingen*, trans. Hilty, P., New York, Frederick Ungar Pub. Co, 1982

Novalis, *Hymns to the Night and Other Selected Writings*, trans. Passage, C., Indianapolis, Bobbs-Merrill Company Inc, 1960

O'Brien, T. K. (ed.), *The Spiral Path*, St Paul, MN., 1988

Olson, C., *The Book of the Goddess*, New York, Crossroad, 1987

The Other Bible, ed. Barnstone, W., San Francisco, Harper & Row, 1984

Ovid, *Metamorphoses*, trans. Innes, M. M., Harmondsworth, Penguin, 1955

The Oxford Classical Dictionary, ed. Hammond, N. G. L. and Scullard, H. H., Oxford Univ. Press, 1970

Oxford Dictionary of the Christian Church, ed. Cross, F. L., Oxford Univ. Presss, 1974

Patai, R., *The Hebrew Goddess*, New York, Avon Books, 1978

Pausanius, *Guide to Greece* (vol 2), trans. Levi, P., Harmondsworth, Penguin, 1971

Perera, S. B., *Descent to the Goddess*, Toronto, Inner City Books, 1981

Phillips, J. A., *Eve: the History of an Idea*, San Francisco, Harper & Row, 1983

Philo, *The Contemplative Life, the Giants and Selections*, trans. and ed. Winston, D., SPCK, 1981

Pindar, *The Odes*, trans. Bowra, C. M., Harmondsworth, Penguin, 1969

Plato, *The Collected Dialogues*, ed. Hamilton, E. and Cairns, H., Princeton, NJ, Princeton Univ. Press, 1961

Plotinus, *The Enneads*, trans. MacKenna, S., Faber, 1956

Plutarch, *Moralia* (vol. 5) trans. Babbitt, F. C., Heinemann, 1957

Pollack, R. and Matthews, C., *Tarot Tales*, Century, 1989

Pope, M., *Song of Songs*, Garden City, NY, Doubleday & Co, 1977

Preston, J. J. (ed.), *Mother Worship*, Chapel Hill, NC, Univ. of North Carolina Press, 1982

Pritchard, J. B. (ed.), *Solomon and Sheba*, Phaidon, 1974

Querido, R., *The Golden Age of Chartres*, Edinburgh, Floris Books, 1987

Quest of the Holy Grail, trans. Matarasso, P., Harmondsworth, Penguin, 1969

Quispel, G., *The Secret Book of Revelation*, Collins, 1979

Redemptoris Mater, Catholic Truth Society, 1987

Reese, J. M., *Hellenic Influence on the Book of Wisdom and its Consequences*, Rome, Biblical Institute Press, 1970

Reeves, M., *Joachim of Fiore and the Prophetic Future*, SPCK, 1976

Ringgren, H., *Word and Wisdom*, Lund, H. Ohlssons Boktryckeri, 1947

Robertson, O., *Pantheia: Initiations and Festivals of the Goddess*, Clonegal, Cesara Publications, 1988

Robertson, O., *Sophia: Cosmic Consciousness of the Goddess*, Clonegal, Cesara Publications, n.d.

Robertson, O., *Urania: Ceremonial Magic of the Goddess*, Clonegal, Cesara Publications, n.d.

Robinson, J. M., *Aspects of Wisdom in Judaism and Early Christianity*, Notre Dame, Univ. of Notre Dame Press, 1975

Robinson, J. M., *The Future of Our Religious Past*, SCM Press, 1971

Roerich, N., *Shambhala*, New York, Nicholas Roerich Museum, 1985

Ross, A., *Pagan Celtic Britain*, Paladin, 1974

Ruether, R. R., *Sexism and God-Talk: Toward a Feminist Theology*, Boston, Beacon Press, 1983

Ruether, R. R., *Woman-Church*, San Francisco, Harper & Row, 1985

de Saint Hilaire, P., *L'Ardennes Mystérieux*, Brussels, Rossel editions, 1976

de Saint Hilaire, P., *Bruxelles Mystérieux*, Brussels, Rossel editions, 1976

Sandars, N. K., trans., *Poems of Heaven and Hell from Ancient Mesopotamia*, Harmondsworth, Penguin, 1971

Scholem, G., *Kabbalistic Ritual and the Bride of God* in Scott, W. (ed.), *Hermetica* (4 vols), Boulder, CO, Hermes House, 1982

'Shepherd of Hermes' in *The Apostolic Fathers* (vol 2), ed. Lake, K., Heinemann, 1976.

Semmelroth, O., *Mary, Archetype of the Church*, Dublin, Gill & Son, 1964

Sharp, W., *Vistas*, Heinemann, 1912

Sheldrake, R., *The Presence of the Past*, Collins, 1988

Sherrard, P., *The Rape of Man and Nature*, Ipswich, Golgonooza Press, 1987

A Simple Prayer Book, Catholic Truth Society, 1977

Singer, J., 'A Necessary Heresy' in *Gnosis* vol 4, Spring/Summer 1987

Spence, L., *The Minor Traditions of British Mythology*, Rider & Co, 1948

Springborg, P., *Royal Persons*, Unwin Hyman, 1990

Steiner, R., *The Search for the New Isis, the Divine Sophia*, Spring Valley, NY, Mercury Press, 1983

Tavard, G. H., *Woman in Christian Tradition*, Notre Dame, Ind, Univ of Notre Dame, 1973

Taylor, T., *Selected Writings*, ed. Raine, K. and Harper, G. M., Princeton, Princeton Univ. Press, 1969

Thompson, W. I., *The Time Falling Bodies Take to Light*, Rider, 1981

Thune, N., *The Behmenists and the Philadelphians*, Uppsala, Almquist & Wiksells Boktryckeri, 1948

Tulku Thondup Rinpoche, *Hidden Teachings of Tibet*, Wisdom Publications, 1986

Vaughan, H., *The Complete Poems*, Harmondsworth, Penguin, 1976

Vermaseren, M., *Cybele and Attis*, Thames & Hudson, 1977

Von Franz, M.-L. (ed.), *Aurora Consurgens*, New York, Bollingen Foundation, 1966

Von Franz, M.-L., *C. G. Jung: His Myth in Our Time*, Hodder & Stoughton, 1975

Ware, K., *The Orthodox Way*, Mowbrays, 1979

Wetherbee, W., *Platonism and Poetry in the Twelfth Century*, Princeton, Princeton Univ. Press, 1972

Whitson, R. E., *The Shakers*, SPCK, 1983.

Wili, W., 'The History of the Spirit in Antiquity' in *Spirit and Nature*, ed. Buonaiuti, E. et al, Routledge & Kegan Paul, 1955

Wilken, R. L. (ed.), *Aspects of Wisdom in Judaism and Early Christianity*, Notre Dame, Ind, Univ. of Notre Dame Press, 1975

Williams, C., *The Descent of the Dove*, Faber, 1949

Wilson, P. and Pourjavady, N., *The Drunken Universe: an Anthology of Persian Sufi Poetry*, Grand Rapids, Phanes Press, 1987

Wilson, P. L., *Scandal: Essays in Islamic Heresy*, New York, Autonomedia, 1987

Winston, D., *The Wisdom of Solomon*, Garden City, NY, Doubleday & Co, 1979

Witt, R. E., *Isis in the Graeco-Roman World*, Thames & Hudson, 1971

Wolfram von Eschenbach, *Parzival*, trans. Hatto, A. T., Harmondsworth, Penguin, 1980

Wolkstein, D. and Kramer, S. N., *Inanna: Queen of Heaven and Earth*, Rider, 1984

Wynne-Tyson, E., *The Philosophy of Compassion: the Return of the Goddess*, Vincent Stuart Ltd, 1962

Zaehner, R. C., *The Dawn and Twilight of Zoroastrianism*, Weidenfeld & Nicholson, 1961

Zenkovsky, S. A., *Medieval Russia's Epics, Chronicles and Tales*, New York, E. P. Dutton, 1963

Zolla, E., *The Androgyne: Fusion of the Sexes*, Thames & Hudson, 1981

Zolla, E., *Archetypes*, Allen & Unwin, 1971

Zundel, M., *Our Lady of Wisdom*, trans. Sheed, F. J. Sheed & Ward, 1941

Select discography

(* = record   † = tape)

†   *Cant de la Sibilla*, Monserrat Figueras (Astrée E 8705)
†   Aaron Copland *Appalacian Spring*
*   Hildegard of Bingen *A Feather on the Breath of God*, Gothic Voices, (Hyperion A 66039)
†   Hildegard of Bingen, *Symphoniae*, Sequentia (Harmonia Mundi D7800)
†   Georgia Kelly, *Eros and Logos*, (Heru 108)
†   Esther Lamandier, *Chants Chrétien Aramaens*, (Alienor ALM 1034)
†   Orlandus Lassus, *Missa Osculetus Me* (Gimell 158T-18)
*   *Liber Sapientiae*, Schola Hungarica (Hungaraton SKPD 12534)
*   Gustav Mahler, *Symphony of a Thousand, no 8*, Raphael Kubelik & Der Bayerischen Rundfunks (Deutscher Grammaphon 2562 087)
*   Claude Marti, *L'Agonie du Languedoc*, 1976 (Reflexe 1C 063–30 132)
*   Mozart, *Die Zauberflote*

† R. Carlos Nakai, *Earth Spirit*, Canyon Records (CR 612, 1987)
* Francis Poulenc, *Litanies à la Vièrge Noire*, French Church Music (Abbey LPB 780)
* Szymanowski, *Stabat Mater*, (HMV 27 00271)

Caitlín Matthews is available to give workshops, seminars and courses. Please write to *Domus Sophiae Terrae et Sancte Gradalis*, BCM – Hallowquest, London WC1N 3XX, enclosing an SAE within UK or three international reply-paid tokens.

INDEX

Italicized numbers indicate illustrations

dragon 22, 303, 312
drakaina (Pythoness) 22, 29, 205–7
duality of body and spirit 35
Dumuzi 36, 39, 40, 41, 47, 112, 133, 134

Earth
  as witness of vows 22, 48, 288
  destruction of. 23, 29, 54
  ecology of 8, 25
  groans of 279–80, 303, 307, 312–15, 326
  honouring the 317, 325ff, 342ff
  lights and other phenomena 310–12
  Mother 8, 22, 24, 25, 26, 31, 34, 57, 194, 251, 288
  planet 242, 326ff, 336
Eastern spiritual traditions 2, 9, 16, 17
Ecclesia (Church) 47, 102, 134–5, 136, 199, 200ff, 226, 227, 229, 230, 231, 291, 304, 315, 323, 328
  as sister of Wisdom 200, 230
Ecclesia Gnostica Mysteriorum 338–40
ecumenism 148, 149
Edelson, Mary Beth *343*
Eden, 42, 44
Eleusinian mysteries 37, 58, 59ff
Elucidation 208, 215ff
engendering 54
Enkidu 36, 167
Ephesus
  as centre of Goddess worship 193–4
  Council of 192, 193
Epinoia 153, 159
Ereshkigal 39, 40–1, 123
Erigena, John Scotus 134, 231, 235–6
Erinyes 22, 48, 51, 85
Eros 36, 133, 137, 253
Evdokimov, Paul 294, 302
Eve 22, 43, 45, 52, 57, 62, 64, 83, 89, 151, 153, 154, 156, 165, 166, 174, 175, 241, 250, 265, 271, 278, 312
  as Black Goddess 222
  as *Hawwah* 223, 322
  responsible for Fall 221ff
Exegesis of the Soul 162, 167

Fall
  as loss of paradise 218, 224, 227, 312
  as necessary experience 65, 223–5, 251
  the Christian 57, 133, 165, 174, 175, 186, 221ff
  the Gnostic 156, 165, 174
Fatima
  daughter of Muhammed 179, 180, 189, 190
  in Portugal 308–9

Faustus 168, 280–2
Feirfitz 217
Fellowship of Isis 335, 357
female ordination 11, 329
feminist
  scholarship 10, 58
  views of mythology 21
fire as spiritual experience 77, 168, 213–4, 306, 341
Florensky, Pavel 297–8
Fortuna 77, 232–3
Fortune, Dion 271
frashkart 181, 303
Fredriksen, Paula 316
fundamentalism as spiritual wasteland 314ff

Gaia/Ge
  as metaphor of Earth 26, 86, 266, 325, 343
  as Titanic Goddess 21, 22, 26, 27, 71, 151, 160
Galahad 42, 217
Galen 162
Gayomart 182
Gilgamesh 36, 167
Giordano, Bruno 249
gnosis 150, 336–40
Gnosticism
  future of 178, 321ff, 331, 338ff
Gnostics 36, 150–2, 153ff, 257, 269, 295, 345
  attitude to women 161–7
  fundamentalism of 164
Goddess *see also* Divine Feminine
  and evil 335
  as a lost mother country 5, 8–9, 57
  as creative source 216–17, 225
  as *paredros* 48, 52, 96, 97, 98, 106, 115, 136, 139, 151, 324
  as sacred site 25
  birthing 23, 25, 27
  communion with the 41, 56
  creation myths of the 19, 134
  decline of the 77–80, 159
  descent of the 37, 38, 63
  diminished metaphors of the 16, 89, 191
  in medieval allegory 239ff
  initiation into death 37, 59
  leaves the earth 48
  many-aspected 26, 31–2
  matriarchal 10
  mediation of the 247
  mirror of the 3, 11, 59, 342
  mutable nature of the 16, 158, 231–4
  mysteries of the 10, 33, 58–9, 68, 247